Who Gains from Free Trade?

Since the late 1980s, almost all Latin American countries have gone through a process of far-reaching economic reforms, featuring in particular trade, financial and capital account liberalization. At first the reforms seemed to be working as promised and trade expanded. However, at the turn of the century, the economies have shown unstable and rather dismal growth. Some argue trade liberalization is partly to be blamed for this.

Who Gains from Free Trade? examines the extent to which trade reforms have been an important source of the slowdown of economic growth, rising inequality and rising poverty as observed in many parts of the region. This volume presents an comprehensive analysis of this important topic, utilising research based on 16 country narratives of policy reform and economic performance; rigorous general equilibrium (CGE) modelling of the economy-wide effects of trade reform for all country cases; alongside application of an innovative method of microsimulations to assess the employment and factor income distribution impact of policy reforms on poverty and inequality at the household level.

The study finds that trade liberalization and the switch to export-led growth are not the cause of the growth slowdown in Latin America. Nor are they the cause of rising poverty and inequality. If anything, the impact on growth and poverty in general has been positive, but very small. Thus, further trade opening is neither the solution to the region's economic woes, nor should we expect any disastrous implications for aggregate poverty.

Rob Vos is Director of Development Policy and Analysis of the United Nations and Professor of Finance and Development at the Institute of Social Studies, The Hague, The Netherlands.

Enrique Ganuza is Chief Economist for Latin America and the Caribbean of UNDP, New York.

Samuel Morley is Senior Research Fellow at the International Food Policy Research Institute (IFPRI), Washington D.C.

Sherman Robinson is Professor of Economics at University of Sussex and Fellow of the Institute of Development Studies (IDS) at the University of Sussex.

Routledge Studies in Development Economics

Who Gains from Free Trade?

Export-led growth, inequality and poverty in Latin America

Edited by

Rob Vos
Enrique Ganuza
Samuel Morley
Sherman Robinson

Routledge
Taylor & Francis Group

LONDON AND NEW YORK

First published 2006
by Routledge
2 Park Square, Milton Park,
Abingdon, Oxon OX14 4RN

Simultaneously published in the USA and Canada
by Routledge
711 Third Avenue, New York, NY 10017

Routledge is an imprint of the Taylor & Francis Group, an informa business

First issued in paperback 2012

© 2006 Rob Vos, Enrique Ganuza, Samuel Morley and Sherman Robinson

Typeset in Times by Keyword Group Ltd

British Library Cataloguing in Publication Data
A catalogue record for this book is available from the British Library

Library of Congress Cataloging in Publication Data
A catalog record for this book has been requested

ISBN13: 978-0-415-77044-6 (hbk)
ISBN13: 978-0-415-63238-6 (pbk)

Contents

**3   Are export promotion and trade liberalization good
for Latin America's poor?**   55
A comparative macro–micro CGE analysis
ENRIQUE GANUZA, SAMUEL MORLEY, SHERMAN ROBINSON,
VALERIA PIÑEIRO AND ROB VOS

**4   Argentina – the convertibility plan, trade openness,
poverty and inequality**   125
CAROLINA DÍAZ-BONILLA, EUGENIO DÍAZ-BONILLA,
VALERIA PIÑEIRO AND SHERMAN ROBINSON

**5   Bolivia – export promotion and its effects on growth,
employment and poverty**   150
WILSON JIMÉNEZ

9 Ecuador – dollarization, trade liberalization and poverty   270

ROB VOS AND MAURICIO LEÓN

10 Mexico – do the poor benefit from increased openness?   302

SAMUEL A. MORLEY AND CAROLINA DÍAZ-BONILLA

List of tables and figures

Tables

Figures

About the authors

The Editors:

Enrique Ganuza – Chief Economist for Latin America and the Caribbean of United Nations Development Program (UNDP), New York.

Samuel Morley – Senior Research Fellow at the International Food Policy Research Institute (IFPRI), Washington, DC.

Sherman Robinson – Professor of Economics at the University of Sussex and Fellow of the Institute of Development Studies (IDS) at the University of Sussex. At the time of writing, Director of Trade and Macroeconomics Division, International Food Policy Research Institute (IFPRI), Washington, DC.

Rob Vos – Director of Development Policy and Analysis of the United Nations, New York. At the time of writing, Professor of Finance and Development, Institute of Social Studies, The Hague, and Professor of Development Economics, Free University, Amsterdam.

Other Contributors:

Carolina Díaz-Bonilla – Economist at the World Bank. At the time of writing, at the International Food Policy Research Institute (IFPRI), Washington, DC.

Eugenio Díaz-Bonilla – Executive Director for Argentina and Haiti at the Inter-American Development Bank. At the time of writing, at the International Food Policy Research Institute (IFPRI), Washington, DC.

Angela Ferriol – Senior Researcher and Director Social Development Division at Instituto Nacional de Investigaciones Económicas (INIE), Havana.

Francisco Galrão Carneiro – World Bank, Washington, DC. At the time of writing, Catholic University of Brasilia, Brasilia.

Juan García Carpio – Research Assistant at Grupo de Análisis para el Desarrollo (GRADE), Lima.

Alfredo González – Senior Researcher at Instituto Nacional de Investigaciones Económicas (INIE), Havana.

Alina Hernández – Researcher at Instituto Nacional de Investigaciones Económicas (INIE), Havana.

Xuan Hoang – Visiting Researcher at Instituto Nacional de Investigaciones Económicas (INIE), Havana.

Wilson Jiménez – Director Social Development Division, Unidad de Análisis de Política Económica (UDAPE), La Paz.

Silvia Laens – Senior Researcher at Centro de Investigaciones Económicas (CINVE), Montevideo.

Mauricio León – United Nations Development Program (UNDP) consultant. At the time of writing, Director of the Integrated System of Social Indicators of Ecuador (SIISE) at the Technical Secretariat of the Social Cabinet, Quito.

Marcelo Perera – Senior Researcher at Centro de Investigaciones Económicas (CINVE), Montevideo.

Valeria Piñeiro – Research Fellow at the International Food Policy Research Institute (IFPRI), Washington, DC.

Jorge Saba Arbache – University of Brasilia, Brasilia.

Pablo Sauma – Professor at National University of Costa Rica, San José.

Marco V. Sánchez C.– Researcher at UN-ECLAC, Mexico. At the time of writing, researcher at the Institute of Social Studies (ISS), The Hague.

Alonso Seguro Vasi – Consultant at Grupo de Análisis para el Desarrollo (GRADE), Lima.

Preface

For almost a decade, the United Nations Development Program (UNDP) and the Economic Commission for Latin America and the Caribbean of the United Nations (UN-ECLAC) have coordinated a number of comparative studies on the macroeconomic performance, poverty and inequality in Latin America and the Caribbean. Poverty reduction is high on the international development agenda, but still we know relatively little about what determines poverty in the region and how economic reform policies impact on human well-being and income distribution. One thing is clear though, namely, that the effectiveness of particular types of policies may vary greatly from country to country. In this vein, UNDP and UN-ECLAC have joined forces once more to study the impact of economic policies on poverty and inequality through a comparative analysis of a large number of countries from the region.

A common starting point is that across the region exports have become the engine of growth following a decade of so-called structural adjustment policies in the 1980s and even more drastic policy reforms during the 1990s. During the 1980s the countries used mainly macroeconomic instruments to steer the economy towards better export performance, such as through exchange rate policies and fiscal adjustment. From the late 1980s onwards, most countries engaged in deeper, microeconomic reforms, including rapid and drastic trade liberalization, financial liberalization, capital account opening, privatizations, labour market deregulation and tax reforms, among other things. The expectation that this would yield higher, more stable and sustainable growth has not been met, however. Growth has indeed become more reliant on exports and thus on world markets, but it has remained highly volatile. Also, the expected beneficial impact on poverty reduction has not been very visible (or not at all) in most countries of the region. The trends are not uniform though in all countries of the region, even though on the face of it they all implemented similar reforms with similar timing.

So why, unlike what seems to have occurred in East Asia, has export-led growth promoted through trade liberalization not provided the expected welfare and poverty reduction gains for Latin America? Why do outcomes vary so much across country experiences? To find answers to these questions, UNDP and UN-ECLAC joined forces with two prestigious international research institutions, the International Food Policy Research Institute (IFPRI) in Washington, DC, and the Institute of Social Studies (ISS) in The Hague. The present study provides some answers, specifically as to the impact of trade liberalization and other export promotion policies on growth, employment, inequality and poverty in 16 countries of the region during the 1990s. On the basis of country comparative analysis, the study yields both lessons for the region at large and specific policy recommendations for the various country cases.

In order to obtain answers as close as possible to country realities, the project conducted the investigation in collaboration with teams of local experts. Combining country expert knowledge with a common, rigorous modelling methodology to isolate the effects of policy reforms on poverty has been the approach to ensure a high degree of realism in the analysis and maximum comparability. Without the input of the country experts, many appearing as chapter authors in this volume, this undertaking would not have been possible. The investigation took place over a period of two years, during which four workshops were held at which the research methodology was agreed and refined and intermediate results were discussed and compared. UNDP country offices in Nicaragua, Dominican Republic and Argentina offered invaluable support in making these events happen.

The editors of this volume received invaluable research support and backstopping in the application of the general equilibrium models in each of the countries from Valeria Piñeiro, Research Fellow at IFPRI. Niek de Jong of ISS gave important inputs into the methodology and application of the microsimulation method in several countries. Francisco Ferreira of the World Bank participated in the final project meeting in Buenos Aires and gave very useful comments and suggestions for the interpretation of the findings of the study. Edgar Pardo, New School for Social Research, New York, gave valuable research assistance in the analysis of Chapter 3 and Sandra van Ginhoven and Leandro Serino (at ISS) did the same for the core statistical data comprised in Chapter 2.

Kathy Ogle translated half of the chapters from the original Spanish to English and Admasu Shiferaw of ISS provided helpful assistance in the final editing of the English manuscript. The Ford Foundation generously financed various workshops. Manuel Montes from the New York office of the Ford Foundation accompanied the research team throughout this project.

The authors are most grateful to the hosting agencies, UNDP, UN-ECLAC, IFPRI and ISS. They provided all the institutional support required, while leaving all the intellectual freedom needed to conduct this research on issues so central to the well-being of the populations in the countries of the region, but which are also controversial. It goes without saying that the opinions expressed in this volume are exclusively those of the authors.

Rob Vos
Enrique Ganuza
Samuel Morley
Sherman Robinson
New York, Washington, Sussex and The Hague,
May 2005

1 Introduction

Rising exports, slower growth and greater inequality: is trade liberalization to blame?

Rob Vos, Enrique Ganuza and Samuel Morley

1.1 Reforms and dismal growth

Since the late 1980s, almost all Latin American countries have gone through a process of far-reaching economic reforms, featuring in particular trade, financial and capital account liberalization. Economic opening has gone hand in hand with large financial inflows, particularly in the first half of the 1990s. Increased openness has brought new sources of economic growth but it has also increased volatility and sensitivity to external shocks. At first, the reforms seemed to be working as promised. Economic growth increased, inflation declined and there was a big surge in foreign capital inflows. But somewhere around 1995 or thereabouts, growth faltered, particularly in the countries of South America. So did exports. They had been expected to be the leading sector in the post-reform growth model, but unlike the Asian experience, export-led growth in Latin America has proved so far to be anything but a development miracle. Not only has overall growth been far less than during the period of import substitution, but export growth has also slowed down and is still dominated by primary products. Also, income inequality has risen in a context where inequality was already very high to begin with. Not surprisingly, little progress has been made on poverty reduction since 1990. Indeed, poverty has been rising in the region as growth slowed down after 1995.

An important and natural question to ask is whether the reforms are the reason or at least a significant contributing factor for the poor performance of the region since the mid-1990s? Did they contribute to the growth slowdown and the rise in poverty and inequality? These are crucial questions and the more so because the countries in the region are considering further trade integration under the flag of the Free Trade Area of the Americas (FTAA), bilateral free trade treaties with the USA and/or in the context of regional economic integration areas such as Mercosur, the Andean Pact, CAFTA and NAFTA. The countries of the region also have become members of the World Trade Organization (WTO), subscribing to further trade liberalization, including the elimination of export subsidies. Key players from the region, like Brazil, were instrumental in blocking a new global trade agreement under the aegis of WTO in September 2003 precisely because of concerns about the developmental and equity effects of freer world trade.

In this book, we take a dual approach to trying to find answers to what was the impact of the reforms and the switch to an export-led growth strategy. Since we believe that countries differ in structure and that structure matters, we have collected together case studies for 16 of the countries in the region, covering over 90 per cent of its population and of its GDP. The comparative analyses in Chapters 2–3 covers all the 16 countries, while in Chapters 4–12 selected country cases are presented whereby for each country we first present a historical narrative of recent growth and poverty trends.[1] Then, we develop a country-specific computable general equilibrium (CGE) model with which we can simulate the effects on output and employment of trade liberalization, export promotion and various external shocks, holding everything else constant. We also develop a microsimulation model to translate these sectoral impacts into changes in poverty and inequality.

Our brief answer to the main questions posed above is that trade liberalization and the switch to export-led growth are not the cause of the growth slowdown in the region. Nor are they the cause of rising poverty and inequality. On the contrary, for most countries their impact is mildly positive for both growth and poverty reduction. But overall, the impact of the reforms and export growth, while positive, are small. So while the reforms are not to blame for the region's woes, they do not appear to be the solution for them either. The case studies also show that trade reforms increase skill-intensity and that some social groups win (mostly the better educated workers and profit earners) and some lose (often agricultural and unskilled workers) in the process providing the explanation for the rising inequality observed in most country experiences.

1.2 The analytical approach of this study

There are no facile answers about the impact of trade reforms on growth, poverty and income distribution but, whatever they are, they are bound to be country specific, requiring in-depth analysis of the nature and timing of reforms and the prevailing economic structure. Cross-country econometric studies are often used as an alternative way to find answers to the questions raised.[2] Such studies typically are not very enlightening about the mechanisms by which trade liberalization and export promotion affect growth and income distribution and by their nature have little to add to country-level policy debates. Instead, we will rely on country case studies to obtain policy-relevant answers. But even then, how can we separate the effects of specific policy changes from other factors such as external shocks and other policy initiatives? We faced this standard problem of economic analysis by combining four methodological elements.

First, we present country narratives for 9 out of 16 countries discussing policy changes and observed outcomes in a *before-and-after* approach. The country stories start with a basic set of questions and hypotheses and a simple analytical framework suggesting possible channels of causation of the type outlined above.

Second, still within the realm of before-and-after, to identify the importance of changes in the external and domestic policy environment we applied a set of standardized decompositions of sources of output growth and of the forces driving balance-of-payments adjustment (see Chapter 2 for the related methodologies). We use the former type of decomposition to identify to what extent trade has become a more forceful engine of growth since trade liberalization. The second type of decomposition is a standard decomposition of the current account of the balance of payments, which enables us to show the observed relative importance of various types of external shocks (in terms of trade, world demand, interest rates, etc.) and domestic responses (through adjustments in aggregate demand, and import and export ratios) in the pre- and post-liberalization episodes.

Third, to isolate the effects of different types of trade reforms and external shocks, a standardized CGE model framework was set up (see Löfgren *et al.* 2001 and Chapter 3). The country models capture the structural features of each country through a social accounting matrix, country-relevant elasticities of commodity and factor market adjustment to relative price changes and country-specific 'closure rules', which define policy regimes (such as a fixed or flexible exchange rate regime, a fixed or endogenous fiscal balance) and behavioural rules in key markets (endogenous or exogenous capital flows, price or quantity adjustment in different segments of the labour and other factor markets and the degree of factor mobility across sectors). We then perform a common set of counterfactual model simulations for each country (with-and-without) of different trade policies and external shocks and assess the (static) impact on (sectoral) output and export growth, employment, labour–income inequality and household welfare.

Finally, the poverty and inequality impact of the counterfactual CGE analysis is estimated using a microsimulation methodology. This sequential modelling approach fits a recent tradition of assessing the poverty impact of economic policies in developing countries (see Bourguignon *et al.* 2002b). One drawback of the typical CGE model, including the ones used in this study, is that simulation results are only obtained for between-group differentials in terms of employment and factor remuneration. The assessment of the impact on household incomes and consumption is also limited to differentials between highly aggregated groups. In consequence, the CGE model captures only a part of the distribution effects and therefore lacks sufficient detail for a meaningful assessment of the poverty impact of the policy simulations. The microsimulation approach helps to overcome this shortcoming by taking the outcomes of the CGE model simulation and applying the simulated changes in labour market parameters to the full income distribution using household survey data. The microsimulation methodology also resolves the issue of which *individuals* in the distribution are likely to move position in the face of the counterfactual labour market adjustment (e.g. which worker will loose his or her job if the unemployment rate moves up). Most country studies follow the microsimulation approach as developed in a previous study (Ganuza *et al.* 2002), but in a few cases (Argentina, Mexico) the approach as suggested by

Bourguignon *et al.* (2002a) was followed. These methodologies are described in Chapter 3.

1.3 Overview of the main findings

Chapter 2 analyses growth trends and the vulnerability to external shocks of the countries in Latin America and the Caribbean over almost a quarter of a century since 1980. It is shown that as a consequence of the process of economic opening to world markets, growth has become export-led in virtually all countries of the region. However, unlike the experience with export-led growth in East Asia, Latin America's new growth strategy seems to come with a number of less virtuous characteristics. First, while more reliant on exports, economic growth did not significantly increase after trade opening. Instead, growth slowed down and economic performance was worse in the second half of the 1990s than in the first and most countries slipped to negative per capita income growth at the turn of the century. Second, vulnerability to fluctuations in global commodity markets (i.e. terms-of-trade shocks and volatility in global demand) remains high and is a first indication of insufficient diversification of trade. This vulnerability to trade shocks cannot by itself explain the dismal growth performance, as in fact for most countries terms of trade and world demand for their exports improved during the 1990s.

Third, for most countries of the region export growth has been below that of world trade, implying lower export penetration in global markets as a result of losses in competitiveness. At the same time, import dependence has risen more strongly than the capacity to export. As a result, capital flows have become more important to sustain a growth path built on this paradoxical combination of increasing reliance on exports and a structural rise in the trade deficit. Capital flows in turn have both initiated (to the extent exogenous) and reinforced this pattern by pushing up real exchange rates, cheapening imports and squeezing profits for exporters in the short run. As capital flows themselves have been volatile, to a large part for reasons exogenous to the economic conditions of the countries of the region, macroeconomic adjustment has become more difficult to steer, resulting in short-lived booms as access to foreign borrowing eases and demand deflation as it contracts with important implications for employment and wages. Trade reforms therefore must be studied in conjunction with such macroeconomic constraints.

The CGE model framework laid out in Chapter 3 deals with this by the explicit specification of alternative macroeconomic closure rules under which trade reform policies work their way through the economy, labour markets and eventually poverty. Such closure rules define whether in a particular context there is easy or constrained access to foreign savings, whether investment demand is savings constrained or not and whether there is a binding fiscal constraint or not. These macroeconomic conditions also reflect alternative policy regimes: a fixed versus flexible exchange rate regime, a Keynesian demand-constrained versus neoclassical supply-constrained policy environment and a fixed versus flexible target for the fiscal deficit, respectively. By applying the same closure rules across countries we are able to detect the differential impact of trade reform due to differences in economic structure and degree of flexibility in market adjustment. Subsequently, we compare this with the type of macroeconomic closure rules considered relevant for each country case to understand how trade reforms interact with varying macroeconomic constraints. We find that trade liberalization increased output in almost every country in our sample. This finding is consistent across alternative macroeconomic constraints, but output growth is stronger under a regime with easy access to foreign capital and subsequent real exchange rate appreciation. Under the latter scenario, the country models reproduce the pattern observed in reality for most countries, that is, trade liberalization increases the growth rate but it is led by the non-traded goods sector and imports rather than exports. The trade deficit increases. Output effects are dampened visibly if the level of foreign savings is assumed to be fixed before and after trade opening.

In the same vein, trade liberalization leads either to increasing wages or employment depending on the labour market closure used in the country-specific models. Consistent with this, poverty declined in all but one country (Ecuador) in the unilateral trade liberalization scenario. Rising labour inequality, particularly between skilled and unskilled workers, emerges in the majority of cases, but does not necessarily translate into more inequality in per capita household incomes because of offsetting positive employment effects. The inequality effects tend to be stronger in natural resource abundant economies like Argentina, Bolivia, Costa Rica, Ecuador and Peru. The effects on poverty and inequality of further unilateral trade liberalization are small, but positive.

These results are broadly consistent with moving to completely free trade under WTO rules or to a region-wide multilateral trade agreement under FTAA. Both these changes also reduce poverty and inequality in most of the countries, but not in all cases. Poverty rises (modestly) under these scenarios in Costa Rica (only WTO), Ecuador, Paraguay and Venezuela, mainly due to the negative impact on agriculture in these countries, which is not compensated by sufficient employment and income growth in other sectors. Gains from further trade integration are clearly not evenly distributed within countries and this is therefore a legitimate concern in trade negotiations.

With a few exceptions (Brazil and Argentina), unilateral export promotion via export subsidies is also found to be poverty reducing in apparent contradiction with the WTO scenario. In a sense, it works like a tariff cut stimulating aggregate employment as mostly more labour-intensive (e.g. agriculture) sectors benefit from subsidies that are increased in the scenario. Skill-differentials rise in some countries and fall in others. Thus, one cannot say that choosing a more export-led growth strategy will in general favour either the skilled or the unskilled. This depends on the export structure of individual countries. The country stories in Chapters 4–12 present the details.

These model results have to be interpreted with some caution. The reader should note that our findings are general equilibrium, comparative static results that do not reflect the costs of adjusting to a changed production structure. If we assume that the exchange rate is fixed, the simulation determines the long-run or permanent impact of lowering the tariff rate while bringing in more foreign capital to permanently finance a bigger balance-of-payments deficit. As indicated, the latter change is expansionary (though growth is led by non-traded goods rather than exports). If foreign saving is constrained, the exchange rate has to depreciate to allow exports to expand enough to pay for additional imports. But total output and employment increase in both cases and poverty declines. The simulation results also suggest that if no poverty reduction was observed in practice after trade liberalization, it is either because a lot of other poverty-increasing factors were changing at the same time (most typically dealing with macro shocks; see Taylor and Vos 2002) or because the economies are still in the process of adapting their production structures.

Notes

1   The full set of country cases can be obtained from United Nations Development Programme (UNDP) or downloaded at the following website: http://www.undp.org/rblac/drafts/
2   See, e.g. the recent debate spurred by papers of Sachs and Warner (1995), Rodriguez and Rodrik (2000), Dollar and Kraay (2001a, b), Easterly (2001) and Rodrik *et al.* (2002). And see Berg and Krueger (2003) for a summary of the main issues of controversy.

References

Berg, Andrew and Anne Krueger (2003) 'Trade, growth, and poverty: a selective survey', IMF Working Paper WP/03/30, Washington, DC: International Monetary Fund.

Bourguignon, François, Anne-Sophie Robilliard and Sherman Robinson (2002a) 'Representative versus real households in the macro-economic modeling of inequality', Washington, DC: World Bank and IFPRI (mimeo).

Bourguignon, François, Luis Pereira da Silva and Nicholas Stern (2002b) 'Evaluating the poverty impact of economic policies: some analytical challenges', Washington, DC: The World Bank (mimeo).

Dollar, David and Aart Kraay (2001a) 'Trade, growth and poverty', Washington, DC: The World Bank (mimeo).

Dollar, David and Aart Kraay (2001b) 'Growth is good for the poor', World Bank Policy Research Working Paper No. 2587, Washington, DC: The World Bank.

Easterly, William (2001) *The Elusive Quest for Growth. Economists' Adventures and Misadventures in the Tropics*, Cambridge, MA: MIT Press.

Ganuza, Enrique, Ricardo Paes de Barros, Lance Taylor and Rob Vos (eds) (2001) *Liberalización, Desigualdad y Pobreza: América Latina y el Caribe en los 90*, Buenos Aires: EUDEBA (for UNDP and CEPAL).

Ganuza, Enrique, Ricardo Paes de Barros and Rob Vos (2002) 'Labour market adjustment, poverty and inequality during liberalisation', in: Rob Vos, Lance Taylor and Ricardo Paes de Barros (eds) *Economic Liberalisation, Distribution and Poverty: Latin America in the 1990s*, Cheltenham, UK: Edward Elgar Publishers, pp. 54–88.

Löfgren, Hans, Rebecca Lee Harris and Sherman Robinson (2001) 'A standard computable general equilibrium (CGE) model in GAMS', TMD Discussion Paper No. 75, Washington, DC: International Food Policy Research Institute (IFPRI).

Rodriguez, Francisco and Dani Rodrik (2000) 'Trade policy and economic growth: A skeptic's guide to the cross-national evidence', Cambridge, MA: Kennedy School of Government and University of Maryland (mimeo).

Rodrik, Dani, Arvind Subramanian and Francesco Trebbi (2002) 'Institutions role: the primacy of institutions over geography and integration in economic development', Cambridge, MA: Harvard University (mimeo).

Sachs, Jeffrey and Andrew Warner (1995) 'Economic reform and the process of global integration', *Brookings Papers on Economic Activity*, 1: 1–118.

Taylor, Lance and Rob Vos (2002) 'Balance of payments liberalization in Latin America: effects on growth, distribution and poverty', in: Rob Vos, Lance Taylor and Ricardo Paes de Barros (eds) *Economic Liberalization, Income Distribution and Poverty. Latin America in the 1990s*, Cheltenham, UK: Edward Elgar Publishers, pp. 1–53.

Vos, Rob, Lance Taylor and Ricardo Paes de Barros (eds) (2002) *Economic Liberalization, Income Distribution and Poverty. Latin America in the 1990s*, Cheltenham, UK: Edward Elgar Publishers.

2 Bad luck or wrong policies?

External shocks, domestic adjustment and growth slowdown in Latin America and the Caribbean

Samuel Morley and Rob Vos

2.1 Introduction

For most Latin American countries, the 1990s have turned out to be a disappointment. Almost all of them adopted the reforms of the Washington consensus on the promise that these would yield efficiency and hence welfare gains. They controlled inflation, sold off state enterprises, lowered tariffs, opened their capital markets, reformed their tax systems, deregulated financial markets and lowered government deficits. In most cases these reforms were implemented in the late 1980s and early 1990s. Things seemed to be going well in the initial post-liberalization phase, prior to the Tequila Crisis in 1995. Growth rates were much higher than they had been in the 1980s, and for some countries were even higher than they had been in the long period between the Second World War and the debt crisis. Things were expected to get even better in the following years since in many countries the reforms had only recently been adopted and since it takes time to reap their full benefits.

But it is not working out that way for most of the countries in the region. Instead of accelerating, growth has decelerated, especially in the countries of South America. Overall average per capita income growth in the region between 1990 and 1995 was 1.8 per cent per year (Table 2.1). That rate fell to 1.4 per cent per year between 1995 and 2000 and further down to 0.6 per cent in 1999–2001. Only a few countries (Dominican Republic, Haiti, Mexico, Nicaragua and Suriname) did better in the last 5 years than they did in the first five of the decade. However, also these countries saw a steep fall in growth rates towards the end of the decade and into the twenty-first century. About half of the countries listed in Table 2.1 saw average incomes decline during 1999–2001.

This deceleration of growth is particularly pronounced in South America. In the first half of the 1990s, per capita growth in South America averaged 2.5 per cent per year, while it came to a complete stop in Mexico and Central America, which is almost entirely explained by Mexico's poor growth performance up to the Tequila Crisis. However, in the second half of the decade, when the reforms were supposed to bear fruit, growth in South America dropped to 0.8 per cent per year and turned negative around the turn of the century. In Mexico, Central America and the Caribbean, growth recovered to a respectable 3.6 per cent

Table 2.1 Latin America: growth, volatility and recession

	GDP % growth rates						Volatility[1]			Recession years (no.) (1995–2001)[2]
	1960–80	1980–5	1985–90	1990–5	1995–2000	1999–2001[3]	1960s and 1970s	1980s	1990s	
Argentina	1.8	−4.0	−5.8	5.1	1.3	−3.8	4.8	5.5	5.7	4
Bolivia	1.0	−3.8	−3.8	1.6	1.0	−0.5	4.3	2.7	1.6	3
Brazil	4.6	−1.0	−0.8	1.6	0.9	1.6	3.7	4.7	3.0	2
Chile	1.5	−0.7	4.3	6.9	2.9	2.3	5.0	6.3	3.5	1
Colombia	2.7	0.1	2.6	2.5	−1.0	0.2	1.7	1.6	2.7	3
Costa Rica	2.4	−2.6	−1.0	3.0	2.8	−0.5	2.6	4.4	2.8	2
Cuba					4.2	5.4				0
Dominican Republic	3.4	−0.2	0.7	2.4	5.8	3.3	6.9	2.9	4.2	0
Ecuador	3.5	−0.6	−0.9	1.2	−1.9	2.0	5.1	4.4	3.1	3
El Salvador	1.0	−3.5	−2.9	4.0	1.0	0.0	3.0	5.5	1.9	2
Guatemala	2.8	−3.6	−3.2	1.6	1.2	0.2	1.9	2.7	0.7	1
Guyana	1.0	−4.2	−5.9	6.8	2.2	−0.6	5.5	4.9	4.2	2
Haiti	0.5	−2.8	−4.5	−5.2	0.0	−2.2	4.3	2.9	5.4	3
Honduras	1.8	−1.5	−1.4	0.6	0.2	1.2	3.1	2.6	2.7	1
Jamaica	0.6	−1.5	2.6	0.3	−1.4	−0.5	5.6	4.6	2.0	5
Mexico	3.5	−0.3	−0.6	−0.3	3.9	1.6	2.3	4.3	3.6	2
Nicaragua	0.3	−2.4	−7.8	−1.5	3.2	3.0	8.6	4.8	3.2	0
Panama	3.1	1.3	−1.4	3.6	1.8	−0.2	2.9	6.1	2.5	1
Paraguay	3.8	−1.3	−0.6	0.5	−1.9	−1.3	2.7	5.3	1.6	5
Peru	1.6	−2.0	−5.8	3.7	0.8	0.0	2.7	8.0	4.9	3
Suriname		−2.9	−3.3	0.5	2.9	−2.0	2.6	8.8	7.6	2

(Continued)

Table 2.1 (Continued)

	GDP % growth rates						Volatility[1]			Recession years (no.) (1995–2001)[2]
	1960–80	1980–5	1985–90	1990–5	1995–2000	1999–2001[3]	1960s and 1970s	1980s	1990s	
Uruguay	1.5	−4.4	−1.3	3.2	1.4	−3.0	2.8	6.5	3.7	4
Venezuela, RB	0.4	−3.4	−3.4	1.1	−1.4	1.0	3.0	4.8	4.4	3
Weighted averages										
Latin America and Caribbean	2.8	−1.4	−1.6	1.8	1.4	0.6	1.60	2.56	2.03	3
South America	2.7	−1.9	−1.9	2.5	0.8	0.1	2.06	3.43	2.49	3
Central America, Mexico and Carribean (excluding Cuba)[4]	3.2	−0.5	−0.9	0.0	3.6	1.5	1.73	3.58	3.07	2
Unweighted averages										
Latin America and Caribbean	2.0	−2.1	−2.0	2.0	1.3	0.3	0.99	2.05	1.23	2
South America	2.2	−2.1	−1.6	2.7	0.2	−0.2	1.15	3.09	2.20	2
Central America, Mexico and Carribean (excluding Cuba)[4]	1.8	−2.0	−2.4	1.3	2.1	0.7	1.50	1.70	1.04	0

Source: World Bank data

Notes
1 Volatility is defined as standard deviation of per capita income growth rates
2 Number of recession years in a period; recession year is defined as year of negative per capita income growth
3 For Cuba, the period refers to 1999–2000
4 The subregion also includes Suriname and Guyana

per year during 1995–2000, but with a significant slowdown towards the end of the decade.

Although disappointing, the growth performance during the final years of the century was still better than in the lost decade of the 1980s when nearly all countries in the region suffered negative per capita income growth. However, the recent growth performance has been much worse, in South America in particular, than during the heydays of the import substitution policies of the 1960s and 1970s. This dismal performance is characterized though by significant differences between countries, substantial volatility and recurrent crises in a growing number of countries. Defining the years of crisis as cases of negative per capita income growth, there were 16 out of 23 countries with two or more years of crisis during 1995–2001, including Argentina, Paraguay and Jamaica, which have been in an almost permanent state of crisis since 1995 and Bolivia, Colombia, Ecuador, Peru, Uruguay and Venezuela with three crisis years in the period. The South American countries were in recession more than half (52 per cent) of the time between 1995 and 2001. In Mexico, Central America and the Caribbean the comparable figure was 26 per cent, or, excluding Jamaica, one-fifth of the time. For most of the region, matters have not improved since 2000, as marked by the severe deepening of the crises in Argentina, Uruguay and Venezuela and the emergence of a recession in Mexico and much of Central America and the Caribbean following the slowdown of the US economy and the steep decline in *maquila* industrial activity.

In thinking about growth rates or evaluating country performance, it is appropriate to compare current with past performance avoiding periods of extreme volatility. However, obtaining estimates of long-term growth is very difficult for periods that are marked both by recession and recovery. For Latin America, this suggests a comparison of growth in the 1990s with growth in the 20-year period prior to the debt crisis (Figure 2.1a). Eight of the 23 countries significantly improved their performance (Argentina, Chile, Costa Rica, Dominican Republic, Guyana, El Salvador, Peru and Uruguay). Growth rates in Bolivia and Nicaragua are about the same and the rest of the countries did worse or much worse than usual. If one looks at just the last 5 years, there are only three countries (Dominican Republic, Mexico and Nicaragua) whose performance has been significantly better than in the base period[1] and 12 (Argentina, Chile, Colombia, Ecuador, El Salvador, Guyana, Jamaica, Panama, Paraguay, Peru, Uruguay and Venezuela) for which per capita growth during 1995–2000 was at least two percentage points per year below the base period (see Figure 2.1b).

Latin America clearly remains a very volatile region as compared to most other parts of the world (IDB 1995; Rodrik 1999; De Ferranti *et al.* 2000). The above description of patterns confirms such volatility. However, in terms of growth performance it is not true that volatility has increased during the 1990s. As Table 2.1 shows, volatility (defined as the standard deviation of the per capita income growth rate) in the 1990s was somewhat lower than during the 1980s, though generally higher than during the period of high growth of the 1960s and 1970s.

In short, at least since 1995 something seems to have gone wrong already, especially in South America, and throughout the region since 2000. What could

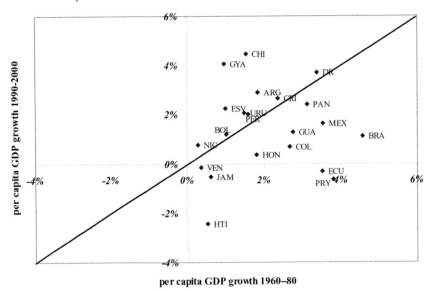

per capita GDP growth 1960–80

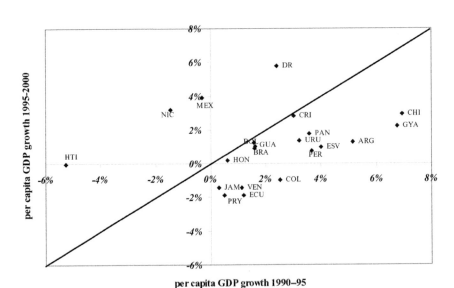

per capita GDP growth 1990–95

Figure 2.1 (a) Upper panel: Growth performance in the 1990s compared to 1960–80. (b) Lower panel: Bright and dark sides of growth in the 1990s. (From World Bank data.)

it be? There are a number of possibilities. It could be that the investment rate has never recovered from the decline it suffered in the 1980s. In that case, the growth rate would be lower simply because the growth rate of fixed capital is lower. It could also be that trade liberalization has reduced the domestic production of importables by more than the hoped for expansion of exports. It could also be that the international environment is now less favourable than it used to be in the 1950–80 period or than it was earlier in the 1990s. Reductions in capital flows after the Tequila Crisis in 1995 and the East Asia financial crisis in 1998 coupled with the falling world prices for commodities may also have a negative impact on the prospects and growth of Latin America. Finally, the effect on growth of the reforms themselves could be perverse. We now consider each of these possibilities.

2.2 Bad luck? External shocks during the 1990s

A changing external outlook

The growth strategy of Latin American countries during the 1980s and 1990s is analysed through the performance of their economies, taking into account external shocks and the domestic responses as factors of the current account deficit trends.[2] The objective of the present analysis is to identify the nature of the shocks Latin American countries experienced during the 1980s and 1990s, to compare the cross-country differences in experiences and to assess the relationship between external shocks and domestic macroeconomic adjustment. This section concentrates on the nature and size of the external shocks.

The analytical distinction between external shocks and domestic response as causal factors in current account deficits and external debt accumulation has been central to the debates on structural adjustment and economic reforms in developing countries. The exogenous and endogenous factors typically show a complex interaction, more complex than standard textbook approaches to macroeconomic adjustment typically assume. Our aim here is to identify the nature of the shocks and their relative size through fairly straightforward and standard decomposition analysis. The same methodology also allows us to assess how key macroeconomic aggregates have responded to changes in the external environment.

The economic reforms of the 1980s and 1990s have led to greater openness and hence one could expect greater sensitivity to shocks emanating from the global economy. However, at the same time, the reforms should be expected to have shifted resources towards more competitive and diversified export sectors, reducing the traditional sensitivity to terms-of-trade shocks caused by the region's heavy reliance on primary exports. Further, the financial opening process would make capital flows more endogenous to domestic market conditions and facilitate its movement into more diversified portfolios.

The aggregate picture suggests significant export orientation of the Latin American economies, with the region's export share in GDP doubling from about 9 to 20 per cent between 1980 and 2000. The export structure also appears to have become more diversified, reducing the heavy reliance on primary exports in favour of non-traditional manufactures (Figure 2.2a). However, this outcome is strongly influenced by Mexico's performance, which showed the largest shift away from primary-export dependence during the 1990s. As shown by Figure 2.2b and Table 2.2, Brazil and the rest of South America barely reduced their reliance

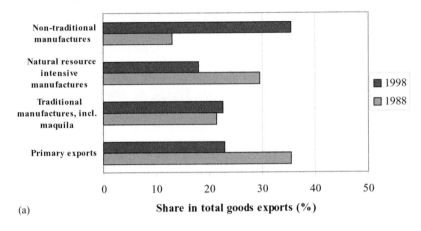

(a)   **Share in total goods exports (%)**

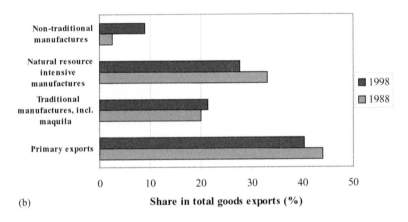

(b)   **Share in total goods exports (%)**

Figure 2.2 (a) Latin America and the Caribbean: export structure, 1988 and 1998.
(b) South America (excluding Brazil): export structure, 1988 and 1998. [From
CEPAL data (see Table 2.2).]

on agricultural and mining exports and also manufactured exports remained strongly
natural resource-based. The Central American economies followed Mexico's
patterns influenced by substantial growth of *maquila* industries.

There was a recovery of capital flows towards the region in the 1990s facilitated by the settling of much of the commercial bank debt overhang of the 1980s
under Brady agreements, the financial opening, privatization of public enterprises
and macroeconomic stabilization policies. However, probably equally important
were events in global capital markets exogenous to the region, including the entrance
of large institutional investors (such as pension funds) as global investors. Capital
inflows to Latin America averaged 3 per cent of GDP per year during the decade.
However, much of the boom took place in the early 1990s, particularly towards
Argentina, Brazil, Chile, Colombia and Mexico, with a larger share going to some

Table 2.2 Latin America and the Caribbean: changing export structures in the 1990s

	Mexico		Brazil		South America (excluding Brazil)		Central America		Caribbean (English speaking)		Latin America and Caribbean	
	1988	1998	1988	1998	1988	1998	1988	1998	1988	1998	1988	1998
Primary exports	42.9	10.0	18.8	19.6	44.0	40.4	63.8	41.7	27.8	28.2	35.5	22.9
Manufactures	56.7	89.9	80.1	79.2	55.6	57.8	35.7	58.2	72.0	70.2	63.9	76.2
Traditional manufactures[1]	10.8	20.0	29.2	28.9	20.0	21.3	23.6	31.1	19.1	21.0	21.3	22.6
Natural resource-intensive manufactures[2]	20.6	8.3	31.5	24.1	33.1	27.6	6.9	8.9	50.4	47.3	29.5	18.1
Non-traditional manufactures[3]	25.3	61.6	19.4	26.2	2.5	8.9	5.2	18.2	2.5	1.9	13.1	35.5
Other	0.4	0.1	1.1	1.2	0.4	1.8	0.5	0.1	0.2	1.6	0.6	0.9
Total	100	100	100	100	100	100	100	100	100	100	100	100

Source: CEPAL

Notes
1 Includes food processing, textiles as well as *maquila*
2 Refers to natural resource-based products with large-scale economies; includes petrochemicals, paper, cement and basic metals
3 Includes durable consumption goods, machinery and equipment and other manufactures

of the smaller economies in the latter part of the decade. However, by that time several global financial crises led to sudden stops in capital flows, particularly portfolio investments, temporarily after the 1995 Mexican peso crisis and most strongly after the 1997–8 Asian and Russian financial crises. From 2000 onwards, also direct foreign investment to the region declined (except for Brazil), affecting most, in particular *maquila* industries in Mexico and Central America (CEPAL 2003).

Decomposition methodology

In short, external structures of the economies of the region have changed and with that the degree of vulnerability to shocks in the global economy, but with clear differences across the countries. To assess the nature and degree of shocks, we adopt a basic balance-of-payments decomposition methodology originating from Balassa (1981) and refined by Avila and Bacha (1987) and FitzGerald and Sarmad (1997). We follow the latter approach here. The methodology is detailed in Appendix A2.1.

In the methodology, external shocks and policy responses are determinants of changes in the current account of the balance of payments. Imports are linked to the domestic absorption, and the export volumes are linked to the world trade volume (a measure of export penetration). Interest payments are linked to the dollar interest rate and the debt stock. The primary external shocks refer to the terms of trade (export and import prices), the interest rate to be paid on the external debt, and the world trade volume. Secondary external shocks are the debt accumulation burden and other external variables such as investment income, remittances and official transfers. Though determined by external variables, these are also sensitive to domestic policies and private adjustment behaviour. Finally, the domestic response variables comprise domestic absorption and trade ratios (import demand and export supply). The former is influenced in first instance by fiscal and monetary policies, the latter by trade policies.

Since 1980, most Latin American countries were subject to a large number of external shocks, such as the changes in terms of trade during the 1980s, the increase in world interest rates in the early 1980s, the fluctuations in the volume of world trade (downward trend in the early 1980s and upwards since then), the bank credit crunch (in the 1980s), and the portfolio and direct foreign investment boom (both in the early 1990s). More recent shocks to most Latin American countries were the Mexican crisis (1994–5), the rise in the international price of oil (1996 and 2000), the Asian financial crisis (1997), the Russian crisis (1997), the collapse of international oil prices and coffee prices (1998–9), the Brazilian financial crisis (1999), and the slowdown of the global economy and collapse of global stock market prices in 2001 and 2002. In almost half of the countries under analysis, structural reforms started during the second half of the 1980s; for the others, reforms started during the first half of the 1990s. As a result, the periods 1985–9 and 1990–4 present imbalances and instabilities in some economies, resulting from incomplete reforms and even lags. The period 1995–9 and beyond is then useful in identifying post reform new trends in domestic policies to face external shocks and in growth strategies.

For the sake of the comparative analysis we have harmonized the periods, even though the timing of major shocks may differ from country to country. The country studies use a periodization that fits the economic history of the country. In the analysis below, we show 5-year period averages for external shocks and domestic adjustment. This allows us to focus on patterns of adjustment in the medium run rather than on annual fluctuations. The limitation of this approach is, of course, that the observed shifts may obscure substantial within-period volatility.

External shocks

Table 2.3 shows the weighted regional average effect of the external shocks and domestic adjustment on the current account deficit (change from the previous period as percentage of GNP).[3] Countries are classified by major shocks in Table 2.4, and the frequencies of shocks are shown in Table 2.5. Please note that in Table 2.4 we report changes in the current account *deficit*, meaning that a positive sign refers to an increase in the deficit and an adverse external shock.

Table 2.3   Latin America and the Caribbean: sources of changes in the current account deficit (weighted period averages, changes with respect to the preceding 5-year period as percentage of GNP)

	1985–9 from 1980–4	1990–4 from 1985–9	1995–9 from 1990–4	1999–2001 from 1995–9
Observed change in current account deficit	−0.18	0.98	−0.22	−3.08
External shocks	4.28	0.48	−3.64	−9.66
Terms of trade shock	5.31	1.84	−0.39	−3.83
Interest-rate shock	0.74	−0.09	−0.07	−0.07
World trade shock	−1.77	−1.27	−3.18	−5.75
Other external variables	−0.96	−0.37	0.35	−0.65
Domestic adjustment	−2.72	2.66	4.13	6.88
Consumption contraction	−0.17	−0.24	−0.03	0.18
Investment reduction	−0.28	0.21	0.10	0.06
Trade ratios	−2.28	2.69	4.06	6.64
Import ratio	−0.94	4.18	5.48	2.03
Export penetration	−1.34	−1.49	−1.43	4.62
Interaction effects	−0.77	−1.78	−1.05	0.35

Source: Appendix A2.2. Please note that in the table we report changes in the current account *deficit*, meaning that a positive sign refers to an increase in the deficit and an adverse external shock

Table 2.4 Classification of countries by major shocks and domestic adjustment shifts (>|2| per cent of GNP)[1]

Type of external shock and domestic adjustment	1985–9 Negative	1985–9 Positive	1990–4 Negative	1990–4 Positive	1995–9 Negative	1995–9 Positive	1999–2001 Negative	1999–2001 Positive
Terms of trade	Brazil, Chile, Ecuador, Mexico, Paraguay, Peru, Venezuela	Bolivia	Argentina, Bolivia, Brazil, Colombia, Costa Rica, Uruguay, Venezuela	El Salvador	Ecuador, Nicaragua	Costa Rica, El Salvador, Guatemala, Honduras, Nicaragua, Paraguay	Costa Rica, El Salvador, Nicaragua	Venezuela
Interest-rate Shock	Argentina, Brazil	Chile, Costa Rica, Ecuador	Chile	Mexico	Ecuador	Nicaragua		
World trade		Argentina, Bolivia, Ecuador, El Salvador, Guatemala, Mexico, Peru, Uruguay, Venezuela		Bolivia, Brazil, Dominican Republic, Ecuador, Honduras, Mexico, Paraguay, Peru, Uruguay,		Bolivia, Brazil, Colombia, Costa Rica, Dominican Republic, Ecuador, El Salvador, Guatemala, Honduras,		Argentina, Bolivia, Chile, Colombia, Costa Rica, Dominican Republican, Honduras, Mexico, Paraguay,

(Continued)

Table 2.4 (Continued)

Type of external shock and domestic adjustment	1985–9		1990–4		1995–9		1999–2001	
	Negative	Positive	Negative	Positive	Negative	Positive	Negative	Positive
				Venezuela		Mexico, Nicaragua, Paraguay, Uruguay, Venezuela		Peru, Venezuela
Debt accumulation burden	Chile	Argentina, Brazil, Peru	Argentina, Brazil, Peru	Chile, Costa Rica	Brazil	Nicaragua		Nicaragua
Other external variables	Argentina, Chile, Ecuador, Peru	Dominican Republic, El Salvador, Honduras		Argentina, Bolivia, Costa Rica, Ecuador, El Salvador, Honduras, Peru	Costa Rica	Dominican Republic, Ecuador, Peru	Costa Rica	Honduras
Domestic spending		Chile	El Salvador, Honduras, Paraguay	Costa Rica, Ecuador	Paraguay	Nicaragua		Chile, Costa Rica, Dominican Republic, El Salvador, Nicaragua

(Continued)

Table 2.4 *(Continued)*

Type of external shock and domestic adjustment	1985–9		1990–4		1995–9		1999–2001	
	Negative	*Positive*	*Negative*	*Positive*	*Negative*	*Positive*	*Negative*	*Positive*
Trade ratios	Bolivia, Costa Rica, Dominican Republic, El Salvador	Brazil, Chile, Colombia, Ecuador, Mexico, Paraguay	Argentina, Brazil, Colombia, Dominican Republic, El Salvador, Guatemala, Honduras, Mexico, Paraguay, Peru, Uruguay		Argentina, Bolivia, Brazil, Chile, Colombia, Costa Rica, Ecuador, El Salvador, Guatemala, Honduras, Mexico, Nicaragua, Paraguay, Peru, Uruguay, Venezuela		Guatemala, Honduras, Mexico, Nicaragua, Venezuela	

Source: Appendix A2.2

Note: 1 Negative shock or negative domestic adjustment effect refers to contributions to rising current account deficit

Table 2.5 Frequency of sizeable shocks and domestic adjustment shifts[1] per period: number of countries (out of 17)

Type of shock and domestic adjustment	1985-9[2]		1990-4[2]		1995-9		1999-2001[3]	
	Negative	Positive	Negative	Positive	Negative	Positive	Negative	Positive
Terms of trade	7	1	7	1	2	6	3	1
Interest rate	2	3	0	1	1	1	0	0
World trade	0	9	1	10	0	14	0	11
Debt accumulation	1	3	3	2	1	1	0	1
Other external variables	4	3	0	7	1	3	1	1
Domestic spending	0	1	3	2	1	1	0	5
Trade ratios	4	6	11	0	16	0	5	0
Import ratio	3	5	12	0	14	0	6	1
Export penetration	4	7	2	5	7	5	4	4

Source: Appendix A2.2

Notes:
1 Sizeable shocks are larger than |2| per cent of GNP (period average); negative shock refers to contribution to rising current account deficit
2 Does not include Nicaragua, hence 16 country cases
3 Does not include Ecuador, hence 16 country cases

Current account deficits widened for the region as a whole during the first half of the 1990s and reduced somewhat in the second half and strongly during 1999–2001, consistent with the surge and stops in capital inflows. In the aggregate, most of the external shocks came through the trade channel, both negatively and positively. On the bright side, the region benefited from growing world trade (helping to reduce the external imbalance). On the dark side, there was, on average, a negative effect due to the falling terms of trade during the late 1980s and early 1990s. Shifting trade ratios have dominated domestic adjustment patterns. World trade expansion had an increasing positive effect in reducing the current account deficit in more than 60 per cent of the countries under analysis. Interest-rate shocks and debt accumulation were relatively unimportant in explaining shifts in the external imbalance during the 1990s.

Terms-of-trade shocks have been large and mostly negative in at least half of the country cases. They were particularly strong and adverse in the first half of the 1990s, explaining on average 1.8 per cent points of GNP of the widening current account deficit (of 1.0 per cent of GNP). Terms of trade have moved more favourably in the latter half of the 1990s and 1999–2001, particularly because of falling import price costs. Central American and Caribbean countries, in particular, witnessed positive terms-of-trade shocks during 1995–9, but declining export prices produced strong adverse shocks during 1999–2001, explaining part of the declining economic performance in the subregion in the final period. Adverse terms-of-trade shocks do not seem to be a prime candidate to explain the growth slowdown in South America, as only oil exporters Ecuador and Venezuela witnessed a major adverse shock due to declining oil prices in 1995–9.

World trade growth has provided a positive effect on Latin America's external balance for most of the 1980s and 1990s. Nearly all countries in the region witnessed a positive effect on export earnings due to growing world demand for its exports during all episodes. On average, Latin America managed to improve its position in world commodity markets in the late 1980s and early 1990s, as can be seen from the negative sign for the *export penetration ratio*. In effect, already during 1995–9 a substantial number of countries (Bolivia, Colombia, Ecuador, Honduras, Paraguay, and Venezuela) (see Appendix A2.2) suffered important losses of export competitiveness, contributing more than 2 per cent of GNP to widening current account deficits. The overall positive export penetration effect for the region as a whole during that period is mainly explained by the rapid export growth in Chile, Mexico and Central America (except Honduras), but as indicated this dynamics was not sustained in the period thereafter. When taking the simple average (see Appendix A2.2), the region shows a loss of export competitiveness (as measured through the export penetration ratio) during 1995–9. The effect becomes stronger towards the end of the period and the reduction in the penetration ratio of Latin American exports in world markets heavily contributed to widening current account deficits in 1999–2001, when taking both the weighted and the unweighted measures.

We take this dismal export performance in the most recent period as a worrisome empirical fact. The precise causes are not immediately clear. Country experiences seem to vary. In many cases exchange rate appreciation during a surge in capital inflows seems to have been part of the story, as it undermined competitiveness and counteracting export incentives provided by trade liberalization. Lessening of the initial trade creation effects of regional trade agreements, such as Mercosur, NAFTA and the Andean pact, along with financial woes in many countries leading to contractionary macroeconomic adjustment with spillover effects to exports of neighbouring countries, has been a factor in several parts of the region in different degrees. However, macroeconomic factors are very unlikely to provide the full story. Microeconomic adjustment of firms to the trade-opening process seems to have been slow and the capacity to improve efficiency in many sectors appears to have been limited. In part, this could be due to the apparent volatility and footloose nature of foreign direct investment in certain sectors, which has been affecting in particular the *maquila* industry in Mexico and Central America lately. Other factors limiting efficiency improvements in many countries are inadequacies in infrastructure and insufficient supplies of skilled labour. The country case studies discuss these issues at some length.

Perhaps, the most dramatic aspect of the adjustment process of the 1990s has been the rise in import ratios, i.e. import desubstitution, contributing on average 4.2 and 5.5 percentage points of GDP during 1990–4 and 1995–9 to the external imbalance (see Table 2.3). This effect is consistent with the import liberalization policies and rising capital inflows (and associated real exchange rate appreciation). However, the continued steep rise in the import ratio during 1995–9 and 1999–2001, when capital inflows started to slow down, would reflect structurally higher import dependence. Greater reliance on direct investment in financing the external balance and related imports of new technologies and rising intra-industry trade seem important factors behind this trend (De Ferranti *et al.* 2002; CEPAL 2003).

Other external variables, like *worker remittances* and *official transfers* played a substantial role in some countries of the region, but these have not been sources of major shocks for the Latin American economy as a whole. As discussed in the country studies, increases in worker remittances induced substantial positive balance-of-payments shocks of greater than 2 per cent of GNP in Costa Rica, Dominican Republic, Ecuador, El Salvador, Honduras, Nicaragua and Paraguay during the 1990s. In Costa Rica, El Salvador and Nicaragua this effect was largely offset by reductions in official transfers.

2.3 Failed adjustment or policies? The nature of domestic adjustment

Methodology

The external shock decomposition methodology also allows assessing of how domestic variables have shifted in response to the observed shocks (see Appendix A2.1). These results are also reported in Tables 2.3–2.5. We complement this analysis by another macroeconomic decomposition of economic growth with major aggregate demand components. This decomposition provides a link between the external and domestic adjustment process and growth performance as influenced by demand composition effects.[4,5]

Trade adjustment versus domestic spending

As might be expected from the trade opening process, the adjustment of the trade ratios dominates the domestic adjustment process in the 1990s. Neither did consumption booms form (on average) a major source of rising current account deficits, nor was contracting consumption a key source of domestic adjustment. During the 1990s investment, particularly private investment increased to contribute to widening deficits, but the average impact remained rather small. This type of adjustment, together with our earlier conclusion regarding the shift in trade ratios, suggests that the import liberalization and financial opening helped to raise the import content of aggregate demand, thereby compromising a sustainable growth path once access to foreign financing becomes more limited. At the same time, as discussed, the region lost export competitiveness, as is apparent from a lower export penetration ratio contributing to a wider current account deficit (see Table 2.3 and the following).

Only in a few country cases did adjustments in domestic spending make a substantial impact on reducing the current account deficit. In the early 1990s, Costa Rica and Ecuador reduced domestic spending mainly through a contraction of public and private consumption. In contrast, expanding domestic spending contributed to widening deficits in Honduras and El Salvador, where post-war reconstruction pushed up the investment rate financed largely from foreign aid. In Nicaragua, the same elements pushed up public consumption to drive the growth rate in that period. During 1995–9, domestic spending adjustment hardly played a role in explaining the shifts in the external balance in most countries, but during 1999–2001 reductions in aggregate demand helped to achieve substantial reductions in the current account deficit in Chile, Dominican Republic and the Central American countries (again, except Honduras).

Domestic adjustment and economic growth

While only very few countries created an export dynamics exceeding the growth of the world economy (i.e. larger export penetration ratio), there were a growing number of countries in the region whose growth rate mainly, if not entirely, was dependent on export growth. This result following from the macroeconomic decomposition of growth is summarized in Table 2.6(a), (b) and (c) for the 1980s, 1990s and 2000–1, respectively. During the lost decade of the 1980s, there were only three economies with moderate to high growth rates (defined here as GDP growth over 4 per cent per annum) during at least part of the decade and which relied on export-led growth. These are Chile, Colombia and Jamaica, which recovered from weak growth in the early 1980s through export expansion (Table 2.6a).

Table 2.6 Latin America: demand-side sources of growth

	Export led			Public sector demand	Private sector demand
	With private investment	With consumption boom	Exports only		
(a) 1980s					
Negative or zero GDP growth (<0.5%)	Bolivia (−) (1980–4)		Costa Rica (1980–4), El Salvador (−) (1980–4), Guatemala (−) (1980–4), Jamaica (1980–4)	Argentina (+) (85–9), Peru (−) (85–9), Nicaragua (−) (85–9)	Argentina (−) (1980s), Peru (−) (1980–4), Uruguay (−) (1980–4), Venezuela (−) (1980–4)
Low GDP growth (0.5–4%)		El Salvador (1985–9)	Bolivia (1985–9), Costa Rica (1985–9), Ecuador (1980s), Guatemala (1985–9), Mexico (1980s), Paraguay (1980s), Uruguay (1985–9), Venezuela (1985–9)	Brazil (1980s), Colombia (1980–4), Honduras (1980–4), Nicaragua (1980–4)	Chile (1980–4), Dominican Republic (1980s), Honduras (1985–9)
Moderate to high GDP growth (>4%)	Chile (1985–9)		Colombia (1985–9), Jamaica (1985–9)		

(Continued)

Table 2.6 (Continued)

	Export led			Public sector demand	Private sector demand
	With private investment	With consumption boom	Exports only		
(b) 1990s					
Negative or zero GDP growth (<0.5%)	Jamaica (−/+) (1995–2000), Paraguay (+/−) (1995–2000)		Venezuela (1995–2000)		Colombia (−) (1995–2000), Ecuador (1995–2000), Venezuela (1995–2000)
Low GDP growth (0.5–4%)	Ecuador (1990–4), Nicaragua (1990–4), Venezuela (1990–4)	Brazil (1990–4)	Argentina (1995–2000), Brazil (1995–2000), El Salvador (1995–2000), Mexico (1990–4), Paraguay (1990–4), Peru (1995–2000), Uruguay (1990s)	Honduras (1995–2000)	Bolivia (1995–2000), Honduras (1990–4), Jamaica (1990–4)
Moderate to high GDP growth (>4%)	Bolivia (1990–4), Chile (1990–4), Dominican Republic (1995–2000), El Salvador (1990–4), Guatemala (1990s), Mexico (1995–2000), Nicaragua (1995–2000)		Chile (1995–2000), Costa Rica (1990s), Dominican Republic (1990–4)	Argentina (1990–4)	Colombia (1990–4), Peru (1990–4)

(Continued)

Table 2.6 (Continued)

	Export led			Public sector demand	Private sector demand
	With private investment	With consumption boom	Exports only		
(c) 2000–1 Negative or zero GDP growth (<0.5%)	Bolivia (−/+) (2000–2001), Costa Rica (+/−) (2000–1), Dominican Republic (+/−) (2000–1), El Salvador (−/+) (2000–1), Jamaica (+/−) (2000–1), Mexico (2000–1), Peru (−/+) (2000–1)		Uruguay (−) (2000–1)		Argentina (−) (2000–1)
Low GDP growth (0.5–4%)	Colombia (2000–1), Ecuador (2000–1)		Brazil (2000–1), Chile (2000–1), Honduras (2000–1), Nicaragua (2000–1), Paraguay (2000–1), Venezuela (2000–01)	Guatemala (2000–1)	
Moderate to high GDP growth (>4%)					

Source: Appendix A2.4

Note: Cases of negative growth report the main source of output decline. These cases are indicated with (−) added after the country's name. In case of export-led growth in combination with the other major factor (private investment), (−/+) means private investment decline, but export increase and (+/−) means private investment increase but export decline

Throughout the 1990s, only Chile, Costa Rica, Dominican Republic and Guatemala managed to pursue an export-led growth path at moderately high rates (Table 2.6b). Colombia sustained moderate to high growth during the first part of the 1990s, mainly building on a private investment boom, but this bubble burst in the second half of the decade pushing the economy into recession. Jamaica's economy fell into a slump during the entire decade, falling exports being an important factor. In contrast, many other economies in the region (15 out of 18) became export-led growth economies with positive GDP growth at some point during the 1990s. However, only the four aforementioned countries managed to sustain that condition at a moderate to high growth rate. During the second half of the 1990s, they were joined by Mexico and Nicaragua. All represent cases of restructured export sectors and dynamic performance of non-traditional, non-primary commodities. All other cases never managed to achieve even moderately high growth rates based on exports. During 1999–2001, all countries (except Argentina and Guatemala) relied on export-led growth, but with output growing very slowly or falling. For Uruguay, the economic collapse of its major trading partners of Mercosur induced a steep decline in export earnings, explaining most of the economy's decline during 2000–1. The decline of *maquila* exports explains much of the economic downfall of the stellar exporters of the 1990s, Costa Rica, Dominican Republic and Mexico, despite the stimulus given to domestic investment. In Bolivia and El Salvador, in turn, the collapse in domestic investment is the major factor underlying the recession at the beginning of the century, despite positive export growth.

This sums up the gloomy picture for much of the region. Export penetration ratios have fallen during the 1990s, suggesting the region's decrease in export competitiveness. At the same time, in a rising number of countries the growth rate by and large depends on export dynamics. However, less than a handful of countries have managed to convert export-led growth to moderate to high overall growth. All others rely on export growth but lose global competitiveness. With the slowdown of world demand around the turn of the century, this only emphasizes the fundamental weakness in the region's growth strategy and the likelihood of even more gloomy prospects ahead, the more so because – as shown by the current account decomposition – export growth during the 1990s was mainly driven by the expansion of world trade, rather than by greater penetration of world markets by Latin American exports. The global recession of the early 2000s thus has hit hard the region's growth performance.

2.4 Conclusions

Latin America's growth performance in the postmarket reform period has been rather dismal to say the least. In this chapter we have tried to disentangle some patterns across the countries of the region of this poor growth performance. We have done so mainly by looking at some macroeconomic descriptives that likely have influenced the growth outcome. Hence, we come up with a 'what has happened' story rather than a 'why it happened' story. Nonetheless, some indications seem clear. The trade and financial opening process has enhanced trade and exports have become more important as an engine of growth. Compared with the import substitution years, this has made the Latin American economies more volatile, but volatility in the 1990s has not been worse than that in the 1980s. Countries have suffered varying degrees of 'bad luck' in terms of adverse external shocks, particularly in terms of trade. However, they have also been favoured during the liberalization process by strong world trade growth. Import liberalization and increased capital flows, particularly in the early post reform period, have pushed up import demand quite strongly. This, however, has not been matched by an equally strong export growth; instead, most countries in the region have lost competitiveness as measured by the average export penetration ratio. The market reforms do not appear to have unleashed an investment drive in tradable goods production required to achieve the required efficiency improvements to strengthen the region's position in global markets and generate an export-led growth process based on productivity improvements. Instead, the greater reliance on export growth has moderated the aggregate growth performance. This seems to imply that the real challenge of improving the efficiency of the economies of the region towards a sustainable, high-growth path needed to achieve substantive poverty reduction has yet to be taken up. The drastic policy reforms of the early 1990s by themselves clearly have not produced the durable shot in the arm they were supposed to give.

Appendix A2

A2.1 A methodology for estimating external shocks and domestic response[6]

The UNCTAD methodology

The UNCTAD methodology[7] is based on the decomposition of the current account deficit (D) in any 1 year (t) between imports of goods and non-factor services (M), net payments of factor services to other countries (V), exports of goods and non-factor services (E) and unrequited transfers received from abroad (T):

$$D_t = M_t + V_t - E_t - T_t \tag{A1}$$

Imports and exports are disaggregated between price indices (P_m, P_x) and volumes (J, X) at constant domestic currency prices:

$$M_t = P_{mt}J_t \tag{A2}$$
$$E_t = P_{xt}X_t \tag{A3}$$

Import volume is linked to real domestic absorption (A) – in other words, consumption (C) plus investment (I) – by a single coefficient (j):

$$J_t = j_t A_t \tag{A4}$$
$$A_t = C_t + I_t \tag{A5}$$

Export volume (X) is linked to world trade volume (W) by an 'overall export coefficient' (x) which in effect measures export penetration as the country's share of world trade:

$$X_t = x_t W_t \tag{A6}$$

Finally, factor services payments to other countries (V) are broken down into net interest payments abroad (V_i), net investment income payments abroad (V_d) and net workers' remittances from abroad (R). Net interest payments abroad are defined as the product of the current dollar interest rate (r) and the debt stock (in local currency at the official exchange rate) from the previous year (F_{t-1}):

$$V_t = V_{it} + V_{dt} - R_t \tag{A7}$$
$$V_{it} = r_t F_{t-1} \tag{A8}$$

It should be recalled that all the coefficients (x, j, r) are in practice derived from these equations, so that the definitional identities do always sum to the observed current account deficit (D).

Substituting Equations (A2)–(A8) into Equation (1) and dividing through by national income at current prices yields the complete decomposition formula:

$$\frac{D_t}{Y_t} = \frac{p_{mt}j_t(C_t - I_t)}{Z_t} + \frac{r_t F_{t-1}}{Y_t} + \frac{(V_{dt} - R_t)}{Y_t} - \frac{p_{xt}x_t W_t}{Z_t} - \frac{T_t}{Y_t} \tag{A9}$$

where national income at current prices (Y_t) is equal to the product of national income at constant prices (Z_t) and the implicit GNP deflator (P_{yt}):[8]

$$Y_t = P_{yt} Z_t \tag{A10}$$
$$p_{mt} = \frac{P_{mt}}{P_{yt}} \tag{A11}$$
$$p_{xt} = \frac{P_{xt}}{P_{yt}} \tag{A12}$$

Finally, a base year or years (s) is chosen in order to separate out the partial derivatives (d) of the variables, which then define the separate effects identified in the UNCTAD study:

$$d\left[\frac{D_t}{Y_t}\right] = \left[\frac{j_s A_s}{Z_s}\right]dp_{mt} - \left[\frac{x_s W_s}{Z_s}\right]dp_{xt} \quad \text{terms-of-trade effect}$$
$$+ \left[\frac{F_{s-1}}{Y_s}\right]dr_t \qquad\qquad\qquad \text{interest-rate shock}$$
$$- x_s p_{xs} d\left[\frac{W_t}{Z_t}\right] \qquad\qquad\quad \text{world-trade effect}$$

$$+r_s \mathrm{d}\left[\frac{F_{t-1}}{Y_t}\right] \qquad\qquad \text{debt accumulation burden}$$

$$+\mathrm{d}\left[\frac{V_{\mathrm{d}t} - R_t - T_t}{Y_t}\right] \qquad\qquad \text{other external variables}$$

$$+j_s p_{\mathrm{ms}} \mathrm{d}\left[\frac{A_t}{Z_t}\right] \qquad\qquad \text{domestic absorption}$$

$$+\left[\frac{p_{\mathrm{ms}} A_s}{Z_s}\right] \mathrm{d}j_t \qquad\qquad \text{import replacement}$$

$$-\left[\frac{p_{\mathrm{xs}} W_s}{Z_s}\right] \mathrm{d}x_t \qquad\qquad \text{export penetration}$$

$$+\text{interaction terms} \tag{A13}$$

The first three phrases define the exogenous 'external shock'; the next two are 'debt accumulation burden' and 'other external variables', which respond to both internal and external conditions but which are taken as autonomous; the last three are defined as 'domestic policy response', although they should more appropriately be termed as 'domestic adjustment', since the changes may be caused both by policy intervention and by private adjustment behaviour. The difference between the sum of the explicitly defined terms and the observed change in the normalized current account deficit is defined as 'interaction terms' and not further analysed.

The 'residual'

A significant weakness in the UNCTAD methodology is concealed by these 'interaction terms' in the methodology, renamed 'residual' in the corresponding statistical tables in UNCTAD (1987). The missing terms are in fact the second-order effects arising from the product of two or more partial differentials, which should tend to zero for small changes in the variables but which, in the presence of relatively large shifts associated with adjustment to external shock, can be as significant as the current account deficit itself.[9] These effects are particularly important if we are trying to identify the shifts in the structural coefficients over a number of years, which should come about where 'adjustment' (as opposed to demand restriction) has taken place.

In calculus, the derivative of a product is expressed as the limiting value of the sum of the partial differentials:

$$y = uv$$

$$\frac{\delta y}{\delta x} = u\frac{\delta v}{\delta x} + v\frac{\delta u}{\delta x} + \delta u\frac{\delta v}{\delta x}$$

$$\frac{\mathrm{d}y}{\mathrm{d}x} = \lim\left[\frac{\delta y}{\delta x}\right] \quad \text{as } \delta x \text{ tends to } 0$$

$$= u\frac{\mathrm{d}v}{\mathrm{d}x} + v\frac{\mathrm{d}u}{\mathrm{d}x}$$

In Equation (A13), the residual is in fact equivalent to the '$\delta u \delta v / \delta x$' terms, which are not only relatively large but also have economic significance, because they reflect the fact that the variable changes associated with shock and adjustment are not marginal, and thus the simplifications may not in fact be valid. This is particularly true of the terms-of-trade shock.

The difference (R) between the *observed* change in the normalized deficit and the specified terms as defined in Equation (A13) is in fact made up of the following three 'interaction effects': [10]

$R =$ sum of the secondary effects of interactions between:
domestic demand and unit imports

$$\left[\frac{A_t}{Z_t} - \frac{A_s}{Z_s} \right] [j_t p_{mt} - j_s p_{ms}] \text{displacement and import price}$$

$$+ \frac{A_s}{Z_s} [j_t - j_s][p_{mt} - p_{ms}] \textit{less} \text{ interactions between:}$$

world demand and unit exports$- \left[\frac{W_t}{Z_t} - \frac{W_s}{Z_s} \right] [x_t p_{xt} - x_s p_{xs}]$

penetration and export price$- \left[\frac{W_s}{Z_s} \right] [x_t - x_s][p_{xt} - p_{xs}]$

plus interactions between: debt stock and interest rate

$$+ [r_t - r_s] \left[\frac{F_t}{Y_t} - \frac{F_s}{Y_s} \right] \tag{A14}$$

The residual (R) clearly tends to zero for small changes in the variables, but in practice it is significantly large in both the UNCTAD study and our own.

These five phrases might be expected to have determinate signs, derived from the respective demand and supply elasticities. The first phrase (the interaction between the domestic demand level and the cost of the imports generated by a unit increase in that demand) might be expected to have a negative sign through the income effect, unless demand adjustment is in fact 'forced' by external variables. The second phrase (interaction between import displacement and relative import prices) is presumably negative if the real exchange rate stimulates more efficient use of imported inputs and changes consumption patterns. Under the small-country assumption, we can assume that world demand is not affected by export prices, but to the extent that faster world trade improves market opportunities and primary commodity prices, the third interaction phrase (between world demand and unit exports) might be expected to be positive. The fourth (export penetration and relative export prices) should also be greater than zero for a positive supply elasticity, unless the so-called 'backward-sloping supply curve for exports' applies, which is all too common under adjustment to foreign exchange shocks. There is no reason, however, to expect a determinate relationship between changes in the accumulated debt stock and the world interest rate,[11] so that no sign can be assigned to the fifth phrase.

Under the (strong) assumption that all the phrases are 'well behaved' in the sense indicated earlier, the sum of these interaction effects (i.e. the residual, R) might therefore be expected to be negative.

Domestic absorption

In the UNCTAD methodology, real domestic absorption (A_t) as a proportion of real GNP (Z_t) is defined as the indicator of 'domestic spending' and one of the 'domestic policy actions', the other being 'trade ratios'. However,

$$Y = C + I + E - M \tag{A15}$$

so that as in Equation (A5) absorption (A) is

$$A = C + I = Y - E + M \tag{A16}$$

If we set out Equation (A16) in terms of Equations (A2)–(A4) and (A6), we have

$$A_t P_{yt} = Z_t P_{yt} - x_t W_t P_{xt} + j_t A_t P_{mt} \tag{A17}$$

Substituting Equations (A11) and (A12) into (A17) and rearranging, we find that the domestic spending indicator is in fact

$$\frac{A_t}{Z_t} = \left[\frac{1 - p_{xt} x_t \frac{W_t}{Z_t}}{1 - p_{mt} j_t} \right] \tag{A18}$$

All the variables on the right-hand side of Equation (A18) are in fact defined as independent already in the UNCTAD methodology, so the left-hand side should not really be treated as a further variable at all. At most, if, say, investment (I) is treated as autonomous, consumption (C) cannot be taken as independent.

A2.2 Decomposition of changes in current account deficit

(The values in the following tables are changes between period averages, given as percentage of GNP.)

	Latin America			
	Weighted average			
Period average	*1985–9*[1]	*1990–4*[1]	*1995–9*	*1999–2001*[2]
Weights	*1980–4*	*1985–9*	*1990–4*	*1995–9*
	(1)	*(2)*	*(3)*	*(4)*
Observed deficit increase	−0.18	0.98	−0.22	−3.08
External shocks				
Total	4.28	0.48	−3.64	−9.66
Terms trade deterioration	5.31	1.84	−0.39	−3.83
Import price effect	3.10	−2.64	−1.53	−4.71
Export price effect	2.21	4.48	1.14	0.89
Interest rate shock	0.74	−0.09	−0.07	−0.07
World trade retardation	−1.77	−1.27	−3.18	−5.75
Other external variables				
Total	−0.96	−0.37	0.35	−0.65
Debt accumulation burden	−0.73	−0.32	0.44	−0.17
Change in direct investment income	0.19	−0.07	−0.04	−0.65
Change in remittances	−0.20	−0.08	−0.16	0.18
Change in official transfers	−0.21	0.10	0.11	−0.02
Domestic adjustment				
Total	−2.72	2.66	4.13	6.88
Domestic spending	−0.45	−0.04	0.08	0.24
Consumption contraction	−0.17	−0.24	−0.03	0.18
Private consumption	−0.17	−0.28	0.07	−0.03
Public consumption	0.01	0.03	−0.09	0.21
Investment reduction	−0.28	0.21	0.10	0.06
Private investment	0.02	0.28	0.24	−0.64
Public investment	−0.30	−0.08	−0.13	0.71
Trade ratios	−2.28	2.69	4.06	6.64
Import replacement	−0.94	4.18	5.48	2.03
Export penetration	−1.34	−1.49	−1.43	4.62
Interaction effects				
Total	−0.77	−1.78	−1.05	0.35
Import shock	−0.31	−1.10	−0.59	−0.84
Demand/unit imports	−0.11	0.05	−0.14	−0.07
Displacement/price	−0.20	−1.15	−0.45	−0.77
Export shock	0.46	0.84	−0.31	1.19
Demand/unit exports	0.13	0.25	−0.22	1.16
Penetration/price	0.33	0.60	−0.09	0.02
Debt shock	−0.93	−1.53	−0.15	0.01
Stock/interest	−0.93	−1.53	−0.15	0.01

Source: World Bank data and IMF, International Financial Statistics and following country tables

Notes
1 Does not include Nicaragua
2 Excluding Ecuador, and Uruguay for which no complete, comparable data are available

	Latin America			
	Simple average			
Period average	*1985–9*[1]	*1990–4*[1]	*1995–9*	*1999–2001*[2]
Weights	*1980–4*	*1985–9*	*1990–4*	*1995–9*
	(1)	*(2)*	*(3)*	*(4)*
Observed deficit increase	−1.18	0.92	−0.58	−1.05
External shocks				
Total	−0.11	−2.12	−5.96	−1.26
Terms trade deterioration	2.55	1.12	−0.74	1.07
Import price effect	1.77	−1.93	−1.77	0.81
Export price effect	0.78	3.05	1.03	0.26
Interest rate shock	−0.27	−0.56	−0.61	−0.08
World trade retardation	−2.39	−2.68	−4.61	−2.25
Other external variables				
Total	0.05	−1.28	−1.00	−0.88
Debt accumulation burden	0.30	0.50	−0.50	−0.06
Change in direct investment income	0.76	−1.00	−0.13	−0.07
Change in remittances	−0.15	−1.13	−1.14	−0.72
Change in official transfers	−0.85	0.34	0.76	−0.03
Domestic adjustment				
Total	−0.12	5.28	6.39	0.77
Domestic spending	−0.20	0.27	0.21	−1.30
Consumption contraction	0.07	−0.26	−0.25	−0.96
Private consumption	0.22	0.01	−0.14	−0.90
Public consumption	−0.14	−0.27	−0.11	−0.06
Investment reduction	−0.27	0.54	0.46	−0.34
Private investment	0.14	0.50	0.44	−2.11
Public investment	−0.41	0.04	0.02	1.77
Trade ratios	0.07	5.00	6.18	2.07
Import replacement	0.40	6.59	5.71	0.75
Export penetration	−0.32	−1.59	0.47	1.32
Interaction effects				
Total	−1.00	−0.95	−0.01	0.33
Import shock	−0.59	−1.35	−0.62	−0.55
Demand/unit imports	−0.13	0.11	−0.01	−0.09
Displacement/price	−0.45	−1.45	−0.60	−0.46
Export shock	0.08	1.15	0.49	0.84
Demand/unit exports	0.28	0.41	0.43	0.28
Penetration/price	−0.19	0.74	0.06	0.56
Debt shock	−0.50	−0.74	0.11	0.04
Stock/interest	−0.50	−0.74	0.11	0.04

Source: World Bank data and IMF, International Financial Statistics and following country tables

Notes
1 Does not include Nicaragua
2 Excluding Ecuador, and Uruguay for which no complete data are available

Country Tables[12]

	Argentina			
Period average	1987–90 1980–6	1990–4 1987–90	1995–9 1990–4	1999–2001 1995–9
Observed deficit increase	−3.37	5.61	1.32	−0.59
External shocks	2.42	1.19	−2.33	−1.93
Terms trade deterioration	0.62	3.11	−1.00	−0.01
Import price effect	−0.50	−0.55	−0.73	−0.69
Export price effect	1.12	3.66	−0.27	0.68
Interest rate shock	4.91	−1.45	0.11	0.30
World trade retardation	−3.11	−0.47	−1.44	−2.22
Other external variables	−3.14	6.98	0.61	0.20
Debt accumulation burden	−3.39	8.02	0.82	0.69
Change in direct investment income	0.95	−1.43	−0.35	−0.55
Change in remittances	−0.01	0.09	−0.01	−0.01
Change in official transfers	−0.70	0.31	0.15	0.08
Domestic adjustment	−0.87	4.92	3.64	0.80
Domestic spending	−0.50	−0.04	−0.07	−0.06
Trade ratios	−0.37	4.95	3.72	0.87
Import replacement	−0.75	4.82	4.60	0.15
Export penetration	0.38	0.13	−0.89	0.72
Interaction effects	−1.78	−7.48	−0.60	0.33

Note: Change in periods: 1980–6 instead of 1980–4 and 1987–90 instead of 1985–90 to avoid measurement problems due to change in exchange rate regime after hyperinflation

	Bolivia			
Period average	1987–90 1980–7	1990–4 1987–90	1995–9 1990–4	1999–2001 1995–9
Observed deficit increase	−4.21	1.54	0.80	−1.17
External shocks	−10.09	3.62	−3.77	−1.51
Terms trade deterioration	−5.52	4.79	0.05	0.71
Import price effect	−6.54	1.05	−1.69	−1.13
Export price effect	1.02	3.75	1.74	1.84
Interest rate shock	−0.72	1.05	−0.18	−0.26
World trade retardation	−3.85	−2.22	−3.64	−1.96
Other external variables	−1.20	−3.53	−1.03	−0.50
Debt accumulation burden	0.87	−0.58	−0.19	−0.04
Change in direct investment income	−1.39	−1.92	−1.11	0.31
Change in remittances	−0.01	0.01	−0.37	−0.41
Change in official transfers	−0.67	−1.05	0.64	−0.35
Domestic adjustment	8.85	1.00	5.29	0.51

(Continued)

(Continued)

Domestic spending	−0.11	0.19	−0.18	−1.22
Trade ratios	8.97	0.81	5.47	1.73
Import replacement	7.35	2.93	2.93	−1.46
Export penetration	1.62	−2.12	2.54	3.18
Interaction effects	−1.78	0.45	0.31	0.34

Note: Change in periods: 1980–7 instead of 1980–4 and 1987–90 instead of 1985–9 to avoid measurement problems due to change in exchange rate regime after hyperinflation

	Brazil			
Period average	*1985–9* *1980–4*	*1990–5* *1985–9*	*1995–9* *1990–5*	*1999–2001* *1995–9*
Observed deficit increase	*−1.66*	*2.63*	*1.98*	*0.48*
External shocks	5.15	−0.92	−4.13	−0.03
Terms trade deterioration	3.21	2.84	−1.73	1.65
Import price effect	−2.30	1.27	−2.73	3.17
Export price effect	5.51	1.58	1.00	−1.52
Interest rate shock	1.93	−0.71	−0.39	−0.18
World trade retardation	0.02	−3.05	−2.00	−1.50
Other external variables	−2.80	1.24	1.77	1.56
Debt accumulation burden	−2.90	2.90	1.31	1.02
Change in direct investment income	0.08	−1.22	0.26	0.54
Change in remittances	−0.02	−0.34	0.17	0.02
Change in official transfers	0.04	−0.11	0.02	−0.02
Domestic adjustment	−4.05	2.88	5.59	−0.46
Domestic spending	−0.31	0.41	0.77	0.27
Trade ratios	−3.74	2.47	4.83	−0.73
Import replacement	−1.14	2.11	3.90	−0.38
Export penetration	−2.60	0.37	0.93	−0.35
Interaction effects	0.04	−0.56	−1.26	−0.58

Note: Change in periods: 1990–5 instead of 1990–4 to avoid problems with deflator and currency regime change

	Chile			
Period average	*1985–9* *1980–4*	*1990–4* *1985–9*	*1995–9* *1990–4*	*1999–2001* *1995–9*
Observed deficit increase	*−6.74*	*−0.88*	*1.17*	*−2.71*
External shocks	0.53	3.16	−2.38	−0.67
Terms trade deterioration	3.85	0.83	−1.35	1.79
Import price effect	11.58	−6.32	−7.05	0.50
Export price effect	−7.73	7.15	5.70	1.29

(Continued)

(Continued)

Interest rate shock	−3.24	−1.08	−0.43	0.22
World trade retardation	−0.07	3.41	−0.60	−2.68
Other external variables	5.79	−3.92	−1.10	−0.05
Debt accumulation burden	3.89	−3.18	−0.68	0.51
Change in direct investment income	2.21	−0.73	−0.56	−0.55
Change in remittances	0.01	0.10	−0.02	0.00
Change in official transfers	−0.31	−0.10	0.16	0.00
Domestic adjustment	−8.39	−0.73	5.62	−2.06
Domestic spending	−2.04	−0.04	1.58	−2.42
Trade ratios	−6.35	−0.69	4.03	0.36
Import replacement	−2.87	8.10	6.68	0.87
Export penetration	−3.47	−8.79	−2.64	−0.51
Interaction effects	−4.67	0.61	−0.97	0.06

	Colombia			
Period average	*1985–9* *1980–4*	*1990–4* *1985–9*	*1995–9* *1990–4*	*1999–2001* *1995–9*
Observed deficit increase	−5.31	2.58	3.99	−5.02
External shocks	0.98	0.00	−5.67	−2.50
Terms trade deterioration	0.49	2.37	−0.73	0.75
Import price effect	2.35	−1.32	−3.38	1.85
Export price effect	−1.86	3.69	2.65	−1.10
Interest rate shock	0.65	−0.64	−0.37	−0.03
World trade retardation	−0.16	−1.73	−4.57	−3.22
Other external variables	−0.31	−1.34	0.39	−0.23
Debt accumulation burden	0.96	−0.42	−0.25	0.67
Change in direct investment income	0.50	−0.73	−1.03	0.34
Change in remittances	−0.97	0.06	0.43	−0.93
Change in official transfers	−0.80	−0.24	1.24	−0.31
Domestic adjustment	−5.56	3.80	9.36	−2.17
Domestic spending	−0.73	−0.11	1.24	−1.36
Trade ratios	−4.83	3.91	8.12	−0.81
Import replacement	−2.05	6.70	5.73	−1.71
Export penetration	−2.78	−2.79	2.39	0.90
Interaction effects	−0.43	0.12	−0.09	−0.13

	Costa Rica			
Period average	*1985–9* *1980–4*	*1990–4* *1985–9*	*1995–9* *1990–4*	*1999–2001* *1995–9*
Observed deficit increase	−3.55	−1.52	−1.14	0.05
External shocks	−7.79	2.35	−8.47	0.22
Terms trade deterioration	−1.82	2.98	−1.99	3.25
Import price effect	−10.78	−4.76	−2.59	0.20
Export price effect	8.96	7.74	0.60	3.06
Interest rate shock	−4.67	0.52	0.03	−0.12
World trade retardation	−1.30	−1.15	−6.51	−2.90
Other external variables	−0.61	−4.68	3.69	2.69
Debt accumulation burden	−0.36	−2.49	−0.89	0.02
Change in direct investment income	0.97	−2.90	3.84	2.49
Change in remittances	1.02	−2.43	−0.67	0.17
Change in official transfers	−2.23	3.14	1.41	0.01
Domestic adjustment	5.93	0.42	4.87	−2.91
Domestic spending	0.92	−0.48	−0.05	−2.45
Trade ratios	5.02	0.90	4.92	−0.46
Import replacement	7.69	9.61	9.46	3.58
Export penetration	−2.68	−8.71	−4.53	−4.03
Interaction effects	−1.08	0.39	−1.23	0.04

	Dominican Republic			
Period average	*1985–9* *1980–4*	*1990–4* *1985–9*	*1995–9* *1990–4*	*1999–2001* *1995–9*
Observed deficit increase	1.93	−1.91	−4.35	1.87
External shocks	−1.18	−6.99	−1.58	3.53
Terms trade deterioration	−0.21	−0.11	0.46	1.42
Import price effect	−1.26	−0.71	0.51	1.05
Export price effect	1.05	0.59	−0.05	0.37
Interest rate shock	−0.30	−0.71	0.39	0.12
World Trade Retardation	−0.67	−6.17	−2.44	1.99
Other external variables	−1.74	0.47	−2.80	−0.35
Debt accumulation burden	1.00	−0.09	−0.49	−0.20
Change in direct investment income	0.36	1.42	0.85	−0.14
Change in remittances	−2.21	−0.63	−2.01	−0.42
Change in official transfers	−0.89	−0.22	−1.14	0.42
Domestic adjustment	4.91	3.62	0.00	−1.10
Domestic spending	1.26	−0.38	−1.52	−2.01
Trade ratios	3.65	4.00	1.52	0.90
Import replacement	12.69	−0.23	−0.65	−0.52
Export penetration	−9.04	4.23	2.16	1.43
Interaction effects	−0.06	0.99	0.03	−0.21

	Ecuador			
Period average	*1985–9* *1980–4*	*1990–4* *1985–9*	*1995–9* *1990–4*	*2000–2002* *1995–9*[1]
Observed deficit increase	8.93	−10.54	−5.71	−0.59
External shocks	10.99	−4.34	−4.33	−4.13
Terms trade deterioration	15.31	1.76	2.50	0.76
Import price effect	14.08	−2.88	2.03	3.45
Export price effect	1.23	4.64	0.47	−2.68
Interest rate shock	−2.05	−1.81	3.15	0.64
World trade retardation	−2.26	−4.29	−9.98	−5.53
Other external variables	7.01	−3.95	−7.04	−3.80
Debt accumulation burden	1.93	0.86	−0.57	0.07
Change in direct investment income	5.87	−3.69	−2.01	0.53
Change in remittances	0.00	−1.66	−4.60	−3.57
Change in official transfers	−0.79	0.53	0.14	−0.76
Domestic adjustment	−6.27	−2.57	4.78	6.05
Domestic spending	−1.91	−2.47	−0.84	0.53
Trade ratios	−4.35	−0.10	5.62	5.52
Import replacement	−1.80	1.70	1.24	0.82
Export penetration	−2.56	−1.80	4.38	4.70
Interaction effects	−2.81	0.32	0.88	1.23

Note: 1 The data of the last column are not strictly comparable with the previous period changes, as they are based on a new set of balance-of-payments data using a revised methodology. The revised data series are available only for 1993–2002

	El Salvador			
Period average	*1985–9* *1980–4*	*1990–4* *1985–9*	*1995–9* *1990–4*	*1999–2001* *1995–9*
Observed deficit increase	−1.21	−0.17	−1.19	0.71
External shocks	−4.98	−6.13	−5.73	2.52
Terms trade deterioration	0.19	−4.45	−3.46	3.01
Import price effect	−4.02	−5.59	−5.47	2.25
Export price effect	4.21	1.14	2.02	0.77
Interest rate shock	0.01	0.04	−0.19	0.01
World trade retardation	−5.18	−1.73	−2.09	−0.50
Other external variables	−3.59	−6.27	0.83	−0.22
Debt accumulation burden	0.13	−0.34	−0.20	0.09
Change in direct investment income	−0.40	−0.18	0.03	0.49
Change in remittances	0.15	−8.59	−0.99	−1.63
Change in official transfers	−3.46	2.85	1.98	0.83

(Continued)

(Continued)

Domestic adjustment	6.27	14.21	5.08	−1.23
Domestic spending	0.85	2.35	0.20	−3.19
Trade ratios	5.41	11.86	4.89	1.95
Import replacement	−3.02	10.55	9.40	5.57
Export penetration	8.44	1.31	−4.51	−3.62
Interaction effects	1.09	−1.98	−1.36	−0.35

	Guatemala			
Period average	*1985–9 1980–4*	*1990–4 1985–9*	*1995–9 1990–4*	*1999–2001 1995–9*
Observed deficit increase	0.07	0.87	−0.54	0.82
External shocks	−1.52	−4.20	−5.95	−1.57
Terms trade deterioration	1.61	−1.87	−2.38	−0.50
Import price effect	4.90	−1.21	−4.33	0.52
Export price effect	−3.30	−0.66	1.95	−1.02
Interest rate shock	0.03	−0.45	−0.16	0.08
World trade retardation	−3.15	−1.89	−3.41	−1.14
Other external variables	−0.55	−1.57	−0.28	−1.23
Debt accumulation burden	0.66	−0.13	−0.21	−0.02
Change in direct investment income	0.26	−0.45	0.22	−0.37
Change in remittances	−0.38	−1.28	−0.61	−0.33
Change in official transfers	−1.08	0.29	0.33	−0.50
Domestic adjustment	1.51	6.86	6.14	3.48
Domestic spending	0.27	0.32	−0.03	−0.26
Trade ratios	1.25	6.54	6.18	3.74
Import replacement	−3.58	5.90	5.23	2.30
Export penetration	4.83	0.63	0.94	1.44
Interaction effects	0.63	−0.22	−0.45	0.14

	Honduras			
Period average	*1985–9 1980–4*	*1990–4 1985–9*	*1995–9 1990–4*	*1999–2001 1995–9*
Observed deficit increase	−3.82	3.53	−3.08	0.74
External shocks	−4.14	−2.40	−10.40	−3.66
Terms trade deterioration	−1.44	0.14	−2.67	1.29
Import price effect	−2.55	11.63	12.53	−0.27
Export price effect	1.11	−11.48	−15.20	1.56
Interest rate shock	−1.41	1.46	−1.21	−0.62
World trade retardation	−1.29	−3.99	−6.52	−4.33

(Continued)

(Continued)

Other external variables	−0.78	−2.46	−1.74	−4.66
Debt accumulation burden	0.67	0.73	−0.05	−0.39
Change in direct investment income	0.46	−0.81	−1.68	−0.91
Change in remittances	0.57	−2.27	0.38	−2.12
Change in official transfers	−2.49	−0.11	−0.40	−1.24
Domestic adjustment	1.16	6.01	6.54	8.41
Domestic spending	−0.29	2.12	−1.17	−1.64
Trade ratios	1.45	3.89	7.71	10.05
Import replacement	−1.77	−1.86	−0.46	1.70
Export penetration	3.22	5.74	8.17	8.35
Interaction effects	−0.06	2.38	2.52	0.65

	Mexico			
Period average	1985–9 1980–4	1990–4 1985–9	1995–9 1990–4	1999–2001 1995–9
Observed deficit increase	2.49	4.65	−3.49	0.69
External shocks	7.15	−6.08	−3.89	−3.32
Terms trade deterioration	11.42	−1.33	1.12	−1.40
Import price effect	9.60	−6.50	1.24	−7.36
Export price effect	1.82	5.17	−0.12	5.95
Interest rate shock	−1.70	−2.15	0.30	0.03
World trade retardation	−2.56	−2.61	−5.31	−1.95
Other external variables	−0.21	0.61	−0.28	−1.00
Debt accumulation burden	1.18	−0.93	0.24	−0.35
Change in direct investment income	−0.87	1.30	−0.15	−0.67
Change in remittances	−0.43	0.18	−0.43	0.00
Change in official transfers	−0.08	0.06	0.06	0.02
Domestic adjustment	−3.21	13.54	2.89	6.24
Domestic spending	−0.55	0.85	−0.87	0.76
Trade ratios	−2.66	12.69	3.76	5.48
Import replacement	−0.74	12.87	10.85	8.90
Export penetration	−1.92	−0.18	−7.08	−3.42
Interaction effects	−1.25	−3.42	−2.21	−1.23

	Nicaragua			
Period average	1985–9 1980–4	1990–4 1985–9	1995–9 1991–4	1999–2001 1995–9
Observed deficit increase			−0.35	−3.38
External shocks			−12.25	4.81
Terms trade deterioration			2.62	6.91

(Continued)

(Continued)

Import price effect	6.29	2.77
Export price effect	−3.67	4.13
Interest rate shock	−10.69	−1.42
World trade retardation	−4.18	−0.68
Other external variables	−5.94	−7.27
Debt accumulation burden	−6.80	−3.08
Change in direct investment		
income	1.23	0.22
Change in remittances	−7.30	−4.60
Change in official transfers	6.93	0.18
Domestic adjustment	14.36	−1.52
Domestic spending	1.76	−3.61
Trade ratios	12.60	2.09
Import replacement	15.88	5.38
Export penetration	−3.28	−3.28
Interaction effects	3.49	0.60

Note: Change in the period 1991–5 instead of 1990–5 to avoid problems with deflators and currency reform following period of hyperinflation

	Paraguay			
Period average	*1985–9* *1980–4*	*1990–4* *1985–9*	*1995–9* *1990–4*	*1999–2001* *1995–9*
Observed deficit increase	−4.22	7.86	2.25	−1.71
External shocks	2.90	−3.10	−12.99	−5.50
Terms trade deterioration	4.00	0.15	−2.62	−0.56
Import price effect	11.26	−10.60	−9.05	13.33
Export price effect	−7.26	10.75	6.43	−13.89
Interest rate shock	0.17	0.27	−0.86	0.22
World trade retardation	−1.26	−3.51	−9.51	−5.16
Other external variables	0.61	−2.14	−0.45	−0.20
Debt accumulation burden	0.61	−0.32	0.00	0.31
Change in direct investment				
income	0.36	−1.55	0.82	−0.28
Change in remittances	0.03	−0.51	−2.66	−0.70
Change in official transfers	−0.39	0.25	1.39	0.47
Domestic adjustment	−4.18	16.56	15.08	−1.09
Domestic spending	−0.82	2.32	2.79	−1.53
Trade ratios	−3.36	14.24	12.28	0.44
Import replacement	1.47	28.09	6.11	−14.67
Export penetration	−4.83	−13.85	6.18	15.10
Interaction effects	−3.55	−3.47	0.60	5.08

	Peru			
Period average	*1985–9* *1980–4*	*1990–4* *1985–9*	*1995–9* *1990–4*	*1999–2001* *1995–9*
Observed deficit increase	2.34	0.74	−0.52	−3.47
External shocks	2.24	−5.26	−2.48	0.21
Terms trade deterioration	3.99	1.52	−1.31	1.75
Import price effect	−0.07	−2.66	−2.29	1.22
Export price effect	4.06	4.19	0.99	0.53
Interest rate shock	1.46	−0.44	0.27	0.44
World trade retardation	−3.21	−6.34	−1.44	−1.97
Other external variables	0.48	1.66	−2.08	−1.28
Debt accumulation burden	−2.06	4.97	0.36	0.12
Change in direct investment income	2.31	−2.42	−2.27	−1.24
Change in remittances	−0.10	−0.79	−0.31	−0.15
Change in official transfers	0.32	−0.10	0.13	−0.01
Domestic adjustment	0.48	7.34	4.45	−2.40
Domestic spending	−0.26	−0.19	0.48	−1.26
Trade ratios	0.74	7.53	3.97	−1.14
Import replacement	−3.60	5.72	4.44	−0.84
Export penetration	4.34	1.80	−0.47	−0.30
Interaction effects	−0.86	−3.00	−0.40	0.00

	Uruguay			
Period average	*1985–9* *1980–4*	*1990–4* *1985–9*	*1995–9* *1990–4*	*1999–2001* *1995–9*
Observed deficit increase	−4.51	1.78	0.14	n.a.
External shocks	−7.02	−2.53	−6.50	n.a.
Terms trade deterioration	−0.04	2.22	−1.72	0.24
Import price effect	−2.15	−4.91	−4.88	−0.48
Export price effect	2.11	7.13	3.16	0.72
Interest rate shock	−0.88	−1.44	−0.18	0.02
World trade retardation	−6.10	−3.31	−4.60	n.a.
Other external variables	1.22	−1.96	−0.55	n.a.
Debt accumulation burden	1.13	−1.09	0.23	0.63
Change in direct investment income	0.11	−0.78	−0.71	−1.00
Change in remittances	0.03	−0.02	−0.01	0.00
Change in official transfers	−0.05	−0.07	−0.06	n.a.
Domestic adjustment	1.04	6.42	7.78	n.a.
Domestic spending	1.38	0.70	1.15	0.41
Trade ratios	−0.34	5.71	6.63	n.a.
Import replacement	−0.55	7.04	5.25	0.17
Export penetration	0.21	−1.33	1.38	n.a.
Interaction effects	0.26	−0.14	−0.60	n.a.

	Venezuela			
Period average	*1985–9* *1980–4*	*1990–4* *1985–9*	*1995–9* *1990–4*	*1999–2001* *1995–9*
Observed deficit increase	3.94	−2.00	−1.14	−2.98
External shocks	2.65	−2.31	−8.85	−9.54
Terms trade deterioration	5.15	3.02	1.65	−4.01
Import price effect	4.80	3.27	−8.42	−5.31
Export price effect	0.35	−0.25	10.07	1.30
Interest rate shock	1.50	−1.44	−0.02	−0.07
World trade retardation	−4.00	−3.89	−10.48	−5.47
Other external variables	0.65	0.31	−1.03	−0.65
Debt accumulation burden	0.47	0.08	−1.05	−0.20
Change in direct investment income	0.32	0.06	0.44	−0.67
Change in remittances	−0.05	0.06	−0.41	0.26
Change in official transfers	−0.09	0.10	−0.01	−0.04
Domestic adjustment	0.38	0.14	7.43	6.98
Domestic spending	−0.29	−1.22	−1.66	0.39
Trade ratios	0.67	1.36	9.09	6.59
Import replacement	−0.99	1.39	6.45	2.39
Export penetration	1.65	−0.03	2.64	4.20
Interaction effects	0.26	−0.13	1.30	0.22

A2.3 Average current account balance

(Values are given as percentage of GNP.)

	1980–4	*1985–9*	*1990–4*	*1995–9*	*1999–2001*
Argentina	−0.14	3.23	−2.38	−3.71	−3.12
Bolivia	−9.21	−5.00	−6.54	−7.33	−6.16
Brazil	−1.18	0.48	−2.15	−4.13	−4.61
Chile	−10.63	−3.89	−3.01	−4.18	−1.47
Colombia	−4.38	0.93	−1.65	−5.64	−0.62
Costa Rica	−11.15	−7.60	−6.08	−4.94	−4.99
Dominican Republic	−6.18	−8.11	−6.20	−1.85	−3.72
Ecuador	−4.32	−13.25	−2.72	2.99	n.a.
El Salvador	−3.80	−2.59	−2.42	−1.23	−1.94
Guatemala	−3.91	−3.98	−4.85	−4.31	−5.13
Honduras	−10.84	−7.02	−10.55	−7.47	−8.21
Mexico	1.40	−1.09	−5.73	−2.25	−2.94
Nicaragua	n.a.	n.a.	−37.31	−36.97	−33.59
Paraguay	−6.99	−2.77	−10.63	−12.88	−11.18
Peru	−3.32	−5.66	−6.40	−5.88	−2.41
Uruguay	−3.67	0.84	−0.95	−1.08	n.a.
Venezuela	4.07	0.13	2.13	3.27	6.25

Source: World Bank data and IMF, International Financial Statistics

Note: For Argentina, the periods are 1980–6 and 1987–90; for Bolivia, 1980–7 and 1987–90; for Brazil, 1990–5 and for Nicaragua, 1991–5. See also footnotes to country tables

A2.4 Macroeconomic decomposition of economic growth

(Values are average annual growth rates, in %.)

	Private sector			Public sector			External sector			Interaction effects	GDP growth
	Total	Investment	Savings leakage	Total	Government	Tax leakage	Total	Exports	Import leakage		
Argentina											
1980–4	−6.8	−9.5	2.7	0.0	0.0	0.0	1.7	1.1	0.5	2.6	−2.5
1985–9	−2.9	−0.7	−2.2	1.9	1.3	0.6	1.7	1.7	0.0	−1.2	−0.5
1990–4	2.6	3.4	−0.9	4.6	5.5	−0.8	−0.7	0.7	−1.3	0.0	6.6
1995–2000	0.8	0.4	0.4	0.5	0.5	0.0	1.3	1.7	−0.3	−0.1	2.6
2000–1	−2.3	−5.0	2.7	3.1	2.9	0.3	4.2	3.3	0.8	−9.5	−4.5
Bolivia											
1980–4	−0.5	−1.6	1.0	0.2	0.8	−0.6	−1.8	−2.2	0.5	0.1	−2.0
1985–9	0.4	0.1	0.4	−2.0	−2.1	0.1	3.5	5.2	−1.7	0.2	2.2
1990–4	1.2	1.3	−0.1	0.4	0.6	−0.2	2.5	2.9	−0.4	0.1	4.1
1995–2000	2.1	1.5	0.6	0.5	0.8	−0.2	0.6	1.1	−0.6	0.2	3.4
2000–1	−6.6	−6.4	−0.2	1.6	1.6	0.1	4.4	2.1	2.3	1.8	1.2
Brazil											
1980–4	−0.5	−0.6	0.1	1.9	1.6	0.3	1.4	1.3	0.1	−1.7	1.1
1985–9	−0.2	−0.1	−0.1	2.8	3.6	−0.9	0.0	0.1	−0.1	−0.6	2.0
1990–4	3.3	1.4	1.9	−0.9	−1.1	0.2	1.3	1.5	−0.2	−0.6	3.1
1995–2000	0.1	0.1	0.1	0.3	0.6	−0.3	1.0	1.0	0.0	0.8	2.2
2000–1	−1.5	0.7	−2.1	1.3	−0.4	1.6	2.0	2.0	0.0	−0.3	1.5
Chile											
1980–4	−1.5	−0.8	−0.7	0.3	0.0	0.3	1.7	−1.2	2.9	0.4	0.9
1985–9	3.9	4.5	−0.7	−0.4	−0.7	0.3	3.2	4.8	−1.5	0.0	6.7
1990–4	4.7	4.2	0.5	0.2	0.3	−0.1	3.7	5.4	−1.7	0.1	8.7

(Continued)

	Private sector			Public sector			External sector			Interaction effects	GDP growth
	Total	Investment	Savings leakage	Total	Government	Tax leakage	Total	Exports	Import leakage		
1995–2000	0.4	0.3	0.1	0.3	0.3	0.0	3.6	4.0	-0.4	0.1	4.3
2000–1	-4.4	-4.7	0.4	0.5	0.6	-0.1	6.6	5.2	1.4	0.0	2.8
Colombia											
1980–4	0.7	0.9	-0.3	1.1	1.1	0.0	0.5	0.2	0.3	0.0	2.2
1985–9	0.6	1.0	-0.4	1.2	1.2	0.0	2.7	2.7	0.0	0.0	4.5
1990–4	3.5	3.8	-0.3	0.6	0.6	0.1	0.1	1.8	-1.7	0.2	4.5
1995–2000	-3.9	-3.8	-0.1	2.8	3.1	-0.3	1.8	1.4	0.4	0.1	0.9
2000–1	1.8	1.6	0.2	-0.9	-0.9	0.0	0.5	1.6	-1.1	0.0	1.4
Costa Rica											
1980–4	-1.1	-1.1	-0.1	0.0	0.1	-0.1	1.3	0.3	1.0	0.2	0.3
1985–9	1.8	1.6	0.2	-0.3	-0.2	-0.1	3.0	5.0	-2.0	0.1	4.6
1990–4	0.9	0.8	0.1	0.1	0.0	0.1	4.3	5.3	-0.9	0.0	5.5
1995–2000	0.1	0.3	-0.3	-0.2	-0.1	0.0	4.9	6.0	-1.1	0.2	5.0
2000–1	4.2	3.6	0.6	0.4	0.6	-0.2	-3.7	-3.9	0.3	0.0	0.9
Dominican Republic											
1980–4	-0.7	1.4	-2.1	0.9	0.9	0.0	1.7	-3.0	4.8	0.4	2.3
1985–9	0.8	3.4	-2.5	-0.3	-0.2	0.0	1.6	-0.5	2.1	0.7	2.8
1990–4	0.6	0.1	0.5	0.6	0.6	-0.1	2.6	1.1	1.5	0.4	4.2
1995–2000	2.8	3.2	-0.4	1.6	1.7	-0.1	2.5	2.8	-0.2	0.5	7.6
2000–1	3.1	10.2	-7.1	2.1	-2.2	4.4	-2.6	-4.8	2.3	0.0	2.7

(Continued)

	Private sector			Public sector			External sector			Interaction effects	GDP growth
	Total	Investment	Savings leakage	Total	Government	Tax leakage	Total	Exports	Import leakage		
Ecuador											
1980–4	−1.3	−1.7	0.4	0.1	0.6	−0.5	3.2	2.0	1.2	0.1	2.1
1985–9	−0.5	0.0	−0.4	−0.3	−1.3	1.0	2.8	2.1	0.7	0.0	2.0
1990–4	1.3	1.5	−0.2	−0.7	−0.6	−0.1	2.8	3.5	−0.7	0.0	3.4
1995–2000	0.6	1.0	−0.3	−0.4	−0.6	0.2	−0.2	0.0	−0.2	0.0	0.1
2000–2001	6.0	8.2	−2.2	0.2	−1.9	2.1	−2.6	1.2	−3.8	0.0	3.7
El Salvador											
1980–4	−1.3	−1.4	0.1	0.9	1.1	−0.2	−2.5	−2.9	0.4	0.1	−2.8
1985–9	2.4	0.3	2.0	−1.6	−2.1	0.5	0.3	1.2	−1.0	1.0	2.1
1990–4	4.1	2.4	1.7	−0.4	−0.1	−0.3	2.3	5.5	−3.2	0.1	6.2
1995–2000	−1.4	−1.4	0.0	−0.2	−0.2	0.0	4.6	6.7	−2.2	0.2	3.1
2000–2001	−2.5	−2.4	−0.1	−0.3	−0.1	−0.2	4.7	5.5	−0.8	0.0	1.8
Guatemala											
1980–4	−1.1	−1.0	−0.1	1.1	0.8	0.4	−1.3	−2.7	1.4	0.1	−1.1
1985–9	1.0	1.0	0.1	0.7	0.7	−0.1	1.1	1.7	−0.7	0.2	2.9
1990–4	2.2	1.7	0.5	0.8	0.9	−0.1	1.2	2.2	−1.0	0.1	4.3
1995–2000	1.3	2.6	−1.3	0.8	−0.3	1.1	1.5	2.3	−0.8	0.3	3.9
2000–1	−0.3	−0.6	0.2	2.3	2.3	0.0	0.7	0.3	0.4	−0.5	2.1
Honduras											
1980–4	−2.8	−2.7	−0.1	2.7	2.7	0.0	1.6	0.0	1.5	0.3	1.7
1985–9	0.6	0.8	−0.1	1.1	1.2	−0.1	1.0	0.9	0.1	0.5	3.1
1990–4	3.9	4.0	0.0	−0.5	−0.4	−0.1	−0.1	0.2	−0.3	0.3	3.5

(Continued)

	Private sector			Public sector			External sector			Interaction effects	GDP growth
	Total	Investment	Savings leakage	Total	Government	Tax leakage	Total	Exports	Import leakage		
1995–2000	0.4	0.4	0.1	1.8	1.7	0.0	0.6	0.6	0.0	0.1	2.9
2000–1	1.0	0.4	0.6	-0.5	-0.3	-0.2	2.1	2.3	-0.2	0.0	2.6
Jamaica											
1980–4	0.1	-0.7	0.8	0.4	0.6	-0.2	-0.3	2.3	-2.6	-0.1	0.1
1985–9	-0.2	-0.1	-0.1	0.8	0.8	0.0	2.1	2.6	-0.5	2.3	5.0
1990–4	4.6	4.1	0.6	-1.5	-1.5	0.0	-1.0	-0.6	-0.4	-0.9	1.3
1995–2000	-1.8	-2.1	0.3	0.7	0.8	-0.1	0.7	0.1	0.6	-0.2	-0.6
2000–1	3.8	3.6	0.2	-0.3	-0.3	0.1	-1.9	-2.0	0.2	0.0	1.7
Mexico											
1980–4	-2.4	-1.7	-0.6	1.4	1.5	0.0	2.3	1.6	0.7	0.6	1.9
1985–9	-0.2	-0.6	0.4	-0.1	-0.2	0.1	1.3	2.3	-1.0	0.6	1.7
1990–4	-1.8	-1.6	-0.2	-0.2	-0.2	0.1	3.3	4.0	-0.7	0.2	1.5
1995–2000	2.7	2.7	-0.1	-0.8	-0.7	0.0	3.5	6.5	-3.1	0.0	5.4
2000–1	-0.9	-2.8	2.0	0.6	0.8	-0.3	0.0	-0.7	0.7	0.0	-0.3
Nicaragua											
1980–4	-0.2	2.1	-2.4	3.8	4.8	-1.0	-3.3	-4.6	1.3	0.4	0.6
1985–9	-3.0	-0.5	-2.5	-5.3	2.3	-7.6	1.8	0.9	0.9	3.2	-3.3
1990–4	2.2	4.1	-2.0	-4.0	0.7	-4.6	2.3	3.4	-1.0	0.9	1.5
1995–2000	2.3	1.0	1.4	-0.1	0.4	-0.5	2.8	4.9	-2.1	0.3	5.4
2000–1	-0.9	0.5	-1.4	1.6	1.1	0.5	2.3	1.9	0.4	0.0	3.0
Paraguay											
1980–4	-1.7	-1.8	0.1	0.5	0.4	0.1	2.2	0.5	1.6	0.7	1.7
1985–9	-0.9	-0.9	0.0	0.2	0.2	0.0	4.0	6.7	-2.7	0.6	3.9

(Continued)

(Continued)

	Private sector			Public sector			External sector				GDP growth
	Total	Investment	Savings leakage	Total	Government	Tax leakage	Total	Exports	Import leakage	Interaction effects	
1990–4	−0.8	−2.4	1.5	0.6	0.6	0.0	3.2	7.7	−4.5	0.3	3.2
1995–2000	2.3	2.2	0.1	2.5	2.5	0.0	−4.3	−8.1	3.9	0.2	0.7
2000–1	−1.9	−5.3	3.4	0.3	0.2	0.1	4.3	3.4	0.9	0.0	2.7
Peru											
1980–4	−3.7	−3.6	−0.1	1.8	1.6	0.2	1.9	1.3	0.6	0.4	0.3
1985–9	0.3	1.1	−0.8	−1.2	−1.6	0.4	−1.3	−0.8	−0.5	0.4	−1.9
1990–4	4.3	3.9	0.4	0.1	0.5	−0.3	1.0	2.1	−1.1	0.1	5.5
1995–2000	−1.1	−0.4	−0.7	0.9	0.8	0.1	2.6	2.3	0.3	0.0	2.5
2000–1	−2.9	−3.8	0.9	0.2	0.3	−0.1	3.0	3.2	−0.2	0.0	0.2
Uruguay											
1980–4	−6.0	−5.8	−0.2	0.5	0.5	−0.1	1.8	0.5	1.3	0.0	−3.8
1985–9	0.9	0.5	0.4	0.6	0.6	−0.1	2.4	3.5	−1.1	0.0	3.9
1990–4	2.6	1.4	1.2	−0.3	−0.1	−0.2	1.6	4.7	−3.0	0.1	3.9
1995–2000	−0.4	−0.8	0.4	0.3	0.3	0.0	2.0	3.1	−1.1	0.3	2.3
2000–1	−1.3	−0.1	−1.2	0.2	−0.3	0.5	−3.8	−6.9	3.1	0.0	0.0
Venezuela											
1980–4	−2.0	−2.8	0.9	0.3	0.5	−0.2	0.1	0.4	−0.3	0.6	−0.9
1985–9	−2.5	−1.7	−0.8	0.9	0.7	0.3	3.8	2.9	0.9	0.3	2.6
1990–4	2.2	2.9	−0.7	−0.3	−0.6	0.3	1.2	2.5	−1.2	0.3	3.4
1995–2000	0.1	0.2	−0.1	−0.1	−0.1	0.0	0.6	1.5	−0.9	0.1	0.6
2000–1	0.8	0.7	0.1	0.8	0.6	0.2	1.0	2.3	−1.2	0.0	2.7

Source: World Bank data (Word Development Indicators 2003), unless indicated otherwise

A2.5 Sectoral growth decomposition

Some of the country case studies also report a sectoral decomposition of output growth. The Keynesian income multiplier decomposition as reported in this chapter is in practice difficult to implement at the sector level. The so-called Chenery decomposition provides a method of decomposing sectoral output growth by demand components grouped into three effects: domestic demand growth, import substitution and export growth dynamics.[13]

$$(X_t - X_{t-i}) = \alpha_{t-i}(D_t - D_{t-i}) + (\alpha_t - \alpha_{t-i})S_t + \alpha_{t-i}(E_t - E_{t-i})$$

where

$X = $ GDP
$D = $ domestic demand$(= X + M - E)$
$S = $ total supply$(= X + M)$
$E = $ total exports of goods and services (fob)
$M = $ total imports of goods and services (cif)
$\alpha = $ GDP as a share of total supply $\left(\dfrac{X}{S}\right)$
$t = $ final year of the period
$t - i = $ initial year of the period.

The equation expresses an identity. By adding a subscript i for sectors, it will be clear that the decomposition can also be done by sector/type of commodity. Variable X can also be defined as total output (instead of GDP), in which case an additional variable for intermediate demand should be factored in, however, without changing the overall idea of the equation (see the suggested readings for such 'sophistications'). In principle, of course, we are interested here in volume changes (constant prices).

Now we can identify the following growth sources:

$\alpha_{t-i}(D_t - D_{t-i})$ domestic demand contribution
$(\alpha_t - \alpha_{t-i})S_t$ import substitution effect[14]
$\alpha_{t-i}(E_t - E_{t-i})$ export growth effect.

Acknowledgements

The authors are grateful to Sandra van Ginhoven and Leandro Serino for excellent research assistance.

Notes

1 Actually four, if we include Haiti, which had no per capita income growth during 1995–2000, but stopped the downhill performance of 1990–5 when average income fell at a rate of 5 per cent per year.

2 The countries under analysis are Argentina, Bolivia, Brazil, Chile, Colombia, Costa
   Rica, Dominican Republic, Ecuador, El Salvador, Guatemala, Honduras, Mexico,
   Nicaragua, Paraguay, Peru, Uruguay and Venezuela. Cuba could not be included due to
   lack of macroeconomic data for the period at large and Jamaica was excluded because
   of a lack of consistency in the series.
3 The complete table is provided in Appendix A2.2. The appendix also provides the decomposition results for the unweighted regional average and those for the individual countries.
4 Emphasizing demand effects, one may explain output growth as a result of changes in
   exogenous spending, and the parameters imports, consumption and taxes according to
   the Keynesian model:

$$Y = C + I + G + E - M$$
$$C = c(1 - t)Y$$
$$M = mY$$
$$T = tY$$

where C is private consumption, I is gross private investment, G is total government
spending, E is exports, M is imports and c, t and m are average propensity to consume,
average tax rate and import ratio, respectively.

With this simple Keynesian model it follows that

$$Y = \frac{1}{(s + t + m - ts)}(G + I + E)$$

where s is average private saving rate out of disposable income.

The overall change in aggregate output can now be calculated. The impact of a
change in exports over any time period is the observed change in E times the multiplier
$\frac{1}{(s+t+m-ts)}$. The impact of a change in investment and government spending is
calculated in the same way. The impact of changes in imports, savings and taxes is the
change in the multiplier resulting from the change in s, t or m times the initial level of
I, G and E. Each of these component changes measures the change in aggregate demand
that would be observed if that variable, and only that variable, were changed. By construction, these six sources of change sum to the overall observed change except for a
small cross-product term, which is caused by the fact that the observed changes are not
instantaneous. The decomposition in growth rates becomes

$$\frac{\Delta Y}{Y} = m\frac{\Delta E}{Y} + \Delta m_m\frac{E}{Y} + m\frac{\Delta G}{Y} + \Delta m_t\frac{G}{Y}$$
$$+ m\frac{\Delta I}{Y} + \Delta m_s\frac{I}{Y} + \text{interaction terms}$$

where m is the Keynesian multiplier and Δm_m, Δm_t and Δm_s are the changes in the
multiplier due to changes in the respective leakage effects (imports m, taxation t and
savings s).
5 Some of the country studies also report on a sectoral decomposition of output growth
   (see Appendix A2.5). We do not compare those results here as comparable results are
   only available for a reduced number of countries.
6 Adapted from FitzGerald and Sarmad (1997).

7   Set out in Avila and Bacha (1987: 177–204).
8   The UNCTAD study uses the GDP deflator as the GNP deflator was apparently unavailable; the authors recognize that this is not technically correct, but suggest that the resultant error is small – our own estimates did not bear this out.
9   For instance, appendix table B (UNCTAD 1987: 175) shows a mean modular value for the residual of 1 per cent of GNP, while the mean modular value of the observed deficit increase is itself only 4 per cent of GNP. Thus, in this case the effects listed in Equation (A13) only explicitly account for three-quarters of the observed variations in D_t, although, being based on national accounting identities, it should 'explain' the variations entirely.
10 The algebra is rather intricate, but the method can be clearly seen by taking just the debt term, which is the last phrase in Equation (A14). Leaving aside the normalization procedure and the lag for simplicity of exposition and taking the differences between 2 years (1, 2), the observed change in the contribution of the debt term (V_i) in Equation (A8) to the current account deficit (D) in Equation (A9) has the form

$$dV_i = r_2 F_2 - r_1 F_1$$

while what is in fact estimated by the UNCTAD methodology in Equation (A13) is

$$dV_i^* = F_1[r_2 - r_1] + r_1[F_2 - F_1]$$

The difference between these two is the contribution (Rf) of the debt term to the residual (R), formed by the product of the changes in the debt and the interest rate, and appearing as the last phrase in Equation (A14):

$$R_f = dV_i - dV_i^*$$
$$= [r_2 - r_1][F_2 - F_1]$$

This residual clearly tends to zero for small changes in the variables (r, F) but in fact their changes are large (frequently greater than 10 per cent in 1 year) and thus their product becomes significant compared to $d\left[\dfrac{D}{Y}\right]$ itself, which is measured in single percentage points of GNP.
11 In principle, a possible exception could be the interest rate charged to LDCs (r), which might be regarded as reflecting the world capital market valuation of the creditworthiness of individual countries, which in turn would reflect domestic policy. However, in practice it would appear that credit – and aid – is rationed to reflect sovereign risk, the interest rate premium being relatively small and not reflecting LDC country risk (Vos 1994).
12 More detailed country tables, including a disaggregation of domestic spending and interaction effects, are available upon request from the authors. Please write to vos@iss.nl
13 For further references to this decomposition, see Yotopoulos and Nugent (1976) and Chenery (1979).
14 This may become clear if we express the term in full:

$$\left[\left(\frac{X}{X+M}\right)_t - \left(\frac{X}{X+M}\right)_{t-i}\right](X+M)_t$$

References

Avila, L. and E. Bacha (1987) 'Methodological note', in: UNCTAD, *International and Monetary Issues for Developing Countries*, Geneva: UNCTAD, pp. 177–204.

Balassa, Bela (1981) 'The newly-industrializing developing countries after the oil crisis', *Welwirtschaftliches Archiv*, 117: 142–94.

CEPAL (2003) *La inversión extranjera en América Latina y el Caribe. Informe 2002*, Santiago: UN-ECLAC.

Chenery (1979) *Structural Change and Development Policy*, Oxford, NY: Oxford University Press.

De Ferranti, David, Guillermo Perry, Indermit Gil and Luis Serven (2000) *Securing Our Future in a Global Economy*, Washington, DC: World Bank.

De Ferranti, David, Guillermo Perry, Daniel Lederman and William F. Maloney (2002) *From Natural Resources to the Knowledge Economy: Trade and Job Quality*, World Bank Latin American and Caribbean Studies Viewpoints, Washington, DC: The World Bank.

FitzGerald, E. V. K. and Khwaja Sarmad (1997) 'External shocks and domestic adjustment in the 1970s and 1980s', in: Karel Jansen and Rob Vos (eds) *External Finance and Adjustment: Failure and Success in the Developing World*, London, New York: Macmillan and St. Martin's Press, pp. 63–89.

IDB (1995) *Economic and Social Progress in Latin America: Overcoming Volatility*, Baltimore: Johns Hopkins U.P. (for Inter-American Development Bank).

Jansen, Karel and Rob Vos (eds) (1997) *External Finance and Adjustment: Failure and Success in the Developing World*, London, New York: Macmillan and St. Martin's Press.

Morley, Samuel (2001) 'Why has the growth rate in Latin America slowed down?', Washington, DC: IFPRI (mimeo).

Rodrik, Dani (1999) 'Why is there so much economic insecurity in Latin America?', Harvard University (mimeo).

UNCTAD (1987) *International and Monetary Issues for Developing Countries*, Geneva: UNCTAD.

Vos, Rob (1994) *Debt and Adjustment in the World Economy. Structural Asymmetries in North–South Interactions*, London, New York: Macmillan and St. Martin's Press.

Yotopoulos, Pan and Jeffrey Nugent (1976) *Economics of Development. Empirical Investigations*, New York: Harper & Row Publishers.

3 Are export promotion and trade liberalization good for Latin America's poor?

A comparative macro–micro CGE analysis

Enrique Ganuza, Samuel Morley, Sherman Robinson, Valeria Piñeiro and Rob Vos

3.1 Macro-micro modelling of trade reforms

Trade reforms have economy-wide effects requiring a general equilibrium approach in order to be able to assess the full impact of such reforms. In this chapter, we compare the impact of trade reforms (and external shocks) in our sample of 16 countries using a standardized computable general equilibrium (CGE) model framework to assess relative price adjustment, sectoral output and employment effects, labour income and household consumption effects and their interactions. The model framework allows us to isolate the impact of specific policies and external shocks. Country-specific social accounting matrices were constructed defining the economic structure of each country case and the accounting framework for each country model. A drawback of the typical CGE model is that income distribution is captured as between-group differentials for relatively aggregate labour categories and household groups. This makes it difficult to get at the impact of, say, trade reforms on poverty, since we need the full distribution. To overcome this, we apply a 'top down' multiple modelling framework with the CGE model as the first layer and a methodology of microsimulations as the second layer. The latter translates the general equilibrium effects of trade reform on the labour market onto the impact on poverty and inequality at the household level making use of the full income distribution from micro (household survey) data.

Section 3.2 details the methodology and underlying assumptions of this approach and thereby also its limitations. Section 3.3 describes the main findings of the CGE simulations. In order to make the analysis as comparable as possible, we have standardized the simulations imposed on each country model as well as the so-called 'closure rules' of the models that define the macroeconomic adjustment of the corresponding economies and the nature of the labour market. This way, differences in simulation results per country are reduced to differences in economic structure and capacity to respond to relative price changes. Subsequently, we compare the results of this exercise in 'elasticity structuralism' with the simulation results obtained from the country models with the nature of macroeconomic and labour market adjustment defined specifically for each economy by the authors dealing with the respective countries. Section 3.4 reports on the poverty and inequality outcomes as obtained from the application of the microsimulation approach. In Section 3.5, we conclude that trade liberalization, as isolated from other policies and factors of influence, appears to have a poverty-reducing effect in most of the Latin American economies. The same applies for multilateral trade scenarios, like the Free Trade Area of the Americas and the worldwide adaptation of World Trade Organization (WTO) rules. Poverty reduction from further trade reform is rather small however, such that the present analysis leads us to conclude that export-led growth stimulated this way is no panacea and does not suffice to give the region the economic shot in the arm it needs to lift itself from poverty and do away with its deeply rooted inequality.

3.2 CGE model strategy

The country studies in this project have all used a common economy-wide, multisector modelling framework: a CGE model. The model is a 'standard' CGE model described in detail in Löfgren *et al.* (2001).[1] Such models are used extensively in policy analysis, and provide a framework for capturing linkages between economy-wide changes or shocks; the sectoral structures of production, trade and employment; and distributional outcomes. A CGE model captures the circular flow of income in an economy, as shown in Figure 3.1. The circular flow framework and models based on it are closed in the sense that the framework accounts for all flows of goods and services across markets, the corresponding flows of payments and all other transfers among agents. All economic transactions in the economy are captured, and the accounts of each agent in the model must balance.

Social accounting matrix

The accounts of the various agents, and much of the underlying data for a CGE model, can conveniently be summarized in the form of a social accounting matrix (SAM) – see Figure 3.2. A SAM is a square matrix that, for a period of time

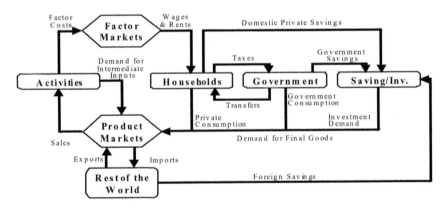

Figure 3.1 Circular flow in a SAM/CGE model.

		Expenditures								
Receipts	Activities	Commodities	Factors	Households	Enterprises	Government	Savings–Investment	Rest of the World	TOTAL
Activities		marketed outputs							activity income
Commodities	intermediate inputs			private consumption		government consumption	investment	exports	demand
Factors	value-added								factor income
Households			factor income to households	inter-household transfers	surplus to households	transfers to households		transfers to households	household income
Enterprises			factor income to enterprises			transfers to enterprises		transfers to enterprises	enterprise income
Government	producer and value-added tax	sales taxes, tariffs, export taxes	factor taxes	transfers, direct taxes	direct taxes			transfers to government	government income
Savings–Investment				household savings	enterprise savings	government savings		foreign savings	savings
Rest of the World (RoW)		imports	factor income to RoW		surplus to RoW	government transfers			foreign exchange outflow
TOTAL	activity expenditures	commodity supply	factor expenditures	household expenditures	enterprise expenditures	government expenditures	investment	foreign exchange inflow	

Source: Adapted from Löfgren, Harris, and Robinson (2001).

Figure 3.2 National SAM used in the CGE model.

(typically a year), accounts for the economy-wide circular flow of incomes and payments. Each entry represents a payment by a column account to a row account. Since the income–expenditure accounts of each agent must balance, the corresponding row and column accounts in the SAM must also balance exactly. Although SAMs are most commonly constructed for countries, they may be applied at widely different levels of aggregation: households, villages, regions, countries and the entire world. A SAM summarizes the structure of an economy, including its internal and external links, and the roles of different actors and sectors. A national SAM brings disparate data (including input–output tables, household surveys, producer surveys, trade statistics, national accounts data, balance of payments statistics and government budget information) into a unified framework, and provides the underlying conceptual framework for the system of national accounts.

The 'agents' in a CGE model based on the SAM in Figure 3.2 include producers (activities), factors of production, households, enterprises, government, savings–investment and the rest of the world. The aggregate 'savings–investment' account collects savings and purchases capital goods – a macro agent that essentially represents the financial system and the loanable funds market. The SAM is a compact way to present the national accounts, and nicely traces out the circular flow from production activities to factor payments to incomes of 'institutions' and back to demand for commodities.

The SAM incorporates the three macro balances: government deficit, trade deficit and savings–investment balance. The macro balances are expressed as flows – the SAM does not include asset accounts – and any macro relationship in this framework will be in flow terms. All models in the SAM framework must 'explain' how balance is achieved in the three macro accounts. Given that the SAM is always balanced, determining two of the macro balances necessarily determines the third. The SAM represents a closed system – all economic transactions are included – and models in this framework will incorporate Walras' law in some form. They need (indeed, only can) explain one less than the total number of accounts in the SAM.

The 'standard' CGE model[2]

Producers ('activities' in the SAM) and consumers interact across product and factor markets, buying and selling goods and services. Producers are assumed to maximize profits, purchasing inputs and selling outputs in competitive markets, constrained by their production technology. In the model, production functions include intermediate inputs according to fixed input–output coefficients and primary factors (capital, labour and land) according to constant elasticity of substitution (CES) functions (see Table A3.1, Equations 11–15). Households receive factor income (wages and profits) from producers, pay taxes, save and spend the rest to consume goods and services ('commodities' in the SAM). Households are assumed to maximize utility, and their demand for commodities is given by the linear expenditure system (see Table A3.1, Equations 33–34).

A CGE model is Walrasian in spirit, incorporating all the flows in the SAM, including production, distribution and demand, and determining equilibrium wages and prices by simulating the operation of all markets. The model is an empirical special case of the neoclassical Arrow–Debreu general equilibrium model. The model can only determine relative prices, and some price or price index is chosen as numéraire – the consumer price index in the models used in this project. The absolute price level is undetermined and must be specified exogenously. The supply and demand equations in the model are all homogeneous of degree zero in prices – double all prices and equilibrium production and demand do not change – so the absolute price level does not matter to the real side. In macro terminology, the model displays strong neutrality of money. Introducing some mechanism to determine the absolute level of prices such as a simple transactions demand for money plus a fixed money supply would determine the absolute price level, but would not affect relative prices or any real magnitudes.

Typically, classic CGE models specify fixed supplies of primary factors of production (e.g. labour and capital) and assume that all markets 'clear' in that prices and wages (defined broadly to include rental rates for all factors) adjust to achieve supply–demand equilibrium in all product and factor markets. In macro terms, the model will always generate full employment of all factors and hence the economy is always operating on the production possibility frontier. Many applications of CGE models focus on introducing various distortions to the price system and calculating the resulting inefficiencies and loss of welfare. By assuming full employment, however, 'inefficiency' is always in terms of being at the wrong place on the production possibility frontier, not from ending up at some point inside the frontier.

To capture the characteristics of labour markets in developing countries, it is common to specify an alternative treatment of the labour market. Instead of a fixed labour supply, some labour categories are assumed to be available in unlimited supplies at a fixed real wage. This treatment is consistent with the dual economy models of Lewis and Ranis and Fei, and has been used in most of the country models in this project.[3] In this specification, any changes in the economic environment that would normally lead to a rise in the real wage will instead lead to an increase in employment and aggregate gross domestic product (GDP).

Imports, exports and the balance of trade

Extending the classic Walrasian CGE model to incorporate foreign trade was a major part of the work programme in the development of CGE models. The specification in the standard model follows what has become a broad consensus for 'trade-focused' CGE models and incorporates imperfect substitutability between domestically produced and traded goods, citing early work on specifying import demand functions by Paul Armington.[4] The Armington insight is extended to the treatment of exports, and the model specifies import demand based on sectoral CES 'import aggregation' functions and export supply based on sectoral CET (constant elasticity of transformation) 'export transformation' functions (see, respectively, Equations 24 and 21 of Table A3.1). This model is an extension of the Salter–Swan model and is a theoretically consistent generalization of the 'standard' trade model with non-traded goods, introducing degrees of substitutability and transformability rather than assuming a rigid dichotomy between tradable and non-tradable goods. The theoretical properties of this model have been worked out in detail.[5]

Adding exports, imports and the trade balance also raises the issue of how the receipt–expenditure account of the new actor, the world, is brought into balance, or equilibrated. As with the Salter–Swan model, trade-focused CGE models include a new equilibrating variable, the real exchange rate, which is the relative price of aggregates of traded and non-traded goods. There is an implicit functional relationship between the real exchange rate and the trade balance. Increasing foreign savings always yields an appreciation of the real exchange rate – the price of non-traded goods rises relative to the price of traded goods (exports and imports).[6] Exports fall as producers shift production towards domestic markets and imports rise as consumers shift demand in favour of imports, bringing the trade balance into equilibrium with the new exogenous higher level of foreign savings.

Most trade-focused CGE models, and the standard model, introduce the exchange rate as an explicit variable, with units of domestic currency per unit of foreign currency. However, the 'currency' is not money but simply defines the units of domestic and world prices – domestic prices in local currency units and world prices in foreign currency units (e.g. dollars). The model still contains no assets or money, and the exchange rate is not a 'financial' variable in any sense. Changes in the exchange rate work only by changing the relative prices of traded to non-traded goods on domestic markets, affecting export supply and import demand.

Savings, investment and government

In addition to the trade balance, CGE models applied to actual economies incorporate savings and the demand for investment goods. The introduction of the savings–investment account, which collects savings and purchases investment goods, is standard. A new flow equilibrium condition is added to the model – the flow of savings must be made to equal the flow demand for investment goods – and some mechanism is introduced to achieve the savings–investment balance (see Equation 45 in Table A3.1). Typically, CGE models specify fixed savings rates by households and assume that whatever is saved is then spent on investment goods. The result is a 'savings-driven' model of aggregate investment demand.[7]

The government in a classic CGE model collects taxes, makes and receives transfer payments and purchases goods and services. It is hard to see the government as being a utility maximizing actor; so most CGE models treat government as following specified rules of behaviour.[8] For example, a common specification is that government expenditure is fixed in real terms, including transfers; government revenue is determined by fixed tax rates; and government savings is determined residually as the gap between revenue and expenditure. The model treats the government deficit or surplus as coming from the loanable funds market, and so any government deficit 'crowds out' private investment.

The discussion above has described a typical CGE model that achieves macro balances (or macro 'closure') in a particular way, which can be termed 'neoclassical macro closure'. The model assumes full employment, with wages and prices adjusting to achieve equilibrium in factor and product markets. The balance of trade is fixed exogenously, which determines foreign savings. The real exchange adjusts to achieve the specified trade balance through its effect on aggregate imports and exports. The government has a simple rule-based specification: fixed real expenditure, fixed tax rates and government savings determined residually. Households and firms have fixed savings rates, which determine private savings. Finally, given that all the components of savings are determined by various rules and behavioural parameters, aggregate investment is specified as 'savings driven' and equal to the sum of private, government and foreign savings.

Macro closure

There is a large literature on issues of macro closure of CGE models.[9] The issue is how the model achieves flow equilibrium in the three macro balances: savings–investment, government deficit and the balance of trade. Since the model satisfies Walras' law, the macro closure issue is to specify equilibrating mechanisms for achieving balance in two of the three accounts – the third account will then necessarily balance as well.

The standard model offers a number of different choices of macro closure. For the trade balance, one can either assume that the trade balance is fixed and the real exchange rate adjusts to equilibrate aggregate exports and imports or that the real exchange rate is fixed and the trade balance is endogenous. For savings–investment balance, one can assume that the model is 'savings driven' as discussed earlier with fixed savings rates for various actors determining aggregate savings, which in turn determines investment. Alternatively, one can assume that aggregate investment is either fixed or set by some macro relationship and that the savings rate of some actor or actors adjusts to generate the savings required to finance aggregate investment – the model is 'investment driven'. Similarly, government expenditure can either be assumed to be fixed or set by some macro relationship, and that government savings is determined residually as the difference between government earnings and expenditure. Alternatively, one can assume that government savings is fixed and that some tax instruments are determined endogenously to generate the needed funds.

In general, both the extreme savings- and investment-driven macro closures seem unrealistic, forcing all macro adjustments in either aggregate savings or aggregate investment. Looking at the historical experience of countries undergoing macro shocks and structural adjustment programmes, a specification of some kind of 'balanced' macro closure seems more realistic, spreading the macro adjustment burden evenly among aggregate investment, consumption and government expenditure. Specification of such a balanced closure is an option in the standard model, and was used in about a quarter of the country studies in the project.

Labour Market Closures

These various macro closures can be linked to different specifications of the operation of factor markets to generate a rich menu of possible macro-employment interactions. The essential issue is that the classic Walrasian CGE model, in which all markets clear, yields a full-employment equilibrium and market-clearing prices and wages, while short-run macro models typically involve wage and price rigidities, partial adjustment mechanisms and equilibrium without market clearing, including unemployment. The two paradigms embody very different notions of equilibrium.[10] If the CGE model assumes factor markets clear, then any choice of macro closure will have no effect on aggregate employment and little or no effect on aggregate GDP. In this situation, different macro closures will have 'compositional' effects – the balance between aggregate investment, consumption, government spending and the trade balance – but no effect on the level of real economic activity and employment.

There is a literature on 'structuralist' CGE models, which embody elements of short-run macro models, including 'demand-driven' Keynesian models that yield equilibria with unemployment.[11] These models do not explicitly incorporate financial variables and asset markets, but manage to work within the flow-equilibrium structure of CGE models. They effectively impose a macro story onto the CGE model structure that involves the assumption that labour markets do not clear and that macro shocks can have effects on aggregate employment and GDP. Most structuralist models start from the assumption that the labour market does not clear with flexible wages, but is limited in its adjustment. In a Keynesian structuralist model, the labour market is driven by macro phenomena, and employment is affected by aggregate demand via a Keynesian multiplier process. In such a model, the real wage is viewed as a macro-equilibrating variable, with employment determined only by the demand for labour.[12]

Most of the country studies in this project specify a combination of structuralist features in the labour market and Keynesian multipliers. The comparative analysis described in Section 3.3 define a set of 'standardized' closure rules for all countries, using a 'balanced' macroeconomic closure, i.e. with weak Keynesian demand adjustment, and a fixed real wage in all sectors assuming an unlimited supply of labour at that wage. The implication, as described earlier, is that any change that would normally lead to an increase in the real wage (e.g. increased productivity or capital stock growth) will instead lead to an increase in the demand for labour and higher aggregate employment.

Macro–micro linkages: economy-wide shocks, distribution and poverty

A major focus of the country studies has been to translate changes at the macro or economy-wide level to resulting impacts on the distribution of income and

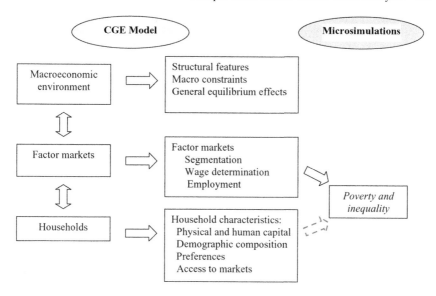

Figure 3.3 Mapping from macro changes to poverty outcomes.

poverty. All the studies have used household survey data and microsimulation methods, which are described later, to analyse distributional impacts. The methodological issue facing the various studies is how to track the mechanisms by which economy-wide shocks involving macro variables work their way through the economy, finally affecting household livelihoods. Figure 3.3 provides a schematic picture of the mechanisms involved.

The 'top–down' causal chain works from macro shocks through the operation of factor and product markets yielding prices, wages and employment, and finally to household income and expenditure. A crucial part of analysing and modelling distributional outcomes at the household level is the specification of the various sources of income at the household level and how those sources are linked to the operation of factor and product markets. In terms of the SAM data framework and SAM-based analysis, it is crucial to disaggregate the factor markets, including data on the ownership of factors by households. In various settings, it may be important to disaggregate production and employment by categories such as region, sector, skill category, gender, age and nature of employment (e.g. self-employed, informal sector or formal sector), all of which could be relevant in determining how households earn their income. In addition, the extent to which households operate in commercial or formal markets can be important – for example, home consumption can represent a significant part of real income and consumption for poor farmers.

The country studies vary widely in the extent to which they have been able to disaggregate the sources and uses of household income – essentially limited by data availability. All the studies were able to use household survey data, but vary in their ability to link household income to changes at the macro and economy-wide levels. The modelling framework can accommodate such analysis, but estimating the underlying SAM was always the binding constraint.

In the country studies, the analysis is 'top–down' in that the goal was to translate from economy-wide changes to outcomes at the household level. No attempt was made to determine feedbacks from changes at the household level back through the operation of factor markets to macro variables.[13] A major advantage of the top–down approach is that the analysis and modelling of households, based on survey data, can be done separately from the economy-wide analysis, and there is no need to reconcile the household data with the national data. The communication between the two strands is in the form of information about changes in prices, wages and employment – there is no need to reconcile data on levels.[14] The microsimulation analysis at the household level is discussed in more detail next.

Microsimulation methodology

The country analyses in this study focus on the labour market as the main transmission channel of the modelled impact of trade reforms on poverty and distribution. To go from the counterfactual labour market effects simulated with the CGE model to poverty and income distribution at the household level we need to deal with two methodological issues. First, how to incorporate both between- and within-group effects into the distribution analysis? That is, how can we account for the full distribution and thus for the heterogeneity of the population within households when assessing the poverty and inequality effects? Second, people may change position in the labour market (hence also affecting household income) due to trade reforms, external shocks or other simulated macro changes. Workers may shift from one sector to another, change occupation or lose their job. The methodological issue is to find a procedure that can account for such labour market shifts and identify which individuals are most likely to shift position in order to be able to simulate a new, counterfactual income distribution.

Various microsimulation methodologies have been proposed in the literature to deal with these problems.[15] We mention two types that try to answer the type of questions raised in this study. The first involves the estimation of a microeconomic, partial-equilibrium household income generation model through a system of equations that determine occupational choice, returns to labour and human capital, consumer prices and other household (individual) income components (see, for instance, Bourguignon *et al.* 2001a, b). Combining this methodology in 'top–down' fashion with a CGE model has been probed by Bourguignon *et al.* (2002a) for the case of Indonesia.

A second microsimulation approach of less modelling intensity assumes that occupational shifts may be proxied by a random selection procedure within a segmented labour market structure. This procedure allows the imposition of counterfactual changes in key labour market parameters (participation rate, unemployment, employment composition by sectors, wage structure, etc.) on a given distribution derived from household survey data and estimate the impact of each change on poverty and income distribution at the household level. This type of methodology of counterfactual microsimulations originates with Orcutt (1957) for tax incidence analysis in developed countries and Oaxaca (1973) and Blinder (1973) for between-group differentials in mean earnings and, more recently, with Almeida dos Reis and Paes de Barros (1991) for an analysis of inequality in the full distribution of earnings.[16] The latter approach was subsequently generalized to analyse total per capita household income inequality and poverty (see Paes de Barros and Leite 1998; Paes de Barros 1999; Frenkel and González 2000; Ganuza *et al.* 2002).

In both types of methods, total per capita household income is defined as

$$ypc_{hi} = \frac{1}{n_h} \left[\sum_{i=1}^{n_h} yp_{hi} + yq_h \right]$$

(1)

where n_h is the size of household h, yp_{hi} the labour income of member i of household h and yq_h the sum of all non-labour incomes of the household, defined as

$$yq_h = \sum_{i=1}^{n_h} yqp_{hi} + yqt_h$$

(2)

In Equation (2), yqp_{hi} = individual non-labour income of member i of household h and yqt_h = other household incomes. In the simulations, yp_{hi} is altered for some individuals i of household h as a result of changes in the labour market parameters.

The second microsimulation approach as applied in Ganuza *et al.* (2002) is followed in most country studies and defines the labour market structure in terms of rates of economic participation (P_j) and unemployment (U_j) among different groups j of the population at working age defined according to sex and skill, the structure of employment (defined according to sector of activity S and occupational category O) and remuneration W_1, as well as overall level of remuneration W_2. The skill composition of the population is represented by variable M. The labour market structure can be written as $\pi = \pi(P, U, S, O, W_1, W_2, M)$.

For all types of individuals, the unemployment rates determine part of the labour market structure. The latter is further determined by the structure of employment. The employed workforce is classified according to segment k, defined on the basis of sector of activity and occupational category. For both skill groups within segments k in the labour market, the average remuneration is calculated and these averages are expressed as a ratio of the overall average. The effect of alteration of parameters of the labour market structure on poverty and inequality can now be analysed using the accounting identities of Equations (1) and (2). The impact of changes in the labour market can be analysed both separately and sequentially.

The Ganuza–Barros–Vos approach introduces a number of important assumptions about the labour market. First, as indicated, for lack of a full model of the labour market, a randomized process is applied to simulate the effects of changes in the labour market structure. That is, random numbers are used to determine: which persons at working age change their labour force status; who will change occupational category; which employed persons obtain a different level of education; and how are new mean labour incomes assigned to individuals in the sample. Hence, the assumption is that, on average, the effect of the random changes correctly reflects the impact of the actual changes in the labour market.[17] Because of the introduction of a process of random assignation, the microsimulations are repeated a large number of times in Monte Carlo fashion.[18] This allows constructing 95% confidence intervals for the indices of inequality and poverty, except in the case of the simulations of the effect of change in the structure and level of remuneration, which do not involve random numbers. In each simulation, the incidence, depth and severity of poverty and the Gini and Theil coefficients of the distribution of both per capita income and primary incomes are calculated.[19]

It should be noted that the case studies of Argentina and Mexico follow a hybrid approach to the microsimulations. Rather than randomly selecting the individuals in the simulations as done by Ganuza *et al.* (2002), a probability function is estimated to determine who, given personal characteristics, is most likely to move and which is the likely income he or she will obtain after the shift. Subsequently, the estimated parameters replace the randomized procedure in the Ganuza *et al.* methodology, thereby moving closer to the first type of microsimulations. In terms of Figure 3.3, there is a *closed-line* arrow from labour market outcomes to poverty and inequality at the household level, representing the link as established through the Ganuza–Barros–Vos approach. The alternative microsimulation approach as in Bourguignon *et al.* (2002b) would add a probabilistic specification of household labour supply behaviour, adding an additional link as represented by the arrow with the *dotted* lines in Figure 3.3.

In Section 3.4 and in the country studies we report results for the poverty incidence (P_0) and the Gini coefficients for labour and per capita household incomes. Unless reported otherwise, directions of change of the microsimulations are the same for all alternative poverty and distribution measures.

3.3 Macro CGE simulations: counterfactual analysis of effects of trade reforms and external shocks

Standardized simulations

In this section, we report the main findings of the CGE simulations for alternative trade reform and trade integration scenarios and a number of external shocks for the 16 Latin American countries in our sample. In order to make the outcomes as comparable as possible, we ran the same simulations (with shocks of equal size) in two steps. First, we apply the policy shocks for a standardized set of 'macro and labour-market' closures. Second, we then compare those outcomes with the 'actual' closures as used by the country studies. Since we have a 'standard' model, imposing standardized closures implies that we focus in the first set of simulations on differences in outcomes of the imposed policy changes and shocks that are due to differences in economic structure and the capacity of markets to respond to relative price shifts. One could call this an exercise in 'elasticity structuralism' as we assume roughly identical behaviour and functioning of the economies. The country-specific closures should identify how macro and labour market adjustment is working out in reality as justified in the country studies and differences in outcomes of the simulations are a result of both differences in economic structure and adjustment behaviour.

The standardized closure rules involve: (a) alternatively, a *fixed* or *endogenous* level of foreign savings for the external balance (i.e. respectively corresponding to a flexible and a fixed exchange-rate regime); (b) a balanced savings–investment closure rule (see Section 3.2); and (c) endogenous government savings (i.e. fixed tax rates). For the labour market closure, we assume a fixed real wage for all labour categories, implying that all adjustment falls on quantities (employment), rather than prices (wages).

The country-specific closures involve in half of the cases a fixed exchange-rate regime; the other half assumes a flexible regime.[20] Most countries (except Argentina, Brazil and Venezuela) had the same government balance closure as in the standard simulations, but only four countries (Bolivia, El Salvador, Mexico and Paraguay) used a 'balanced' savings–investment closure. Two countries assumed a neoclassical macro closure (Peru and Brazil) and the rest (10) assumed a Keynesian, investment-driven closure. In most cases, factor market closures assumed segmented markets with different adjustment mechanisms by type of factor, mostly allowing for unemployment in the formal and unskilled labour segments and with price (wage) adjustment predominating in the informal and/or skilled labour segments. The various closure mechanisms are summarized in Table A3.2.

Given the structure of the CGE model, we expect that trade liberalization will shift relative prices in favour of tradables. If the tradable goods sector has a higher average productivity and labour intensity than non-traded activities, this should lead to an expansion of aggregate output and employment along the lines of the dependent-economy model. The expansionary effect may be compounded, in the short run, by reduced import cost and a larger influx of foreign capital to finance a rising trade deficit if import demand responds more strongly than exports to trade opening. Thus, if the given conditions hold we would expect a stronger expansionary effect of trade liberalization under a fixed exchange-rate regime as in this case rising domestic demand and a widening external balance will not hit a foreign exchange constraint. The ensuing real exchange-rate appreciation depresses the positive impact on exports and traded-goods output, but if trade elasticities are relatively low (which would hold in particular for point-sourced primary exporters, such as Bolivia, Ecuador, Venezuela and several other cases) the foreign capital impulse and expansion of non-traded goods tend to outweigh the effects on export production. For similar reasons, devaluations tend to be contractionary. Under a flexible exchange-rate regime, we allow the real exchange rate to depreciate to accommodate a rising trade deficit triggered by import liberalization and keep the level of foreign savings fixed. If all the other conditions are the same as indicated above, the expected result would now be a strengthening of the export drive and tradable goods output and employment, but more restricted aggregate demand growth as access to external borrowing is restricted.

The employment effects of trade liberalization under the standard closure rules will depend on the labour and skill intensity of the main sectors in the economy. Recall that we assume (unrealistically) a fixed labour supply and fixed real wages in all sectors, such that all labour market adjustment falls on shifts in quantities of labour. Standard trade theory would predict trade liberalization to lead to rising demand for unskilled labour if that is the abundant factor and rising overall employment assuming the country will specialize in the production for which it has a comparative advantage. However, many of the countries in our sample may equally be defined as natural resource abundant and probably are less unskilled-labour abundant than competitors in Asia for world market production. Point-source natural resource abundant countries, like those mentioned earlier, likely have relatively low labour intensity in export production and have weak or negative employment gains from trade liberalization, while skill intensity may rise if the non-traded sector is high on demand for more educated workers. As suggested earlier, the latter effect may be stronger if we assume that the inflow of foreign capital is endogenous. These effects may differ in economies with more diffuse natural resource endowments (i.e. more diversified primary exports and predominance of small holders in exports, such as coffee) and a basis for manufacturing exports (including *maquila*). Such conditions would fit Mexico and the Central American countries, for instance. Positive employment effects are likely stronger under these conditions, even though skill intensity may still rise if the average level of education of workers in the mentioned activities is higher than the average for the rest of the economy.

The results for the key macroeconomic variables and employment for the standardized simulations are displayed in Tables 3.1–3.3. Results for simulation results for the country-specific closure rules are given in Table 3.4.

We begin the discussion with policies such as tariff reduction, export subsidies, devaluations and foreign capital inflows that are related to liberalization of trade and capital flows, and export promotion. Apart from these scenarios of unilateral trade reform, we study the effects of two multilateral trade agreements: a WTO scenario of free trade and worldwide elimination of export subsidies and the much debated option of a Free Trade Area of the Americas (FTAA). We then look at two exogenous trade-related issues, namely terms of trade shock, represented here by a rise in the price of all imports, and the impact of an across the board increase in productivity, which is a quick way of exploring the effect of long-term growth on poverty reduction and income distribution.

Table 3.1 CGE simulations – standardized closures: macroeconomic indicators (real values and percentage change from base)

| | | | | | | | | Costa | | El | | | | | | Dom. | | |
	Argentina	Bolivia	Brazil	Cuba	Chile	Colombia	Rica	Ecuador	Salvador	Honduras	Mexico	Paraguay	Peru	Rep.	Uruguay	Venezuela
BASE																
GDP (factor prices)	274	38	74,388		2,907	1,218	2,979	28,424	1,091	70	2,424	20,090	98	118	126	20,687
Absorption	276	40	74,777		2,927	1,290	3,092	28,464	1,223	67	2,370	27,893	94	124	124	23,757
Household consumption	205	28	48,422		1,747	825	2,166	19,869	937	46	1,694	20,939	65	100	91	18,767
Investment	48	6	14,888		819	254	538	5,412	178	16	488	5,420	21	21	18	3,477
Government consumption	23	5	11,466		361	210	389	3,182	109	5	189	1,534	9	4	15	1,513
Exports	16	8	5,546		852	180	1,220	7,128	271	26	999	3,604	13	47	22	10,370
Imports	23	11	7,148		1,139	266	1,422	8,127	419	37	968	13,946	22	57	25	6,083
Real exchange rate	100	90	97		94	100	100	100	100	91	100	93	87	100	100	90
Tariff cut																
GDP (factor prices)	0.1	0.8	−0.1		1.1	4.7	0.9	1.6	0.1	1.5	0.4	0.1	0.4	0.8	0.6	0.6
Absorption	0.1	0.8	−0.3		1.2	4.3	0.9	1.5	0.2	1.6	0.4	0.5	0.5	1.1	0.6	0.5
Household consumption		0.8	0.2		1.2	4.4	0.9	1.6	0.2	1.5	0.4	0.5	0.4	0.8	0.6	0.4
Investment	0.5	1.5	−0.8		1.4	4.3	1.3	1.6	0.5	1.7	0.4	0.0	1.1	2.7	1.1	0.5
Government consumption		0.3	0.0		0.5	3.8	0.0	0.7	−0.1	1.7	0.3	1.3	0.2	1.5	0.3	0.0
Exports	2.8	2.2	1.1		2.5	7.4	2.1	2.6	1.6	3.3	0.5	1.8	4.0	5.6	1.8	0.9

Foreign savings fixed (flexible exchange rate)

(Continued)

Table 3.1 (Continued)

							Costa		El					Dom.		
	Argentina	Bolivia	Brazil	Cuba	Chile	Colombia	Rica	Ecuador	Salvador	Honduras	Mexico	Paraguay	Peru	Rep.	Uruguay	Venezuela
Imports	2.4	1.8	0.7		2.1	5.3	1.9	2.4	1.1	2.8	0.5	0.9	3.3	5.1	1.6	0.9
Real exchange rate	2.4	1.4	0.5		1.3	1.4	1.1	2.1	0.9	0.7	0.3	1.3	1.4	0.7	1.0	3.4
Foreign savings increase																
GDP (factor prices)	0.4	1.0	0.0		0.8	1.6	0.7	1.2	0.5	2.2	3.1	1.6	0.1	−0.3	0.3	4.2
Absorption	1.0	2.9	0.0		3.6	2.7	4.5	3.8	2.3	5.5	7.2	2.1	1.3	3.3	2.1	4.7
Household consumption	0.9	2.9	0.0		3.5	2.8	4.4	3.4	2.3	5.1	7.2	2.0	1.2	3.1	1.8	0.0
Investment	1.2	3.4	0.0		4.0	2.7	5.1	5.3	2.7	6.4	7.6	2.3	1.6	4.7	3.9	12.2
Government consumption	0.9	2.9	0.0		3.1	2.6	4.0	3.0	1.7	6.6	6.0	2.0	1.3	2.6	1.9	0.0
Exports	−5.1	−4.2	0.0		−5.1	−3.7	−4.9	−3.5	−3.8	−5.3	−5.5	−2.4	−6.2	−12.7	−5.5	−6.2
Imports	3.8	4.8	0.0		4.3	4.5	4.6	6.1	4.2	3.8	4.8	2.6	3.1	−2.0	4.2	10.7
Real exchange rate	−4.7	−3.9	0.0		−4.8	−2.3	−3.0	−5.4	−3.2	−5.3	−6.9	−2.7	−3.7	−5.4	−4.8	−3.3
Terms-of-trade shock: import price increase																
GDP (factor prices)	−1.4	−6.2	−0.1		−6.6	−16.5	−7.4	−8.2	−4.6	−11.8	−11.8	−9.3	−2.3	−8.4	−4.2	−3.2
Absorption	−1.5	−5.9	−1.1		−6.6	−15.1	−7.2	−8.0	−4.4	−11.3	−11.9	−7.1	−2.5	−8.2	−4.5	−13.0
Household consumption	−1.3	−5.6	−1.6		−6.6	−15.4	−7.2	−8.0	−4.4	−10.8	−12.1	−6.9	−2.2	−7.3	−4.1	−12.2
Investment	−2.1	−8.0	−0.2		−7.3	−15.2	−8.7	−9.9	−5.1	−12.3	−12.0	−8.2	−3.7	−12.2	−7.4	−17.2

(Continued)

Table 3.1 (Continued)

								Costa		El					Dom.		
							Foreign savings fixed (flexible exchange rate)										
	Argentina	Bolivia	Brazil	Cuba	Chile	Colombia	Rica	Ecuador	Salvador	Honduras	Mexico	Paraguay	Peru	Rep.	Uruguay	Venezuela
Government consumption	-1.3	-4.6	0.0		-5.0	-13.7	-4.8	-5.3	-4.0	-12.6	-10.0	-6.9	-2.2	-9.6	-3.5	0.0
Exports	1.7	-2.2	5.4		-1.1	-17.2	-0.9	-3.8	-2.2	-5.0	-0.8	-2.2	1.5	-26.1	-0.6	-8.9
Imports	-8.0	-10.7	-6.1		-9.4	-20.2	-9.8	-12.3	-10.5	-12.6	-9.9	-9.8	-8.2	-29.4	-9.6	-17.2
Real exchange rate	7.7	5.3	-11.6		6.2	3.6	5.5	4.3	5.8	8.7	7.9	8.9	6.6	13.5	6.6	-9.1
Terms-of-trade shock: export price increase																
GDP (factor prices)	1.2	6.0	0.0		6.6	21.0	7.4	8.3	4.7	11.3	11.9	6.9	2.3	8.5	4.2	1.3
Absorption	1.2	5.4	0.0		6.5	18.7	6.9	8.1	3.6	10.3	12.1	3.7	2.2	8.5	4.3	-3.3
Household consumption	1.1	5.2	0.0		6.6	19.2	7.0	8.1	3.5	10.0	12.4	3.6	1.9	7.5	3.9	-0.9
Investment	1.8	7.6	0.0		7.2	18.7	8.5	10.1	4.1	11.1	12.2	4.4	3.3	13.1	7.1	7.0
Government consumption	1.0	3.9	0.0		4.7	16.8	4.3	4.9	3.3	11.6	9.8	3.5	1.9	9.8	3.3	0.0
Exports	-0.3	2.9	0.0		1.3	23.8	1.3	4.0	4.3	4.4	0.4	6.4	0.2	17.1	1.0	-10.0
Imports	7.6	10.8	0.0		10.0	25.8	10.4	13.5	9.9	12.5	11.0	6.0	8.3	25.4	10.1	7.1
Real exchange rate	-5.7	-4.1	0.0		-5.4	-2.7	-4.8	-4.0	-4.0	-7.4	-7.3	-3.6	-5.4	-14.2	-5.6	-13.0
Productivity shock																
GDP (factor prices)	15.0	18.5	10.1		20.7	81.6	14.9	27.6	14.9	23.0	26.9	12.4	13.8	13.9	23.0	10.1
Absorption	15.7	18.2	9.6		20.8	76.9	14.8	26.8	13.7	21.6	27.0	10.8	13.9	13.8	23.7	14.5

(Continued)

Table 3.1 (Continued)

															Dom.		
	Argentina	Bolivia	Brazil	Cuba	Chile	Colombia	Costa Rica	Ecuador	El Salvador	Honduras	Mexico	Paraguay	Peru	Rep.	Uruguay	Venezuela
Foreign savings fixed (flexible exchange rate)																
Household consumption	14.8	18.0	7.1		20.3	77.6	14.4	27.5	13.4	22.2	27.5	10.9	13.4	13.3	22.9	13.6
Investment	16.7	17.4	25.4		21.1	74.0	15.1	25.6	14.7	21.1	23.9	10.0	14.5	14.5	26.5	19.8
Government consumption	21.4	20.0	0.0		22.1	77.6	16.4	24.3	14.1	17.6	30.5	12.0	16.3	22.0	25.0	0.0
Exports	19.2	21.2	13.7		20.6	100.0	15.6	27.1	19.7	22.1	18.9	25.5	17.0	21.0	22.4	12.0
Imports	14.9	17.4	8.4		19.6	71.5	14.2	25.2	13.2	19.4	20.0	8.9	13.4	18.4	20.5	13.9
Real exchange rate	1.0	4.3	-6.3		2.2	4.2	1.2	6.6	1.6	2.0	5.6	8.5	1.1	-0.7	2.0	2.8
Export subsidy increase																
GDP (factor prices)	0.3	2.8	-0.1		3.2	17.8	2.7	5.0	1.8	5.3	5.4	3.2	1.0	5.0	2.2	1.4
Absorption	0.3	2.5	-0.1		3.0	15.9	2.4	4.6	1.2	4.8	5.4	1.6	0.9	5.0	2.2	-2.8
Household consumption	0.2	2.3	0.8		3.2	16.3	2.5	4.9	1.1	4.8	5.7	1.5	0.7	4.3	2.1	-3.1
Investment	0.6	4.3	-3.0		3.3	15.9	3.4	5.1	1.4	4.8	5.1	2.0	1.8	8.0	3.3	3.9
Government consumption	0.1	1.0	0.0		1.7	14.1	0.4	2.0	1.6	5.0	4.1	1.5	0.6	7.2	1.5	0.0
Exports	4.9	7.3	3.6		6.9	29.3	6.1	8.2	8.7	10.4	6.3	9.2	7.2	33.8	6.6	2.0
Imports	3.9	6.0	2.2		6.0	20.9	5.7	7.6	5.9	8.9	6.7	3.3	5.8	29.2	6.0	1.9
Real exchange rate	-5.5	-4.8	2.0		-5.9	-4.5	-6.6	-3.4	-5.2	-6.9	-6.1	-3.4	-7.0	-12.6	-5.7	-3.7

(Continued)

Table 3.1 (Continued)

| | | | | | | | | | | | | | | | Dom. | | |
		Argentina	Bolivia	Brazil	Cuba	Chile	Colombia	Costa Rica	Ecuador	El Salvador	Honduras	Mexico	Paraguay	Peru	Rep.	Uruguay	Venezuela

Foreign savings fixed (flexible exchange rate)

	Argentina	Bolivia	Brazil	Cuba	Chile	Colombia	Costa Rica	Ecuador	El Salvador	Honduras	Mexico	Paraguay	Peru	Dom. Rep.	Uruguay	Venezuela
FTAA scenario																
GDP (factor prices)	0.1	1.2	0.0		1.1	7.6	1.3	2.4	0.3	2.2	0.3	−0.3	0.4	1.1	0.7	−0.9
Absorption	0.2	1.3	0.0		1.1	7.0	1.2	2.3	0.4	2.2	0.3	0.5	0.6	1.7	0.8	−4.6
Household consumption	0.1	1.2	0.2		1.2	7.2	1.3	2.4	0.4	2.1	0.3	0.6	0.3	1.2	0.7	−0.3
Investment	0.5	2.2	−0.7		1.3	7.0	1.9	2.8	0.6	2.3	0.2	−0.3	1.7	3.9	1.2	−11.5
Government consumption	0.1	0.5	0.0		0.5	6.2	0.1	1.1	−0.1	2.4	0.2	2.0	0.0	2.1	0.4	0.0
Exports	3.0	3.2	0.9		2.5	12.0	2.8	3.5	2.2	4.1	0.2	2.9	7.7	7.7	2.0	−1.6
Imports	2.6	2.8	0.7		2.0	8.7	2.8	3.5	1.6	3.7	0.3	1.1	5.4	7.1	2.0	−1.1
Real exchange rate	2.3	2.2	0.6		1.4	2.2	1.2	2.4	1.1	0.4	0.1	2.6	2.8	0.6	1.0	−1.5
WTO scenario																
GDP (factor prices)	0.9	4.2	0.0		0.5	13.9	2.5	6.7	−0.1	10.3	−0.9	−2.1	2.4	0.2	2.5	−1.7
Absorption	1.0	3.8	−0.1		0.5	11.3	2.4	6.3	0.1	9.5	−0.6	−1.2	1.8	1.0	2.5	−6.2
Household consumption	0.8	3.9	0.4		0.6	11.7	2.4	6.6	0.1	9.4	−0.9	−1.0	1.0	0.4	2.5	−1.6
Investment	2.1	4.9	−1.6		0.7	11.2	3.9	7.2	0.7	9.8	0.3	−2.6	4.5	4.2	3.2	−14.2
Government consumption	0.6	2.3	0.0		−0.4	9.7	0.0	2.9	−0.2	9.5	−0.7	0.7	1.3	0.4	1.3	0.0
Exports	7.6	4.4	2.2		5.1	17.7	3.9	8.3	2.5	8.1	−0.4	4.6	8.9	4.6	4.0	−1.5
Imports	10.3	6.8	1.5		1.7	14.6	5.2	9.7	1.0	12.0	−0.6	−0.9	22.8	4.2	7.1	−3.7
Real exchange rate	−0.6	2.7	1.2		4.3	2.4	−0.9	3.0	2.1	−2.8	−0.8	6.3	−20.7	2.0	−0.8	−0.5

Source: Author's calculations

Note: Cuba was not included in this exercise because it is not realistic to assume a flexible exchange rate.

Table 3.2 CGE simulations – standardized closures: macroeconomic indicators (real values and percentage change from base)

							Costa		El					Dom.		
	Argentina	Bolivia	Brazil	Cuba	Chile	Colombia	Rica	Ecuador	Salvador	Honduras	Mexico	Paraguay	Peru	Rep.	Uruguay	Venezuela
BASE																
GDP (factor prices)	274	38	74,388	29	2,907	1,218	2,979	28,424	1,091	70	2,424	20,090	98	118	126	20,687
Absorption	276	40	74,777	30	2,927	1,290	3,092	28,464	1,223	67	2,370	27,893	94	124	124	23,757
Household consumption	205	28	48,422	22	1,747	825	2,166	19,869	937	46	1,694	20,939	65	100	91	18,767
Investment	48	6	14,888	2	819	254	538	5,412	178	16	488	5,420	21	21	18	3,477
Government consumption	23	5	11,466	6	361	210	389	3,182	109	5	189	1,534	9	4	15	1,513
Exports	16	8	5,546	4	852	180	1,220	7,128	271	26	999	3,604	13	47	22	10,370
Imports	23	11	7,148	5	1,139	266	1,422	8,127	419	37	968	13,946	22	57	25	6,083
Real exchange rate	100	90	97		94	100	100	100	100	91	100	93	87	100	100	90
Tariff cut																
GDP (factor prices)	0.2	1.3	0.0	-0.1	1.4	6.2	1.4	2.1	0.3	2.0	0.6	1.1	0.4	0.6	0.0	0.9
Absorption	0.6	2.3	0.1	-0.7	2.7	7.0	4.6	3.3	1.3	2.9	0.9	1.9	1.3	2.2	1.2	0.7
Household consumption	0.5	2.2	0.3	-0.7	2.7	7.1	4.6	3.2	1.3	2.8	0.9	1.9	1.1	1.8	1.1	0.3
Investment	1.1	3.2	-0.5	0.1	3.0	7.0	5.6	4.2	1.7	3.2	1.0	1.6	2.0	4.1	2.2	0.0
Government consumption	0.5	1.8	0.0	-1.1	1.8	6.3	3.4	2.2	0.7	3.3	0.7	2.7	1.0	2.3	0.8	0.0
Exports	0.0	0.0	0.2	0.0	0.2	3.4	-1.9	0.7	-0.2	1.9	0.1	0.1	-0.3	1.8	0.2	0.4

Exchange rate fixed

(Continued)

Table 3.2 (Continued)

								Costa		El					Dom.		
	Argentina	Bolivia	Brazil	Cuba	Chile	Colombia	Rica	Ecuador	Salvador	Honduras	Mexico	Paraguay	Peru	Rep.	Uruguay	Venezuela
Imports	4.4	4.2	1.2	0.3	3.8	9.8	5.8	5.4	2.9	3.7	0.9	2.6	4.9	4.5	2.8	0.7
Real exchange rate	-0.2	-0.5	1.7		-0.6	-0.9	-1.4	-0.6	-0.4	-0.6	-0.2	-0.6	-0.5	-0.8	-0.3	-2.6
Devaluation																
GDP (factor prices)	-0.8	-2.7	-0.1	1.7	-1.4	-2.6	-2.1	-2.1	-1.0	-3.7	-3.7	-6.7	-0.1	2.0	-0.3	-2.3
Absorption	-2.2	-9.8	-1.1	1.0	-16.3	-10.9	-22.6	-7.8	-11.3	-11.9	-12.1	-9.6	-4.4	-9.2	-5.1	-14.6
Household consumption	-2.1	-9.6	-0.7	1.1	-15.9	-11.0	-22.2	-7.2	-11.4	-11.0	-12.1	-9.4	-4.2	-8.7	-4.4	-10.0
Investment	-2.7	-10.6	-3.0	-1.4	-17.4	-10.8	-24.9	-10.6	-12.8	-13.8	-12.6	-10.8	-5.1	-11.9	-8.9	-44.6
Government consumption	-2.1	-10.0	0.0	1.6	-15.5	-10.7	-21.5	-7.2	-8.3	-14.0	-10.7	-9.3	-4.3	-7.4	-4.7	0.0
Exports	12.1	15.7	8.4	10.0	32.7	35.6	25.1	8.3	23.9	12.6	11.2	12.3	23.6	33.1	15.0	6.6
Imports	-7.5	-13.6	-3.7	7.1	-12.9	-17.2	-19.8	-11.2	-16.3	-7.0	-6.4	-11.4	-8.5	4.4	-8.2	-17.9
Real exchange rate	10.5	12.4	-8.8		12.1	12.4	12.8	11.1	13.1	11.7	11.5	13.7	11.4	10.9	10.9	-8.4
Terms-of-trade shock: import price increase																
GDP (factor prices)	-1.3	-6.7	0.0	-10.4	-6.8	-18.8	-8.2	-8.9	-4.6	-11.5	-11.8	-10.4	-2.3	-8.3	-4.2	-2.3
Absorption	-1.1	-7.4	-0.3	-10.6	-7.3	-19.7	-13.1	-10.0	-6.5	-10.4	-11.2	-8.6	-2.3	-3.0	-4.4	-9.6
Household consumption	-1.0	-7.1	-1.0	-8.4	-7.3	-20.0	-13.1	-9.8	-6.4	-10.0	-11.4	-8.3	-2.0	-2.4	-4.0	-10.2
Investment	-1.7	-9.7	1.8	0.4	-8.1	-19.8	-15.3	-12.4	-7.5	-11.3	-11.3	-9.8	-3.5	-5.4	-7.2	-5.7

(Continued)

Table 3.2 (Continued)

								Exchange rate fixed								
	Argentina	Bolivia	Brazil	Cuba	Chile	Colombia	Costa Rica	Ecuador	El Salvador	Honduras	Mexico	Paraguay	Peru	Dom. Rep.	Uruguay	Venezuela
Government consumption	-1.0	-6.2	0.0	-23.3	-5.6	-18.1	-10.5	-7.1	-5.6	-11.6	-9.4	-8.3	-2.1	-5.3	-3.5	0.0
Exports	-0.1	0.1	-0.5	0.0		-8.1	5.8	-2.1	1.5	-5.8	-1.4	-0.5	0.4	-41.3	-0.8	-8.1
Imports	-6.9	-12.9	-3.5	0.6	-10.2	-27.1	-15.0	-15.0	-13.7	-12.1	-9.5	-11.5	-8.0	-29.9	-9.4	-12.8
Real exchange rate	6.0	7.4	-5.5		7.1	9.0	9.4	7.1	8.8	7.7	7.1	11.0	6.5	6.3	6.4	-7.6
Terms-of-trade shock: export price increase																
GDP (factor prices)	0.4	4.0	0.0	0.3	5.7	18.5	6.0	7.5	3.9	7.5	7.9	3.7	2.2	14.3	4.0	4.0
Absorption	-1.0	-2.0	0.0	-0.5	-4.9	11.7	-7.7	3.0	-4.3	-2.4	-1.0	-1.1	-2.1	-5.8	-0.7	-4.6
Household consumption	-1.0	-2.0	0.0	-1.4	-4.5	12.1	-7.4	3.4	-4.4	-1.9	-0.7	-1.1	-2.2	-5.8	-0.4	-4.2
Investment	-0.9	-0.6	0.0	-0.9	-5.2	11.7	-7.9	2.7	-4.8	-3.5	-1.6	-1.0	-1.6	-6.3	-1.7	-6.3
Government consumption	-1.1	-3.5	0.0	3.3	-5.7	10.0	-8.9	0.5	-2.3	-3.4	-1.5	-1.1	-2.3	-1.3	-1.2	
Exports	12.1	14.5	0.0	2.9	22.4	41.2	17.0	10.5	20.5	18.6	12.6	12.7	23.1	77.9	15.8	1.0
Imports	-0.7	-0.6	0.0	1.6	-1.0	13.6	-4.1	4.9	-2.4	4.8	3.2	0.0	-0.5	36.9	1.3	-3.4
Real exchange rate	4.5	4.9	0.0		4.9	3.4	3.6	3.9	4.2	3.9	4.3	2.6	4.9	4.6	4.4	5.4
Productivity shock																
GDP (factor prices)	15.1	19.7	10.1	20.2	21.1	88.2	15.1	28.7	15.1	24.9	30.2	17.6	13.8	14.1	23.1	7.5
Absorption	15.9	21.6	10.5	19.8	23.0	87.8	16.6	32.5	14.9	26.6	34.9	18.0	14.3	12.9	24.8	5.3

(Continued)

Table 3.2 (Continued)

							Exchange rate fixed									Dom.		
	Argentina	Bolivia	Brazil	Cuba	Chile	Colombia	Costa Rica	Ecuador	El Salvador	Honduras	Mexico	Paraguay	Peru	Rep.	Uruguay	Venezuela
Household consumption	15.0	21.3	7.7	40.3	22.5	88.6	16.2	32.7	14.7	26.9	35.4	17.9	13.7	12.5	23.8	9.3
Investment	16.9	21.3	27.8	25.6	23.6	84.7	17.3	33.8	16.2	26.8	32.1	18.1	15.0	13.4	28.5	11.4
Government consumption	21.6	23.5	0.0	-59.3	24.1	88.2	18.1	28.9	15.1	23.4	37.4	19.1	16.7	21.3	26.0	0.0
Exports	17.4	16.4	6.9	0.0	17.3	87.1	13.6	19.7	17.3	17.2	12.6	16.5	15.0	24.1	19.4	12.1
Imports	15.5	22.8	11.7	5.3	22.1	88.4	16.1	34.5	15.3	22.7	24.8	17.7	14.1	18.9	22.6	0.7
Real exchange rate	0.4	0.4	0.6	-0.9	-0.1	-0.6	0.0	-0.8	0.2	-2.0	-0.5	-0.1	0.4	0.3	-0.1	0.9
Export subsidy increase																
GDP (factor prices)	-0.3	1.4	-0.1	1.6	2.1	16.4	1.1	4.7	0.9	2.8	3.3	1.3	0.6	7.2	2.0	0.3
Absorption	-1.0	-2.0	-0.8	-0.4	-4.9	11.7	-8.1	2.9	-4.3	-2.4	-1.0	-1.1	-2.1	-5.8	-0.6	-7.4
Household consumption	-1.0	-2.0	0.3	-0.2	-4.5	12.1	-7.8	3.4	-4.4	-1.9	-0.8	-1.1	-2.2	-5.9	-0.3	-9.9
Investment	-0.9	-0.6	-5.1	-0.1	-5.2	11.7	-8.3	2.6	-4.8	-3.5	-1.6	-1.0	-1.6	-6.3	-1.6	-8.0
Government consumption	-1.1	-3.5	0.0	-0.9	-5.7	10.0	-9.2	0.5	-2.3	-3.4	-1.5	-1.1	-2.3	-1.3	-1.1	0.0
Exports	12.1	14.5	8.9	8.4	22.4	41.2	17.4	10.5	20.5	18.7	12.8	12.7	23.1	78.6	15.1	5.1
Imports	-0.7	-0.6	-0.2	-0.9	-1.0	13.6	-4.3	4.9	-2.4	4.8	3.2	0.0	-0.5	37.4	1.3	-5.3
Real exchange rate	0.1	0.4	-3.6	0.0	0.0	-0.8	-1.1	-0.9	0.2	-0.8	-0.8	0.0	0.4	-0.1	-0.3	-3.5

(Continued)

Table 3.2 (Continued)

								Costa		El					Dom.		
	Argentina	Bolivia	Brazil	Cuba	Chile	Colombia	Rica	Ecuador	Salvador	Honduras	Mexico	Paraguay	Peru	Rep.	Uruguay	Venezuela
FTAA scenario																
GDP (factor prices)	0.3	2.0	0.0	1.7	1.4	10.2	1.9	2.9	0.5	2.6	0.4	1.4	0.3	0.9	0.8	0.7
Absorption	0.7	3.7	0.1	1.0	2.8	11.6	6.0	4.5	1.8	3.3	0.6	2.8	1.1	2.9	1.4	−6.9
Household consumption	0.6	3.5	0.3	1.4	2.8	11.9	6.0	4.3	1.8	3.2	0.6	2.8	0.7	2.3	1.3	−1.5
Investment	1.1	5.0	−0.4	0.5	3.1	11.6	7.3	5.9	2.2	3.6	0.6	2.2	2.3	5.6	2.4	−18.9
Government consumption	0.6	2.8	0.0	−0.1	1.9	10.5	4.3	2.9	0.9	3.8	0.5	4.2	0.5	3.0	1.0	0.0
Exports	0.2	−0.3	0.1	0.0	−0.1	5.4	−2.3	1.2	−0.2	2.9	0.0	0.2	4.4	3.0	0.2	−1.5
Imports	4.6	6.6	1.1	0.2	3.9	16.5	7.8	7.0	4.1	4.4	0.5	4.0	5.8	6.4	3.2	−4.7
Real exchange rate	−0.2	−1.0	1.5		−0.7	−1.5	−2.0	−0.9	−0.7	−0.7	−0.3	−0.5	2.6	−1.2	−0.5	−0.9
WTO scenario																
GDP (factor prices)	0.7	4.3	0.0	−2.9	0.7	13.9	2.4	6.9	0.1	9.0	−1.8	−1.5	0.3	−0.1	2.5	0.9
Absorption	0.2	4.3	0.2	−3.5	1.9	13.5	0.8	8.1	1.1	5.2	−3.1	0.0	−6.4	2.9	1.4	−6.7
Household consumption	0.1	4.3	0.6	−3.2	2.0	14.0	0.9	8.2	1.0	5.5	−3.4	−0.2	−6.3	2.1	1.6	−1.9
Investment	1.1	5.5	−1.0	−0.5	2.2	13.4	2.1	9.8	1.9	4.9	−2.4	−1.6	−6.5	6.7	1.3	−15.9
Government consumption	−0.2	2.8	0.0	−5.8	0.9	11.7	−1.4	4.4	0.5	4.3	−2.8	1.5	−6.3	2.1	0.4	0.0
Exports	13.9	3.7	0.3	1.5	2.8	14.7	5.7	6.0	0.8	12.8	1.7	3.6	32.7	−1.5	6.8	−1.5
Imports	7.5	7.7	2.5	1.0	3.3	18.3	3.7	12.8	2.7	9.1	−2.1	0.1	−8.9	3.7	5.2	−4.5
Real exchange rate	2.5	1.9	3.4		2.5	0.7	0.0	0.1	0.7	1.2	1.7	5.1	20.3	−0.5	1.3	−0.9

Source: Author's calculations

Exchange rate fixed

Macroeconomic simulations results

Tariff reduction

In this experiment, we reduce tariffs by 10 per cent relative to their base period level. Since base levels vary significantly between countries, the absolute size of the impact of this trade liberalization on output, employment and poverty will also differ across countries. The impact of trade liberalization is unambiguously expansionary in every country in our sample except for Brazil. Total output and employment both increase and by non-trivial amounts. Exports are the engine of growth in all the simulations in which we fix foreign savings, and they lag behind overall growth when we fix the exchange rate, and in fact decline absolutely in three countries. The opposite is true for fixed investment. When the exchange rate is fixed and tariffs are reduced, there is an increase in imports financed mainly by an increase in foreign savings. If foreign savings is fixed, the increase in import demand has to be financed by an increase in exports. That requires a real devaluation. Since an increase in foreign savings or an exchange-rate appreciation is itself expansionary, as we will see in a moment, the impact of the tariff reduction on output and employment is larger in the fixed rate case than it is with fixed foreign savings in all but the Dominican Republic.

All of this is relevant to understanding the history of trade liberalization in Latin America. With fixed foreign savings, when tariffs are reduced there is a real devaluation and export-led growth, which is just what the advocates of trade liberalization expect. But if the exchange rate is fixed instead there is even faster growth but it is not led by exports. In Chapter 2, we pointed out that in many countries exports have not been growing very rapidly. One of the reasons for that is that the reduction in tariffs was accompanied by a large inflow of foreign capital. That inflow permitted the monetary authorities to fix the exchange rate to help control inflationary pressures. Investment and consumption grew rapidly, but exports lagged behind. The fact that trade liberalization did not bring fast, export-led growth in Latin America is not merely due to a competitive failure of Latin-American export industries as some have claimed, since one cannot ignore the importance of the fact that liberalization was accompanied by a big inflow of foreign capital or equivalently of exchange-rate appreciation.

Devaluation and an increase in foreign savings

Here we look at two policies that should have opposing effects on the economy. In the first experiment, we devalue the nominal exchange rate by 10 per cent. In the second, we treat foreign savings as exogenous and increase it by 10 per cent of the value of exports in the base run.[21] In all countries except the Dominican Republic, devaluation is contractionary and an increase in foreign savings (or exchange-rate appreciation) is expansionary. Employment falls in the one case and rises in the other.

These results may seem surprising, but one must think carefully about what the model is telling us. Recall that this is a comparative static result. We are asking what will happen if there is a permanent increase in the equilibrium inflow of foreign savings. This is not a temporary or one-time increase, but a permanent shock. When there is such an increase in equilibrium inflows, there will be an equilibrium or permanent increase in absorption, a real exchange-rate appreciation and a shift in production away from traded goods. Both total output and employment will be higher. Similarly, in this comparative statics exercise devaluation operates as a permanent policy shock, lowering the level of foreign capital inflow structurally depressing aggregate demand and thus output and employment.

The model does not tell us anything about the short-run costs of adjusting to the change in production structure. When there is a change in relative prices, factors must be transferred between sectors. But that takes time, partly because it will require capital formation, and partly because labour has to be found, hired and trained. That may well mean that during the adjustment process, output may fall even if it is going to be higher in the new long-run equilibrium solution.

What lessons does all this hold for Latin America? The main one is that foreign savings or capital inflows far from being constant as assumed in the general equilibrium solution are actually highly variable. Many countries reduced tariffs and enjoyed big capital inflows until the late 1990s. Output and employment increased just as the theory predicts that it should. But the problem was that these inflows were not sustainable. When foreign exchange crises hit Mexico in 1994, then in Russia and Brazil in 1998, and Argentina in 1999, these capital flows abruptly reversed. That forced exchange-rate devaluations in countries with a flexible regime or heavy domestic demand cuts in those with a fixed regime; both provoking a sharp decline in growth rates all over the region, again just as the theory would predict. The lesson here is that if a country is liberalizing trade with variable foreign savings, it should try to keep its exchange rate at a level at which the level of foreign savings required in equilibrium is also sustainable in fact. If it is able to do that, trade liberalization will be expansionary.

Export subsidies

In this experiment, we increased export subsidies uniformly by 10 per cent of their base period level. Where the subsidies were negative, we made them 10 per cent less negative. Subsidizing exports is expansionary in every country in either closures (fixed or flexible exchange rates) except for Brazil in both closures and Argentina for the fixed exchange-rate case. Not surprisingly growth is led by exports, which appear to be quite sensitive to this kind of subsidy in most countries of the region. When foreign savings is fixed (i.e. under a flexible exchange rate), the real exchange rate appreciates enough to raise imports and cut back the growth of exports. When the exchange rate rather than foreign savings is fixed, the growth in exports is far greater and the growth in imports far less. But the increase in total output (while still positive in all but Brazil and Argentina) is smaller than it is with the subsidy and fixed foreign savings. In effect, there is a reduction in foreign savings and a large improvement in the current account balance all of which is reflected by a reduction in absorption in most countries.

WTO

In this experiment, we eliminated all domestic tariffs and export subsidies and used a vector of the hypothetical world prices for major traded goods groups under a scenario worldwide enforcement of WTO regulations (see Table A3.3). The new set of world traded goods prices was generated by simulating such a scenario using the GTAP world model.[22] In the WTO scenario, generally higher (agricultural) commodity prices are expected as subsidies to agricultural production in the developed countries would disappear, which – depending on the export structure – may compensate producers for the loss of export subsidies in the Latin American countries. Each country author applied the new price vector in accordance with the commodity breakdown in his or her country SAM/CGE. The world price increases produce a substantial positive impact to agriculture in those Latin American countries where agriculture is neither protected nor subsidized.

Indeed, in most of the countries of the region (9/15) moving to full free trade is expansionary under either fixed or flexible exchange rates. The main exceptions are Mexico and the Dominican Republic each of whom has special trading relationships with the United States whose value disappears under full free trade; Cuba, Paraguay and Venezuela who would lose protection of domestic agriculture without benefiting sufficiently from higher world prices; and Brazil for whom free trade has little effect one way or the other. For most other countries agricultural production rises, however, and if foreign savings is fixed, they become more open, with a rise in both exports and imports and a real appreciation of the exchange rate. If the exchange rate is fixed the overall growth is similar but the composition is different. In about half of the countries there is a fall in the trade deficit (i.e. a reduction in foreign savings) as the growth rate of exports at higher world prices exceeds the effect of the fall in domestic protection. That is the case in Argentina, Costa Rica, Honduras, Paraguay, Peru and Uruguay, where agricultural products are an important component of exports.

FTAA

The second multilateral trade agreement simulation is a scenario of the creation of a FTAA. As in the WTO simulation, we used the hypothetical vector of world prices for traded goods calculated by the GTAP world model that would be observed if Latin America and the United States successfully created a hemisphere-wide free trade area. Here, each of the Latin American countries was assumed to reduce its tariffs on trade with other countries in the region, which we approximated by reducing average tariffs by the proportion of each sector's imports coming from other Latin American countries.

Because the impact of this partial move towards full free trade on world commodity markets is far smaller than the WTO, the changes in world prices are much smaller. These results are based on a scenario where all tariffs between countries in the Western Hemisphere are eliminated, but producer subsidies are left at the current levels (see Morley and Piñeiro 2003). In particular, average world agricultural prices go up by less than 0.009 per cent (there is an increase in the agricultural prices but a decrease in the manufacturing prices) rather than 5 per cent as they do in the WTO simulation. This does not imply, as one might expect, that output would rise by more under WTO. In fact, in seven countries (Chile, Cuba, El Salvador, Mexico, Paraguay, Venezuela and the Dominican Republic) the reverse is true. For Mexico and the Dominican Republic, as noted earlier, this is because going to the full WTO reduces output rather than increasing it. In Paraguay and Venezuela, FTAA would negatively affects output as under the WTO scenario, but less so under the former.

In all cases the FTAA causes a big rise in imports and a smaller rise in exports. With a fixed exchange rate there is an expansionary rise in foreign savings and absorption whereas if foreign savings is fixed there is a devaluation and a bigger increase in exports. It is likely that this simulation underestimates the full effect of a FTAA on exports within the region. By assumption, in almost all countries all sector commodity markets are treated as homogenous. That means that each sector in each country is assumed to see its output at world prices adjusted by tariffs or subsidies. How much is consumed nationally and how much is exported depends on internal demand elasticities. No distinction is made for the nationality of the buyer.

Terms-of-trade shock

We simulate an adverse terms-of-trade shock represented by a uniform 10 per cent increase in import prices. Not surprisingly, an increase in the price of imports is highly contractionary in every country, whether we fixed the exchange rate or foreign savings. Absorption, investment and employment all fall and there is a significant depreciation of the real exchange rate. With fixed foreign savings there is also a substantial reduction in exports as domestic productive capacity is switched to the production of import substitutes.

Productivity shock

Our CGE models are not dynamic. They do not link changes in the sectoral production functions to investment or the growth in labour. To obtain a simple approximation of dynamic growth effects, we increase the constant term (technology parameter) in each sector's production function by 10 per cent (it works as a parallel shift in the production function). This, of course, generates a large positive impact on output, employment and poverty. The magnitude of the impact depends in part on our assumption that all labour supplies are endogenous, so that any increase in productivity permits a large increase in employment, virtually doubling the effect of the change in productivity on output. Exports grow rapidly under either closure, but if the nominal exchange rate is fixed imports and foreign savings grow even more rapidly.

It is not at all surprising that productivity growth would have such a large growth effect given the assumptions underlying the model. However, the size of the impacts on poverty, which are larger than any of the trade-related shocks or reforms, serve to remind us of the crucial importance of investment and growth in the struggle to reduce poverty.

Country-specific closures

The country studies have used a mixture of country closures, but the key difference of most is the use of a Keynesian macro closure with investment driving savings adjustments through income multiplier effects. Under the specifications of the CGE model, this implies an independent investment function that leaves the level of investment fixed under the given closure rule. The upshot is that despite the demand-driven macroeconomic adjustment imposed by this closure rule, output effects tend to be smaller than under the balanced savings–investment closure of the standardized simulations, as this allows for some endogenous investment adjustment. Otherwise the macroeconomic results under the country-specific results are broadly consistent with the findings mentioned earlier, showing expansionary effects of both unilateral trade liberalization (tariff cuts) and the FTAA scenario in all cases but Brazil and Venezuela (the latter only in case of FTAA). The same countries plus Mexico also would lose (mildly) under the WTO scenario.

Skill intensity and the total demand for labour under different scenarios

We find that in almost all cases removing barriers to trade and increasing openness lead to an equilibrium increase in output and, as we will see, an increase in total employment. The question we wish to address here is what the change in production structure does to skill intensity. That is, does increased openness imply an increase in the relative demand for skilled labour or does it favour Latin America's more abundant unskilled labour? Under the standardized labour market closure rule we use the simplifying assumption that there is an excess supply of all types of labour, or in other words that relative wages are fixed at their base period level in each country. Therefore, in the simulations reported here, the results will be stated in terms of increases in the quantity demanded of labour. When we speak of an increase or decrease in skill intensity, we mean that this is what would happen if relative wages were constant. If we were to drop that assumption, an increase in skill intensity would also be reflected in a rise in earnings differentials by skills. In the country case studies, a variety of different assumptions were used. In some cases, all of labour supply was assumed fixed; in others, the supply of *skilled* labour was exogenous and fixed and *unskilled* labour was flexible and demand-determined. When we discuss the simulation results for poverty and distribution, derived from the country studies, we will revert to the country assumptions on labour market closures.

Skill intensity may rise or fall following trade opening depending on whether skilled or unskilled labour is more important in traded goods sectors. Our CGE models can shed important light on these questions because they are based on observed, sector-specific production functions and skill intensities. Each country has a different disaggregation of labour, but in all cases the disaggregation permits us to separate factor demand by skill, generally defined in terms of education level. In some cases rural and urban labour are reported separately so that we can see what happens to rural–urban differentials in addition to what happens for the entire economy or in the urban sector considered separately. In most countries, there was a finer disaggregation of labour than we show here. In Table 3.3, we have chosen one category of urban (male) labour, generally defined as unskilled salaried male labour in the formal sector and compared it to skilled salaried labour in the formal sector. Where there is a disaggregation into rural and urban labour, we have compared the change in the demand for rural unskilled labour to urban unskilled labour.

Does trade liberalization or reducing tariffs increase skill intensity? According to the left-hand columns of Table 3.3, the brief answer is that it depends. In about half of our countries it does while in the other half it does not. Recall that when foreign savings is fixed, tariff reductions lead to a depreciation of the real exchange rate and export-led growth. When trade liberalization occurs with fixed exchange rates there is an increase in foreign savings, an appreciation of the real exchange rate and growth is led by non-traded goods as well as investment. But despite this difference in the composition of growth, factor intensity moves in the same direction in all but two cases. Essentially, the pattern depends on skill intensities in the traded goods industries, both those producing export and import substitutes. For the fixed exchange-rate regime, the result depends as well on factor intensities in the non-traded goods and investment sectors, both of which lead the response to tariff reduction when the nominal exchange rate is fixed.

One further pattern is that in all but one of the cases where we have information on rural labour, trade liberalization increased the demand for urban labour relative to rural or agricultural labour. While the demand for agricultural labour seldom falls absolutely, it rises by significantly less than either of the urban labour categories. In this way, trade liberalization is likely to be accompanied by rising labour and income inequality even though the expansion in total output will reduce poverty at the same time.

Are traded or non-traded goods more skill intensive? We can address that question by seeing what happens to labour demand when there is either a devaluation or an appreciation of the real exchange rate in response to a rise in foreign savings. Results show that skill intensity widens in eight countries and falls in four as the economy shifts over to the production of more non-traded goods in response to the rise in foreign savings. Rural workers lose in most of the countries for which we have information because they are dependent on agricultural traded goods production.

Traded goods can, of course, be either import substitutes or exports. In the right-hand side column of Table 3.3, we show the results of the simulation in which we increased all export subsidies by 10 per cent. When we do that there is an expansion of employment in those sectors producing exports. Skill intensity falls in eight countries and rises in five. In all but two of those cases the changes

Table 3.3 CGE simulations – standardized closure rules: changes in skill intensity of urban and rural labour

	Tariff reduction				Increase foreign savings			Increase export subsidies			
	Urban unskilled/Agr. unskilled		Urban skilled/ unskilled		Urban/ rural unskilled	Urban skilled/ unskilled		Urban unskilled/Agr. unskilled		Urban skilled/ unskilled	
	Fixed ER	Flex ER	Fixed ER	Flex ER	Flex ER	Fixed ER	Flex ER	Fixed ER	Flex ER	Fixed ER	Flex ER
Argentina	Rises	Rises	Falls	Falls	Falls	Rises	Falls	Rises	Rises	Rises	Falls
Bolivia			No change	Falls			Rises			Falls	Falls
Brazil			Rises	Rises			Rises			Falls	Falls
Chile			Falls	Falls			Rises			Falls	Falls
Colombia			Rises	Rises			Falls			Rises	Rises
Costa Rica	Rises	Falls	Rises	Falls	Rises	Falls	Rises	Falls	Falls	Falls	Falls
Ecuador			Falls	Falls			No change			Falls	Rises
El Salvador			Falls	Rises			Falls				Rises
Honduras	Falls		Rises	Rises	Rises	Rises	Falls	Rises	Rises	Rises	Rises
Mexico	Rises	Rises	Rises	No change	Rises	Falls	Rises	Falls	Rises	Rises	Rises
Paraguay			Rises	No change			No change			No change	Rises
Peru	Rises	Rises	Falls	Falls	Falls	Rises	Rises	Rises	Rises	Falls	Falls
Dom. Rep.	Rises	Rises	Falls	Rises	Rises	Rises	Rises	Rises	Rises	Falls	Falls
Uruguay			Falls	Falls			Rises			Falls	Falls
Venezuela											

Note: Directions of change refer to relative growth rates in demand for labour categories. They tell whether growth was relatively skill intensive or whether it favoured unskilled urban or rural workers. Since classifications of factors in the country CGE models do not always exactly coincide with those of this table, we take for agriculture/non-agriculture specifications in country CGE's unskilled formal sector labour relative to agricultural unskilled labour. For urban breakdowns we use formal sector skilled relative to formal sector unskilled. Where there is a gender breakdown, we use the series for males

Table 3.4 CGE macro–micro simulations – country-specific closures (changes represent deviations from base)

	Macro outcomes			Labour demand			Wages		Microsimulations	
	Output	Exports	Employment	Unskilled	Skilled	Skill intensity	Average	Skill diff.	Poverty	Inequality
Devaluation										
Argentina	-0.9	57.6	+	+	+	+/0	+	+/0	1.6	0.4
Bolivia	-1.1	6.3	-	-	-	+	0	0	1.3	0.9
Brazil	-0.04	9.0	-	-	-	-	-	+/0	-0.2	-0.2
Cuba	0.9	0.0	+	+	+	+/0	+	+	-0.1	-0.01
Chile	-0.6	7.7	-	-	-	-	-/0	-/0	1.4	0.8
Colombia	-1.2	31.5	0	0	0	0	-	-/0	0.6	0.0
Costa Rica	-0.1	6.5	-	-	0	-	-	-	1.6	-0.2
Ecuador	0.0	5.7	-	-	0	+	-	-	0.4	-0.7
El Salvador	-0.7	17.3	+	+	-	-	-	-	5.1	1.8
Honduras	-10.4	15.5	-	-	+	+	-	+	4.8	2.3
Mexico	-0.1	22.1	-	-	0	+	-	0	1.9	-0.1
Paraguay	-3.7	11.3	-	-	-	0	0	0	4.8	1.4
Peru	-1.5	40.5	-	-	-	-	+	0	1.2	0.3
Dom Rep.	1.2	27.3	+/0	+	-	-	+	+	-2.8	-0.5
Uruguay	-1.7	12.5	0	+/0	0	0	-	+	0.4	-0.4
Venezuela	1.5	-9.4	-	-	-	+	-	0	1.2	-0.3
Tariff cut										
Argentina	0.3	4.2	++	++	+	0	-	-/0	-0.9	0.3
Bolivia	0.8	0.3	++	++	+	0	0	0	-1.8	0.7
Brazil	-0.1	0.1	+	+	+	0	+	+/0	-1.2	-0.2
Cuba	0.0	0.0	-/0	-/0	-/0	0	-/0	+/0	n.a.	n.a.

(Continued)

Table 3.4 (Continued)

	Macro outcomes			Labour demand			Wages		Microsimulations	
	Output	Exports	Employment	Unskilled	Skilled	Skill intensity	Average	Skill diff.	Poverty	Inequality
Chile	0.7	1.8	+	+	+	-/0	+/0	0	-4.5	-0.3
Colombia	0.3	3.8	0	0	0	0	+	-/0	-5.6	0.0
Costa Rica	0.3	-0.4	+	+	+	+/0	+	+	-0.3	0.1
Ecuador	0.3	0.1	+	+	0	-	+	+	0.3	0.2
El Salvador	0.3	-0.2	+	+	+	+	+	+	-0.7	-1.0
Honduras	1.9	1.3	+	+	0	-	+	-	-1.3	-0.5
Mexico	0.1	0.4	+/0	+/0	+	-	0	0	-0.3	-0.1
Paraguay	1.1	0.1	+	+	+	-	+	0	-2.4	-0.6
Peru	0.4	3.4	+	+	-	-	+	0	-1.3	0.7
Dom Rep.	0.7	6.8	+	+	0	-	+	+	-1.4	-0.2
Uruguay	0.0	1.8	0	0	0	0	+	-	-0.4	-0.1
Venezuela	0.1	0.5	+	+	+	+	+	0	-1.0	-0.1
Export subsidy increase										
Argentina	0.3	5.7	+	+	+	-	++	0	2.5	0.5
Bolivia	1.2	7.2	+	+	+	+	0	0	-4.2	-1.8
Brazil	-0.5	-3.1	+/0	+/0	+/0	-/0	+	+	-4.4	-0.2
Cuba	1.0	5.4	+	+	+	-	+/0	+	-0.1	-0.01
Chile	1.9	5.0	+	+	0	-	+	-/0	-11.9	-0.9
Colombia	0.6	8.9	0	0	0	0	+	-	-1.0	0.0
Costa Rica	0.0	0.4	+/0	+/0	+/0	-/0	+/0	-/0	-0.1	0.1
Ecuador	0.2	0.6	+	+	0	-	+/0	+	0.0	-0.1

(Continued)

Table 3.4 (Continued)

	Macro outcomes			Labour demand			Wages		Microsimulations	
	Output	Exports	Employment	Unskilled	Skilled	Skill intensity	Average	Skill diff.	Poverty	Inequality
El Salvador	1.1	15.4	+	+	+	−	+/0	−	1.6	−3.1
Honduras	−0.04	0.2	−/0	−/0	0	+/0	+/0	0	0.1	0.1
Mexico	0.9	1.5	+	+	0	−	+	−	−2.4	−0.5
Paraguay	1.3	12.0	+	+	+	−	0	0	−4.0	−1.1
Peru										
Dom Rep.	1.3	16.4	+	+	−	−	+	+	−3.1	−0.7
Uruguay	0.0	0.3	0	0	0	0	+/0	0	−0.1	0.0
Venezuela	0.2	3.2	−	−	−	−	+	0	−2.0	0.2
FTAA										
Argentina	0.4	4.3	+	+	+	0	−	0	−1.7	0.3
Bolivia	1.2	0.5	+	+	++	+	0	0	−3.9	−2.3
Brazil	−0.4	1.0	+	+	+	+	+	+	−1.2	−0.3
Cuba	0.1	5.4	+	+	+	0	+	+	n.a.	n.a.
Chile	0.7	1.6	+	+	0	−	+	−/0	−4.9	−0.3
Colombia	0.4	5.9	0	0	0	0	+	−/0	−6.9	0.0
Costa Rica	0.2	4.7	+	+	+	+	+	+	−0.4	0.3
Ecuador	0.4	3.4	+	+	0	−	+	+	0.2	0.1
El Salvador	0.5	−0.2	+	+	+	−	+	+	−1.3	−0.7
Honduras	1.2	2.4	+	+	0	−	+	−	−0.7	−0.3
Mexico	0.1	0.6	+/0	+/0	0	−	+	−	−0.3	−0.1
Paraguay	0.3	0.0	+	+	+	+	0	0	0.7	0.4

(Continued)

Table 3.4 (Continued)

	Macro outcomes			Labour demand			Wages		Microsimulations	
	Output	Exports	Employment	Unskilled	Skilled	Skill intensity	Average	Skill diff.	Poverty	Inequality
Peru	0.6	4.8	+	+	+	−	+	+	−1.6	0.4
Dom Rep.	1.0	9.7	+	+	0	0	+	+	−2.7	−0.3
Uruguay	0.0	2.2	0	0	0	0	+	−	−0.6	0.0
Venezuela	−0.1	−0.4	−	−	−	0	−	0	0.3	−0.4
WTO										
Argentina	1.7	10.0	+	+	+	+	++	+	−1.2	0.1
Bolivia	1.1	5.3	+	+	++	+	0	0	−3.1	−3.2
Brazil	−0.4	2.0	+	+	+	+	+	+	−1.4	−0.2
Cuba	0.1	5.4	+	+	+	−/0	+	−/0	n.a.	n.a.
Chile	0.9	3.9	0	+	0	−	+	−	−6.0	−0.5
Colombia	0.4	7.8	0	0	0	0	+	−	−7.4	0.0
Costa Rica	0.1	−1.2	+	−	+	+	+	+	0.9	0.6
Ecuador	1.0	2.6	+	+	0	−	+	++	0.2	0.3
El Salvador	0.5	0.9	+	+	+	+	+	−	−1.0	−0.7
Honduras	2.2	9.8	+	+	+	−	+	−	−1.2	−0.4
Mexico	−0.2	−1.9	−/0	−/0	0	+	−	+	0.0	−0.1
Paraguay	0.5	4.0	+	+	+	−	0	0	0.1	−0.3
Peru	0.5	6.5	+	++	+	−	+	+	−2.0	0.9
Dom Rep.	1.2	8.1	+	0	0	−	+	+	−3.8	−1.2
Uruguay	0.0	5.0	0	0	0	0	+	−	−2.0	−0.3
Venezuela	−0.3	1.6	−	−	−	+	+	0	0.2	−0.1

(Continued)

Table 3.4 (Continued)

	Macro outcomes			Labour demand			Wages		Microsimulations	
	Output	Exports	Employment	Unskilled	Skilled	Skill intensity	Average	Skill diff.	Poverty	Inequality
Foreign savings increase										
Argentina	0.3	−7.4	0	0	0	0	+	−/0	1.3	0.5
Bolivia	0.1	0.5	+	+	+	+	0	0	−0.1	−0.8
Brazil	n.a.	n.a.	n.a.	n.a.	n.a.	n.a.	n.a.	n.a.	n.a.	n.a.
Cuba	n.a.	n.a.	n.a.	n.a.	n.a.	n.a.	n.a.	n.a.	n.a.	n.a.
Chile	0.1	−0.7	+/0	+/0	+/0	+/0	0	0	−0.4	0.0
Colombia	0.2	−2.0	0	0	0	0	+	−	−0.2	0.0
Costa Rica	0.1	−0.4	+	+	+	+	+	+	0.2	0.1
Ecuador	0.1	−3.8	+	+	++	−	+	++	0.6	0.3
El Salvador	4.0	−26.8	++	++	++	+	+	+	−4.6	−5.0
Honduras	2.1	−3.4	+	+	−	−	+	−	−1.4	−0.5
Mexico	−0.5	−10.3	+	+	0	−	+	−	−1.9	−0.4
Paraguay	0.8	−2.3	+	+	+	0	0	0	−1.5	−0.4
Peru	0.1	−2.7	+/0	+/0	+/0	0	−/0	0	−0.1	0.1
Dom Rep.	n.a.	n.a.	n.a.	n.a.	n.a.	n.a.	n.a.	n.a.	n.a.	n.a.
Uruguay	1.5	−19.8	0	0	0	0	+	+	−3.2	0.4
Venezuela	1.9	−3.3	++	+	+	−	+	0	−3.1	−1.0

Note: +, increase; +/0, slight increase (could be insignificant); ++, strong increase; 0, no (significant) change; −, decrease; −/0, slight decrease (could be insignificant); −−, strong decrease

in skill intensity are the opposite of what was observed with the increase in foreign savings. That is, increasing export production has the opposite effect on skill intensity of increasing non-traded goods, which implies that there is no important difference in most cases between the import-substituting part of tradables and the exporting part. The experiment also tells us that in most countries exports are not relatively skill intensive, which implies that pursuing export-led growth should not increase inequality.

However, when introducing the country-specific segmented labour market assumptions, this picture remains equally mixed and does not show an across-the-board widening of the earnings gap between skilled and unskilled workers due to trade liberalization (unilaterally or multilaterally). If countries apply a uniform tariff cut, the earnings gap between skilled and unskilled workers is expected to increase in six country cases (Brazil, Cuba, Costa Rica, Ecuador, El Salvador and Dominican Republic) and only in Honduras, Mexico and Uruguay a smaller earnings gap is expected (see Table 3.4). In all other countries, the simulation of further unilateral trade opening shows no substantial shifts in skill inequality. The multilateral trade liberalization scenarios show a somewhat stronger upward skill bias, partly compounded by negative effects on agricultural employment. Under the FTAA scenario, Peru is added to the country cases with rising wage gap between skilled and unskilled workers and under WTO scenario this also is the outcome for Argentina. Average real wage levels increase almost without exception in all trade opening scenarios for the country-specific labour market closures as a consequence of the generally expansionary effect on the economy. The poverty effects of these labour market outcomes will depend on the net impact of these shifts in aggregate and sector employment, mean earnings and earnings differentials. This will be taken up in the next section.

3.4 The impact of policy simulations on poverty and inequality

Observed trends in the 1990s

It is useful to begin the discussion of poverty and inequality with an overview of observed trends in these two variables. We have used the ECLAC estimations on household data to preserve comparability. ECLAC uses poverty lines that reflect the cost of a market purchased basket of necessities and they make a correction for underreporting of survey-based incomes and for income in kind, which was generally not done by our country authors. For these reasons, the country-level estimates shown in Table A3.4 may differ from the poverty estimates in the country papers. That is of less concern to us here because what we want to determine are the trends in poverty over the 1990s rather than the levels of poverty. For that the estimates shown in the table are useful. For the region as a whole the total and extreme poverty incidence are presented in Table 3.5 for the period 1980–99, including estimations for 2002.[23]

Overall, both in absolute and relative terms, total poverty and extreme poverty worsened between 1980 and 1990 and then improved somewhat in the period

Table 3.5   Poverty in Latin America

	Total poverty		Extreme poverty	
	Millions	*Per cent*	*Millions*	*Per cent*
1980	136	40.5	62	18.6
1990	200	48.3	93	22.5
1997	204	43.5	89	19.0
1999	211	43.8	89	18.5
2002	221	44.0	99	20.0

Source: ECLAC (2002)

before 1997. But even in the early 1990s the numbers in poverty continued to increase even though there was a decline in the headcount ratio. Table 3.5 also suggests that after 1997 there was no further progress in reducing either poverty or indigence. Reducing current extreme poverty rates by half towards 2015 has been defined as the central objective of the United Nation's Millennium declaration. Reaching this goal will require a major effort for many countries in the region (UNDP, ECLAC and IPEA 2003).

The region totals for the 1990s shown in Table 3.5 hide a great deal of heterogeneity among the different countries (see Table A3.4). Brazil, Chile, Costa Rica, Guatemala, Panama and Uruguay all made significant progress in poverty reduction, particularly between 1990 and 1997, while Argentina, Paraguay, Ecuador and Venezuela had large increases in poverty particularly after 1997. Because of its size, Brazil's good performance makes the performance for the region seem better than it is for most of the other countries. Between 1990 and 1999 Brazil cut its indigent population by 13 million people. Indigence in the rest of Latin America rose by nine million. Thus, for most countries observed trends in poverty followed the performance of the economy. Countries in crisis after 1997 such as Argentina, Ecuador, Paraguay and Uruguay or Mexico in 1995–6 had big increases in poverty whereas poverty fell rapidly in countries growing rapidly, such as Chile, the Dominican Republic and Mexico after 1996.

The region did not manage to decrease inequality in per capita household income distribution during the 1990s, with the subcontinent remaining the world's most unequal area (ECLAC 2002). By measuring inequality by the Gini coefficient, the available evidence shows that inequality increased further in at least 11 out of 18 countries between 1990 and 1999 (see Table A3.4). Two countries (Honduras and Uruguay) show decreasing inequality, while it is unchanged in four countries (Chile, Guatemala, Nicaragua and Panama).

Effects of export-led economic strategies on poverty and inequality

We have seen what happened to output, employment and earnings differentials in the simulations reported in Section 3.3. What we now want to know is what these changes might mean for poverty and the distribution of income at the household level. As explained in Section 3.2, we do this by taking the CGE model simulation outcomes and applying these through the microsimulation approach as counterfactuals to the observed labour market parameters using the full distribution as given by household surveys of each country case.

We report the comparative results of the microsimulations in two ways. First, the final two columns of Table 3.4 report the poverty and income inequality effects as percentage changes from the base for each of the policy simulations using the country-specific closures for the CGE models. Second, since the absolute changes in policy variables and the distribution of income differ across countries we also report the changes as elasticities, defined as the percentage change in poverty or inequality percentage change in a policy variable. To make the changes easier to visualize, for each policy simulation we have transferred the elasticities into four quadrant diagrams, and calculated the elasticity for both earned income and household income per capita (see Figures 3.4 and 3.5). The diagrams put poverty on the vertical axis and the Gini coefficient of per capita household income on the horizontal axis. Thus, poverty increases in the two top quadrants, and inequality increases in the two right hand quadrants of each diagram.

Poverty effects of trade liberalization

Unilateral trade liberalization reduces poverty and raising tariffs increases it. There is only one point-source natural resource abundant country where that is not the case (Ecuador) and even in this case the increase in poverty is small as a consequence of a unilateral tariff cut. More generally, the poverty effects are not very big. Income inequality at the household level rises (slightly) in most natural resource abundant economies as predicted (Argentina, Bolivia, Costa Rica, Ecuador and Peru), although Venezuela provides an exception to this rule. The small effects on poverty and inequality should not be surprising, as under this scenario we are cutting tariffs further from already low, post-reform levels. A key conclusion is that pre-reform counterfactual (raising tariffs) would enhance poverty suggesting that trade liberalization is indeed poverty reducing. These results are broadly consistent with moving to completely free trade under the WTO or to a region-wide multilateral trade agreement under FTAA. Both of these changes also reduce poverty and inequality in most of the countries. However, poverty rises (modestly) under these scenarios in Costa Rica (only WTO), Ecuador, Paraguay and Venezuela, mainly due to the negative effects on the agricultural sectors in these countries, which is not sufficiently picked up with employment and income growth in other sectors.

Across-the-board increases in export subsidies are generally poverty reducing as well (in apparent contradiction with the WTO scenario), with a few exceptions. Under this scenario export production is stimulated in a broad sense and given the small-economy assumption is assumed not to affect world prices. In this sense, it works like a tariff cut stimulating aggregate employment as mostly more labour-intensive (e.g. agriculture) sectors benefit from subsidies that are increased in the scenario.

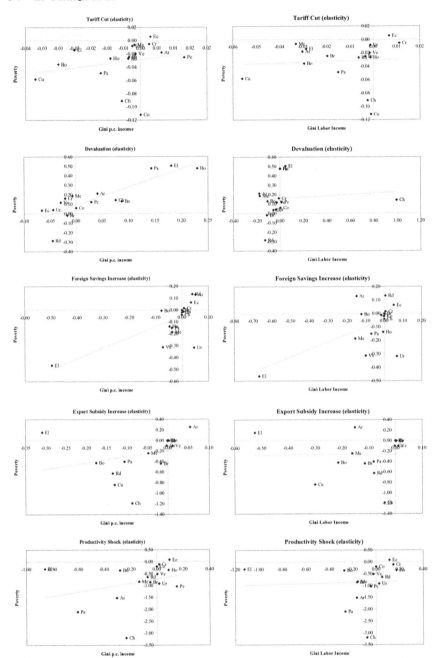

Figure 3.4 Poverty and inequality responses to CGE simulations – domestic policy scenarios (elasticities with respect to indicated policy scenario).

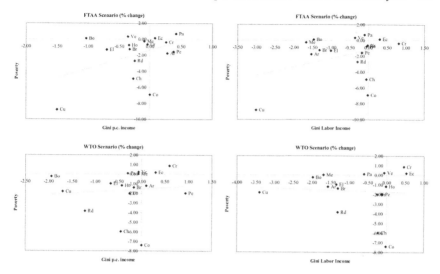

Figure 3.5 Poverty and inequality responses to CGE simulations – FTAA and WTO scenarios (percentage changes with respect to indicated policy scenario).

These results have to be interpreted with some caution though. These are general equilibrium, comparative static results that do not take into account the costs of adjusting to a changed production structure. If the exchange rate is fixed, the simulation determines the impact of lowering the tariff rates and bringing in more foreign capital to permanently finance a bigger balance of payments deficit. In the previous section we saw that this change is expansionary (though growth is led by non-traded goods rather than exports). If foreign savings is fixed, the exchange rate has to depreciate to allow exports to expand enough to pay for additional imports. But total output and employment increase in both cases and poverty declines. The simulation results also suggest that if no poverty reduction was observed in practice after trade liberalization, it is either because a lot of other poverty-increasing factors were changing at the same time (most typically dealing with macro shocks; see Taylor and Vos 2002) or because the economies are still in the process of adapting their production structures.

Poverty and external balance shifts

As we saw in the previous section devaluation is contractionary and an increase in foreign savings is expansionary. These changes have the expected effects on poverty. Devaluation increases poverty, in some cases by quite large amounts and foreign savings reduces it. It is also clear that devaluation increases income inequality. Curiously enough, however, it does not increase earnings inequality. This suggests that traded goods are in most countries not skill intensive. Thus, while total output and employment go down with a devaluation (or a fall in foreign savings), for those who keep their jobs skill intensity falls.

Productivity increases

Far and away the largest amount of poverty reduction comes from increasing productivity. That is true whether the change is measured in absolute amounts or in elasticities. In most cases increasing productivity also reduces inequality. This quite clearly underlines the obvious and important role that economic growth plays in poverty reduction.

Labour market adjustment and poverty impact

As explained earlier, the study assumed that the labour markets are the main transmission channel of the impact of trade reforms on poverty and distribution. The effect of alteration of parameters of the labour market structure on poverty and inequality was analysed in the country cases and is summarized in Table A3.5. This table indicates, for each country, the labour market parameter that shows the largest change, in absolute terms, when explaining total changes in poverty and inequality for different simulations. The following stylized facts can be observed:

- Mean wage (and other labour earnings) adjustments (W_1 as defined in Section 3.2) tend to have the largest effect on the poverty incidence in most simulations.
- Changes in the remuneration structure (W_2) are also the most important variable explaining absolute changes in income inequality at the household level (rather than quantity shifts in the employment structure or reductions in unemployment) in most country cases. Unsurprisingly, this also applies to the simulated effects on the Gini coefficient of labour income inequality for the full distribution.
- Quantity adjustment in the form of a falling rate of unemployment are key in explaining poverty reduction under trade liberalization in a few cases, most notoriously Brazil and Peru, as well as in Cuba and Venezuela in the FTAA scenario.

3.5 Conclusions

The purpose of this project was to determine the impact of trade liberalization, external shocks and domestic policy responses on output, employment, poverty and the distribution of income. We found that trade liberalization increased output in almost every country in our sample. It also increased either wages or employment depending on the closure used in the country-specific models. Consistent with this, poverty declined in all but one country in the unilateral trade liberalization scenario. Rising labour inequality, particularly between skilled and unskilled workers, emerges in the larger number of cases, but does not necessarily translate into more inequality in per capita household incomes because of offsetting positive employment effects. These results are very different from the historical experience of most Latin American countries in the period after trade liberalization. This is partly due to the many other disturbances that affected the region during the period and partly because ours are comparative static equilibrium results that say nothing at all about the adjustment period during which the economy adjusts to changes in tariff protection.

Two alternative trade liberalization scenarios, WTO and FTAA, have exactly the same positive effects on output, employment and poverty as a uniform and unilateral tariff reduction case in most countries.

In contrast, devaluation as an isolated policy measure is contractionary according to our results. It causes a decline in output and employment almost everywhere and an increase in poverty. The opposite is true for an increase in foreign borrowing. In both cases, the simulation assumes a permanent change in the exchange rate or the inflow of foreign savings, which is very different than the short run effect of devaluation on an economy out of equilibrium and in either a recession or a balance of payments crisis. The model results also do not consider likely negative effects of increased debt servicing following an increase in foreign borrowing, neither do they take account of the possibility of emerging debt-solvency constraints.

Subsidizing exports is expansionary in all but Brazil and Argentina (for the fixed exchange-rate closure). Employment increases and poverty declines in most cases. Skill differentials, however, rise in some countries and fall in others. Thus, one cannot say that choosing a more export-led growth strategy will in general favour either the skilled or the unskilled. This depends on the export structure of individual countries.

In terms of results on poverty, the analysis confirms the main results of the macro CGE simulations shown in Section 3.3. Policy measures with contractionary effects on the level of economic activity have negative results on poverty, leading to increased poverty incidence in most of the countries. This is the case for nominal devaluation and increase in tariffs. On the other hand, tariff reductions, productivity increases and trade and integration agreements in line with FTAA and WTO have positive effects on the level of economic activity and contribute to reduce the poverty incidence in a majority of the countries.

If labour market parameters are crucial to explain poverty and inequality variations, and most of the evidence point in that direction, wage levels and relative wage structures seem to explain most of the variations in those welfare outcomes. Aggregate employment changes as a consequence of trade reforms are mostly not big enough to exercise a significant impact on poverty and inequality.

In sum, export-led economic strategies have not been the panacea for welfare improvements, in the form of poverty and inequality reduction, many of its supporters expected when advocating these policy choices. But they have not been the devil its detractors predicted either. To reduce poverty and inequality from the severe levels most of the countries of the region are showing at the beginning of the new century may require policy mixes far more complicated and tailored to country specificities than the Washington medicine predicted a decade ago.

Table A3.1 Mathematical summary statement for the standard CGE model

Symbol	Explanation
Sets	
$a \in A$	Activities
$a \in ACES(\subset A)$	Activities with a CES function at the top of the technology nest
$a \in ALEO(\subset A)$	Activities with a Leontief function at the top of the technology nest
$c \in C$	Commodities
$c \in CD(\subset C)$	Commodities with domestic sales of domestic output
$c \in CDN(\subset C)$	Commodities not in CD
$c \in CE(\subset C)$	Exported commodities
$c \in CEN(\subset C)$	Commodities not in CE
$c \in CEN(\subset C)$	imported commodities
$c \in CMN(\subset C)$	Commodities not in CM
$c \in CT(\subset C)$	Transaction service commodities
$c \in CX(\subset C)$	Commodities with domestic production
$f \in F$	Factors
$i \in INS$	Institutions (domestic and rest of world)
$i \in INSD(\subset INS)$	Domestic institutions
$i \in INSDNG(\subset INSD)$	Domestic non-government institutions
$h \in H(\subset INSDNG)$	Households
Parameters	
$\overline{qg}_c$	Base-year quantity of government demand
$\overline{qinv}_c$	Base-year quantity of private investment demand
$shif_{if}$	Share for domestic institution i in income of factor f
$shii_{ii'}$	Share of net income of i' to i ($i' \in INSDNG'$; $i \in INSDNG$)
$cwts_c$	Weight of commodity c in the CPI
$dwts_c$	Weight of commodity c in the producer price index
ica_{ca}	Quantity of c as intermediate input per unit of activity a
$icd_{cc'}$	Quantity of commodity c as trade input per unit of c' produced and sold domestically
$ice_{cc'}$	Quantity of commodity c as trade input per exported unit of c'
ta_a	Tax rate for activity a

(Continued)

Symbol	Explanation	Symbol	Explanation
$icm_{cc'}$	Quantity of commodity c as trade input per imported unit of c'	te_c	Export tax rate
$inta_a$	Quantity of aggregate intermediate input per activity unit	tf_f	Direct tax rate for factor f
iva_a	Quantity of aggregate intermediate input per activity unit	$\overline{tins}_i$	Exogenous direct tax rate for domestic institution i
$\overline{mps}_i$	Base savings rate for domestic institution i	$tins01_i$	0–1 parameter with 1 for institutions with potentially flexed direct tax rates
$mps01_i$	0–1 parameter with 1 for institutions with potentially flexed direct tax rates	tm_c	Import tariff rate
		tq_c	Rate of sales tax
pwe_c	Export price (foreign currency)	$trnsfr_{i,f}$	Transfer from factor f to institution i
pwm_c	Import price (foreign currency)	tva_a	Rate of value-added tax for activity a
$qdst_c$	Quantity of stock change		
Greek letters			
α_a^a	Efficiency parameter in the CES activity function	δ_c^t	CET function share parameter
α_a^{va}	Efficiency parameter in the CES value-added function	δ_{fa}^{va}	CES value-added function share parameter for factor f in activity a
α_c^{ac}	Shift parameter for domestic commodity aggregation function	γ_{ch}^m	Subsistence consumption of marketed commodity c for household h
α_c^q	Armington function shift parameter	γ_{ach}^h	Subsistence consumption of home commodity c from activity a for household h
α_c^t	CET function shift parameter	θ_{ac}	Yield of output c per unit of activity a

(Continued)

Table A3.1 (Continued)

Symbol	Explanation
β_{ach}^{h}	Marginal share of consumption spending on home commodity c from activity a for household h
β_{ch}^{m}	Marginal share of consumption spending on marketed commodity c for household h
δ_{a}^{a}	CES activity function share parameter
δ_{ac}^{ac}	Share parameter for domestic commodity aggregation function
δ_{c}^{q}	Armington function share parameter

Exogenous variables

Symbol	Explanation
$\overline{CPI}$	Consumer price index
$\overline{DTINS}$	Change in domestic institution tax share (= 0 for base; exogenous variable)
$\overline{FSAV}$	Foreign savings (FCU)
$\overline{GADJ}$	Government consumption adjustment factor
$\overline{IADJ}$	Investment adjustment factor

Endogenous variables

Symbol	Explanation
DMPS	Change in domestic institution savings rates (= 0 for base; exogenous variable)
DPI	Producer price index for domestically marketed output

Symbol	Explanation
ρ_{a}^{a}	CES production function exponent
ρ_{a}^{va}	CES value-added function exponent
ρ_{c}^{ac}	Domestic commodity aggregation function exponent
ρ_{c}^{q}	Armington function exponent
ρ_{c}^{t}	CET function exponent
$\overline{MPSADJ}$	Savings rate scaling factor (= 0 for base)
$\overline{QFS}_{f}$	Quantity supplied of factor
$\overline{TINSADJ}$	Direct tax scaling factor (= 0 for base; exogenous variable)
$\overline{WFDIST}_{fa}$	Wage distortion factor for factor f in activity a
QF_{fa}	Quantity demanded of factor f from activity a
QG_{c}	Government consumption demand for commodity

(Continued)

Table A3.1 (Continued)

Symbol	Explanation	Symbol	Explanation
EG	Government expenditures	QH_{ch}	Quantity consumed of commodity c by household h
EH_h	Consumption spending for household	QHA_{ach}	Quantity of household home consumption of commodity c from activity a for household h
EXR	Exchange rate (LCU per unit of FCU)	$QINTA_a$	Quantity of aggregate intermediate input
$GOVSHR$	Government consumption share in nominal absorption	$QINT_{ca}$	Quantity of commodity c as intermediate input to activity a
$GSAV$	Government savings	$QINV_c$	Quantity of investment demand for commodity
$INVSHR$	Investment share in nominal absorption	QM_c	Quantity of imports of commodity
MPS_i	Marginal propensity to save for domestic non-government institution (exogenous variable)	QQ_c	Quantity of goods supplied to domestic market (composite supply)
PA_a	Activity price (unit gross revenue)	QT_c	Quantity of commodity demanded as trade input
PDD_c	Demand price for commodity produced and sold domestically	QVA_a	Quantity of (aggregate) value added
PDS_c	Supply price for commodity produced and sold domestically	QX_c	Aggregated quantity of domestic output of commodity
PE_c	Export price (domestic currency)	$QXAC_{ac}$	Quantity of output of commodity c from activity a
$PINTA_a$	Aggregate intermediate input price for activity a	$TABS$	Total nominal absorption
PM_c	Import price (domestic currency)	$TINS_i$	Direct tax rate for institution i ($i \in$ INSDNG)

(Continued)

Table A3.1 (Continued)

Symbol	Explanation
PQ_c	Composite commodity price
PVA_a	Value-added price (factor income per unit of activity)
PX_c	Aggregate producer price for commodity
$PXAC_{ac}$	Producer price of commodity c for activity a
QA_a	Quantity (level) of activity
QD_c	Quantity sold domestically of domestic output
QE_c	Quantity of exports

Symbol	Explanation
$TRII'_{ii}$	Transfers from institution i' to i (both in the set INSDNG)
WF_f	Average price of factor
YF_f	Income of factor f
YG	Government revenue
YI_i	Income of domestic non-government institution
YIF_{if}	Income to domestic institution i from factor f

Equations

No.	Equation	Domain	Description
	Price block		
1	$PM_c = pwm_c \cdot (1 + tm_c) \cdot EXR + \sum\limits_{c' \in CT} PQ_{c'} \cdot icm_{c'c}$ $\begin{bmatrix} \text{import} \\ \text{price} \\ (LCU) \end{bmatrix} = \begin{bmatrix} \text{import} \\ \text{price} \\ (FCU) \end{bmatrix} \cdot \begin{bmatrix} \text{tariff} \\ \text{adjust-} \\ \text{ment} \end{bmatrix} \cdot \begin{bmatrix} \text{exchange rate} \\ (LCU \text{ per} \\ FCU) \end{bmatrix} + \begin{bmatrix} \text{cost of trade} \\ \text{inputs per} \\ \text{import unit} \end{bmatrix}$	$c \in CM$	Import price

(Continued)

Table A3.1 (Continued)

No.	Equation	Domain	Description
2	$PE_c = pwe_c \cdot (1 - te_c) \cdot EXR - \sum_{c' \in CT} PQ_{c'} \cdot ice_{c'c}$ $\begin{bmatrix} export \\ price \\ (LCU) \end{bmatrix} = \begin{bmatrix} export \\ price \\ (FCU) \end{bmatrix} \cdot \begin{bmatrix} tariff \\ adjust- \\ ment \end{bmatrix} \cdot \begin{bmatrix} exchange\ rate \\ (LCU\ per \\ FCU) \end{bmatrix} - \begin{bmatrix} cost\ of\ trade \\ inputs\ per \\ export\ unit \end{bmatrix}$	$c \in CE$	Export price
3	$PDD_c = PDS_c + \sum_{c' \in CT} PQ_{c'} \cdot icd_{c'c}$ $\begin{bmatrix} domestic \\ demand \\ price \end{bmatrix} = \begin{bmatrix} domestic \\ supply \\ price \end{bmatrix} + \begin{bmatrix} cost\ of\ trade \\ inputs\ per \\ unit\ of \\ domestic\ sales \end{bmatrix}$	$c \in CD$	Demand price of domestic non-traded goods
4	$PQ_c \cdot (1 - tq_c) \cdot QQ_c = PDD_c \cdot QD_c + PM_c \cdot QM_c$ $\begin{bmatrix} absorption \\ (at\ demand \\ prices\ net\ of \\ sales\ tax) \end{bmatrix} = \begin{bmatrix} domestic\ demand\ price \\ times \\ domestic\ sales\ quantity \end{bmatrix} + \begin{bmatrix} import\ price \\ times \\ import\ quantity \end{bmatrix}$	$c \in (CD \cup CM)$	Absorption
5	$PX_c \cdot QX_c = PDS_c \cdot QD_c + PE_c \cdot QE_c$ $\begin{bmatrix} producer\ price \\ times\ marketed \\ output\ quantity \end{bmatrix} = \begin{bmatrix} domestic\ supply\ price \\ times \\ domestic\ sales\ quantity \end{bmatrix} + \begin{bmatrix} export\ price \\ times \\ export\ quantity \end{bmatrix}$	$c \in CX$	Marketed output value

(Continued)

Table A3.1 (Continued)

No.	Equation	Domain	Description
6	$PA_a = \sum_{c \in C} PXAC_{ac} \cdot \theta_{ac}$ $\left[\begin{array}{c} activity \\ price \end{array}\right] = \left[\begin{array}{c} producer\ prices \\ times\ yields \end{array}\right]$	$a \in A$	Activity price
7	$PINTA_a = \sum_{c \in C} PQ_c \cdot ica_{ca}$ $\left[\begin{array}{c} aggregate \\ intermediate \\ input\ price \end{array}\right] = \left[\begin{array}{c} intermediate\ input\ cost \\ per\ unit\ of\ aggregate \\ intermediate\ input \end{array}\right]$	$a \in A$	Aggregate intermediate input price
8	$PA_a \cdot (1 - ta_a) \cdot QA_a = PVA_a \cdot QVA_a + PINTA_a \cdot QINTA_a$ $\left[\begin{array}{c} activity\ price \\ (net\ of\ taxes) \\ times\ activity\ level \end{array}\right] = \left[\begin{array}{c} value\text{-}added \\ price\ times \\ quantity \end{array}\right] + \left[\begin{array}{c} aggregate \\ intermediate \\ input\ price\ times \\ quantity \end{array}\right]$	$a \in A$	Activity revenue and costs
9	$\overline{CPI} = \sum_{c \in C} PQ_c \cdot cwts_c$ $[CPI] = \left[\begin{array}{c} prices\ times \\ weights \end{array}\right]$		Consumer price index
10	$DPI = \sum_{c \in C} PDS_c \cdot dwts_c$ $\left[\begin{array}{c} Producer\ price\ index \\ for\ non\text{-}traded\ outputs \end{array}\right] = \left[\begin{array}{c} prices\ times \\ weights \end{array}\right]$		Producer price index for non-traded market output

(*Continued*)

Table A3.1 (Continued)

No.	Equation	Domain	Description
	Production and commodity block		
11	$QA_a = \alpha_a^a \cdot \left(\delta_a^a \cdot QVA_a^{-\rho_a^a} + (1 - \delta_a^a) \cdot QINTA_a^{-\rho_a^a}\right)^{-\frac{1}{\rho_a^a}}$ $\begin{bmatrix} activity \\ level \end{bmatrix} = CES \begin{bmatrix} quantity\ of\ aggregate\ value\text{-}added, \\ quantity\ aggregate\ intermediate\ input \end{bmatrix}$	$a \in ACES$	CES technology: activity production function
12	$\dfrac{QVA_a}{QINTA_a} = \left(\dfrac{PINTA_a}{PVA_a} \cdot \dfrac{\delta_a^a}{1-\delta_a^a}\right)^{\frac{1}{1+\rho_a^a}}$ $\begin{bmatrix} value\text{-}added\text{-} \\ intermediate\text{-} \\ input\ quantity \\ ratio \end{bmatrix} = f \begin{bmatrix} intermediate\text{-}input \\ \text{-}value\text{-}added \\ price\ ratio \end{bmatrix}$	$a \in ACES$	CES technology: value-added–intermediate-input ratio
13	$QVA_a = iva_a \cdot QA_a$ $\begin{bmatrix} demand\ for \\ value\text{-}added \end{bmatrix} = f \begin{bmatrix} activity \\ level \end{bmatrix}$	$a \in ALEO$	Leontief technology: demand for aggregate value-added
14	$QINTA_a = inta_a \cdot QA_a$ $\begin{bmatrix} demand\ for\ aggregate \\ intermediate\ input \end{bmatrix} = f \begin{bmatrix} activity \\ level \end{bmatrix}$	$a \in ALEO$	Leontief technology: demand for aggregate intermediate input
15	$QVA_a = \alpha_a^{va} \cdot \left(\sum_{f \in F} \delta_{fa}^{va} \cdot QF_{fa}^{-\rho_a^{va}}\right)^{-\frac{1}{\rho_a^{va}}}$ $\begin{bmatrix} quantity\ of\ aggregate \\ value\text{-}added \end{bmatrix} = CES \begin{bmatrix} factor \\ inputs \end{bmatrix}$	$a \in A$	Value-added and factor demands

(Continued)

Table A3.1 (Continued)

No.	Equation	Domain	Description
16	$W_f \cdot \overline{WFDIST}_{fa} = PVA_a \cdot (1 - tva_a) \cdot QVA_a \cdot \left(\sum_{f \in F'} \delta^{va}_{fa} \cdot QF^{-\rho^{va}_a}_{fa} \right)^{-1} \cdot \delta^{va}_{fa} \cdot QF^{-\rho^{va}_a - 1}_{fa}$ $\left[\begin{array}{c} \textit{marginal cost of} \\ \textit{factor f in activity a} \end{array} \right] = \left[\begin{array}{c} \textit{marginal revenue product} \\ \textit{of factor f in activity a} \end{array} \right]$	$a \in A$ $f \in F$	Factor demand
17	$QINT_{ca} = ica_{ca} \cdot QINTA_a$ $\left[\begin{array}{c} \textit{intermediate demand} \\ \textit{for commodity c} \\ \textit{from activity a} \end{array} \right] = f \left[\begin{array}{c} \textit{aggregate intermediate} \\ \textit{input quantity} \\ \textit{for activity a} \end{array} \right]$	$a \in A$ $c \in C$	Disaggregated intermediate input demand
18	$QXAC_{ac} + \sum_{h \in H} QHA_{ach} = \theta_{ac} \cdot QA_a$ $\left[\begin{array}{c} \textit{marketed quantity} \\ \textit{of commodity c} \\ \textit{from activity a} \end{array} \right] + \left[\begin{array}{c} \textit{household home} \\ \textit{consumption} \\ \textit{of commodity c} \\ \textit{from activity a} \end{array} \right] = \left[\begin{array}{c} \textit{production} \\ \textit{of commodity c} \\ \textit{from activity a} \end{array} \right]$	$a \in A$ $c \in CX$	Commodity production and allocation
19	$QX_c = \alpha^{ac}_c \cdot \left(\sum_{a \in A} \delta^{ac}_{ac} \cdot QXAC^{-\rho^{ac}_c}_{ac} \right)^{-\frac{1}{\rho^{ac}_c}}$ $\left[\begin{array}{c} \textit{aggregate} \\ \textit{marketed} \\ \textit{production of} \\ \textit{commodity c} \end{array} \right] = CES \left[\begin{array}{c} \textit{activity-specific} \\ \textit{marketed} \\ \textit{production of} \\ \textit{commodity c} \end{array} \right]$	$c \in CX$	Output aggregation function

(Continued)

Table A3.1 (Continued)

No.	Equation	Domain	Description
20	$PXAC_{ac} = PX_c \cdot QX_c \cdot \left(\sum_{a \in A'} \delta_{ac}^{ac} \cdot QXAC_{ac}^{-\rho_c^{ac}} \right)^{-1} \cdot \delta_{ac}^{ac} \cdot QXAC_{ac}^{-\rho_c^{ac}-1}$ $\left[\begin{array}{l}\text{marginal cost of com-}\\ \text{modity } c \text{ from activity } a\end{array}\right] = \left[\begin{array}{l}\text{marginal revenue product of}\\ \text{commodity } c \text{ from activity } a\end{array}\right]$	$a \in A$ $c \in CX$	First-order condition for output aggregation function
21	$QX_c = \alpha_c^t \cdot \left(\delta_c^t \cdot QE_c^{\rho_c^t} + (1 - \delta_c^t) \cdot QD_c^{\rho_c^t} \right)^{\frac{1}{\rho_c^t}}$ $\left[\begin{array}{l}\text{aggregate marketed}\\ \text{domestic output}\end{array}\right] = CET \left[\begin{array}{l}\text{export quantity, domestic}\\ \text{sales of domestic output}\end{array}\right]$	$c \in (CE \cap CD)$	Output transformation (CET) function
22	$\dfrac{QE_c}{QD_c} = \left(\dfrac{PE_c}{PDS_c} \cdot \dfrac{1-\delta_c^t}{\delta_c^t} \right)^{\frac{1}{\rho_c^t-1}}$ $\left[\begin{array}{l}\text{export–domestic}\\ \text{supply ratio}\end{array}\right] = f \left[\begin{array}{l}\text{export–domestic}\\ \text{price ratio}\end{array}\right]$	$c \in (CE \cap CD)$	Export–domestic supply ratio
23	$QX_c = QD_c + QE_c$ $\left[\begin{array}{l}\text{aggregate}\\ \text{marketed}\\ \text{domestic output}\end{array}\right] = \left[\begin{array}{l}\text{domestic market}\\ \text{sales of domestic}\\ \text{output [for}\\ c \in (CD \cap CEN)]\end{array}\right] + \left[\begin{array}{l}\text{exports [for}\\ c \in (CE \cap CDN)]\end{array}\right]$	$c \in$ $(CD \cap CEN)$ $\cup$ $(CE \cup CDN)$	Output transformation for non-exported commodities
24	$QQ_c = \alpha_c^q \cdot \left(\delta_c^q \cdot QM_c^{-\rho_c^q} + (1 - \delta_c^q) \cdot QD_c^{-\rho_c^q} \right)^{-\frac{1}{\rho_c^q}}$ $\left[\begin{array}{l}\text{composite}\\ \text{supply}\end{array}\right] = f \left[\begin{array}{l}\text{import quantity, domestic}\\ \text{use of domestic output}\end{array}\right]$	$c \in (CM \cap CD)$	Composite supply (Armington) function

(Continued)

Table A3.1 (Continued)

No.	Equation	Domain	Description
25	$\underbrace{\dfrac{QM_c}{QD_c}}_{\substack{\text{import–domestic}\\\text{demand ratio}}} = \left(\dfrac{PDD_c}{PM_c} \cdot \dfrac{\delta_c^q}{1-\delta_c^q}\right)^{\frac{1}{1+\rho_c^q}} = f\underbrace{\left[\begin{array}{c}\text{domestic-import}\\\text{price ratio}\end{array}\right]}$	$c \in (CM \cap CD)$	Import–domestic demand ratio
26	$QQ_c = QD_c + QM_c$ $\underbrace{\left[\begin{array}{c}\text{composite}\\\text{supply}\end{array}\right]}= \underbrace{\left[\begin{array}{c}\text{domestic use of}\\\text{marketed domestic}\\\text{output [for}\\ c \in (CD \cap CMN)]\end{array}\right]} + \underbrace{\left[\begin{array}{c}\text{imports [for}\\ c \in (CM \cap CDN)]\end{array}\right]}$	$c \in$ $(CD \cap CMN)$ $\cup$ $(CM \cap CDN)$	Composite supply for non-imported outputs and non-produced imports
27	$QT_c = \sum_{c' \in C'} (icm_{cc'} \cdot QM_{c'} + ice_{cc'} \cdot QE_{c'} + icd_{cc'} \cdot QD_{c'})$ $\underbrace{\left[\begin{array}{c}\text{demand for}\\\text{transactions}\\\text{services}\end{array}\right]}= \underbrace{\left[\begin{array}{c}\text{sum of demands}\\\text{for imports, exports,}\\\text{and domestic sales}\end{array}\right]}$	$c \in CT$	Demand for transactions services

Institution block

No.	Equation	Domain	Description
28	$YF_f = \sum_{a \in A} WF_f \cdot \overline{WFDIST}_{fa} \cdot QF_{fa}$ $\underbrace{\left[\begin{array}{c}\text{income of}\\\text{factor } f\end{array}\right]}= \underbrace{\left[\begin{array}{c}\text{sum of activity payments}\\\text{(activity-specific wages}\\\text{times employment levels)}\end{array}\right]}$	$f \in F$	Factor income
29	$YIF_{if} = shif_{if} \cdot \left[(1-tf_f) \cdot YF_f - trnsfr_{rowf} \cdot EXR\right]$ $\underbrace{\left[\begin{array}{c}\text{income of}\\\text{institution } i\\\text{from factor } f\end{array}\right]}= \underbrace{\left[\begin{array}{c}\text{share of income}\\\text{of factor } f \text{ to}\\\text{institution } i\end{array}\right]} \cdot \underbrace{\left[\begin{array}{c}\text{income of factor } f\\\text{(net of tax and}\\\text{transfer to RoW)}\end{array}\right]}$	$i \in INSD$ $f \in F$	Institutional factor incomes

(Continued)

Table A3.1 (Continued)

No.	Equation	Domain	Description
30	$YI_i = \sum_{f \in F} YIF_{if} + \sum_{i' \in INSDNG'} TRII_{ii'} + trnsfr_{i,gov} \cdot \overline{CPI} + trnsfr_{i,row} \cdot EXR$ $\begin{bmatrix} income\ of \\ institution\ i \end{bmatrix} = \begin{bmatrix} factor \\ income \end{bmatrix} + \begin{bmatrix} transfers \\ from\ other\ domestic \\ non\text{-}government \\ institutions \end{bmatrix} + \begin{bmatrix} transfers \\ from \\ government \end{bmatrix}$ $+ \begin{bmatrix} transfers \\ from \\ RoW \end{bmatrix}$	$i \in INSDNG$	Income of domestic, non-government institutions
31	$TRII_{ii'} = shii_{ii'} \cdot (1 - MPS_{i'}) \cdot (1 - TINS_{i'}) \cdot YI_{i'}$ $\begin{bmatrix} transfer\ from \\ institution\ i'\ to\ i \end{bmatrix} = \begin{bmatrix} share\ of\ net\ income \\ of\ institution\ i' \\ transferred\ to\ i \end{bmatrix} \cdot \begin{bmatrix} income\ of\ institution \\ i',\ net\ of\ savings\ and \\ direct\ taxes \end{bmatrix}$	$i \in INSDNG$ $i' \in INSDNG'$	Intra-institutional transfers
32	$EH_h = \left(1 - \sum_{i \in INSDNG} shii_{ih}\right) \cdot (1 - MPS_h) \cdot (1 - TINS_h) \cdot YI_h$ $\begin{bmatrix} household\ income \\ disposable\ for \\ consumption \end{bmatrix} = \begin{bmatrix} household\ income,\ net\ of\ direct \\ taxes,\ savings,\ and\ transfers\ to \\ other\ non\text{-}government\ institutions \end{bmatrix}$	$h \in H$	Household consumption expenditure

(Continued)

Table A3.1 (Continued)

No.	Equation	Domain	Description
33	$$QH_{ch} = \gamma_{ch} + \frac{\beta_{ch}^m \cdot \left(EH_h - \sum_{c'\in C} PQ_{c'} \cdot \gamma_{c'h}^m - \sum_{a\in A}\sum_{c'\in C} PXAC_{ac'} \cdot \gamma_{ac'h}^h\right)}{PQ_c}$$ $$\underbrace{\begin{bmatrix} \text{quantity of} \\ \text{household demand} \\ \text{for commodity } c \end{bmatrix}}_{} = f \underbrace{\begin{bmatrix} \text{household} \\ \text{consumption} \\ \text{spending,} \\ \text{market price} \end{bmatrix}}_{}$$	$c \in C$ $h \in H$	Household consumption demand for marketed commodities
34	$$QHA_{ach} = \gamma_{ach}^h + \frac{\beta_{ach}^h \cdot \left(EH_h - \sum_{c'\in C} PQ_{c'} \cdot \gamma_{c'h}^m - \sum_{a\in A}\sum_{c'\in C} PXAC_{ac'} \cdot \gamma_{ac'h}^h\right)}{PXAC_{ac}}$$ $$\underbrace{\begin{bmatrix} \text{quantity of} \\ \text{household demand} \\ \text{for home commodity } c \\ \text{from activity } a \end{bmatrix}}_{} = f \underbrace{\begin{bmatrix} \text{household} \\ \text{disposable} \\ \text{income,} \\ \text{producer price} \end{bmatrix}}_{}$$	$a \in A$ $c \in C$ $h \in H$	Household consumption demand for home commodities
35	$$QINV_c = \overline{IADJ} \cdot \overline{qinv_c}$$ $$\underbrace{\begin{bmatrix} \text{fixed investment} \\ \text{demand for} \\ \text{commodity } c \end{bmatrix}}_{} = \underbrace{\begin{bmatrix} \text{adjustment factor} \\ \text{times} \\ \text{base-year fixed} \\ \text{investment} \end{bmatrix}}_{}$$	$c \in CINV$	Investment demand
36	$$QG_c = \overline{GADJ} \cdot \overline{qg_c}$$ $$\underbrace{\begin{bmatrix} \text{government} \\ \text{consumption} \\ \text{demand for} \\ \text{commodity } c \end{bmatrix}}_{} = \underbrace{\begin{bmatrix} \text{adjustment factor} \\ \text{times} \\ \text{base-year government} \\ \text{consumption} \end{bmatrix}}_{}$$	$c \in C$	Government consumption demand

(Continued)

Table A3.1 (Continued)

No.	Equation	Domain	Description
37	$$YG = \sum_{i \in INSDNG} TINS_i \cdot YI_i + \sum_{f \in F} tf_f \cdot YF_f + \sum_{a \in A} tva_a \cdot PVA_a \cdot QVA_a$$ $$+ \sum_{a \in A} ta_a \cdot PA_a \cdot QA_a + \sum_{c \in CM} tm_c \cdot pwm_c \cdot QM_c \cdot EXR + \sum_{c \in CE} te_c \cdot pwe_c \cdot$$ $$XQE_c \cdot EXR + \sum_{c \in C} tq_c \cdot PQ_c \cdot QQ_c + \sum_{f \in F} YF_{gov\,f} + trnsfr_{gov\,row} \cdot EXR$$ $$\begin{bmatrix} government \\ revenue \end{bmatrix} = \begin{bmatrix} direct\ taxes \\ from \\ institutions \end{bmatrix} + \begin{bmatrix} direct\ taxes \\ from \\ factors \end{bmatrix} + \begin{bmatrix} value\text{-} \\ added \\ tax \end{bmatrix}$$ $$+ \begin{bmatrix} activity \\ tax \end{bmatrix} + \begin{bmatrix} import \\ tariffs \end{bmatrix} + \begin{bmatrix} export \\ taxes \end{bmatrix}$$ $$+ \begin{bmatrix} sales \\ tax \end{bmatrix} + \begin{bmatrix} factor \\ income \end{bmatrix} + \begin{bmatrix} transfers \\ from \\ RoW \end{bmatrix}$$		Government revenue
38	$$EG = \sum_{c \in C} PQ_c \cdot QG_c + \sum_{i \in INSDNG} trnsfr_{i\,gov} \cdot \overline{CPI}$$ $$\begin{bmatrix} government \\ spending \end{bmatrix} = \begin{bmatrix} government \\ consumption \end{bmatrix} + \begin{bmatrix} transfers\ to\ domestic \\ non\text{-}government \\ institutions \end{bmatrix}$$		Government expenditures

System constraint block

No.	Equation	Domain	Description
39	$$\sum_{a \in A} QF_{fa} = \overline{QFS}_f$$ $$\begin{bmatrix} demand\ for \\ factor\ f \end{bmatrix} = \begin{bmatrix} supply\ of \\ factor\ f \end{bmatrix}$$	$f \in F$	Factor market

(Continued)

Table A3.1 (Continued)

No.	Equation	Domain	Description
40	$$QQ_c = \sum_{a \in A} QINT_{ca} + \sum_{h \in H} QH_{ch} + QG_c + QINV_c + qdst_c + QT_c$$ $\begin{bmatrix} composite \\ supply \end{bmatrix} = \begin{bmatrix} intermediate \\ use \end{bmatrix} + \begin{bmatrix} household \\ consumption \end{bmatrix} + \begin{bmatrix} government \\ consumption \end{bmatrix}$ $+ \begin{bmatrix} fixed \\ investment \end{bmatrix} + \begin{bmatrix} stock \\ change \end{bmatrix} + \begin{bmatrix} trade \\ input\ use \end{bmatrix}$	$c \in C$	Composite commodity markets
41	$$\sum_{c \in CM} pwm_c \cdot QM_c + \sum_{f \in F} trnsfr_{rowf} = \sum_{c \in CE} pwe_c \cdot QE_c + \sum_{i \in INSD} trnsfr_{i\,row} + \overline{FSAV}$$ $\begin{bmatrix} import \\ spending \end{bmatrix} + \begin{bmatrix} factor \\ transfers \\ to\ RoW \end{bmatrix} = \begin{bmatrix} export \\ revenue \end{bmatrix} + \begin{bmatrix} institutional \\ transfers \\ from\ RoW \end{bmatrix} + \begin{bmatrix} foreign \\ savings \end{bmatrix}$		Current account balance for RoW (in foreign currency)
42	$$YG = EG + GSAV$$ $\begin{bmatrix} government \\ revenue \end{bmatrix} = \begin{bmatrix} government \\ expenditures \end{bmatrix} + \begin{bmatrix} government \\ savings \end{bmatrix}$		Government balance
43	$$TINS_i = \overline{tins}_i \cdot (1 + \overline{TINSADJ} \cdot tins\,01_i) + \overline{DTINS} \cdot tins\,01_i$$ $\begin{bmatrix} direct\ tax \\ rate\ for \\ institution\ i \end{bmatrix} = \begin{bmatrix} base\ rate\ adjusted \\ for\ scaling\ for \\ selected\ institutions \end{bmatrix} + \begin{bmatrix} point\ change \\ for\ selected \\ institutions \end{bmatrix}$	$i \in INSDNG$	Direct institutional tax rates
44	$$MPS_i = \overline{mps}_i \cdot (1 + \overline{MPSADJ} \cdot mps\,01_i) + \overline{DMPS} \cdot mps\,01_i$$ $\begin{bmatrix} savings \\ rate\ for \\ institution\ i \end{bmatrix} = \begin{bmatrix} base\ rate\ adjusted \\ for\ scaling\ for \\ selected\ institutions \end{bmatrix} + \begin{bmatrix} point\ change \\ for\ selected \\ institutions \end{bmatrix}$	$i \in INSDNG$	Institutional savings rates

(Continued)

Table A3.1 (Continued)

No.	Equation	Domain	Description
45	$$\sum_{i \in INSDNG} MPS_i \cdot (1 - TINS_i) \cdot YI_i + GSAV + EXR \cdot \overline{FSAV}$$ $$= \sum_{c \in C} PQ_c \cdot QINV_c + \sum_{c \in C} PQ_c \cdot qdst_c$$ $$\left[\begin{array}{c}\text{non-govern-}\\\text{ment savings}\end{array}\right] + \left[\begin{array}{c}\text{government}\\\text{savings}\end{array}\right] + \left[\begin{array}{c}\text{foreign}\\\text{savings}\end{array}\right] = \left[\begin{array}{c}\text{fixed}\\\text{investment}\end{array}\right] + \left[\begin{array}{c}\text{stock}\\\text{change}\end{array}\right]$$		Savings–investment balance
46	$$TABS = \sum_{h \in H}\sum_{c \in C} PQ_c \cdot QH_{ch} + \sum_{a \in A}\sum_{c \in C}\sum_{h \in H} PXAC_{ac} \cdot QHA_{ach}$$ $$+ \sum_{c \in C} PQ_c \cdot QG_c + \sum_{c \in C} PQ_c \cdot QINV_c + \sum_{c \in C} PQ_c \cdot qdst_c$$ $$\left[\begin{array}{c}\text{total}\\\text{absorption}\end{array}\right] = \left[\begin{array}{c}\text{household}\\\text{market}\\\text{consumption}\end{array}\right] + \left[\begin{array}{c}\text{household}\\\text{home}\\\text{consumption}\end{array}\right]$$ $$+ \left[\begin{array}{c}\text{government}\\\text{consumption}\end{array}\right] + \left[\begin{array}{c}\text{fixed}\\\text{investment}\end{array}\right] + \left[\begin{array}{c}\text{stock}\\\text{change}\end{array}\right]$$		Total absorption
47	$$INVSHR \cdot TABS = \sum_{c \in C} PQ_c \cdot QINV_c + \sum_{c \in C} PQ_c \cdot qdst_c$$ $$\left[\begin{array}{c}\text{investment-}\\\text{absorption}\\\text{ratio}\end{array}\right] \cdot \left[\begin{array}{c}\text{total}\\\text{absorption}\end{array}\right] = \left[\begin{array}{c}\text{fixed}\\\text{investment}\end{array}\right] + \left[\begin{array}{c}\text{stock}\\\text{change}\end{array}\right]$$		Ratio of investment to absorption
48	$$GOVSHR \cdot TABS = \sum_{c \in C} PQ_c \cdot QG_c$$ $$\left[\begin{array}{c}\text{government}\\\text{consumption-}\\\text{absorption}\\\text{ratio}\end{array}\right] \cdot \left[\begin{array}{c}\text{total}\\\text{absorption}\end{array}\right] = \left[\begin{array}{c}\text{government}\\\text{consumption}\end{array}\right]$$		Ratio of government consumption to absorption

Table A3.2 Closure rules for standardized and country-specific CGE simulations

	Argentina	Bolivia	Brazil	Cuba	Chile	Colombia	Costa Rica	Ecuador	El Salvador	Honduras	Mexico	Paraguay	Peru	Dom. Rep	Uruguay	Venezuela
Standardized closure rules																
External balance	1 and 2	1 and 2	1 and 2	2	1 and 2	1 and 2	1 and 2	1 and 2	1 and 2	1 and 2	1 and 2	1 and 2	1 and 2	1 and 2	1 and 2	1 and 2
Government balance	1	1	1	1	1	1	1	1	1	1	1	1	1	1	1	1
Savings–investment	4	4	4	4	4	4	4	4	4	4	4	4	4	4	4	4
Factor markets																
Labour market	3	3	3	3	3	3	3	3	3	3	3	3	3	3	3	3
Capital	1	1	1	1	1	1	1	1	1	1	1	1	1	1	1	1
Country-specific closure rules																
External balance	3	1	2	2*	1	2	2	2	2	2	1	2	1	1	2	1
Government balance	4	1	3	1	1	1	1	1	1	1	1	1	1	1	1	2
Savings–investment	2	4	3	1	1	1	1	1	4	1	5	4	3	1	1	1
Factor markets																
Labour market																
Formal – skilled	3	3	3	3	3	1	3	1	3	3	5	3	3	1	1	5
Informal – skilled	3	1	5	3	3	1	3	1	3	3	5	3	3	1	1	5
Formal – unskilled	3	3	5	3	3	1	3	3	3	3	5	3	3	3	1	5

(*Continued*)

Table A3.2 (Continued)

	Argentina	Bolivia	Brazil	Cuba	Chile	Colombia	Costa Rica	Ecuador	El Salvador	Honduras	Mexico	Paraguay	Peru	Dom. Rep	Uruguay	Venezuela
Informal – unskilled	3	1	5	3	3	1	3	3	3	3	1	3	3	3	1	5
Capital	2	2	2	2	2	2	2	2	1	2	1	1	1	2	2	1

*Cuba has dual foreign exchange market with fixed official exchange rate and flexible informal market rate

Notes: *Definition of closures*

Value for savings-investment closure:

1. Investment-driven savings (uniform mps rate point change for selected institutions)
2. Investment-driven savings (scaled mps for selected institutions)
3. Investment is savings driven
4. Balanced closure (1): investment and government are fixed (absolute shares)
5. Balanced closure (2): investment is fixed (abs share); scaled mps (cf. 2)

mps = marginal propensity to save

Value for rest of world closure:

1. Flexible exchange rate, fixed foreign savings
2. Fixed exchange rate, endogenous foreign savings
3. Fixed exchange rate and fixed foreign savings (Argentina: has flexible money supply and CPI)

Value for government closure:

1. Government savings are flexible, dir tax rate is fixed
2. Government savings are fixed, uniform dir tax rate point change for selected institutions
3. Government savings are fixed, scaled dir tax rate for selected institutions

Factor market closures:

1. Factors are fully employed and mobile
2. Factors are fully employed and activity-specific
3. Factors are unemployed and mobile

Other closure:

ARG: (a) Labour is unemployed and mobile. For each activity, the real wage is fixed. (b) Labour supply and nominal wage are market-clearing variables for unified labour market. Wage distortion factor (WFDIST) clears labour demand and supply in each sector

BRA: Wage curve for most urban workers (imperfect wage adjustment)

MEX: (a) Skilled labour: fixed wage, flexible WFDIST, mobile, fixed labour supply. (b) Unskilled labour: faces upwards sloping labour supply function: market-clearing wage, total stock endogenous, mobile among sectors. (c) Agricultural labour: fully employed and mobile within agricultural sectors

VEN: Fixed nominal wage for all workers, real wages and unemployment adjust to balance labour supply and demand

Table A3.3 GTAP model: simulated world market prices for FTAA and WTO scenarios (indices; changes from baseline)

	FTAA	WTO
Rice	1.013	1.149
Wheat	1.001	1.231
Other cereals	1.002	1.204
Fruits and vegetables	1.005	1.052
Oil seeds	1.000	1.113
Sugar	1.009	1.106
Natural fibres	0.998	1.011
Other crops	1.002	1.015
Wool	0.995	1.066
Forestry	0.996	1.001
Fishing	0.996	1.016
Meat and meat products (bovine)	1.009	1.213
Other meat products	1.002	1.190
Vegetable oils	1.000	1.044
Dairy products	1.007	1.262
Other food products	1.002	1.068
Beverages and tobacco	1.000	1.087
Energy products	0.997	0.980
Mining products	0.995	0.998
Textiles	0.998	1.014
Clothing	0.997	0.993
Leather products	0.997	0.992
Paper and printing	0.998	1.010
Oil products	0.997	0.996
Chemicals, rubber and plastics	0.998	1.013
Mineral products	0.997	1.012
Automobiles and parts	0.999	1.013
Other transport equipment	0.997	1.002
Electronic equipment	0.997	1.000
Machinery	0.997	1.007

Source: Simulation results of the GTAP model, prepared by E. Díaz Bonilla and X. Diao

Table A3.4 Poverty and inequality indicators[1] for Latin America during the 1990s

	Poverty incidence	Extreme poverty incidence	Gini coefficient
Argentina			
1990[2]	21.2	5.2	0.501
1997[2]	17.8	4.8	0.530
1999[2]	19.7	4.8	0.542
2001*	31.3	10.9	—
Bolivia			
1989[3]	53.1	23.2	0.538
1997	62.1	37.2	0.595
1999	60.6	36.5	0.586
2001*	61.2	37.3	—

(Continued)

Table A3.4 (Continued)

	Poverty incidence	Extreme poverty incidence	Gini coefficient
Brazil			
1990	48.0	23.4	0.627
1996	35.8	13.9	0.638
1999	37.5	12.9	0.640
2001*	36.9	13.0	—
Chile			
1990	38.6	12.9	0.554
1996	23.2	5.7	0.553
2000	20.6	5.7	0.559
2001*	20.0	5.4	—
Colombia			
1991	56.1	26.1	0.531
1997	50.9	23.5	0.569
1999	54.9	26.8	0.572
2001*	54.9	27.6	—
Costa Rica			
1990	26.2	9.8	0.438
1997	22.5	7.8	0.450
1999	20.3	7.8	0.473
2001*	21.7	8.3	—
Ecuador			
1990[4]	62.1	26.2	0.461
1997[4]	56.2	22.2	0.469
1999[4]	63.6	31.3	0.521
2001*	63.5	28.9	—
El Salvador			
1995	54.2	21.7	0.507
1997	55.5	23.3	0.510
1999	49.8	21.9	0.518
2001*	49.9	22.5	—
Guatemala			
1989	69.1	41.8	0.582
1998	60.5	34.1	0.582
2001*	60.4	34.4	—
Honduras			
1990	80.5	60.6	0.615
1997	79.1	54.4	0.558
1999	79.7	56.8	0.564
2001*	79.1	56.0	—
Mexico			
1989	47.8	18.8	0.536
1996	52.1	21.3	0.526
2000	41.1	15.2	0.542
2001*	42.3	16.4	—

(Continued)

Table A3.4   (Continued)

	Poverty incidence	Extreme poverty incidence	Gini coefficient
Nicaragua			
1993	73.6	48.4	0.582
1998	69.9	44.6	0.584
2001*	67.4	41.5	—
Panama			
1991	42.8	19.2	0.560
1997	33.2	13.0	0.570
1999	30.2	10.7	0.557
2001*	30.8	11.6	—
Paraguay			
1990[5]	42.2	12.7	0.447
1996[4]	46.3	16.3	0.493
1999	60.6	33.9	0.565
2001*	61.8	36.1	—
Peru			
1997	47.6	25.1	0.532
1999	48.6	22.4	0.545
2001*	49.0	23.2	—
Dominican Rep.			
1997	37.2	14.4	0.517
2001*	29.2	10.9	—
Uruguay			
1990[4]	17.8	3.4	0.492
1997[4]	9.5	1.7	0.430
1999[4]	9.4	1.8	0.440
2001*	12.5	2.8	—
Venezuela			
1990	40.0	14.6	0.471
1997	48.1	20.5	0.507
1999	49.4	21.7	0.498
2001	48.5	21.2	—

Source: ECLAC (2002)

Notes
*Estimates based on microsimulations keeping the Gini coefficient constant
1 Estimate for per capita household incomes
2 Gran Buenos Aires
3 Eight largest cities and El Alto
4 Total urban
5 Metropolitan area of Asunción

Table A3.5 Microsimulations: main labour market adjustment impact on poverty and inequality

	Nominal devaluation			Foreign savings increase			Export subsidy increase			Productivity shock		
	Poverty incidence	Gini p.c. income	Gini labour income	Poverty incidence	Gini p.c. income	Gini labour income	Poverty incidence	Gini p.c. income	Gini labour income	Poverty incidence	Gini p.c. income	Gini labour income
Argentina	6	5	5	6	5	5	6	5	5	5	5	5
Bolivia	2	4	4	2	4	4	2	4	4	2	4	4
Brazil*	2	2	6	n.c.	n.c.	n.c.	6	2	6	6	2	6
Colombia*	6	6	2	6	6	2	6	6	2	6	6	2
Costa Rica	3	3	3	3	6a	6a	3	3	3	3	3	6a
Cuba												
Chile	4	7	4	3	3	3	3	3	3	6	3	3
Ecuador	5	5	5	5	5	5	5	5	5	5	5	4
El Salvador	3	3	3	4	7	4	3	3	4	4	3	3
Honduras	5	4	4	6	4	7	6	4	7	5	6	4
Mexico	6	5	5	6	3	5	6	5	5	6	6	5
Paraguay	3	3	6	4	4	6	4	4	4	2	2	4
Peru	2	2	4	5	2	3	4	4	4	2	2	4
Dominican Republic	6	3	3	2	2	2	6	5	2	2	2	5
Uruguay	6	5	5	6	5	5	5	5	7	6	5	5
Venezuela*	2	2	2	2	2	2	6	6	6	6	2	2
Argentina		5	5	5			5	5	6		5	5
Bolivia		2	4	4		2	4	4	2		4	4
Brazil*		2	2	2		6	2	6	6		2	6

(Continued)

Table A3.5 (Continued)

	Tariff cut			FTAA scenario			WTO scenario		
	Poverty incidence	Gini p.c. income	Gini labour income	Poverty incidence	Gini p.c. income	Gini labour income	Poverty incidence	Gini p.c. income	Gini labour income
Colombia*	6	6	2	6	6	2	6	6	2
Costa Rica	3	3	6a	3	3	6a	3	3	6a
Cuba	5	5	5	2	2	2	5	5	5
Chile	6	3	3	6	7	3	6	3	3
Ecuador	5	5	5	5	5	5	5	5	5
El Salvador	3	3	3	7	3	3	3	3	4
Honduras	6	4	7	6	4	7	6	4	7
Mexico	5	5	5	5	5	5	5	5	5
Paraguay	4	4	4	4	3	6	3	4	3
Peru	2	2	2	2	2	3	2	2	3
Dominican Republic	6	5	5	6	5	5	2	2	3
Uruguay	6	n.c.	n.c.	6	5	5	6	5	5
Venezuela*	6	2	2	2	6	6	2	2	2

Source: Authors' calculations

Notes:

Phase	Symbol	Definition
1	P	Participation rate
2	U	Unemployment rate
3	S1	Employment structure by sectors
4	O	Employment by occupational category
5	W1	Remuneration structure
6	W2	Change in mean remuneration level
6a	W1 + W2	Combined effect of W1 and W2
7	M	Employment structure by education level
*		Only two phases simulated (U + W2)
n.c.		No change from baseline

Notes

1 The model is in the family of trade-focused CGE models developed by Dervis *et al.* (1982) and Robinson *et al.* (1999). The model is implemented in the GAMS modelling language. The description given in the text draws on the monograph by Löfgren *et al.* (2001).
2 See Table A3.1 for a formal description of the model.
3 See Lewis (1954) and Ranis and Fei (1961).
4 Armington (1969).
5 See, for example, Dervis *et al.* (1982), de Melo and Robinson (1989), Devarajan *et al.* (1990, 1993), de Melo and Tarr (1992) and Thierfelder and Robinson (2002).
6 The theoretical properties of the real exchange rate in this model are worked out in Devarajan *et al.* (1993).
7 This is an example of a macro 'closure' of the CGE model. Other examples will be discussed below.
8 There are exceptions in the public finance literature where government is treated as analogous to a household, with its own utility function. See Shoven and Whalley (1992).
9 See, for example, Sen (1963), Taylor (1983, 1990), Rattsø (1982), Robinson (1989, 1991) and Dewatripont and Michel (1987). For a recent discussion of macro closure issues in CGE models, see Robinson (2003).
10 Malinvaud (1977) discusses the different notions of 'equilibrium' in macro and general equilibrium models.
11 See Taylor (1983, 1990).
12 The multiplier process works through changes in the real wage. An increase in final demand (e.g. investment or government demand) requires an increase in savings, which requires an increase in income, which requires an increase in output, which requires an increase in employment, which requires a decrease in the real wage (as firms are assumed to be on their demand curves for labour).
13 To the extent the CGE differentiates various groups of households, it does account for the feedback effects of changes in their relative incomes and consumption levels on the rest of the economy through differences in spending behaviour across those household groups.
14 Such an integrated analysis requires a modelling framework that can accommodate many households, using the household survey data. It is not necessary to model all the households in a sample survey. For a discussion of the use of 'representative' households in models, see Löfgren *et al.* (2003).
15 See Bourguignon *et al.* (2002a) for an overview of related methods. It should be noted that the approach is fairly new in its application to the developing country context, but that combinations of macro or CGE policy models and microsimulations, for instance to assess distributional effects of tax reforms, are quite common in applications in developed countries.
16 It should be noted that both Orcutt and Oaxaca–Blinder essentially involve accounting methods assuming fixed positions of workers and household groups. For a recent overview of applications of microsimulation approaches for assessing the impact of government policies in OECD countries, see Gupta and Kapur (2000).
17 The possibility of incorporating conditional probabilities to decide which individuals change status within the labour force will be explored in future research.
18 Experiments with the methodology for several household survey data sets show that about 30 iterations are sufficient. Repeating the simulations a larger number of times does not alter the results.
19 Mean incomes per decile are calculated in the simulations. These means are subsequently assigned to newly employed or to already employed persons who changed sector of employment, occupational category or moved from one educational group to

another. In principle, to assess the impact of changes in the labour market structure, one would have to calibrate the database prior to simulating the effect of said changes – that is, replace the original labour incomes by mean incomes per decile. A test showed that both the direction of change and the magnitude of the effect do not change if one uses the original values of the labour incomes instead of calibrated values.

20   The external closure in the Cuban model is slightly more complex as it assumes a dual foreign exchange market. The exchange rate is fixed in the official market and flexible in the informal segment.

21   We did the experiment this way because the base-year level of foreign savings was positive in some countries and negative in others.

22   We are grateful to E. Díaz Bonilla and X. Diao of IFPRI for generating this vector of world market prices. For a description of the GTAP model, see Hertel and Tsigas (1997).

23   Information detailed by country can be found in Table A3.5. Estimations may differ from official national estimates, as well as to those reported by the country authors, due to adjustments made by ECLAC to keep income definitions comparable over time (and as much as possible, across countries), to deal with non-reported incomes, to deal with statistical discrepancies between household surveys and national accounts data and are, last but not in the least, due to differences in poverty lines. The direction of change should be emphasized therefore, rather than the precise estimates.

References

Almeida dos Reis, José G. and Ricardo Paes de Barros (1991) 'Wage inequality and the distribution of education: A study of the evolution of regional differences in inequality in metropolitan Brazil', *Journal of Development Economics*, 36: 117–43.

Armington, Paul A. (1969) 'A theory of demand for products distinguished by place of production', *IMF Staff Papers* 16(1): 159–78.

Blinder, Alan (1973) 'Wage discrimination: reduced form and structural estimates', *Journal of Human Resources*, 8: 436–55.

Bourguignon, François, Francisco Ferreira and Nora Lustig (2001a) 'MIDD: the microeconomics of income distribution dynamics. A comparative analysis of selected developing countries', Paper presented at the Latin American Meeting of the Econometric Society, Buenos Aires, July (mimeo).

Bourguignon, F., M. Fournier and M. Gurgand (2001b) 'Fast development with stable income distribution: Taiwan, 1979–1994', *Review of Income and Wealth*, 43(3): 139–64.

Bourguignon, François, Luis Pereira da Silva and Nicholas Stern (2002a) 'Evaluating the poverty impact of economic policies: some analytical challenges', Washington, DC: The World Bank (mimeo).

Bourguignon, François, Anne-Sophie Robilliard and Sherman Robinson (2002b), 'Representative versus real households in the macro-economic modeling of inequality', Washington, DC: World Bank and IFPRI (mimeo).

De Jong, Niek (2001) 'Decomposing changes in poverty and inequality: the case of urban Panama in the 1990s', Paper presented in the Economic Research Seminar, Institute of Social Studies, The Hague (mimeo).

De Melo, Jaime and Sherman Robinson (1989) 'Product differentiation and the treatment of foreign trade in computable general equilibrium models of small economies', *Journal of International Economics*, 27(1–2): 47–67.

De Melo, Jaime and David Tarr (1992) *A General Equilibrium Analysis of US Foreign Trade Policy*, Cambridge, MA: The MIT Press.

Dervis, Kemal, Jaime de Melo and Sherman Robinson (1982) *General Equilibrium Models for Development Policy*, Cambridge: Cambridge University Press.

Devarajan, Shantayanan, Jeffrey D. Lewis and Sherman Robinson (1990), 'Policy lessons from trade-focused two-sector models,' *Journal of Policy Modeling*, 12(4): 625–57.

Devarajan, Shantayanan, Jeffrey D. Lewis and Sherman Robinson (1993) 'External shocks, purchasing power parity, and the equilibrium real exchange rate', *World Bank Economic Review*, 7(1): 45–63.

Dewatripont, M. and G. Michel (1987) 'On closure rules, homogeneity, and dynamics in applied general equilibrium models', *Journal of Development Economics*, 26(1): 65–76.

ECLAC (2002) *Panorama Social de América Latina y el Caribe, 2002*, Santiago: Economic Commission for Latin America and the Caribbean.

Frenkel, Roberto and Martin González Rozada (2000) 'Liberalización del balance de pagos. Efectos sobre el crecimiento, el empleo y los ingresos en Argentina – Segunda parte', Buenos Aires: CEDES (mimeo).

Ganuza, Enrique, Ricardo Paes de Barros and Rob Vos (2002) 'Labour market adjustment, poverty and inequality during liberalisation', in: Rob Vos, Lance Taylor and Ricardo Paes de Barros, R. (eds) *Economic Liberalisation, Distribution and Poverty: Latin America in the 1990s*, Cheltenham (UK) and Northampton (US): Edward Elgar Publishers, pp. 54–88.

Gupta, Anil and Vishnu Kapur (eds) (2000) *Microsimulation in Government Policy and Forecasting*, Amsterdam: North-Holland.

Hertel, T.W. and M.E. Tsigas (1997), Structure of GTAP, in: T.W. Hertel (ed.) *Global Trade Analysis: Modeling and Applications,* Cambridge: Cambridge University Press.

Lewis, W. Arthur (1954) 'Economic development with unlimited supplies of labour', *Manchester School* 22(2) (May): 140–91.

Löfgren, Hans, Rebecca Lee Harris and Sherman Robinson (2001) 'A standard computable general equilibrium (CGE) model in GAMS', TMD Discussion Paper No. 75, Washington, DC: International Food Policy Research Institute (IFPRI).

Löfgren, Hans, Sherman Robinson and Mohamed El-Said (2003) 'Poverty and inequality analysis in a general equilibrium framework: the representative household approach', in: François Bourguignon and Luis Pereira da Silva (eds) *Evaluating the Poverty and Distributional Impact of Economic Policies*, Washington, DC: The World Bank and Oxford University Press.

Malinvaud, Edmund (1977) *The Theory of Unemployment Reconsidered*, Oxford: Basil Blackwell.

Oaxaca, Ronald (1973) 'Male–female wage differentials in urban labour markets', *International Economic Review*, 14: 673–709.

Orcutt, Guy H. (1957) 'A new type of socio-economic system', *Review of Economics and Statistics* 80: 1081–1100.

Paes de Barros, Ricardo (1999) 'Evaluando el impacto de cambios en la estructura salarial y del empleo sobre la distribución de renta', IPEA, Rio de Janeiro (mimeo).

Paes de Barros, Ricardo and Philippe Leite (1998) 'O Impacto da Liberaliçao sobre Distribuiçao de Renda no Brasil', IPEA, Rio de Janeiro (mimeo).

Ranis, Gustav and John Fei (1961) 'A theory of economic development', *American Economic Review* 51: 533–65.

Rattsø, Jørn (1982) 'Different macroclosures of the original Johansen model and their impact on policy evaluation', *Journal of Policy Modeling* 4(1): 85–97.

Robinson, Sherman (1989) 'Multisectoral models', in H. Chenery and T.N. Srinivasan (eds) *Handbook of Development Economics*, Volume 2, Amsterdam: North-Holland, pp. 886–947.

Robinson, Sherman (1991) 'Macroeconomics, financial variables, and computable general equilibrium models', *World Development,* 19(11): 1509–25.

Robinson, Sherman (2003) 'Macro models and SAM multipliers: Leontief, Stone, Keynes and CGE models', Paper presented at Conference 'Poverty, Inequality and Development' in Honor of Erik Thorbecke, Ithaca: Cornell University (October).

Robinson, Sherman, Antonio Yuñez-Naude, Raúl Hinojosa, Jeffrey D. Lewis and Shantayanan Devarajan (1999) 'From stylized to applied models: Building multisector CGE models for policy analysis', *The North-American Journal of Economics and Finance* 10: 39–67.

Sen, Amartya K. (1963) 'Neo-classical and neo-Keynesian theories of distribution', *Economic Record* 39: 53–66.

Shoven, John B. and John Whalley (1992) *Applying General Equilibrium*, Cambridge: Cambridge University Press.

Taylor, Lance (1983) *Structuralist Macroeconomics. Applicable Models for the Third World*, New York: Basic Books.

Taylor, Lance (1990) 'Structuralist CGE models', in: Lance Taylor (ed.) *Socially Relevant Policy Analysis*, Cambridge, MA: MIT Press.

Taylor, Lance and Rob Vos (2002) Balance of payments liberalization in Latin America: effects on growth, distribution and poverty', in: Rob Vos, Lance Taylor and Ricardo Paes de Barros (eds) *Economic Liberalization, Distribution and Poverty: Latin America in the 1990s*, Cheltenham (UK), Northampton (US): Edward Elgar Publishers, pp. 1–53.

Thierfelder, Karen and Sherman Robinson (2002) 'An analysis of the skilled–unskilled wage gap using a general equilibrium trade model', TMD Discussion Paper No. 93, Washington, DC: International Food Policy Research Institute.

UNDP, ECLAC and IPEA (2003) *Meeting the Millennium Poverty Reduction Targets in Latin America and the Caribbean*, Santiago: Economic Commission for Latin America and the Caribbean (with UNDP and IPEA).

Vos, Rob, Lance Taylor and Ricardo Paes de Barros (eds) (2002) *Economic Liberalisation, Distribution and Poverty: Latin America in the 1990s*, Cheltenham (UK) and Northampton (US): Edward Elgar Publishers.

4   Argentina – the convertibility plan, trade openness, poverty and inequality

Carolina Díaz-Bonilla, Eugenio Díaz-Bonilla, Valeria Piñeiro and Sherman Robinson

Abstract

Argentina's economy and society underwent dramatic changes during the 1990s. The economy entered a period of higher growth and low inflation after the 1991 Convertibility Plan created a currency board and the economy was liberalized, privatized and deregulated. A puzzling fact was that even during the periods of high growth, unemployment began to increase, eventually reaching levels not experienced before in Argentina's modern history. Poverty and income distribution indicators deteriorated significantly. The collapse of the whole economic programme in late 2001 and early 2002 has given rise to many interpretations. This chapter focuses on a limited set of issues, linked to trade and balance-of-payments developments, and their impact on poverty and income distribution during the 1990s. In particular, it analyses the separate impact of ten possible policy scenarios: changes in trade protection, a devaluation of the peso, overall improvements in productivity in Argentina, terms of trade and capital flows shocks, an increase in export subsidies, the possible implementation of a Free Trade Area of the Americas (FTAA) and a comprehensive global agreement in the World Trade Organization (WTO) negotiations.

To evaluate the impact of the different policies, we combine a relatively detailed computable general equilibrium model of Argentina and microsimulations utilizing household surveys. Policy changes are simulated one at a time, and poverty and income distribution indices recomputed. The simulations show that trade liberalization helped to reduce poverty, with a decrease of or no effect on income inequality. A devaluation would worsen poverty, although it may help expand employment by a small amount and put the external accounts on a sounder footing going forward (which requires a dynamic framework to analyse). The pure, static trade effects of increased capital flows has a negative impact on exports and poverty, but a full evaluation requires a dynamic framework. Increases in export prices and export subsidies increase poverty slightly, although the extreme poor are better off and inequality is lower under the higher export price and export subsidies scenarios. Finally, a generalized (exogenous) productivity increase will reduce poverty and increase employment.

4.1 Introduction

In Argentina, as in most Latin American countries, the decade of the 1990s began with high hopes: growth had picked up after the disappointing 1980s, inflation was down and capital flows were streaming back to the region (see Table 4.1). Argentina's economic policies since 1991 (commonly known as the 'Convertibility Plan' because of the popular name of the currency board arrangement at the heart of the economic programme) seemed to usher in a new era of growth and stability. The second half of the 1990s in Latin America has been far less encouraging. In Argentina, the economic deceleration of the second half of the 1990s turned into an all-out crisis with the economy imploding in 2002. However, a puzzling fact of Argentina's experience has been that unemployment climbed up steadily even during the times of rapid growth. Obviously, once economic growth declined and finally collapsed in 2001–2, unemployment and poverty rates jumped to levels not experienced before in modern times in the country's history.

There have been different analyses of the causes of economic problems in Argentina, but all agree that the country's tragedy is the result of a combination of factors: external shocks, both economic and political; weak internal economic policies and fragile domestic political and institutional frameworks (see, for example, Díaz-Bonilla and Schamis 2001; Calvo *et al.* 2002; De la Torre *et al.* 2002; Mussa 2002; Perry and Serven 2002). Disentangling the specific contribution

Table 4.1 Argentina: main economic indicators, 1970–2001

	1970s	*1980s*	*1990–4*	*1995–9*	*2000–1*
Growth % change year	2.9	(0.7)	6.8	2.2	(2.6)
Inflation % change year	132.9	565.7	505.1	0.8	(0.8)
Unemployment % year	4.3	4.8	8.4	15.6	16.2
Poverty % year	8.0[1]	17.9[2]	21.8	26.3	32.2
Public sector deficit % GDP[3]	n.a.	(3.8)	0.2	(1.8)	(2.6)
Public sector deficit % GDP[4]	n.a.	n.a.	(1.6)	(3.3)	(5.0)
Public debt US dollars (average in millions)	n.a.	n.a.	75,375	115,809	158,479
Public debt US dollars (average in millions)	n.a.	n.a.	25,700	32,870	37,882
Current account balance % GDP[5]	1.4	(3.1)	(1.5)	(3.6)	(2.4)
Trade balance % GDP[5]	2.5	2.0	—	(1.5)	0.9
External debt US dollars (average in millions)	9,636	48,717	67,168	125,095	146,172
Public external debt	4,039	31,566	47,774	69,264	86,599
Total debt service % exports[5]	31.7	56.4	30.8	50.7	71.3

Source: World Bank, WDI; IMF
Notes
1 Only 1974
2 1980–8
3 Central Government World Bank
4 Central and provincial public sector IMF
5 For the 1970s, information available covers 1976–9

of the different factors exceeds the purpose of this chapter. Here, we rather focus on a more limited set of issues, linked to trade and balance-of-payments developments, and their impact on poverty and income distribution.

Specifically, the policies considered include changes in trade protection, a devaluation of the peso, overall improvements in productivity in Argentina, terms of trade and capital flows shocks, an increase in export subsidies and, looking to the future, the implementation of a FTAA and a global agreement for the WTO negotiations launched at Doha, Qatar, in November 2001. Trade liberalization has been singled out by some analyses as the main reason for the increase in unemployment and poverty. An overvalued exchange rate and the perceived lack of competitiveness of Argentina's exports feature in many evaluations of that country's problems (Feldstein 2002; Perry and Serven 2002). External shocks in the form of changes in export and import prices, or in the levels of capital flows, have been further emphasized as contributors to Argentina's performance (Calvo *et al.* 2002). Others have noticed the important improvements in productivity during the period 1990–8, and linked it to the general policies followed during the 1990s (Pou 1998; Kehoe 2002). Finally, future scenarios of trade negotiations, particularly a WTO agreement including the elimination of distortions in agricultural markets, help to visualize the impact on Argentina of current protectionist policies, mainly in industrialized countries.

To evaluate the impact of the different policies, we use a computable general equilibrium (CGE) model of Argentina and a microsimulations framework. Discrete changes in trade policies and related balance-of-payments events are simulated one at a time, and the impacts on the variables of interest for the analysis of poverty and income distribution are imposed on the microsimulations. Employment, its sectoral, skill and gender composition, and wages are modified according to the CGE results, and the estimated regressions for sector of employment and income allocate people and households to different (un)employment categories and income levels. Poverty and income distribution indices are then recomputed from household data.

The rest of the chapter is organized as follows.[1] The next section presents an overview of the economic policy framework and performance in Argentina from 1990 to early 2002. In Section 4.3 trade policies and the current account are discussed. Section 4.4 presents the CGE model and the results of the simulations performed. Section 4.5 discusses the methodology for the microsimulations and the impacts on poverty and income distribution. Section 4.6 concludes the chapter.

4.2 General policy framework and economic performance

In March 1991, Congress passed the Convertibility Law, which pegged the peso one-to-one to the dollar[2] and transformed the monetary and exchange rate functions of the Central Bank in effect into a currency board (see Liviatan 1993). The Central Bank had to maintain liquid international reserves to cover (almost) 100 per cent of the monetary base (but not broader monetary aggregates), and thus could not increase the monetary base except when international reserves expanded

Table 4.2   Growth indicators for Argentina, 1961–2000

	Import substitution (1961–75)	Pre-debt crisis (1976-81)	Debt crisis (1982–90)	Convertibility (1991–2001)	Total (1961–2001)
GDP growth (% year)	3.7	1.5	−0.9	3.9	2.4
% time in recessions	26.7	50	55.6	36.4	39
CV (absolute value)[1]	1.2	4.3	6	1.6	2.3

Source: World Bank, WDI
Note: 1 Coefficient of variation: standard deviation/mean (absolute value) of GDP growth rate

(through trade surplus or net capital inflows).[3] Since then, the exchange rate remained fixed for about 11 years (until early 2002), the longest period of exchange rate stability in more than half a century.[4]

Along with the stabilization component, there were wide-ranging structural reforms that included trade liberalization, privatization of public enterprises and deregulation of markets. Trade quotas were significantly reduced, import tariffs were cut, about 90 per cent of public enterprises were privatized, the economy was opened to foreign investment and a significant number of regulatory laws and public agencies were abolished.

From 1991 to 1994 the country experienced high rates of economic growth, averaging about 9 per cent per year. The complete period of the Convertibility Plan (1991–2001) experienced higher growth rates than the 1980s, which were slightly higher than in the import substitution industrialization (ISI) period (running up until 1975). However, the ISI phase was clearly less volatile than the Convertibility Plan (Table 4.2).

Inflation rates declined dramatically, from about 3,100 per cent per year in 1989 and 2,300 per cent in 1990 to about 4.2 per cent in 1994. The real exchange rate (RER) began to appreciate in 1990 until about 1994, thereafter very slowly depreciating in real terms against the US dollar when inflation first converged to and then dropped below international (US) inflation rates. Inflows of foreign capital and expansionary fiscal and monetary policies further increased aggregate demand in a procyclical manner. This led to rapid credit creation and increased public expenditures, which fuelled the consumption boom and high economic growth of 1991–4.

The combination of a fixed exchange rate regime, with an initial value for the peg that appeared 'too tight', trade liberalization and expansionary monetary and fiscal policies had negative effects on sectors producing tradable goods, some of which shrunk under foreign competition, while others reoriented production towards the domestic market and/or resorted to fast technological innovation to compete in the new economic environment. High growth and appreciation of the RER caused trade balances to move from surpluses in 1989–90 to deficits that peaked at about 5 per cent of GDP in 1994 (measured in real terms).

After the hyperinflations of 1989–90, real wages [deflated by the consumer price index (CPI)] recovered and increased from 1991 to 1993, stabilized in 1994

Table 4.3 Argentina: real wages

	1960s	1970s	1980s	1990s
Consumption wage[1]	2,624	2,983	3,166	2,243
Production wage[2]	2,201	2,723	2,915	3,143
Dollar wage official exchange rate[3]	5,230	9,081	7,040	8,254
Dollar wage World Bank adjusted exchange rate[4]	5,231	6,073	5,292	8,258

Source: World Bank data, INDEC
Notes
1 Nominal salary in pesos deflated by CPI 1990
2 Nominal salary in pesos deflated by GDP deflator 1990
3 Nominal salary in pesos transformed in current US dollars using the official exchange rate and deflated by US CPI 1995
4 Nominal salary in pesos transformed in current US dollars using the official exchange rate adjusted by the World Bank and deflated by US CPI 1995

and dropped afterwards. However, even at their peak they stayed below the levels of previous decades. Yet, wages in dollars and deflated by the GDP deflator, which better reflected the cost of labour from the producer's point of view, clearly increased during the 1990s (Table 4.3). Also, there was a 30 per cent decline of the relative price of capital with respect to labour during 1990–4 (IMF 1995). All considered, and although the economy grew at about 7 per cent annually during 1991–4, employment increased only by 1.6 per cent during a comparable period (IMF 1995). In fact, there was not much creation of full-time jobs during the 1990s. As a result, unemployment, which moved between 4 and 8 per cent for most of the period previous to the Convertibility Plan, began to climb steadily from the mid-1990s, even in a context of economic growth (Table 4.1).

After the Mexican crisis of 1995, Argentina grew at 4.3 per cent in 1996 and at a strong 8.4 per cent in 1997. The full implementation of MERCOSUR in 1995, plus strong growth and a progressively overvalued exchange rate in Brazil as a consequence of the Real Plan of 1994, helped Argentina's return to growth in the following years. Another important development was that world agricultural prices strengthened significantly during 1996–7 (see Díaz-Bonilla *et al.* 2003). However, unemployment, although declining, remained high at about 17 per cent in 1996 and 14 per cent in 1997. On the other hand, inflation dropped to 0.1–0.3 per cent in 1996–7, and then became negative.

Poverty and income distribution, which were worsening during the hyper-inflationary episodes of 1989–90, improved somewhat during the first half of the 1990s (the golden period of the Convertibility Plan) only to deteriorate since the mid-1990s.

Another worrisome trend was the slow but steady weakening of fiscal accounts, and the accumulation of public debt (Table 4.1). Part of the problem was related to the change from the previous pay-as-you-go social security system to the new scheme based mostly on private accounts. Yet, while fiscal accounts were deteriorating, the supportive international environment of the first part of the 1990s (declining interest rates, rising capital flows to emerging economies and a depreciating dollar) reversed after a sequence of external financial crises in Asia (1997), Russia (1998) and Brazil (1999). The higher agricultural prices of 1996–7 collapsed in the wake of the Asian crisis, and capital flows to emerging markets dried up after the Russian crisis of 1998. In addition, the dollar had begun to appreciate since the mid-1990s, while in 1999 Brazil devalued its exchange rate, exporting part of its crisis to Argentina.

From 1998, the economic performance deteriorated significantly, posting negative growth rates in every year from 1999 to 2002. The economy is estimated to have collapsed by about 12 per cent in 2002, unemployment soared to 22 per cent and more than 50 per cent of the population dropped below the poverty line. While the collapse in growth since 1999 certainly explains to a great extent the evolution of unemployment and poverty, the question is why there were problems in those variables even during the period of rapid growth.

4.3 Current account and trade performances

After the hyperinflation and economic recession of 1989–90, when Argentina posted a current account surplus, the current account turned negative at an average of about 3.5 per cent of GDP during the 1990s (and 4.5 per cent at the end of the decade). The deterioration of the current account was mainly associated with debt accumulation and rising import demand (see the decomposition of the changes in the current account in Table 4.4). However, and contrary to the view that links the current account deficit to government borrowing (see, for instance, Feldstein 2002), the increase in external debt was mainly the result of private sector decisions, which explained a larger share of accumulated debt during the 1990s than public sector external indebtedness. Also, the argument that Argentina's exports declined for lack of competitiveness does not fit the facts: exports gained market share in the world markets since the beginning of the 1980s. In fact, Argentina's exports of goods and services more than doubled between 1992 and 2001, growing faster than Brazil, Chile, other Latin American countries (excluding Mexico) and OECD countries during that period. The change in the trade balance is basically explained by increased imports. And, again, contrary to some interpretations (Feldstein 2002) the causality for those increased imports seems to depend on the dynamics of private capital: business opportunities in Argentina generated increases in external borrowing and foreign direct investment, which helped maintain growth rates and an appreciated exchange rate leading to growing imports.

Although exports grew faster than in comparable countries, the additional foreign exchange earnings generated by the economy at large (and not just those related to external borrowing and investment decisions) did not keep up with the increase in international factor payments associated with the rising external debt and stock of FDI (see Tables 4.5 and 4.6). The debt service-to-GDP ratio progressively deteriorated, reaching levels comparable to those of the 1980s debt crisis. Along with worsening solvency indicators for the public sector, these

Table 4.4 Argentina: decomposition of current account deficit (per cent GNP)

Period average Weights	1980–2 1976–9 (1)	1983–6 1980–2 (2)	1987–90 1983–6 (3)	1991–5 1987–90 (4)	1996–9 1991–5 (5)
Observed deficit increase	−0.32	−1.59	−3.44	8.01	8.82
External shocks					
Total	−1.00	0.38	11.07	−0.75	−2.91
Terms trade deterioration	−2.81	3.30	−1.09	2.59	2.39
Import price effect	−2.01	3.23	−1.75	−0.74	−0.88
Export price effect	−0.80	0.07	0.66	3.33	3.27
Interest rate shock	2.37	−1.80	14.60	−2.73	−2.71
World trade retardation	−0.56	−1.12	−2.44	−0.61	−2.59
Other external variables					
Total	−2.90	5.04	−2.88	22.45	36.52
Debt accumulation burden	0.10	5.95	−3.85	19.79	34.38
Change in direct investment income	−3.03	−0.93	1.65	2.23	1.62
Change in remittances	0.01	0.02	−0.68	0.42	0.56
Change in public transfers	0.01	0.00	0.00	0.00	−0.05
Domestic policy actions					
Total	4.13	−2.73	0.61	5.99	8.60
Domestic spending	0.30	−0.05	−0.06	0.04	0.11
Consumption contraction	0.44	0.29	0.00	−0.03	−0.06
Investment reduction	−0.14	−0.34	−0.06	0.07	0.17
Private investment	0.19	−0.29	0.00	0.18	0.05
Public investment	−0.33	−0.05	−0.05	−0.11	0.11
Trade ratios	3.82	−2.68	0.66	5.96	8.49
Import replacement	3.57	−2.55	0.23	5.87	9.89
Export penetration	0.25	−0.13	0.43	0.09	−1.40
Interaction effects					
Total	−0.55	−4.27	−12.24	−19.68	−33.39
Import shock	−1.12	−1.17	−0.05	−0.86	−1.62
Demand/unit imports	0.02	0.00	0.01	0.03	0.16
Displacement/price	−1.14	−1.17	−0.06	−0.89	−1.78
Export shock	−0.01	−0.01	0.24	0.16	0.97
Demand/unit exports	−0.04	−0.01	0.27	0.19	0.55
Penetration/price	0.03	0.00	−0.03	−0.03	0.42
Debt shock	0.58	−3.09	−12.43	−18.98	−32.74
Stock/interest	0.58	−3.09	−12.43	−18.98	−32.74

factors contributed to maintaining Argentina's country risk premium above that of countries such as Chile or Mexico. The current account decomposition suggests a different interpretation to the Argentine crisis, more in line with a modified version of the hypothesis of 'sudden stops' of capital flows (see Calvo *et al.* 2002): enhanced business opportunities in Argentina (including the overvalued peso that augmented profitability in non-tradables, but whose fixity ensured repayment of external debt and transfer of profits) led to a combination of decisions by the private sector regarding external indebtedness and the volume and allocation of investments (in general, and not only that of FDI) that did not support the intertemporal sustainability of the current account.

Table 4.5   Argentina: external debt, public and private, and FDI

	1991	1995	1999	2001
Total debt (million US dollars)	61,337	99,147	145,289	140,190
Public	52,739	67,192	84,750	88,250
Private	8,598	31,955	60,539	51,940
Change over 1991 (million US dollars)		37,810	83,952	78,853
Public		14,453	32,011	35,511
Private		23,357	51,941	43,342
Contribution to change (%)		100.0	100.0	100.0
Public		38.2	38.1	45.0
Private		61.8	61.9	55.0
FDI total (million US dollars)	11,524	27,991	61,926	75,998
Change over 1991 (million US dollars)		16,467	50,402	64,474

Source: MECON Argentina

Table 4.6   Argentina: relative growth of exports[1] (index base 1991 = 1)

Against	1991–4	1995–9	2000
Brazil	0.95	1.25	1.17
Chile	1.02	1.13	1.08
Mexico	0.98	0.88	0.62
LAC-Mexico	1.00	1.18	1.08
East Asia and Pacific	0.92	0.87	0.72
Low and middle income	0.99	1.08	0.91
Upper middle income	1.01	1.11	0.94
High income OECD	1.06	1.38	1.36
World	1.04	1.29	1.21

Note: 1 Argentina's exports in current US dollars/other country or region exports

4.4 Structure of the CGE model and simulation results

To estimate the impacts of different shocks and policies in Argentina, we utilized a modified version of the standard CGE model (see the general description in Löfgren *et al.* 2001). The first main change from the standard framework is the inclusion of a cash-in-advance technology (Clower 1967) that can be utilized to anchor the nominal variables.[5] If all nominal variables are free to move, money is a 'veil' and the model behaves as in the classical dichotomy in Walrasian models between the determination of relative prices and the determination of absolute levels (Patinkin 1965). If there is any rigidity in a nominal variable, then changes in money supply or demand will have real effects. The cash-in-advance technology combines constraints for both consumption sales (Feenstra 1986) and production (Fischer 1974), equally weighted.

Second, the modified model includes real wage variables, defined as consumption wages (i.e. nominal wages deflated by the CPI). There is a real wage for the whole economy, but also by sector, which allow modelling different degrees of real wage rigidity among sectors (perhaps because of unions or some forms of sectoral efficiency wages). With fixed real wages the equilibrating variables are total and sectoral employment and the wage gaps between sectors.

Data for the model are included in a social accounting matrix (SAM) that corresponds to national accounts, trade data and household surveys for 1993. This year captures the beginning of the impact of the 1991 programme. The SAM includes 44 sectors ('activities') and commodities, 9 factors of production and the standard accounts for households, firms, the government and the rest of the world. The final SAM is disaggregated into 11 primary agricultural products, 4 non-agricultural primary sectors, 11 food-manufacturing sectors, 14 non-food-manufacturing sectors, 3 service sectors and the government. The nine factors of production include eight labour types and capital. The labour force is divided among rural male and female labour (2), and urban unskilled, urban semiskilled and urban skilled male and female labour (6). Unskilled labour is defined as those with at most completed primary schooling. Semi skilled labour means those who have no more than a high school education or vocational training, while those with university education or more are considered skilled labour.

The closures are as follows. For the labour markets, the model considers the existence of unemployment, allows labour to be mobile across sectors and maintains fixed real (consumption) wages by sectors. In terms of capital, total national stock is fixed at the 1993 levels, but its sectoral allocation may vary (i.e. capital is mobile across sectors). Therefore, the results of the simulations reflect a time horizon in which capital stock can be redeployed in the economy.

Argentina had a fixed exchange rate during this period, and capital flows are considered exogenous, therefore the nominal exchange rate and the level of capital flows are fixed in the model, except in the devaluation simulation in which the money supply is fixed and the level of capital flows (i.e. foreign savings) is flexible. For the government, the level of the real deficit and its consumption of real goods and services are fixed across simulations. Income taxes are changed to adjust public sector accounts (which are affected by changes in import taxes in several simulations, or simply by changes in the nominal value of expenditures due to movements in prices). Investment demands for capital goods and inventories are kept constant in real values, and savings by households are adjusted.

There are ten simulations. In the first two simulations (labelled TARINCR and TARDECR in the tables), we estimated the effects of a 50 per cent increase and 50 per cent decrease in tariffs, respectively. Trade restrictions are measured as *ad valorem* tariff equivalents.

Then, there are two simulations of future trade scenarios: a possible FTAA (labelled ALCA, the Spanish acronym for FTAA) and an agreement under the current WTO negotiations initiated in November 2001 (OMC). The simulations impose on the country CGE model the world prices and the import tariff levels assumed to result from each agreement. The WTO scenario is a generalized liberalization across sectors, so all import tariffs are set to zero. Changes in world prices in dollar terms, which are exogenous, were calculated separately using the multicountry International Food Policy Research Institute model from the Trade and Macroeconomic Division.[6]

As mentioned before, the 1991 programme seems to have triggered important changes in productivity, which was figured at the time as a reason for the weak employment generation. There may be several reasons for the improvements in productivity that took place during the 1990s. First, trade liberalization may affect a country's productivity through different channels: learning by doing, access to new knowledge and scale effects of increased exports; technological spill-over due to greater availability of better capital and intermediate goods for production and increases in competition in previously protected domestic markets. Second, it has also been argued that monetary stability led to further improvements in productivity to the extent that entrepreneurs would not be distracted by the financial arrangements needed to survive in the previously highly inflationary environment. Thus, in the fifth simulation (ALPHASH) we calculate the effects of a 10 per cent increase in total factor productivity across sectors.

The analysis of the current account showed the importance of changes in capital flows to the Argentine economy. Net capital flows (measured as the difference in net total external debt) to Argentina increased by about 40 per cent between 1991 and 1994. Here, we simulate the effect of an increase in foreign savings by 10 per cent of total export value – about a 22 per cent increase (FSAVINCR).

Then, there are two other simulations of external shocks, in this case changes in the terms of trade: a 10 per cent across-the-board increase in import prices (PWMINCR) and a 10 per cent increase in the export price of agricultural products, both primary and agro-industrial (PWXINCR).

The final simulations are a 10 per cent increase in export subsidies (SUBEXIN) and a 10 per cent nominal devaluation of the Argentine peso (DEVAL).

Table 4.7 presents the main results: the components of real GDP, changes in the CPI, capital flows and the RER. Table 4.8 presents employment indicators by rural/urban, male/female, skill categories, and the aggregated sectors used in the microsimulations.

Increases in protection (TARINCR) and increased openness (TARDECR), as it should be expected, show opposite results. A tariff increase leads to declines in GDP (−0.3 per cent) and employment (−0.7 per cent, about 86,000 jobs), and increases in domestic prices measured by the CPI (1 per cent). With exogenous capital flows (and no changes in non-trade components of the current account), the decline in imports also leads to a decline in exports. Employment declines across all labour categories, with a larger incidence in primary activities (agriculture and others, including mining). On the other hand, increased openness through a 50 per cent decrease in all tariffs increases GDP, exports, imports and employment, leading to a gain of about 93,000 jobs.

The simulation for the FTAA (ALCA) also shows a small increase in GDP (0.4 per cent) and in employment (about 104,128 additional jobs over the base). Prices decline (−1 per cent) while exports and imports increase (about 4.3 and 3.5 per cent, respectively). Employment increases proportionally more for rural, male, unskilled workers, and in the primary sector.[7]

Table 4.7 Argentina – CGE policy simulations: macroeconomic outcomes

	Base	TARINCR	TARDECR	ALCA	OMC	ALPHASH	FSAVINCR	PWMINCR	PWXINCR	SUBEXIN	DEVAL
National accounts constant (million pesos)											
GDP market price	274,246	273,388	275,133	275,309	278,882	320,382	274,943	271,902	276,422	275,035	271,653
Private consumption	204,849	203,991	205,737	205,941	210,612	250,986	207,170	200,567	207,855	205,639	191,772
Fixed investment	47,879	47,879	47,879	47,879	47,879	47,879	47,879	47,879	47,879	47,879	47,879
Change in stocks	3,290	3,290	3,290	3,290	3,290	3,290	3,290	3,290	3,290	3,290	3,290
Government consumption	22,860	22,860	22,860	22,860	22,860	22,860	22,860	22,860	22,860	22,860	22,860
Exports	16,237	15,649	16,915	16,937	17,867	19,622	15,034	16,689	16,708	17,157	25,595
Imports	−20,870	−20,282	−21,548	−21,598	−23,626	−24,255	−21,291	−19,384	−22,170	−21,790	−19,743
National accounts constant (% change from base)											
GDP market price		−0.3	0.3	0.4	1.7	16.8	0.3	−0.9	0.8	0.3	−0.9
Private consumption		−0.4	0.4	0.5	2.8	22.5	1.1	−2.1	1.5	0.4	−6.4
Fixed investment		0.0	0.0	0.0	0.0	0.0	0.0	0.0	0.0	0.0	0.0
Change in stocks		0.0	0.0	0.0	0.0	0.0	0.0	0.0	0.0	0.0	0.0
Government consumption		0.0	0.0	0.0	0.0	0.0	0.0	0.0	0.0	0.0	0.0
Exports		−3.6	4.2	4.3	10.0	20.8	−7.4	2.8	2.9	5.7	57.6
Imports		−2.8	3.2	3.5	13.2	16.2	2.0	−7.1	6.2	4.4	−5.4
Other indicators											
CPI (% change from base)		1.04	−0.967	−0.937	6.655	0.899	2.196	−0.272	8.476	6.577	5.968
Net capital flows (million dollars)	7,547	7,547	7,547	7,547	7,547	7,547	9,170.7	7,547	7,547	7,547	−2,938
Real exchange rate (base = 100)	100.0	99.0	100.9	100.8	93.6	99.3	97.9	100.4	92.0	93.7	103.8

Table 4.8 Argentina – CGE policy simulations: employment and wages

	Base	TARCUT1	TARCUT2	ALCA	OMC	ALPHASH	FSAVINCR	PWMINCR	PWXINCR	SUBEXIN	DEVAL
Area											
Rural	2,131.0	2,111.4	2,152.2	2,154.7	2,204.2	2,584.4	2,131.1	2,095.0	2,172.0	2,152.3	2,170.6
Urban	10,521.0	10,454.9	10,592.5	10,601.4	10,832.3	11,879.2	10,521.8	10,393.8	10,646.8	10,591.2	10,614.7
Sex											
Male	8,248.9	8,190.6	8,312.5	8,320.3	8,515.5	9,333.1	8,235.3	8,155.8	8,362.0	8,310.1	8,437.1
Female	4,403.1	4,375.7	4,432.3	4,435.8	4,521.1	5,130.5	4,417.6	4,333.0	4,456.8	4,433.5	4,348.2
Labour category											
Unskilled[1]	3,902.0	3,875.1	3,931.2	3,934.6	4,009.3	4,426.0	3,898.7	3,855.0	3,952.4	3,932.4	3,966.9
Semiskilled[1]	4,003.9	3,981.4	4,028.0	4,031.2	4,101.5	4,498.0	4,008.3	3,955.0	4,045.9	4,029.2	4,006.7
Skilled[1]	2,615.2	2,598.4	2,633.4	2,635.6	2,721.5	2,955.2	2,614.9	2,583.8	2,648.5	2,629.7	2,641.2
Sector											
Primary	1,605.9	1,573.3	1,643.4	1,646.4	1,747.5	1,883.0	1,555.1	1,612.8	1,672.8	1,634.7	2,032.5
Industry	1,564.8	1,558.1	1,571.6	1,573.4	1,589.4	1,789.5	1,565.5	1,547.4	1,569.4	1,577.7	1,543.6
Electricity	88.2	87.8	88.7	88.7	90.3	102.4	88.9	86.7	89.2	88.7	84.7
Construction	739.6	736.7	742.7	742.8	749.5	742.2	739.9	733.3	743.3	743.5	739.6
Services	8,653.4	8,610.4	8,698.4	8,704.7	8,859.9	9,946.5	8,703.6	8,508.7	8,744.1	8,699.0	8,384.9
					Changes from base year						
Area											
Rural		-0.92	1.00	1.12	3.44	21.28	0.01	-1.69	1.93	1.00	1.86
Urban		-0.63	0.68	0.76	2.96	12.91	0.01	-1.21	1.20	0.67	0.89
Sex											
Male		-0.71	0.77	0.87	3.23	13.14	-0.16	-1.13	1.37	0.74	2.28
Female		-0.62	0.66	0.74	2.68	16.52	0.33	-1.59	1.22	0.69	-1.25
Labour category											
Unskilled[1]		-0.69	0.75	0.84	2.75	13.43	-0.08	-1.20	1.29	0.78	1.66
Semiskilled[1]		-0.56	0.60	0.68	2.44	12.34	0.11	-1.22	1.05	0.63	0.07
Skilled[1]		-0.64	0.70	0.78	4.06	13.00	-0.01	-1.20	1.27	0.56	0.99

(*Continued*)

Table 4.8 (Continued)

	Base	TARCUT1	TARCUT2	ALCA	OMC	ALPHASH	FSAVINCR	PWMINCR	PWXINCR	SUBEXIN	DEVAL
Sector											
Primary		-2.03	2.34	2.52	8.82	17.26	-3.16	0.43	4.17	1.79	26.57
Industry		-0.43	0.44	0.55	1.57	14.36	0.05	-1.11	0.30	0.82	-1.36
Electricity		-0.47	0.48	0.57	2.31	16.10	0.70	-1.77	1.04	0.49	-4.00
Construction		-0.39	0.42	0.43	1.34	0.35	0.04	-0.86	0.50	0.52	0.00
Services		-0.50	0.52	0.59	2.39	14.94	0.58	-1.67	1.05	0.53	-3.10
Total employment	12,652.0	12,566.4	12,744.8	12,756.1	13,036.6	14,463.6	12,652.9	12,488.8	12,818.8	12,743.5	12,785.3
Change in thousands		-85.6	92.8	104.1	384.6	1,811.7	1.0	-163.2	166.8	91.5	133.3
Change in %		-0.68	0.73	0.82	3.04	14.32	0.01	-1.29	1.32	0.72	1.05

Note: 1 These are only for the urban sector

Overall, the impact of a WTO agreement is positive on GDP (about 2 per cent). Exports increase by almost 10 per cent in real terms and imports by about 13 per cent. Higher world prices, however, even with the decrease in tariffs, also lead to higher domestic prices: the CPI increases by 6.7 per cent. Total employment increases by about 385,000 jobs or about 3 per cent over the base. Employment goes up more for rural, male and skilled workers, and in the primary sector.

The scenario of a 10 per cent increase in total factor productivity across sectors (ALPHASH) shows important positive effects on all variables. GDP and total employment increase (by 17 and 14 per cent, respectively), as do exports, imports and the level of the CPI (about 21, 16 and 1 per cent, respectively). Of the new 1.8 million jobs, there are more rural, female and unskilled workers, with employment growing relatively more in primary activities.

The devaluation scenario (DEVAL) leads to a decline in real GDP (about −1 per cent). At the same time, there are large increases in exports and a decline in imports (57 vs. 5 per cent). Domestic prices go up by about 6 per cent. Private consumption declines, generating the savings that are now transferred to the rest of the world: net capital inflows of about $7.5 billion become capital outflows of almost $3 billion, a change of about 4 per cent of domestic GDP at base year prices. There is, however, a 1 per cent increase in employment (about 133,000 jobs), with opposite effects on the underlying labour structure. Primary sector employment increases by 26 per cent, while other sectors decrease by as much as 4 per cent. Male employment increases by 2.3 per cent, while female employment decreases by 1.2 per cent. This scenario benefits rural, male and unskilled labour. The decline in value added, however, is due basically to a drop in real income for capital.

The impact of the devaluation in this simulation is a 'pure trade effect' that does not include at least three other possible impacts. One is the additional negative impact of a credit crunch as a result of a banking crisis (which would deepen the decline in GDP). Second, working in the opposite direction, are the future advantages of a more sustainable position of the external accounts to the extent that additional exports and the reductions in the external debt would improve debt-to-exports ratios and thus help avoid future crises (but at the cost of lower levels of consumption in the present). Third, the savings now oriented towards capital markets are not available for immediate domestic uses. The benefit of this transfer will depend on the different internal and external uses of those funds, their respective rates of return and the discount rate for consumption. Remember that the simulations fix real investment and real government consumption, and, therefore, the numbers presented reflect adjustments only in private consumption. The comparison thus would be between investments at home and abroad, yielding a higher or lower average GNP in the future.

The foreign savings simulation has the opposite effect of a devaluation. The scenario consists of an increase in capital inflows (FSAVINCR) by 10 per cent of total export value, or about 22 per cent over the base. There is a small increase in GDP (0.3 per cent) and private consumption (1 per cent). Exports decline (7 per cent) and imports expand (2 per cent) in real terms. Prices go up by 2 per cent.

Overall employment barely moves (+0.01 per cent), however, female labour increases (0.3 per cent), male labour decreases (0.2 per cent), semiskilled labour increases (0.1 per cent) while unskilled labour and skilled labour decrease (0.08 and 0.01 per cent, respectively). The primary sector declines by 3 per cent, while the others increase between 0.04 and 0.7 per cent. The RER appreciates about 2.1 per cent over the base. Again, this is only a pure trade effect. Other important consequences relate to changes in the intertemporal path of the economy when more foreign savings are absorbed by the economy. As before, future consequences will depend on the use of those capital inflows. In our simulations this expands private consumption, while the levels of investment and government expenditures are fixed.

A different type of external shock is a shift in the terms of trade due to movements in export and import prices. A deterioration of the terms of trade resulting from increased import prices (PWMINCR) leads to a decline in imports (−7 per cent), GDP (−1 per cent) and the CPI (−0.3 per cent), and a 0.4 per cent depreciation of the RER. Exports, however, rise by 3 per cent, and employment increases by 0.4 per cent in the primary sector. Yet all other sectors decline, so that overall employment falls by 1.3 per cent (a loss of about 163,000 jobs in the economy).

A positive change in the terms of trade stemming from a 10 per cent increase in agricultural export prices (PWXINCR), would have an overall positive effect on the economy. Exports increase by 3 per cent, tempered by the 8 per cent appreciation of the RER, which then leads to an increase in imports of 6 per cent. As opposed to the previous simulation, the results show an increase in GDP (0.8 per cent), the CPI (9 per cent) and employment (1.3 per cent). Of the 167,000 new jobs, relatively more will be occupied by rural, male, unskilled workers as compared to the base, and mostly in the primary sector.

Last, the results of an increase in export subsidies (SUBEXIN) are qualitatively similar to those of an increase in agricultural export prices. However, the RER appreciates less (6 per cent) and therefore the increase in exports is higher (6 per cent) and the increase in imports is lower (4 per cent). The overall effects on the economy are positive. GDP increases by 0.3 per cent and employment by 0.7 per cent, generating 91,500 new jobs, which benefit rural, male and unskilled workers relatively more. Although employment in all sectors benefits, as under PWXINCR, the export subsidies simulation spreads the impact of the changes more equally across sectors.

4.5 Microsimulations: methodology and results

Background

The CGE model simulation results show the overall effects of the simulations on several key macro variables and on factor supplies and relative prices, but the representative household groups may miss the within-group component of inequality. Using household surveys in a microsimulation model that is integrated with the CGE model incorporates household heterogeneity and allows a better analysis of income distribution and poverty. This section of the chapter will use Argentina's national household survey data to focus on the poverty and income distribution effects at the household level for the ten simulation scenarios presented in the previous section.

An important methodological issue is how to select those individuals who will change sectors when there is a change in labour demand in a simulation, and what level of income to assign to them. Several microsimulation methodologies have been proposed for this in the literature (see, for instance, Bourguignon *et al.* 1998; Alatas and Bourguignon 2000; Bourguignon *et al.* 2001; Bourguignon *et al.* 2002; Ganuza *et al.* 2002).

The methodology that we use combines a 'top-down' methodology to join the CGE and the household variables, and adds a new procedure to the microsimulation: rather than randomly selecting the individuals in the simulations (as in Ganuza *et al.* 2002), we use econometric analysis to determine who moves and the income levels assigned.[8] This approach determines the probability of movement of each individual to the different production sectors based on personal characteristics and estimates the potential wages of non-workers who enter the labour force.

The microsimulation method

The microsimulation approach allows the analysis to move from labour market outcomes to household distribution using information from the Permanent Household Survey of Argentina (EPH in Spanish). The EPH does not include rural areas; therefore, our analysis will basically apply to the urban sector, which covers about 88 per cent of the total population. These surveys consist of demographic and income information for each member of each sampled household.

In our simulations, the consumption real wage for labour by sector of production is fixed. Employment levels adjust to shocks or policy changes both in terms of the total amount of labour utilized and their division among the sectors of production. Average nominal wages and sector-specific nominal wages for each labour type also adjust. Therefore, for each simulation the CGE model calculates the change in the total number of unskilled, semiskilled and skilled men and women in each sector. These totals are passed down to the microsimulation model, where the econometrically estimated functions, rather than random drawings, determine which specific people move to different employment categories and sectors.

The EPH distinguishes five main sectors for urban workers: (1) primary sector (agriculture and mining); (2) industry; (3) construction; (4) electricity, gas and water and (5) services. If for a specific policy simulation in the CGE model, a sector gains workers, the extra workers come first from the unemployed workers within that specific sector. If all the unemployed within a sector find a job, then the remaining demand is met by any unemployed workers in the services sector, and last, if the demand is still not met, by choosing from available inactive working-age men and women. We call this trilevel ordered process the 'choice set'.[9]

The probability of moving is calculated through the use of probit regressions on each person's individual characteristics. For each of the five production sectors, we calculate the probability of each working-age individual entering that sector, whether they are currently employed elsewhere, unemployed or inactive. The individual observations of potential workers in the household survey are now ranked first by the choice set (that is, starting with the unemployed within the sector) and second in order of their probability of moving.

After choosing the people who will move into (out of) a sector of production these new workers receive a wage (new unemployed lose the wage) that corresponds to the change. A series of wage regressions (for the five sectors and both sexes) estimate the sector-specific potential wage of each sector for each person according to his or her personal characteristics.

Since all workers with the same known characteristics will receive the same mean wage, in order to include variation (inequality) we attach an error term to each person who enters the labour market. The error terms are calculated from the sectoral income regression of the workers in each sector. We make no assumption about the distribution of the pool of error terms, but rather draw randomly from this pool (by sector) and attach the error term to the new worker.

Next, the new nominal average wages per sector as calculated from the CGE simulations for each urban labour type are utilized to adjust the income of all workers (whether they moved or not). This results in the final version of wage income per worker for a given simulation. The sum of all income sources for all workers in a household, divided by the adult equivalent number of members, results in the new household per adult equivalent income.

We do not adjust the amount of capital owned or the return to that capital. Although the CGE results show the effects of the simulations on overall capital returns, the household survey data underreport the amount of profit and rent income received. Thus, it is difficult to adjust this source of income without potentially creating a larger bias in the results than by simply calculating the effects on poverty and inequality assuming that capital remains at its initial level.

Finally, in order to calculate the changes in poverty and inequality, we must account not only for changes in household income, but also for changes to the poverty line and the extreme poverty line. The National Institute of Statistics and Census (INDEC) defines a basic food basket to calculate the extreme poverty line. INDEC then takes into account non-food goods and services (such as clothing, transport, education and health) to determine the total basic basket with which to calculate the poverty line in each region. The percentage changes in prices for the different productive sectors from the CGE simulations are used to adjust the poverty lines.

Results of the simulations: poverty and inequality measures

The results in Table 4.9 show the standard poverty indices (see Foster *et al.* 1984): the headcount ratio (P_0), the average normalized poverty gap (P_1) and the average squared normalized poverty gap (P_2). These estimates, for total per adult equivalent household income, are calculated for the poverty and extreme poverty line for the 18 urban agglomerates in Argentina.[10] Table 4.10 shows two measures of

Table 4.9 Argentina – microsimulations: poverty calculations from household survey data (per cent change from base level)

	Base (%)	TARINCR	TARDECR	ALCA	OMC	ALPHASH	FSAVINCR	PWMINCR	PWXINCR	SUBEXIN	DEVAL
P_0											
Poverty	20.53	0.73	-1.72	-2.31	-2.91	-21.24	0.24	1.03	0.42	0.89	1.60
Extreme poverty	5.81	2.15	-2.55	-2.93	-7.56	-29.65	0.33	2.87	-1.34	-0.77	5.67
P_1											
Poverty	8.00	1.65	-1.70	-1.93	-3.79	-25.45	0.23	2.13	0.30	0.47	5.19
Extreme poverty	2.91	3.49	-2.43	-3.00	-9.52	-37.44	-0.33	5.25	-2.28	-1.65	11.60
P_2											
Poverty	4.75	2.35	-1.92	-2.29	-5.63	-30.04	-0.08	3.34	-0.51	-0.27	8.02
Extreme poverty	2.22	4.29	-2.53	-3.21	-10.65	-41.48	-0.87	6.74	-3.27	-2.31	14.59

Note: Poverty (and extreme poverty) estimates relate to total per adult equivalent household income, and are only for the urban sector. For changes in poverty line, prices of basic basket of food and non-food commodities are used; for extreme poverty line, only basic food price index. P_0 = headcount ratio (proportion poor); P_1 = average normalized poverty gap; P_2 = average squared normalized poverty gap

Table 4.10 Argentina – microsimulations: income inequality calculations from household survey data (per cent change from base level)

	Base	TARINCR	TARDECR	ALCA	OMC	ALPHASH	FSAVINCR	PWMINCR	PWXINCR	SUBEXIN	DEVAL
					Gini coefficient						
Labour income	0.3994	4.85	4.71	4.99	4.68	4.64	5.02	4.94	4.84	4.81	5.89
HPAEI[1]	0.4494	0.00	-0.04	-0.02	-0.84	-3.29	-0.14	0.26	-0.53	-0.39	0.42
					Theil index (GE1)						
Labour income	0.2956	6.80	6.48	6.78	6.16	5.63	7.12	6.95	6.57	6.55	9.60
HPAEI	0.3532	-0.32	0.07	0.15	-1.69	-5.68	-0.31	0.18	-1.24	-0.87	-0.01

Note: 1 Gini for HPAEI (household per adult equivalent income) includes households with zero income

income inequality: the Gini coefficient and the Theil index. Using these measures we calculate earnings inequality for the workers as well as inequality of the distribution of household per adult equivalent income. The Gini for the latter distribution is calculated over all households, even those with zero income.

The first two simulations consisted of a direct 50 per cent tariff increase and 50 per cent tariff decrease. These simulations led to basically opposite results in terms of output and employment, which similarly translated into opposite effects on poverty. In the tariff increase scenario, urban poverty increases under all three indices (P_0, P_1 and P_2) for both the poverty line and the extreme poverty line, while all values decrease with the increased openness of the second scenario. In the first simulation, although wages increase for all labour types in all sectors, the drop in all employment levels plus the increase in the cost of the basic basket that determines the poverty line have a larger negative effect on the poverty rate. The largest drop in employment is for unskilled men, and thus the poor (who tend to be unskilled) are hit the hardest. However, it is the increase in the price of basic necessities that has the largest effect on poverty. This follows as well for the tariff decrease simulation, but with the opposite results. The increased openness leads to increased employment, a lower cost for the basic basket of commodities that determines the poverty line and, thus, lower poverty under all measures.

The third and fourth simulations estimated the effects of forming a free trade area for the Americas (ALCA) and the effects of a comprehensive WTO agreement (OMC). Both show an increase in employment, but different wage effects. For the WTO simulation (OMC), the employment increases (in percentage terms) are larger in the primary sector (mainly agriculture). A free trade area for the Americas (ALCA) has one-half to one-third of the labour effect that the WTO agreement would achieve. In terms of nominal wages, under the rules of the WTO these would increase by on average 6.5 per cent, while wages decrease (but by less than 1 per cent) for all sectors under ALCA. The cost of the basket of goods that determines the poverty line increases by about 5 per cent for the OMC simulation while decreasing by 1 per cent for ALCA. Overall, the ALCA effects are very small, while the WTO simulation has a larger impact throughout the whole economy.

The results show that the increased openness of the economy through a decrease in tariffs, the Free Trade Agreement or the WTO framework decreases poverty and extreme poverty for all poverty indices. In addition, the effect on the headcount, poverty gap and poverty depth for the extreme poverty line is stronger than for the poverty line, thus leading to a better welfare effect for the indigent than for the poor in general. In terms of the distribution of household per adult equivalent income, trade liberalization through these scenarios either decreases or has no effect on inequality. Among these, the OMC simulation has the most positive effect, decreasing poverty by 3 per cent, extreme poverty by 8 per cent and inequality by 0.8 per cent. This simulation also shows a relatively stronger positive effect among the poorest of the indigent population.

The fifth simulation estimated the effects of a 10 per cent increase in productivity for the economy. Employment increased by more than 14 per cent in almost every sector (except in construction where there is barely any effect). Nominal wages increased for almost everyone, but mostly by less than 1 per cent. Last, the price of the basic basket of commodities decreased by about 1.5 per cent for food items and less than 1 per cent for the combination of food and non-food. These three effects together led to a dramatic drop in poverty (21 per cent), in particular extreme poverty (30 per cent), and to a strong decrease in inequality.

The sixth simulation allowed for an increase in foreign savings. The effects on poverty were mixed and relatively small. Employment dropped by 3 per cent in the primary sector, increased some for electricity and services and barely changed for manufacturing and construction. Wages increased by an average 2.2 per cent and the price of the basic basket of commodities by about 2.5 per cent. Poverty and extreme poverty increased by 0.2 and 0.3 per cent, respectively. However, the poorest of the extreme poor are slightly better off, and inequality decreases. As mentioned in the previous section, however, our model only captures the pure trade effects of this simulation.

The next simulations were the 10 per cent increase in all import prices and the 10 per cent increase in the export price of agricultural products. These terms of trade changes had opposite effects on employment levels, wages and the basic basket of commodities, but mixed effects on poverty. The increase in import prices led to a decrease in employment by 1–2 per cent in most sectors and for all labour types, a decrease in all wages between 0.2 and 0.3 per cent and a decrease in the basic basket of commodities by around 0.2 per cent. Poverty and extreme poverty rise under all measures but the indigent poor are hurt the most. This effect results in a worsening distribution of household income.

The rise in agricultural export prices, on the other hand, increased employment in all sectors, improved nominal wages between 8 and 8.5 per cent and the price of the basket by about 8 per cent. The poverty results are mixed. According to the headcount ratio, the poor are slightly worse off (a 0.4 per cent increase) since some families have wage increases smaller than the higher prices they now face. The indigent, however, as seen in the extreme poverty results (a 1.3 per cent decrease), are better off in this scenario. The prices of food commodities have not risen as much as the full basket, and so the purchasing power of the extreme poor is better. The results for P_2 also show a welfare benefit for the poorest, and the Gini for household income distribution slightly decreases.

The ninth simulation estimated the effect of increasing subsidies to exports. As mentioned in the previous section, the results on the economy are very similar to the results from an increase in the world price of agricultural exports. Employment goes up in every sector and for all labour types, wages increase between 6.5 and 7 per cent, while the basic basket of commodities increases by about 6.6 per cent. As with the export price simulation, the headcount ratio increases for the poor, but decreases for the extreme poor, while the very poorest are made better off. Inequality in terms of household per adult equivalent income decreases.

The final simulation estimated the effect of a 10 per cent nominal devaluation of the Argentine peso. The devaluation caused the prices of tradables to increase, as well the price of a fixed consumption basket such as the CPI, while total employment did not change much. Therefore, the devaluation in this static model affects poverty negatively: the values of all indicators increase in the simulation, with a particularly negative effect on the poorest of the indigent population, as can be seen by the increase in the P_2 value for extreme poverty. The devaluation improved nominal wages of all labour types for all sectors, increased the employment level of the primary sector (agriculture and mining) by more than that of any other simulation, had little to no effect on employment for construction workers and decreased employment for all other sectors. The price effect (which increased the cost of the basic basket of commodities that determines the poverty line) more than compensated the labour effect, thus leading to a large increase in poverty. The devaluation on impact also has a deteriorating effect on income distribution. Overall, however, the only simulation to have any significant effect (whether positive or negative) on inequality is the productivity shock.

4.6 Conclusions and issues for further research

Argentina's economy and society underwent dramatic changes during the 1990s. The economy appeared to enter a period of higher growth and low inflation after the 1991 Convertibility Plan created a currency board and the economy was liberalized, privatized and deregulated. A puzzling fact was that even during the periods of high growth, unemployment began to increase, eventually reaching levels not experienced before in Argentina's modern history. Poverty and income distribution indicators deteriorated significantly. The collapse of the whole economic programme in late 2001 and early 2002 has led to many interpretations. This chapter has focused on a limited set of issues, linked to developments in the balance of payments and their impact on poverty and income distribution during the 1990s.

What could have been done differently? And what would have been the impact on poverty and income distribution of other policy scenarios and external shocks? There were ten policy changes considered: tariff changes, terms of trade shocks, increased export subsidies and foreign savings, devaluation, overall improvements in productivity in Argentina, the possible implementation of a FTAA and a comprehensive global agreement in the WTO negotiations.

The simulations show that, as a medium-run proposition, trade liberalization helped reduce poverty, with a decrease or no effect on income inequality. The jump of exports under the WTO (OMC) scenario shows the impact of world agricultural protectionism on Argentina, and the better debt/export indicators that could be achieved under such an agreement. The simulated devaluation did not have much effect on employment and deteriorated poverty and inequality indicators. However, it expanded exports and moved the country from net capital inflows to net capital outflows. Whether this allocation of savings is good or bad for the country will depend on the different internal and external uses of those funds, and the respective returns, a question that requires a dynamic framework for its proper answer. The pure trade (i.e. without its potential impact on the expansion of capital) simulation of increased capital flows showed the negative impact on exports and on poverty. But again a full evaluation requires a dynamic assessment of the uses of those capital flows: if they expand investment and, overall although not necessarily directly, lead to larger exports, the dynamics of the current account may be sustainable. The terms of trade simulations and the increase in export subsidies had different effects on poverty and inequality. Through an import price increase, poverty increases, in particular for the poorest, as does inequality, while the other two simulations showed a positive effect for the extreme poor and a decrease in inequality, although a slight increase in poverty. Finally, the simulation of increased productivity showed positive effects overall on growth, inflation, exports and imports, and on poverty indicators. At least in the case of this simulation of broad-based improvements in productivity (as opposed to increases in specific sectors, which were not modelled here), they lead to better results overall and not to displacement of labour.

This analysis leaves us with several puzzles: if trade liberalization did not cause higher unemployment and poverty (and rather the contrary may be the case); if a devaluation would worsen poverty, although it may help expand employment by a small amount (and certainly, put the external accounts on a sounder footing going forward); if the pure trade effects of capital flows do not seem to amount to much and if productivity increases rather than leading to higher unemployment help to increase labour utilization and reduce poverty, then what caused the substantial increase in unemployment and poverty during the 1990s?

Certainly, the 1995 recession and the protracted economic decline since 1999 have a large responsibility for those negative outcomes. But unemployment was growing before 1995 and although it declined in 1996 and 1997, still remained in the uncomfortable range of 14–17 per cent. An important development appears to have been the privatization and downsizing of public sector enterprises, which requires a separate analysis. Also, because the model here is run with labour and capital mobility, it captures, as mentioned, medium-run effects. If productive factors are very sector specific, there are no adequate retraining institutions for labour and/or other rigidities limit labour mobility and the financial markets and legal institutions do not allow a quick redeployment of capital, then there may be significant mismatches in factor supply and demand that would not be captured in the simulations presented here.

In addition, the analysis has been mostly from the labour demand side. But there were also changes in labour supply, including an acceleration in the growth rate of the population in the 15–64-year bracket that added to potential labour supply (the result of demographic events in the previous decades). At the same time, there was an increase in the participation rates by women, but, contrary to the previous effect, this may have been an endogenous result of the decline in consumption wages and the loss of better-paid jobs in previously protected sectors, including public sector enterprises. These hypotheses need to be explored further.

Notes

1 For a more complete overview of the economic policy framework, see Díaz-Bonilla *et al.* (2003).
2 There was also a change of currency from australes to the new peso at a rate of 10,000 australes = 1 peso.

3 The supply of liquidity beyond the monetary base was still affected by Central Bank monetary instruments such as the reserve requirements for the banking system and the use of short-term swaps. This allowed some room for manoeuvre in monetary policy. Also, a percentage of the backing of the monetary base could be covered by the dollar-denominated debt of the Argentine government, which permitted some monetization of fiscal deficits. Hence, the use of 'almost' in the previous paragraphs.
4 The previous record of exchange rate stability was during the period from 1940 to 1946.
5 See Walsh 1998, among others, for a general discussion of cash-in-advance models.
6 The framework is a general equilibrium model with a multiregion and multisector specification (see Diao *et al.* 2002).
7 The trade effects may be more muted than in the case where the simulation would have been able to differentiate between trading partners, and therefore some of the beneficial impacts of the FTAA may be lost.
8 See also Díaz-Bonilla *et al.* (2003) for greater detail on methodology as applied here in the Argentine model, and Díaz-Bonilla and Morley (2003) for an application to Mexico.
9 In practice, most of the microsimulations only needed to use the first of the three levels.
10 Poverty lines come from SIEMPRO and INDEC.

References

Alatas, V. and F. Bourguignon (2000) 'The evolution of the distribution of income during Indonesian fast growth: 1980–1996', Princeton: Princeton University (mimeo).
Bourguignon, F., M. Fournier and M. Gurgand (2001) 'Fast development with stable income distribution: Taiwan, 1979–1994', *Review of Income and Wealth*, 43(3): 139–64.
Bourguignon, François, Francisco Ferreira and Nora Lustig (1998) *The Microeconomics of Income Distribution Dynamics, a Research Proposal*, Washington, DC: Inter-American Development Bank and World Bank (mimeo).
Bourguignon, François, Anne-Sophie Robilliard and Sherman Robinson (2002) *Representative versus Real Households in the Macro-economic Modeling of Inequality*, Washington, DC: World Bank and IFPRI (mimeo, April).
Calvo, G., L. Leiderman and C. Reinhart (1993) 'Capital inflows and real exchange rate appreciation in Latin America: the role of external factors', *IMF Staff Papers* 40: 108–51.
Calvo, G., L. Leiderman and C. Reinhart (1996) 'Capital flows to developing countries in the 1990s: causes and effects', *Journal of Economic Perspectives* 10(2): 123–39.
Calvo, Guillermo, Alejandro Izquierdo and Ernesto Talvi (2002) 'Sudden stops, the real exchange rate and fiscal sustainability: Argentina's lessons', IADB Research Department Working Paper, Washington, DC: Inter-American Development Bank.
Clower, Robert (1967) 'A reconsideration of the microfoundations of monetary theory', *Western Economic Journal*, 6(1): 1–9.
De la Torre, A., E. Yeyati and S. Schmukler (2002) *Argentina's Financial Crisis: Floating Money, Sinking Banking*, Washington DC: World Bank (mimeo).
Diao, Xinshen, Eugenio Díaz-Bonilla and Sherman Robinson (2002) 'Scenarios for trade integration in the Americas', IFPRI Trade and Macroeconomics Division, Discussion Paper no. 90, Washington, DC: IFPRI.
Díaz-Bonilla, Carolina and Samuel Morley (2003) 'The effects of export-led growth on employment, poverty, and inequality: the case of Mexico', this study, chap. 15.
Díaz-Bonilla, Carolina, Eugenio Díaz-Bonilla, Valeria Piñeiro and Sherman Robinson (2003) 'Argentina's growth, trade, and employment during the 1990s. A CGE-microsimulation analysis', IFPRI, TMD Working Paper, Washington, DC: IFPRI.

Díaz-Bonilla, Eugenio (1996) 'The Washington consensus and the myth of the Tequila effect', Fundación Andina Working Papers, Buenos Aires, Argentina: Fundación Andina.

Díaz Bonilla, Eugenio and H. Schamis (2001) 'From redistribution to stability: the evolution of exchange rate policies in Argentina, 1950–98', in: Jeffrey Frieden and Ernesto Stein (eds) *The Currency Game Exchange Rate Politics in Latin America*, Baltimore and Washington, DC: The Johns Hopkins University Press and Inter-American Development Bank.

Feenstra, R. C. (1986) 'Functional equivalence between liquidity costs and the utility of money', *Journal of Monetary Theory*, 17: 271–91.

Feldstein, Martin (2002) 'Argentina doesn't need the IMF', Commentary in *The Wall Street Journal*, May 28.

Fischer, Stanley (1974) 'Money in the production function', *Economic Inquiry* 12(4): 518–33.

Foster, J., J. Greer and E. Thorbecke (1984) 'A class of decomposable poverty measures', *Econometrica*, 52: 761–5.

Ganuza, Enrique, Ricardo Paes de Barros and Rob Vos (2002) 'Labour market adjustment, poverty and inequality during liberalization', in: Rob Vos, Lance Taylor and Ricardo Barros (eds) *Economic Liberalization, Income Distribution and Poverty. Latin America in the 1990s*, Cheltenham, UK: Edward Elgar, pp. 54–88.

IMF (1995) *Argentina, Recent Economic Developments, 1995*, Washington, DC: International Monetary Fund.

IMF (1998) *Argentina, Recent Economic Developments, 1998*, Washington, DC: International Monetary Fund.

Kehoe, T. J. (2002) 'What can we learn from the current crisis in Argentina?', University of Minnesota, Minneapolis (mimeo).

Liviatan, N. (1993) 'Proceedings of a conference on currency substitution and currency boards', World Bank Discussion Paper 207, Washington, DC: World Bank.

Löfgren, Hans, Rebecca Lee Harris and Sherman Robinson (2001) 'A standard computable general equilibrium (CGE) model', IFPRI, TMD Working Paper no. 75, Washington, DC: IFPRI.

Mussa, Michael (2002) 'Argentina and the fund: from triumph to tragedy', *Policy Analyses in International Economics 67*, Washington, DC: Institute for International Economics.

Patinkin, Donald (1965) *Money, Interest, and Prices*, London: Harper and Row.

Perry, Guillermo and Luis Serven (2002) *The Anatomy of a Multiple Crisis: Why Was Argentina Special and What Can We Learn from It?*, Washington, DC: World Bank (mimeo).

Pou, Pedro (1998) 'The economy in political transition', ABRA Convention, 23 June.

Walsh, Carl (1998) *Monetary Theory and Policy*, Cambridge, MA: MIT Press.

Williamson, John (ed.) (1994) *Estimating Equilibrium Exchange Rates*, Washington, DC: Institute for International Economics.

5 Bolivia – export promotion and its effects on growth, employment and poverty

Wilson Jiménez

Abstract

The initial efforts and reforms for stabilization in Bolivia led to moderate but stable growth and some reduction in poverty during most of the 1990s. Towards the end of the decade, nearing the twenty-first century, growth slowed down and poverty increased again. Trade liberalization and capital inflows stimulated export growth and increased the propensity to import. Non-traditional exports took a larger share of overall exports, and exports were the primary source of growth in aggregate output during most of the 1990s. The export-led growth process continues to be based on natural resources, but includes both agricultural (e.g. soya beans) and processed mineral products (e.g. jewels) as new export items. The growth path has not proved to be very stable or sustainable. Performance of exports has been quite vulnerable to economic shocks in neighbouring countries. The growing share of non-traditional exports has been due primarily to the further collapse of traditional exports, particularly natural gas and petroleum products that depend on Argentinean and Brazilian markets. Growth in non-traditional exports has decelerated after 1999 and this has affected the overall growth of the economy. Unemployment rates have increased again to levels close to those recorded at the end of the 1980s, and new emergency employment programmes are being implemented to absorb the social cost of declining economic growth. Real labour income has not shown any increase in the second half of the 1990s, with unskilled workers being the most negatively affected. In 2000, real labour income of unskilled urban workers fell 20 per cent relative to the 1989 levels, while that of skilled urban workers rose approximately 20 per cent. Increased skill intensity and widening wage gaps are also reflected in rising per capita income inequality at the household level. Macro–micro CGE simulations show that the effects of trade liberalization and greater trade integration on aggregate employment and wages would counteract these outcomes. These positive wage and employment outcomes can only materialize, however, if Bolivia's major trading partners are able to emerge from their recessions. Bolivia's dependence on aid and its vulnerability to the volatility of the primary goods markets has not disappeared despite almost two decades of economic reforms. The introduction of social protection programmes provided but small compensation for the economic shocks to which so many Bolivian households remain vulnerable.

5.1 Introduction

Exports contributed to the growth of the Bolivian economy during much of the 1990s; however, trade policies and support to the export sector had little effect in expanding and diversifying the output. Structural bottlenecks in the export sector – primarily low factor productivity, high processing costs, capacity underutilization and low value-added content – have limited export growth and could severely affect growth possibilities for the Bolivian economy in the coming years.

Between 1990 and 1998, the Bolivian economy grew at an annual average rate of 4.4 per cent, generating increases in per capita income and consumption of about 2 per cent per year (Gobierno Nacional de la República 2000; World Bank 2000). The rise in economic activity led to growing employment and labour income, especially for skilled workers in tradable goods sectors as well as in telecommunications and hydrocarbons who benefited from a boost in direct foreign investment (Pereira and Jiménez 2001).

Increased export efforts led to an 88 per cent increase in cumulative export volume between 1991 and 2001. The export value index, however, grew by less than 30 per cent due to adverse shocks in the terms of trade.[1]

In the late 1990s, domestic economic activity slowed down dramatically as the contraction of the region's economy accentuated. Mining and agriculture were particularly affected and pulled other activities into a prolonged recession. The reduction in capital flows to the country and adverse conditions in the region's markets caused a decline in employment rates, an increase in open unemployment and a decline in labour income, especially that of unskilled workers. These aspects likely have led to an increase in poverty between 1999 and 2001 (Hernani 2002; Landa 2002).

This chapter aims to evaluate the contribution of the external sector to economic growth and employment, as well as its effects on poverty and inequality. It uses the CGE model framework spelt out in Chapter 3, which allows the construction of counterfactual scenarios associated with the impact of external shocks and trade policies on economic activity and the labour market. These CGE-based simulation results are applied to household surveys through microsimulations in order to estimate changes in inequality and poverty.

The main findings confirm the hypotheses that external shocks – particularly declining export prices and rising import prices – have a significant contractionary impact leading to rising unemployment rates, which are a transmission mechanism for increased poverty. Conversely, an exogenous increase in the productivity of export activities favours economic growth and poverty reduction.

The prospects for economic recovery and poverty reduction are related to strengthening exports – especially energy production, agricultural products and manufactured goods – that could benefit from an expansion of regional markets and bilateral trade. Economic liberalization policies through import tariff reductions – whether they be uniform or differentiated free trade schemes – could have a favourable impact on growth only if there is an increase in the export of products with high value-added content. In the long run, policies could strengthen linkages between the export sector and products aimed at the domestic market, so that economic growth can have a greater impact on employment and poverty reduction.

Section 5.2 presents a summary of the macroeconomic policies and performance of the economy during the 1990s. It emphasizes the structure of the current account and the decomposition of the changes in sectoral output. Section 5.3 analyses changes in the labour market during the last few years. Section 5.4 presents the results of the general equilibrium model and the impact on employment and poverty, including various simulation exercises, both of external and of internal shocks and trade policies. The final section presents some conclusions and policy recommendations.

5.2 Macroeconomic policies and export promotion

Structural reforms

Opening the economy to world markets was one of the cornerstones of the New Economic Policy (NPE) applied in Bolivia since 1985 within the framework of the adjustment and stabilization programme. These measures favoured fiscal adjustment, domestic price liberalization and exchange rate adjustment. On the expenditure side, the public spending cuts were achieved by reducing employment in public administration and state enterprises through outsourcing of services and transferring of enterprises to the private sector. The tax reform implemented during the adjustment programme was oriented to increasing the collection of fiscal revenue by broadening the tax base and simplifying the tax system (Delgadillo 1996).

Trade liberalization aimed at realigning international and domestic prices through tariff reduction (Zambrana 2002). Given the need to balance the trade account, the government took action to promote exports. In principle, export promotion was based on eliminating licenses and permits for non-traditional exports. The new exchange rate regime established a system of managed floating (the *Bolsín*) that stabilized inflation expectations and became an instrument to cushion the impact of external shocks.[2]

During the 1990s, Bolivia undertook reforms aimed at boosting economic growth by attracting foreign direct investment. Public enterprises were capitalized with contributions from foreign partners. This process generated investments of some US$ 800 million in hydrocarbons, US$ 610 million in telecommunications, US$ 134 million in electricity and US$ 85 million in transportation. Foreign direct investment, which was about US$ 120 million before the capitalization, reached US$ 900 million at the end of the 1990s.[3]

Some of the capitalization resources supported a reform of the pension system. The reforms were complemented by measures intended to deepen the process of decentralization and popular participation, which favoured the expansion of public services and reallocated public investment to 314 municipalities, many of which had not received any central public resources previously.

Actions to reduce the external debt included negotiations on repurchasing debt in secondary markets. The bilateral and multilateral debt was renegotiated in the 'Paris Club' and a restructuring of the debt occurred, which favoured the contracting of concessional loans.[4] In 2000, Bolivia became eligible for the HIPC-II Initiative (heavily indebted poor countries), which allowed reducing a part of the country's debt in exchange for a national commitment to engage in poverty reduction programmes. The reinforced HIPC programme brought US$ 1.5 billion in public external debt relief over a period of 15 years. These resources were transferred to municipal governments to support social investment programmes. In 2002, new emergency employment programmes were introduced and resources were committed to public investment in labour-intensive sectors. For the medium term, the government proposed a pro-poor growth strategy.

Macroeconomic performance

The Bolivian economy began to show some signs of recovery in 1987, after seven consecutive years of recession and high inflation. Between 1989 and 1992, economic activity grew at an annual average of 3.4 per cent aided by the performance of exports and investments (public and private) – both had a positive effect on economic growth at 5.1 and 1.1 per cent, respectively.[5] The impact of public expenditures on fluctuations in short-term growth became gradually smaller, in part due to discipline in spending policy (Table 5.1).

Between 1993 and 1996, the economy grew at an average annual rate of 4.3 per cent of which exports accounted for 3.8 percentage points and investment 1.7 percentage points. In 1997 and 1998, the economy achieved growth rates of 4.9 and 5.2 per cent, respectively – the highest rates since the implementation of the NPE. Nevertheless, in 1997, exports stopped growing at the rates of previous years and actually experienced negative growth (−1.04 per cent). This behaviour shows the initial impact on the Bolivian economy of the crisis in countries elsewhere in the region. The expansion of public investment during this period partially offset the effects of the international crisis and contributed to economic growth. In 1998, the economy benefited from the construction of the gas pipeline to Brazil, which brought about important investments. Exports also accounted for 3.3 percentage points of economic growth in that year.

The Bolivian economy started to slow down dramatically in 1999, showing a growth rate of barely 0.44 per cent. Exports had a negative impact on growth (−5.6 per cent) and lower investment rates were reflected in decreased economic activity. In 2000, the economy recovered at a rate of 2.4 per cent. Exports contributed 2.6 percentage points to this growth largely because of the recovery in the mining sector. There was, however, no recovery in the construction sector and financial services, and the manufacturing industry also performed poorly due to falling domestic demand.

A decline in investment was the main reason behind the slowdown in economic growth in 2001 (to 1.2 per cent). This downturn was partially offset by the recovery

Table 5.1 Bolivia: contribution of the external sector, government, and private sector to GDP growth, 1985–2001 (percentage)

	Public expenditures	Investment	Exports	Savings	Taxes	Imports	Interaction effects	Residual	GDP variation % (annual average)
Average for period									
1985–8	-1.9	1.2	-1.2	6.0	-1.4	-3.7	-0.1	0.0	-1.21
1989–92	0.0	1.1	5.1	-1.0	-0.4	-1.3	0.1	-0.3	3.44
1993–6	0.9	1.7	3.8	-1.3	0.0	-0.5	0.1	-0.3	4.31
1997–2000	0.8	4.4	1.0	-0.1	-0.1	-1.5	0.0	-0.3	4.34
Compared to previous year									
1997	0.71	8.92	-1.04	0.78	-0.13	-4.08	-0.04	-0.17	4.95
1998	0.76	9.62	3.29	-0.38	-0.91	-6.95	0.22	-0.42	5.23
1999	0.47	-7.96	-5.57	3.20	1.36	9.42	-0.54	0.06	0.44
2000	0.21	-0.32	2.57	-0.23	-0.50	0.53	0.11	0.00	2.37
2001	0.68	-9.05	5.58	0.57	-0.14	2.46	-0.02	1.16	1.23

Source: Elaborated with National Accounts database: Central Bank and INE

Note: The sum of the effects is equal to period average of GDP growth. See Chapter 2 for the methodology

in exports, which accounted for 5.6 per cent of growth – a result linked to gas sales to Brazil. Although projections for the following years are still modest, the 2.7 per cent growth achieved in 2002 signals a period of recovery, to be halted by a period of political turmoil in 2003–5.

External shocks: effects on the current account[6]

Variations in the level and structure of the trade balance responded in large part to liberalization and to trade policies. In the first years of adjustment (1985–9), the deficit in the current account represented 8.1 per cent of the GDP, which fell to an average of 5.4 per cent for the period 1989–1992 (Tables 5.2 and 5.3). Variations in the current account[7] as a percentage of GDP were primarily due to the expansion of trade, which helped reduce the current account by −5.5 per cent of GDP. Falling international interest rates (−2.3 per cent) and policies to cut domestic spending (−1.5 per cent) also helped reduce the current account deficit during this period (as compared to the average deficit for 1985–8). These effects offset the adverse impact of falling terms of trade, particularly the collapse of export prices. The growing participation of the informal sector in illegal trade (contraband and drugs) and the decreased Bolivian participation in regional trade are reflected in the 'import substitution' effect (Tables 5.2 and 5.3).

Between 1993 and 1996, the current account deficit dropped slightly to 5.3 per cent of GDP, that is, a decline by 0.13 percentage points relative to the average for 1989–92. Deterioration in the terms of trade and the decrease in trade volumes would have increased the deficit by 1.16 percentage points. Nevertheless, revenue from gas sales to Brazil and the access of Bolivian products to foreign markets compensated for these adverse shocks.

Between 1997 and 2000, the current account deficit widened again to 8 per cent of GDP mainly due to the expansion of import demand.[8] The import substitution effect accounted for 4.66 points and the loss of dynamism in world trade accounted for 1.98 points (Tables 5.2 and 5.3). It is evident in the case of Bolivia that when the economy slows down, the trade deficit tends to widen because of a decreased capacity to export and a high dependency on imported final products and inputs.

Table 5.2   Bolivia: current account of the balance of payments (percentage of GDP)

			Average			
	1985–8	*1989–92*	*1993–6*	*1997–9*	*1985–92*	*1993–9*
Deficit (+)/surplus (−)	8.1	5.4	5.3	8.0	6.2	6.7
Imports	24.1	26.3	27.5	29.8	25.6	28.2
Factor payments	6.8	4.5	3.3	2.3	5.2	3.1
Exports	19.7	21.5	21.7	19.3	21.0	20.6
Unilateral net transfers	3.1	3.8	3.8	4.1	3.6	3.9

Source: INE and Central Bank

Table 5.3 Bolivia: decomposition of changes in the current account deficit (percentage of GDP)

	1989–92 1985–8	1992–6 1985–8	1997–9 1985–8
Observed change in deficit	−2.70	−0.13	3.30
External shocks	−3.85	1.16	1.16
Terms of trade deterioration	3.97	2.00	−0.48
Import price effect	0.54	0.36	−1.05
Export price effect	3.43	1.64	0.57
Interest rate shock	−2.28	−0.95	−0.35
World trade retardation	−5.53	0.11	1.98
Other external variables	−0.77	−0.40	−1.54
Debt accumulation burden	0.15	−0.43	−0.96
Change in direct investment income	−0.19	0.07	−0.30
Change in official transfers	−0.73	−0.04	−0.28
Domestic adjustment	1.23	−1.91	3.67
Domestic spending	−1.48	1.04	−0.83
Import substitution	3.30	−0.41	4.66
Export penetration	−0.59	−2.54	−0.16
Interaction effects	0.71	1.02	0.02

Source: Elaborated with Central Bank database, INE and UDAPE

Note: A (+) sign indicates increase in the deficit, (−) reduction in the deficit. The sum of the outcomes is equal to the difference in the (current account deficit/GDP) indicator between the periods

Adjustment and export growth

The increase in 'non-traditional' exports observed in the 1990s caused a reduction in the current account deficit through the middle of the last decade, even though the share of commodities with a high value-added content was low. Export growth thus failed to spill over to other activities and the economy was not on a sustained growth path (Fundación Milenio 1998).

Value-added growth has been sensitive to fluctuations in both external and domestic demand. On average, the value added of goods[9] for the 1993–6 period grew 17 per cent in real cumulative terms with respect to the average for 1989–92. An increase in exports accounted for 11 per cent while growth in domestic demand[10] contributed 6 per cent. The expansion of domestic demand primarily boosted non-industrial agricultural production and products for local consumption. External demand brought about growth in agro-industries and in the production of wood and various manufactured goods, among others (Figure 5.1 and Table 5.4).

There was a 35.9 per cent cumulative decline in the value added of goods over the period 1997–9 relative to the 1993–6 average. Contraction of external demand accounted for 20 per cent of this decline, while domestic demand and import substitution effects accounted for −9 and −6 per cent, respectively. Reduction in the external demand affected production of hydrocarbons, wood and various manufactured goods, among others. Domestic demand compensated for the deceleration in trade and external demand.

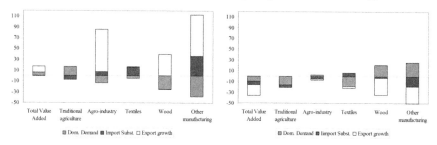

Figure 5.1   Bolivia: decomposition of contribution of domestic and external demand to GDP growth: (a) 1993–6 average relative to 1989–92 and (b) 1997–9 average relative to 1993–6. (Elaborated with INE database.)

Export trends

Structural adjustment measures caused an increase in the volume of traditional and non-traditional exports. After the dramatic fall of traditional mineral prices in the mid-1980s, the mining industry absorbed small producer cooperatives that operated under the free trade and export of minerals. Mining companies benefited from the creation of new credit lines, the Certificate of Tariff Reintegration (CRA) and the lifting of restrictions on the exploitation of gold.

Between 1989 and 1992, exports grew by 38 per cent compared with the previous period (1985–9). The contribution of traditional exports fell due to the decline in the volume of gas sales and the contraction of the export volume of tin and wolfram. Non-traditional products, soya bean in particular, grew at lower rates. Wood exports stagnated and the export value of coffee, cacao and rubber also declined.

Between 1993 and 1996, traditional exports accounted for 52 per cent of the value of exports (41 per cent minerals and 11 per cent hydrocarbons). Non-traditional exports contributed 43 per cent, and re-exports accounted for 4 per cent. During this period, both the volume and the price of silver and gold exports rose. However, hydrocarbon exports were affected by falling sales prices and the deregulation of the energy market, as well as the strong negotiating power of Argentina, the sole purchaser (UDAPE 1997). The value of non-traditional exports tripled with respect to the previous period because of the sale of soya, wood and jewellery products. Favourable performance of exports had to do with the introduction of incentives like the tariff rebate system and the creation of the single export window system (SIVEX) as well as the signing of trade agreements with Peru to operate in free trade zones.

Between 1997 and 2000, the share of traditional exports dropped to 40 per cent with a significant decrease in the sale of minerals (Table 5.5). The finalization of the contract to sell natural gas to Argentina resulted in lower levels of hydrocarbon production. At the same time, transferring operations for exploration and exploitation to the private sector, delays in the building of gas pipelines to Brazil and declining exports of petroleum products all contributed to the export decline. Non-traditional exports fell by −0.2 per cent per year, despite a greater share of

Table 5.4 Bolivia: Chenery decomposition – changes in value added by products 1989–96 (percentage)

	1993–6 Average/1989–92 average				1997–9 Average/1993–6 average			
	Domestic demand %, $\Delta\alpha S_t$	Import substitution %, $\alpha_{t-1}\Delta D$	Variation in export %, $\alpha_{t-1}\Delta E$	Variation % of value added	Domestic demand %, $\Delta\alpha S_t$	Import substitution %, $\alpha_{t-1}\Delta D$	Variation in export %, $\alpha_{t-1}\Delta E$	Variation % of value added
Non-industrial agriculture products	16.3	-7.2	0.2	9.4	-15.5	-5.0	0.1	-20.5
Agro-industrial products	-13.2	7.0	78.7	72.6	2.9	-4.6	-1.8	-3.5
Coca	3.8	0.0	-16.4	-12.6	3.6	0.0	-44.3	-40.7
Livestock products	9.0	-0.1	1.5	10.4	-14.3	0.0	0.1	-14.1
Forestry and fishing	16.3	-3.9	-4.5	7.9	-14.2	-3.0	1.3	-15.8
Crude oil natural gas	1.1	0.0	12.4	13.5	45.3	0.0	-46.3	-0.9
Metallic minerals	4.5	-2.7	16.7	18.5	-5.4	0.8	-22.2	-26.8
Fresh and processed meats	10.7	-1.5	0.8	10.0	-12.2	-1.6	-0.7	-14.6
Dairy products	15.7	-4.0	0.7	12.3	-14.2	-5.0	0.6	-18.6
Milled and baked goods	-3.0	18.8	3.3	19.0	-14.3	-11.3	7.5	-18.1
Sugar	4.4	-13.8	33.2	23.8	29.7	-9.7	-45.1	-25.2
Other food products	-106.3	26.9	147.0	67.6	-91.1	-4.7	94.2	-1.5
Beverages	11.7	-0.2	2.4	13.9	-8.0	-3.5	4.2	-7.4
Processed tobacco	21.1	-14.3	19.2	26.0	-18.2	-1.6	-1.5	-21.3
Textiles and clothing	-4.5	15.8	0.8	12.0	-18.6	6.9	-3.1	-14.8
Wood and wood products	-24.5	-0.7	39.9	14.6	21.1	-2.3	-32.1	-13.3
Paper and paper products	10.3	5.0	1.8	17.2	-15.9	-5.9	0.0	-21.8
Chemical substances and products	19.8	-8.4	0.9	12.3	-13.2	-2.3	1.7	-13.8
Refined petroleum production	25.5	-19.3	3.2	9.4	-18.8	1.7	-4.0	-21.1
Non-metallic mineral products	15.8	12.2	7.3	35.4	-1.3	-3.4	-2.0	-6.7
Basic metal products	5.7	-4.5	16.7	17.9	87.6	-77.0	-44.4	-33.8
Metallic machinery/equipment	26.5	-9.4	3.7	20.8	3.4	-24.3	1.6	-19.3
Miscellaneous manufactured goods	-37.9	36.5	76.2	74.8	25.7	-18.7	-31.4	-24.3
Total	6.0	-0.8	11.4	16.6	-9.1	-6.4	-20.3	-35.9

Source: Elaboration based on the input–output matrix – National Accounts

Note: Output growth ($\Delta X/X$) is expressed in terms of the components of growth of domestic demand (D), supply (S), export promotion (E) and changes in the share of value added in supply (α) (see Chapter 2, Appendix A2.5)

Table 5.5   Bolivia: export structure by product (percentage)

	Average			
	1985–8	*1989–92*	*1993–6*	*1997–9*
Traditional products	84	68	52	40
Minerals	38	44	41	33
Tin	17	12	8	5
Other minerals	21	32	33	28
Hydrocarbons	47	23	11	7
Natural gas	46	23	8	4
Others	1	1	3	3
Non-traditional products	14	28	43	45
Re-exports	2	4	4	15
Total	100	100	100	100

Source: INE – UDAPE

soya bean and soya products (grain, flour, cakes, oils), leather and manufactured goods (UDAPE 1997).

Since 1998, sugar, coffee and cacao prices have declined and have affected export volumes of these products negatively. The devaluation of the Brazilian Real affected the exports of wood and wood products. Sanitary restrictions imposed by Peru on cotton imports from Bolivia, as well as Brazil's and Argentina's administrative requirements for importing Bolivian textiles, were also factors in reducing the value of exports. In addition, adverse climatic factors damaged part of the agricultural production, and restrictions on access to financing and legal insecurity involving foreign investments further caused exports to stagnate (UDAPE 1997).

During the 1990s, exports were diversified and contributed to economic growth. The deceleration in world trade and the unfavourable terms of trade for Bolivian exports, however, reduced the aggregate income effect.

Competitiveness and the exchange rate

During the second half of the 1980s, the exchange rate played an important role in reducing inflationary expectations, especially because of the strong pass-through effect of devaluations on domestic prices (Cupé 2002). The real multilateral exchange rate depreciated between 1990 and 1995, as stabilization policies and reforms were being consolidated (see Figure 5.2). Between 1995 and 1998, the high flow of capital and external financing led to an appreciation of the real exchange rate. The same trend applies for the real multilateral (trade-weighted) exchange rate and is even more accentuated in the real bilateral exchange rates with countries of the Andean Community (CAN). Starting 1999, the real exchange rate depreciated again, but in conjunction with lower domestic inflation.

The effect of the exchange rate on domestic prices has limited the ability to use depreciation as an instrument to promote exports (Antelo *et al.* 1995). Between

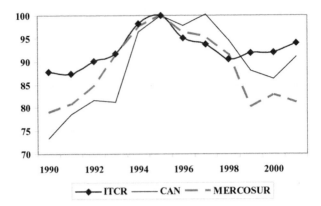

Figure 5.2 Trade-weighted real exchange rates for Bolivia (index, 1995 = 100). ITCR is the overall trade-weighted real exchange rate, CAN that with the Andean countries and Mercosur that with the Southern Cone trading partners. (From UDAPE based on IMF data.)

1994 and 1996, the exchange rate went through a temporary imbalance with respect to its equilibrium level because of exogenous disruptions such as the appreciation of European currencies and the Japanese yen against the dollar in 1994 and 1995 (Lora and Orellana 2001). Between 1998 and 1999 there was an overvaluation associated with declining terms of trade and expansionary fiscal policies. The devaluation of the Brazilian Real in early 1999 caused an appreciation in Bolivian currency of nearly 8 per cent, especially between late 1998 and the first quarter of 1999.

Tariff protection

Import liberalization implied a gradual reduction of the nominal protection rates. In 1985, the tariff system was simplified by setting a 20 per cent uniform customs duty (GAC) for all goods. Between 1988 and 1990 a process of automatic tariff reduction was introduced that resulted in a new GAC structure, maintaining a 10 per cent tariff for capital goods and a 5 per cent investment incentive (Delgadillo *et al.* 2001).

Effective tariff protection was affected by reciprocal concessions derived from subregional trade agreements. The average tariff for imports declined during the 1990s and affected the competitiveness of tradable goods. In 1998, the average tariff was almost half that of the average rates that prevailed in 1990. The reduction of tariffs provoked a fall in revenue from import duties incurring significant fiscal costs, but the fiscal implications did not deter trade liberalization.

Competitiveness and the cost of labour

Bolivia has one of the lowest wage levels in Latin America. In 2001 the minimum wage was US$ 57 per month, a level likely reflecting the low productivity of the economy. Labour legislation, however, establishes substantial non-wage costs that generate disincentives to job creation and create biases against the formal contracting of labour.

Labour legislation in effect since 1985 establishes general regulations for contracting wage labour. Labour regulations establish payments to contribute to social security funds, overtime pay, annual Christmas bonuses and other bonuses, vacation pay, seniority bonuses, severance pay, maternity leave subsidies, interment subsidies and bonuses for some workers living in border areas. Such costs, without considering, for example, the costs of training workers, could double or triple the basic wage of a worker who enjoys such benefits (Paredes 1994).

Non-wage costs and the application of labour regulations also affect competitiveness, in large part because of the uncertainty generated by government intervention in collective bargaining, mediation in labour conflicts and the inadequate regulation of labour unions and monopolies. In recent years, it has become clear that there is a need to formulate a new framework of labour regulations in order to give incentives for job creation, promote labour mobility and increase competitiveness, while at the same time generating systems to protect workers.

The role of export promotion policies

Bolivian exports rely on the exploitation of renewable and non-renewable natural resources. The prospects for growth depend heavily on national negotiations and agreements to participate in regional integration schemes and broader markets.

In the early years of structural adjustment, eliminating import tariffs on inputs for export production and establishing the CRA were ways to promote the export sector, along with reducing import duties on capital goods and inputs. Bolivia's entry into the General Agreement on Tariffs and Trade (GATT) in 1987 permitted the inclusion of other instruments to promote exports, among them the tradable tax credits related to exemptions from the value-added tax, tariff liberalization for exporters, regulating the emission of the CRA and redeemable tax bonds.

The government promoted measures to trim the bureaucracy involved in the administration of foreign trade. To do so, it gave the administration of the customs house to the private sector in concession, created a simplified system for receiving and storing goods, gave tax exemptions to exporters who used national inputs and free trade zones for manufacturing industries and commercial services and suspended payments of taxes and duties on temporary import operations and *maquilas*. In the early 1990s, the SIVEX came into effect, which simplified and centralized the system of export procedures, gave greater access to international credit protected within the framework of the Investments Law, eliminated restrictions on the movement of goods and taxes on inputs for export products, established tax exemptions in free trade zones, and created the Temporary Importation for Exports Regime (RITEX) to exempt export products from the payment of customs duties.

Contracts for the sale of gas to Brazil and the Economic Association Agreement between Bolivia and other Mercosur countries began the modernization of the institutional framework for the creation of a free trade area. The rebate on domestic taxes on inputs for export products and the General Customs Law were put into effect.

The prospects for exporting in the coming years are both controversial and uncertain. Whether selling natural gas to North American and Mexican markets through the Pacific or continuing the gas sales contract with Brazil are real possibilities is the subject of political debate. While both would bring additional income for the government, many factors, such as the terms of sale, prices and costs, externalities derived from building infrastructure, investments and complementary agreements with strategic partners, will play a role.

At the same time, the opportunity to participate in the Free Trade Area of the Americas (FTAA)[11] agreement and the broadening offered by the immediate and short-term Action Plans of the Andean Trade Promotion and Drug Eradication Act (ATPDEA)[12] suggest that strategic actions should be adopted to strengthen the export sector, primarily through support in the form of information and technical assistance, fiscal incentives, simplification of paperwork, promotion of agreements within the private sector – for example, by forming *maquila* industries – or promoting the creation of transportation infrastructure. The time horizon on ATPDEA is limited, policies are essential for promoting exports in an effective manner, oriented towards accelerated technological change and the expansion of the utilized capacities of sectors linked with the external market.

5.3 The labour market and income inequality

Adjustment of the labour market

The fiscal adjustment initiated in the mid-1980s led to a reduction in public sector employment. Firing workers implied payment of benefits and social costs related to higher unemployment. To compensate losses, the government created the Emergency Social Fund, which generated temporary jobs in the maintenance and creation of public infrastructure. Labour reforms implied tying bonuses to the basic wage and simplifying the wage structure a great deal. Business owners used the 3-month trial period contained in the labour legislation as a way to avoid including workers on the rolls for social security and other benefits.

Open contracting under the 1985 labour legislation caused a reduction in open unemployment. Between 1989 and 1997, the open unemployment rate fell from 10.4 to 4.4 per cent (Table 5.6), and less skilled labour saw a decrease in their remunerations (wages). As a result, the informal sector grew significantly, and this led to greater income inequality.

Labour income of unskilled workers fell in real terms during much of the 1990s (1989–95), while income for skilled workers began to recover after 1991 and continued growing until 1997. After 1999, however, income for both skilled and unskilled labour has tended to decline (Table 5.7).

Table 5.6   Bolivia: urban labour market indicators, 1989–2000 (percentage)

	Gross participation rate	Overall participation rate	Employment rate	Open unemployment rate
1989	39.4	52.8	47.3	10.4
1990	38.2	51.3	47.5	7.2
1991	38.3	51.5	48.4	5.9
1992	37.7	50.6	47.8	5.5
1993	39.2	52.6	49.5	6.0
1994	39.9	53.7	52.0	3.1
1995	40.9	55.1	53.1	3.6
1996	42.2	56.6	54.3	4.2
1997	40.6	52.5	50.2	4.4
1999	44.4	56.7	48.3	8.0
2000	43.5	55.9	51.7	7.6
2001	46.8	56.2	51.3	8.6

Source: National Institute of Statistics (INE): household surveys

Table 5.7   Bolivia: urban labour market indicators

	% Skilled workers		Labour income, 1999 = 100	
	Non-tradable	Tradable	Unskilled	Skilled
1989	35.1	31.2	105	78
1990	38.3	31.9	97	83
1991	40.4	33.7	88	71
1992	45.5	39.7	73	78
1993	45.9	38.4	76	89
1994	45.9	40.0	74	92
1995	45.9	40.4	67	89
1996	47.1	39.5	84	95
1997	51.9	41.7	111	115
1999	47.7	36.3	100	100
2000	49.7	40.3	86	95
2001	46.6	42.3	75	86

Source: National Institute of Statistics (INE)

Between 1999 and 2001, unemployment grew to levels comparable to the late 1980s. In 1999, the open unemployment rate was 8 per cent, and it continued to grow to 8.6 per cent in 2001 (Table 5.6). This rapid rise in open unemployment triggered the enactment of the National Emergency Employment Plan (PLANE) aimed at generating short-term employment in works maintenance projects and services. Last year, the plan was able to generate 65,000 jobs in 1 month, primarily benefiting construction workers, unemployed women and unskilled youth.

Table 5.8 Bolivia: poverty and inequality of per capita family income

	1997	1999	2000	2001
Poverty measures[1]				
Incidence of poverty (P_0)	0.632	0.628	0.661	0.648
Poverty gap (P_1)	0.334	0.359	0.399	0.372
Severity (P_2)	0.224	0.257	0.296	0.267
Measures of inequality[1]				
Gini index (national)	0.587	0.578	0.616	0.598
Theil index	0.723	0.635	0.751	0.722

Source: Based on household surveys

Note: 1 Estimate of poverty with per capita family income

Poverty and inequality

Economic growth and reforms put in place during the 1990s fostered a tendency towards poverty reduction. Some studies show that urban income poverty may have fallen nearly 8 percentage points between 1990 and 1995 (Jiménez and Yáñez 1997),[13] and more recent estimates indicate that national poverty fell from 63.2 to 62.8 per cent between 1997 and 1999 (World Bank 2000). Economic deceleration, which began in 1999 and lasted until 2002, once again pushed poverty rates up to 66.1 per cent in 2000 and close to 65 per cent in 2001 (Table 5.8). The growth in poverty levels is attributed, in large part, to an increase in urban unemployment, which practically doubled between 1997 and 2001. At the same time, growing employment in the informal sector accentuated the tendency of falling real labour income of unskilled workers, resulting further in a decline in the family income of poor urban households.

In recent years, increasing poverty was accompanied by a greater concentration of income. Between 1997 and 2001, the Gini coefficient of per capita income increased from 0.587 to 0.598, reflecting the loss of income for households in the lowest percentiles of the income distribution. In the short run, the effects of economic slowdown and recession in a number of activities differed between lower and middle income families, especially because rising unemployment affected the poorest and falling labour income affected workers in the informal sector. In the long run, greater inequality is attributed to increasing differentials in the education levels of the employed population, which is reflected in a rising wage gap between skilled and unskilled labour. It is also probable that workers have lost bargaining power as unemployment rises. This asymmetry explains the tendency increasing towards economic inequality.

5.4 Effects of exports on employment and wages

To evaluate the effect of macroeconomic policies on the labour market we use a CGE model.[14] The basic data for the model are based on the 1996 social accounting matrix for Bolivia (SAM-96). The model allows the generation of simulation scenarios for external shocks and trade policies that affect the levels of remuneration and employment. The CGE results are then used to measure the changes in poverty and inequality using the microsimulation methodology.

CGE model

The CGE represents a group of functional relationships that express decisions that economic agents make to produce, consume and accumulate in order to maximize utility or benefits, given the restrictions related to the price of final goods, inputs and factors. The general equilibrium is established from the balance of macroeconomic aggregates and institutional sectors. The Bolivian CGE follows the basic structure of the Standard Model as outlined in Chapter 3. The base year of the model is 1996 and the accounting identities are laid out in the SAM for that year. Model elasticities and 'closures' are defined in accordance with the nature and adjustment of goods and factor markets reflecting Bolivian reality.

Elasticities

Elasticities are parameters to complete the estimation of functional relationships between the macroeconomic and sector aggregates of the model. They reflect the sensitivity of dependent variables to changes in other model variables. The general equilibrium model considers three types of elasticity: (1) factor substitution, which relates various kinds of labour and capital with the production value generated by the activities; (2) household consumption; and (3) substitutability of domestic products, exports and imports (Table A5.2a). Elasticities are obtained from other CGE analyses for Bolivia (see, for example, Jemio and Wiebelt 2001).

Macro closures

The model's structure allows alternative closures to be considered to reach equilibrium in the function of the characteristics of the economy. The closures permit the definition of macro and factor market variables that are endogenous to the model and those considered to be outside the model (Reinert and Roland-Host 1997). Standardized closures have been adopted for private sector balances, fiscal balance, trade balance and the labour market.

For the closure of the government sector, government savings are endogenous as tax rates are assumed to be fixed (GOV-1). This situation is congruent with the limited degrees of freedom of the government to implement tax reforms as immediate responses to fiscal imbalances.

Closure of the external sector considers the real exchange rate to be flexible (ROW-1), leaving capital inflows fixed. This closure is consistent with the existing exchange rate regime in Bolivia. Savings and investment adjust according to a so-called balanced closure, that is, we assume absorption (part of which is investment) to be fixed at base-year levels. Savings rates of institutional sectors adjust by the same percentage to ensure aggregate ex-post consistency between savings and investment.

Closure of the labour market considers the duality of Bolivia's labour market. On the one hand, wage earners (blue and white collar workers), most of whom are in the formal sector (public and private), tend to receive institutionally fixed real wages and are, therefore, vulnerable to unemployment. On the other hand, many independent workers (own account and employers) are closely associated with the informal sector. We assume real income of this sector to clear any excess demand for labour in this segment of the market. Defined this way, the dichotomy of the labour market implies that an adverse macroeconomic shock tends to reduce wage employment and lower the income of own account workers. Conversely, when there is an expansion in economic activity, wage employment increases along with the income of independent or informal workers. It is probable that the actual functioning of the labour market shows a segmentation that is more complex than the dual economy. Nevertheless, the information contained in SAM-96 does not allow for a more differentiated labour market segmentation.

Simulations based on the general equilibrium model and microsimulations

Counterfactual scenarios constructed with the CGE aim to reflect changes in the economy, in particular those that respond to changes in the external sector and reflect labour market conditions. The simulations consider

1   *external and internal shocks*, considered in conjunction with economic liberalization in the 1990s, among them changes in export prices (+10 and −10 per cent), rising import prices (10 per cent), increased productivity (+10 per cent), higher nominal wages (10 per cent) and higher foreign savings (aid) (+10 per cent), and
2   *trade policies*, reflected in changes in tariffs (+10 and −10 per cent), export subsidies (+10 per cent), a 10 per cent devaluation of the exchange rate, participation in the FTAA agreement (which translates into the reduction of tariffs differentiated by product) and elimination of export subsidies and international price changes brought about by the World Trade Organization's (WTO) liberalization schemes.

Each exercise has two parts. The first is based on macrosimulations from the general equilibrium model with the objective of measuring the impact of external shocks and trade policies on macroeconomic aggregates and labour market variables. The second part contains microsimulations[15] with estimates of the changes in inequality and poverty attributed to the variations in macroeconomic variables.

Variations in the labour market respond to external and internal shocks and are also affected by economic policies. The model supposes that changes will occur in (1) participation rates,[16] (2) unemployment rates, (3) employment structure and (4) the level of labour remunerations according to the skill level and type of worker. Each simulation allows the cumulative effects of variations in the parameters of the labour market to be shown. Workers can move only between types of jobs,[17] not between skill levels.

Simulation of external shocks

Macro effects

Rising import and falling export prices have important contractionary effects on the Bolivian economy. Counterfactual scenarios reveal that for each percentage point decline in the price of the primary export products, real absorption is reduced almost 0.4 per cent, primarily affecting investment (−0.6 per cent), while consumption declines 0.3 per cent (Table 5.9). A reduction in imports tends to contract economic activity and depreciate the exchange rate.

If import prices increase 10 per cent, real absorption could be reduced by about 4 per cent, investment could decrease 9 per cent and private consumption could fall by 6 per cent. The two previous effects would provoke an increase in the balance of trade deficit and unfavourably affect the labour market, reducing the employment and remuneration of the various types of workers.

Conversely, a 10 per cent increase in foreign savings tends to appreciate the exchange rate. At the same time, it increases demand and translates into a 2.4 per cent increase in private consumption and a 3.5 per cent increase in investment. The expansionary effects on economic activity tend to increase the demand for wage earners and the real labour income of independent workers.

A 10 per cent increase in export prices would induce increased investment, absorption would grow by 3.3 per cent and imports would increase by about 9 per cent. The flexible exchange rate regime causes the currency to appreciate. Therefore, exports do not grow significantly. Greater economic activity sets off an increase in the demand for labour and higher labour income.

The simulations of exogenous shocks are complemented by two additional ones: one that reflects a 10 per cent increase in the nominal wage rate of wage earners[18] and another that reflects a 10 per cent increase in labour productivity in export sectors. Higher nominal wages imply higher labour costs, and this would lead to a lower demand for workers. Household consumption could fall 1.9 per cent with respect to the base year level, and government consumption contracts by 5 per cent. The model suggests further that rising nominal wages would cause a contraction in exports and imports in Bolivia's case.

An exogenous increase of 10 per cent in productivity in export sectors (non-traditional agriculture, mining, textiles and wood) would provoke an expansion of macroeconomic aggregates, primarily exports (5 per cent) and absorption (2.7 per cent). The effects on the labour market are expected to be favourable as the aggregate employment level and average remunerations rise.

Effects on poverty and inequality

Negative exogenous shocks are reflected in changes in the welfare indicators of the population. The transmission mechanism is the labour market, which points to changes in the level and structure of employment and remunerations. Negative shocks act through a reduction of employment and real wages.

Increasing import prices and falling export prices cause lower levels of employment and income. These translate into a loss of income sources for workers and

Table 5.9 Bolivia: results of simulations with and without external shocks

	Base (level) Bs 1996	Fall in export price (−10%)	Increase in import price (+10%)	Rise in productivity (+10%)	Increase in nominal wages (+10%)	Increase in export price (+10%)	Increase in foreign savings (+10%)
				% Variation with respect to base			
Macroeconomic indicators							
Absorption	39,566	−3.56	−3.79	2.73	−2.33	3.32	2.57
Household consumption	28,282	−3.21	−3.43	2.76	−1.93	3.01	2.38
Investment	6,095	−6.06	−6.25	3.42	−1.85	5.63	3.54
Government consumption	5,188	−2.53	−2.85	1.81	−5.06	2.24	2.50
Exports	8,394	−0.91	0.10	5.02	−2.00	0.70	−4.07
Imports	−10,238	−8.87	−9.02	4.12	−1.64	8.83	4.86
Real exchange rate	89.7	6.10	6.70	−1.70	−1.10	−5.20	−4.80
Nominal exchange rate	100.0	9.30	−0.60	−1.50	−0.80	−7.90	−4.10
Export prices index	100.0	−10.00	0.00	0.00	0.00	10.00	0.00
Import prices index	100.0	0.00	10.00	0.00	0.00	0.00	0.00
International prices for tradable goods index	100.0	−4.50	5.50	0.00	0.00	4.50	0.00
Domestic prices for non-tradable goods index	111.4	−1.70	−1.70	0.10	0.40	1.50	0.70
Terms of trade	100.0	−10.00	−9.10	0.00	0.00	10.00	0.00
Percentage of nominal GDP							
Investment	16.2	0.10	0.00	−0.10	0.00	−0.10	0.30
Private savings (of households and businesses)	12.1	−0.60	−0.20	0.10	0.20	0.50	−1.40
Foreign savings	4.5	0.60	0.20	−0.20	0.10	−0.50	1.90
Balance of trade deficit	6.6	0.80	0.20	−0.20	0.00	−0.60	1.90
Government savings (−deficit)	−0.5	0.00	0.10	0.10	−0.20	0.00	−0.30
Income from import duties	1.7	0.10	0.10	0.00	0.00	−0.10	0.00
Income from direct taxes	6.9	0.00	0.00	0.00	−0.10	0.00	−0.10

(Continued)

Table 5.9 (Continued)

	Base (level) Bs 1996	Fall in export price (−10%)	Increase in import price (+10%)	Rise in productivity (+10%)	Increase in nominal wages (+10%)	Increase in export price (+10%)	Increase in foreign savings (+10%)
Labour market indicators							
Employment by factor type							
Skilled wage workers	6,659	−3.19	−3.15	2.50	−7.21	2.81	1.22
Unskilled production workers	4,616	−3.06	−3.04	2.36	−6.67	2.71	1.23
Skilled – independent[1]	2,850	—	—	—	—	—	—
Unskilled – independent[1]	4,345	—	—	—	—	—	—
				Average remuneration by factor			
Skilled wage workers[2]	100.0	—	—	—	10.00	—	—
Unskilled production workers[2]	100.0	—	—	—	10.00	—	—
Skilled – independent	100.0	−5.69	−5.52	5.10	−3.48	5.11	1.71
Unskilled – independent	100.0	−5.39	−5.12	1.83	−3.71	4.84	1.09
					Real per capita household consumption		
Urban households	23.5	−3.30	−3.50	2.70	−1.90	3.10	2.50
Rural households	4.8	−2.90	−3.10	2.90	−2.00	2.70	2.00
Total households	28.3	−3.20	−3.40	2.80	−1.90	3.00	2.40

Source: CGE – Bolivia

Notes
1 Supposes full employment of independent workers
2 The wage of wage workers is fixed. Unemployment is considered in this group of workers

consequently lower family income. A 10 per cent reduction in the price of exports causes a 1.27 per cent rise in the incidence of poverty and a 3.13 per cent increase in the poverty gap.[19] Increased poverty is accompanied by greater per capita income inequality (Table 5.10). This means that the increase in poverty comes not only from the contractive effects of the exogenous shocks, but also from the distributive impact of those shocks.

A converse effect could be brought on by an increase in both export prices and foreign savings. Both tend to generate lower poverty levels. If exports go up 10 per cent, the incidence of poverty goes down (cumulative effect) by 0.92 per cent with respect to the level of the base year, and the poverty gap falls by 0.52 per cent. The reduction in poverty is brought on both by higher income levels and by less inequality in the distribution of income.

An increase in wages and productivity would produce opposite effects on poverty and inequality. A higher nominal wage level translates into greater inequality, as a consequence of income disparity generated between those who receive the wage increase (wage earners) and those who do not receive it (own account workers). The consequences of the increased cost of wages, as simulated through the general equilibrium model, are transmitted to the labour market, reducing the demand for labour and generating lower labour income. Conversely, a 10 per cent increase in productivity in export sectors translates into a 4 per cent reduction in the incidence of poverty and a 2.6 per cent reduction in the poverty gap, accompanied by decreasing inequality in income distribution.

Trade policies

Macro effects

The simulation of trade policies relates changes in tariffs, export subsidies, further trade integration in regional and global markets and exchange rate management to macroeconomic aggregates, the labour market, poverty and inequality.

A uniform tariff cut (−50 per cent) tends to promote a greater flow of trade and an appreciation of the exchange rate as exports grow faster than imports. Import liberalization generates an expansion in the demand for consumption and investment (Table 5.11). Though it triggers a reduction in government consumption, real absorption increases 0.27 per cent, caused primarily by an increase in investments (0.88 per cent). Formal sector employment grows around 0.54 per cent and income from independent work grows 1.16 per cent.

A return to greater protectionism, i.e. a uniform tariff increase by 50 per cent with respect to the base year level, reduces imports by 1.1 per cent and lowers exports by 1.4 per cent. Government consumption could increase to 0.84 per cent, but this precipitates contractionary effects on macroeconomic aggregates: investments would be reduced by 0.84 per cent and consumption would contract by 0.21 per cent. The lower economic activity generated by a decrease in trade could translate to a reduction in employment levels and labour income.

A policy of promoting exports based on subsidies (of 10 per cent, for example) would be able to raise the exported value by as much as 5.11 per cent. At the same

Table 5.10 Bolivia: microsimulations with and without internal and external shocks (percentage variations with respect to base)

	Measures of poverty		Inequality of per capita household income		Labour income inequality	
	P_0	P_1	Gini	Theil	Gini	Theil
Value observed in base year (1997)	*0.6247*	*0.3367*	*0.5939*	*0.7275*	*0.5629*	*0.6156*
Reduction of export prices						
(1) Participation rate	0.43	2.02*	−0.17	−1.97	−0.98	−5.00*
(1) + (2) Unemployment rate	1.05*	2.72*	−0.53	−2.46*	−0.98	−5.00*
(1) + (2) + (3) Employment structure	1.18*	3.19*	0.88*	3.73*	−1.15	−4.96*
(1) + (2) + (3) + (4) Wage levels	1.27*	3.13*	0.90	3.82	−1.19	−5.40*
Increase in import prices						
(1) Participation rate	0.48	2.01*	−0.26	−2.30	−0.98	−5.00*
(1) + (2) Unemployment rate	1.21	2.80*	−0.51	−2.29	−0.99	−5.00
(1) + (2) + (3) Employment structure	1.35*	3.22*	0.92	3.85	−1.15	−5.10*
(1) + (2) + (3) + (4) Wage levels	1.28*	3.06*	0.87	3.77	−1.20	−5.42*
Increase in productivity						
(1) Participation rate	0.43	1.79*	−0.32	−2.38	−0.98	−5.00
(1) + (2) Unemployment rate	−0.78	0.64	−0.41	−3.23	−0.99	−5.00*
(1)+(2)+(3) Employment structure	−3.90*	−2.22	−2.24*	−9.97*	−2.57*	−10.15*
(1) + (2) + (3) + (4) Wage levels	−4.04*	−2.56*	−2.66*	−10.73*	−2.35*	−9.62*
Increase in nominal wages						
(1) Participation rate	0.28	2.03*	−0.25	−2.38	−0.99	−5.00*
(1) + (2) Unemployment rate	1.22*	2.89*	−0.52	−2.38	−0.99	−5.00*
(1) + (2) + (3) Employment structure	1.43*	3.64*	1.01	4.07	−1.55*	−5.92*
(1) + (2) + (3) + (4) Wage levels	1.35*	3.71*	1.05*	4.13	−1.36	−6.09*
Increase in price of exports						
(1) Participation rate	0.30	2.14*	−0.39	−2.59	−0.99	−5.00*
(1) + (2) Unemployment rate	−1.06	0.70	−0.48	−3.50	−0.99	−5.00*
(1) + (2) + (3) Employment structure	−0.90	0.64*	−2.35*	−9.01*	−2.83*	−10.94*
(1) + (2) + (3) + (4) Wage levels	−0.92*	0.52	−2.22*	−8.63*	−2.82*	−10.85*

(Continued)

Table 5.10   (Continued)

	Measures of poverty		Inequality of per capita household income		Labour income inequality	
	P_0	P_1	Gini	Theil	Gini	Theil
Increase in foreign savings						
(1) Participation rate	0.37	2.06*	−0.17	−1.99	−0.98	−5.00*
(1) + (2) Unemployment rate	−0.66	0.86	−0.48	−3.27	−0.99	−5.00*
(1) + (2) + (3) Employment structure	−0.58	0.93	−1.30	−5.96*	−1.67*	−7.24*
(1) + (2) + (3) + (4) Wage levels	−2.50*	−0.75	−2.18*	−9.11*	−1.90*	−8.03*

Source: CGE – Bolivia and 1997 INE household survey

Note
*Significant within 95% of the confidence interval with 100 repeated simulations for each case

time, however, it would generate an appreciation in currency. In the short term, this could increase economic activity, employment and labour income.

Scenarios that reflect the possible participation of Bolivia in the FTAA and WTO agreements are manifested in a new structure of tariffs and prices that impact export and import flows. Under the FTAA, import tariffs tend to decrease and, while export prices for minerals and hydrocarbons are lower, the prices of non-food industrial products also go down (Table A5.2b). The import structure shows a high share of manufactured products. Because of this, changes in prices and tariffs due to the FTAA could bring about a reduction in import prices and a depreciation in the exchange rate that would favour Bolivian exports. The boost to investments could have expansionary consequences on economic activity in Bolivia.

The WTO scenario forecasts higher prices for imports and agricultural export products, a decrease in mineral and hydrocarbon prices and an increase in industrial products. The combined effects of the WTO translate into export prices rising at a faster pace than import prices, generating incentives for investment and the expansion of domestic activity. The results of the simulation, both of FTAA and the WTO, depend in large part on the structure of trade and the prospects for strengthening the productive sector.

Effects on poverty and inequality

Economic liberalization through lower import tariffs appears to generate an increase in employment and wages, leading to a fall in poverty incidence (P_0) of 1.5 per cent. However, the poverty gap (P_1) tends to increase, despite a systematic reduction in income inequality (Table 5.12). The interpretation of this ambiguous outcome for poverty is that agricultural sectors are losers of trade liberalization, affecting the incomes of Bolivia's poorest. Hence, the average income

Table 5.11 Bolivia: results of simulations with and without trade policies

	Base (level) Bs 1996	Tariff reductions (−50%)	Tariff increases (+50%)	Export subsidies (+10%)	WTO	FTAA	Exchange rate devaluation (+10%)
Macroeconomic indicators							
		% Variation from base					
Absorption	39,566	0.27	−0.26	0.78	1.16	0.40	−6.77
Household consumption	28,282	0.21	−0.21	0.65	0.99	0.32	−6.34
Investment	6,095	0.88	−0.84	2.29	2.75	1.26	−8.60
Government consumption	5,188	−0.13	0.11	−0.27	0.22	−0.18	−6.96
Exports	8,394	1.49	−1.40	5.11	2.00	2.11	12.51
Imports	−10,238	1.22	−1.14	4.19	4.48	1.82	−10.78
Real exchange rate	89.7	1.30	−1.30	−5.20	0.90	2.00	12.00
Nominal exchange rate	100.0	1.60	−1.50	−4.40	−0.90	2.50	10.00
Export prices index	100.0	0.00	0.00	0.00	4.90	0.00	0.00
Import prices index	100.0	0.00	0.00	0.00	1.60	−0.10	0.00
International prices for tradable goods index	100.0	0.00	0.00	0.00	3.10	−0.10	0.00
Domestic prices for non-tradable goods index	111.4	0.30	−0.20	0.80	1.20	0.40	−1.80
Terms of trade	100.0	0.00	0.00	0.00	3.20	0.10	0.00
Percentage of nominal GDP							
Investment	16.2	0.00	0.00	−0.10	0.00	0.00	−0.90
Private savings (households and businesses)	12.1	0.70	−0.70	2.20	1.80	1.00	4.20
Foreign savings	4.5	0.10	−0.10	−0.20	−0.10	0.10	−5.80
Balance of trade deficit	6.6	−0.70	0.70	−2.50	−1.80	−1.10	−5.80
Government savings (−deficit)	−0.5	−0.70	0.70	−2.00	−1.70	−1.10	0.80
Income from import duties	1.7	−0.80	0.80	0.00	−1.70	−1.20	0.00
Income from direct taxes	6.9	0.10	−0.10	0.20	0.10	0.10	0.20

(Continued)

Table 5.11 (Continued)

	Base (level) Bs 1996	Tariff reductions (−50%)	Tariff increases (+50%)	Export subsidies (+10%)	WTO	FTAA	Exchange rate devaluation (+10%)
Labour market indicators							
Employment by factor type							
Wage workers – skilled	6,659	0.57	−0.54	1.76	1.21	0.82	−2.74
Wage workers – unskilled	4,616	0.54	−0.52	1.54	1.87	0.82	−3.15
Independent – skilled[1]	2,850	—	—	—	—	—	—
Independent– unskilled[1]	4,345	—	—	—	—	—	—
Average remuneration by factor							
Wage workers – skilled[2]	100.0	—	—	—	—	—	—
Wage workers – unskilled[2]	100.0	—	—	—	—	—	—
Independent – skilled	100.0	1.16	−1.12	3.51	4.53	1.83	−4.22
Independent – unskilled	100.0	1.23	−1.21	3.66	8.92	2.14	−3.22
Real per capita household consumption							
Urban households	23.5	0.20	−0.20	0.70	0.70	0.30	−6.50
Rural households	4.8	0.20	−0.30	0.60	2.40	0.50	−5.60
Total households	28.3	0.20	−0.20	0.60	1.00	0.30	−6.30

Source: CGE – Bolivia

Notes
1 Supposes full employment of independent workers
2 The wage of wage workers is fixed. Unemployment is considered in this group of workers

of the poor would decline, while rising employment in other parts of the economy allows some poor to cross the poverty line. This outcome suggests that the social adjustment costs of trade liberalization are potentially high if, as is the case, there is no smooth migration of workers across sectors and from rural to urban areas.

In the short term, export subsidies benefit export sectors. Income gains are mainly concentrated among the non-poor and barely little trickles down to the poor. There is a slight, but barely significant, decrease in poverty incidence, but the poverty gap rises, because agricultural sectors are expected to lose as in the case of import liberalization. The implications are thus the same as under the previous scenario.

A 10 per cent devaluation causes a contraction in employment in the static model simulations. Devaluation of the nominal exchange rate makes imported products more expensive and reduces real wages in terms of tradable goods. Because of the high import dependence of productive sectors, aggregate output and absorption fall and both the poverty incidence (1.08 per cent) and the poverty gap (3.08 per cent) increase.

The expansionary effects of further trade integration through the WTO would work much the same way as the import liberalization scenario, but with hardly any reduction in poverty incidence and a rising poverty gap. However, in this case it seems that industrial and urban informal services are the main losers in the process, causing incomes of the poorest in non-agriculture to decline. The hydrocarbon sector is strongly affected under this scenario and indirectly seems to pull down demand for urban services. In the case of FTAA, such effects are less apparent, as world manufacturing import prices for Bolivia are expected to rise less than under WTO. Also, the hydrocarbon sector is not losing out. In consequence, FTAA could bring benefits to Bolivia in the form of a reduction of poverty incidence (P_0), albeit bringing no income gains to those remaining poor as the poverty gap (P_1) remains virtually unchanged.

5.5 Conclusions and policy implications

Trade liberalization and export promotion contributed to growth in the Bolivian economy during much of the 1990s. Growth options in the future cannot disregard the need to strengthen the export sector, in terms of both the exploitation of natural resources and the inclusion of more processed products.

Export promotion activities were reinforced with structural adjustment, through establishing fiscal incentives, eliminating previous permits, placing a single window for the simplification of procedures, etc. However, this process was not accompanied by structural solutions to improve infrastructure and trade services or to develop the quality of the supply. Such obstacles still impose severe restrictions on the export sector and probably explain much of the stagnation of exports in the last 20 years.

Opening markets, especially through regional integration processes and liberalizing trade, has the potential to broaden export activities. However, it also challenges domestic enterprises to modernize quickly. Lowering tariffs within the framework of liberalization requires the transformation of production with reforms aimed at building competitiveness for national products. It is especially important to lower production costs and improve product quality.

Table 5.12 Bolivia: microsimulations with and without trade policies (percentage change from base)

	Measures of poverty		Per capita family income inequality		Inequality in labour income	
	P_0	P_1	Gini	Theil	Gini	Theil
Values observed in base year (1997)	*0.6247*	*0.3367*	*0.5939*	*0.7275*	*0.5629*	*0.6156*
Reduction in tariffs						
(1) Participation rate	−0.93	1.25	−0.45	−5.57*	−0.70*	−1.69*
(1) + (2) Unemployment rate	−1.20*	1.23	−0.51	−5.86*	−0.99*	−5.00*
(1) + (2) + (3) Employment structure	−1.27*	0.99	−0.89*	−7.04*	−1.35*	−6.25*
(1) + (2) + (3) + (4) Wage levels	−1.49*	0.71	−0.91*	−6.97*	−1.35*	−6.20*
Increase in tariffs						
(1) Participation rate	0.47	2.21*	−0.18	−2.22	−0.98	−5.00*
(1) + (2) Unemployment rate	0.92	2.65*	1.19	4.00*	−0.95	−4.70*
(1) + (2) + (3) Employment structure	0.93	2.52*	1.12*	4.07*	−0.85	−4.49*
(1) + (2) + (3) + (4) Wage levels	0.76	2.22*	1.08	3.89	−0.84	−4.53*
Export subsidies						
(1) Participation rate	0.42	2.11*	−0.21	−2.38	−0.99	−5.00*
(1) + (2) Unemployment rate	−0.58	1.02*	−0.40	−2.90	−0.99	−5.00*
(1) + (2) + (3) Employment structure	−0.60	0.91	−1.95*	−8.05*	−2.03*	−8.48*
(1) + (2) + (3) + (4) Wage levels	−0.30	1.44	−1.63	−7.36*	−2.04*	−8.41*
FTAA						
(1) Participation rate	−0.73	1.49*	−0.42	−5.49	−0.99	−5.00*
(1) + (2) Unemployment rate	−1.12*	0.96*	−0.49	−6.17	−0.99	−5.00*
(1) + (2) + (3) Employment structure	−1.15*	0.98*	−0.98*	−7.25*	−1.47*	−6.66*
(1) + (2) + (3) + (4) Wage levels	−1.93*	−0.14*	−1.14*	−7.73*	−1.47*	−6.59*
WTO						
(1) Participation rate	0.44	2.05*	−0.11	−1.95	−0.99	−5.00*
(1) + (2) Unemployment rate	−0.31	1.46*	−0.11	−2.45	−0.98	−5.00*
(1) + (2) + (3) Employment structure	−0.68	1.20*	−2.05*	−8.41*	−1.70*	−7.39*
(1) + (2) + (3) + (4) Wage levels	−0.23	1.19*	−1.94*	−8.14*	−1.98*	−7.87*

(Continued)

Table 5.12 (Continued)

	Measures of poverty		Per capita family income inequality		Inequality in labour income	
	P_0	P_1	Gini	Theil	Gini	Theil
		Devaluation				
(1) Participation rate	0.51	2.03*	−0.20	−2.16	−0.98	−5.00*
(1) + (2) Unemployment rate	0.97*	2.60*	−0.59	−2.44	−0.98	−5.00*
(1) + (2) + (3) Employment structure	1.19*	3.08*	0.86	3.72	−0.87	−4.35*
(1) + (2) + (3) + (4) Wage levels	1.08*	3.08*	0.89*	3.75	−1.21	−5.42*

Source: CGE – Bolivia and 1997 INE household survey

Note
*Significant within 95% of the confidence interval with 100 repeated simulations for each case

In spite of the great expectations for hydrocarbon exports, they have all the limitations of other primary export strategies. Even if they can generate significant investments and overcome institutional barriers, their impact on employment and economic activities could be insufficient to raise the welfare of the population. The extreme poor appear to be excluded from the gains of freer trade. Along with export-based growth, other potential substitute sectors should be developed, like services or intermediary goods, for both local production and future export.

Recent plans emphasize investment in activities that have the potential to find a place in both internal and external markets. Currently, these are at the centre of attention of the so-called productive chains (clusters) that could have advantages within the ATPDEA framework; among them are textiles, animal skins, leather and wood. Businessmen need to form networks to make better use of the comparative advantages.

It is becoming more costly to create permanent jobs, especially during recessions when economic resources are limited. Direct stimulus to job creation is important as long as it does not create a disincentive to the adoption of new technologies. Activities to broaden training and human resource formation in businesses could be intensified.

External shocks have hampered economic growth, primarily through worsening of the terms of trade and reduction of external demand. These effects are readily transmitted to the labour market. The emergency employment programme and public investment towards unskilled-labour-intensive sectors could counteract the deteriorating labour market conditions as an anticyclical policy device. In addition, one should consider that there are opportunity costs to failing to promote infrastructure investment and policies aiming at removing structural bottlenecks to greater diversification of economic activity.

Table A5.1(a) Social accounting matrix for Bolivia, 1996 (thousands of US$)

	Activities	Products	Transaction costs	Factors	Enterprises	Government	Households	Savings investment	Inventory changes	Income tax	Taxes/sales	Tariffs	Rest of the world	Total
Activities		12,108												12,108
Products	5,676		1,036			1,021	5,564	1,195					1,651	16,148
Transaction costs		1,036							4					1,036
Factors	6,432													6,432
Enterprises				1,108	881	291							28	2,308
Government				0	0	777				509	865	124	9	2,275
Households				5,277	153	238	150						337	5,676
Savings investment					759	−52								1,195
Inventory changes					42	0	−38							4
Income tax				37	472									509
Sales tax		865												865
Tariffs		124		11										124
Rest of the world		2,014		11										2,025
Total	12,108	16,148	1,036	6,432	2,308	2,275	5,676	1,195	4	509	865	124	2,025	38,597

Source: Elaborated based on INE accounting matrix

Table A5.1(b)   Activities and products used in the social accounting matrix

Activities		Products	
A1 Agriculture	A12 Other industries	C1 Agriculture	C11 Communications
A2 Livestock	A13 Electricity, gas	C2 Livestock	C12 Services
A3 Hydrocarbon	and water	C3 Mineral	C15 Restaurants and
extraction	A14 Construction	extraction	hotels
A4 Mineral	A15 Trade	C4 Hydrocarbon	C17 Public
extraction	A16 Transportation	extraction	administration
A5 Food industry	A17 Communications	C5 Food industry	
A6 Textile industry	A18 Financial and	C6 Other	
A7 Wood industry	social services	industries	
A8 Paper industry	A23 Restaurants and	C7 Electricity, gas	
A9 Chemical	hotels	and water	
industry	A25 Public	C8 Construction	
A10 Hydrocarbon	administration	C9 Trade	
derivatives		C10 Transportation	
industry			
A11 Metallic and			
machinery			
minerals industry			

Table A5.2(a)   Elasticities and parameters for Bolivia CGE model

Activity	Elasticity of substitution between factors
Agriculture, livestock	0.2
Mining, hydrocarbons	0.4
Food, textile, wood, paper and other industries	0.6
Services	0.6
Public services	0.4

	Trade elasticity		Elasticity of consumption demand	
	Imports (Armington)	*Exports (CET)*	*Urban households*	*Rural households*
Agricultural products	0.9	0.6	0.7	0.9
Livestock	1.2	1.0	0.8	0.9
Mining	0.8	1.5	0.8	1.0
Hydrocarbons	0.8	1.3	0.8	1.0
Food	0.9	0.9	0.7	0.8
Non-food industrial products	0.8	0.5	1.2	1.3
Electricity, gas, water	0.2	0.2	0.8	1.0
Construction	—	—	0.7	0.7
Transportation	0.8	0.5	0.8	1.0
Communications	0.8	0.5	0.8	1.0
Financial services	1.5	0.9	1.2	1.1
Restaurants and hotels	—	—	0.8	1.0
Public administration	—	—	1.0	1.0

Table A5.2(b)   Parameters for the FTAA and WTO scenario simulations (percent variation with respect to base year)

	FTAA			WTO	
	Import tariffs	*Export prices*	*Import prices*	*Export prices*	*Import prices*
Agricultural products	0.08081	1.000	1.005	1.090	1.159
Fishing	0.67305	1.001	0.996	1.213	1.001
Mining	0.22785	0.995	0.995	0.998	0.998
Hydrocarbons	0.22785	0.997	0.995	0.996	0.998
Food	0.12242	1.002	1.004	1.072	1.135
Non-food industrial products	0.28097	0.997	0.998	1.005	1.005
Electricity, gas, water	0.79857	0.997	1.000	0.980	1.000
Construction	0.91037	1.000	1.000	1.000	1.000
Transportation	0.74077	1.000	1.000	1.000	1.000
Communications	0.74077	1.000	1.000	1.000	1.000
Financial services	0.74077	1.000	1.000	1.000	1.000
Restaurants and hotels	0.74077	1.000	1.000	1.000	1.000
Public administration	0.39862	1.000	1.000	1.000	1.000

Source: GTAP world model

Acknowledgements

The author is grateful for the collaboration of Enrique Ganuza, Sherman Robinson and Valeria Piñeiro and for the comments of Rodney Pereira, Miguel Vera and Rob Vos. This document does not represent the institutional opinion of UDAPE.

Notes

1 Export value and volume indicators correspond to data calculated by Unidad de Análisis de Políticas Sociales y Económicas (UDAPE) (*Dossier de Estadísticas Económicas y Sociales*, vol. 12, La Paz, 2002).
2 During the devaluation of the Brazilian Real and the changes in Argentina's exchange rate policy, the *Bolsín* played an important role in counteracting external shocks.
3 Based on reports evaluating the reforms; internal documents of UDAPE.
4 In 1999, 70 per cent of the public external debt was concessional.
5 The impact of aggregate demand components on growth is calculated using a decomposition of the GDP growth rate (see Chapter 2 of this volume). The 'export effect' measures how much of GDP growth is due to export volume growth.
6 The measure of the current account corresponds to the external balance of the national accounts (exports minus imports, net of factor payments and current transfers), with

the goal of establishing consistent relationships with other macroeconomic aggregates. See Chapter 2.

7 The decomposition of the variations in the trade balance is based on Morley and Vos (this volume). See also Chapter 2 for the decomposition methodology. The current account balance equals exports minus imports of goods and services minus interest and other net factor payments plus net current transfers and remittances received. If the effects of variation in quantity and prices on the flow of goods and services and the interest rates implicit in the factor payments are considered, one can differentiate the impact of external shocks (prices), trade (quantity) and interest rates (on debt payment and servicing), and the interaction effects of these variables.

8 Imports show a sensitivity to increased economic activity, especially consumer goods, which tended to grow more than proportionally to the increase in domestic income (Loza 1999).

9 This includes agricultural products, fish, extraction of minerals and hydrocarbons, industrial products and food and non-food products.

10 The results of the Chenery decomposition show the contribution of domestic demand, import substitution and the growth in exports over the changes in sector output (see Chapter 2, Appendix A2.5).

11 In 1994, 34 countries agreed to promote an FTAA agreement that would take effect in 2005. The objective of this agreement has to do with generating a free trade area over the entire continent and progressively eliminating all trade and investment barriers in the region.

12 ATPDEA promotes access of 6,100 products to the US market beginning in 2002 and coming to an end in December 2006. To take part in the benefits of ATPDEA, countries commit to engaging in a concerted battle against illicit trafficking of narcotics and related crimes, fighting terrorism, supporting democratic governments, eradicating child labour, supporting the formation of FTAA and protecting intellectual property rights.

13 However, not all studies agree that poverty actually fell in the first half of the 1990s. Vos *et al.* (1997) show that poverty remained more or less unchanged when measured through consumption data.

14 SAM-96 distinguishes between 21 activities and 15 products, detailed in Table A5.1(b) in the Appendix. This structure relates to the principal export products. The SAM also distinguishes four groups of workers, classified by their level of education (skilled and unskilled) and occupational category (wage workers and own account workers). There are two groups of households, rural and urban.

15 Methodology is based on an accounting decomposition of per capita income (ypc), related to the median labour income (w_{ij}) and employment rates (l_{ij}) per type of employment i and skill level j, the percentage of adults n and non-labour income (T). The functional relationship of income per capita is expressed in the following equation: $$ypc = \frac{\sum_{i,j} w_{ij} l_{ij}}{n} + \frac{T}{n}$$

Per capita income will change as previous parameters are modified as a consequence of changes simulated in the CGE. Changes in the labour market are reflected in parameters related to the participation rate of unemployment, structure of employment and level of remuneration. The microsimulations model changes in the condition of individuals' activity and occupation in function of decision rules attributed to unobservable variables like ability and random ordering that reflects people's propensity to change their occupational position (see Chapter 3 for a more detailed discussion). Changes in employment bring with it variations in remuneration, distribution of wage income and distribution of family income. Changes in employment and wages permit the elaboration of estimates of poverty and inequality for counterfactual scenarios, keeping in mind that they are elaborated with at least 100 simulations in each exercise due to the introduction of random criteria.

16 The model does not explicitly consider any effect on the participation rate, but systematic changes have been observed in this variable as a function of income. Thus, it has been assumed that the decision to change the labour supply depends on variations in income.
17 Occupational mobility between categories and activities is determined by the propensity of individuals to change their activity. In part, it depends on the kind of skill, the initial occupational category and the unobserved ability of the people involved (Jiménez and Jiménez 2001).
18 The specification of the closure of the labour market in this simulation is modified, supposing fixed wages and unemployment.
19 The magnitudes proposed correspond to the cumulative effects of the variation in participation rates, unemployment, employment structure and remunerations.

References

Adelman, I and S. Robinson (1988) 'Macroeconomic adjustment and income distribution. Alternative models applied to two economies', *Journal of Development Economics* 29.

Antelo, E., L. Jemio, and B. Requena (1995) 'La competitividad en Bolivia', *Revista de Análisis Económico*, 13, La Paz: Unidad de Análisis de Políticas Económicas (UDAPE).

Cupé, E. (2002) 'Efecto "pass-through" de la depreciación sobre la inflación y términos de intercambio internos en Bolivia', *Revista de Análisis Económico*, La Paz: Unidad de Análisis de Políticas Sociales y Económicas (UDAPE).

Delgadillo, M. (1996) 'Es bueno el sistema tributario en Bolivia?', *Revista de Análisis Económico*, 15, La Paz: Unidad de Análisis de Políticas Sociales y Económicas (UDAPE).

Delgadillo, M., I. Loma and R. Pardo (2001) *El Efecto de la apertura del mercado boliviano en las recaudaciones aduaneras*, La Paz: UDAPE (mimeo).

Fundación Milenio (various years). *Informes sobre la Economía Boliviana 1995, 1996, 1997, 1998, 1999 y 2000*, nos. 4 to 9, La Paz.

Gobierno Nacional de la República (2000) *Estrategia Boliviana de Reducción de la Pobreza*, La Paz.

Hernani, W. (2002) 'Mercado laboural, pobreza y desigualdad en Bolivia. Análisis y Estadística', *Revista de Análisis Económico y Social*, La Paz: Instituto Nacional de Estadística, Programa MECOVI (mimeo).

Jemio, L. and M. Wiebelt (2001) *External shocks and anti-shock policies: a CGE analysis for Bolivia*, La Paz: CAF (mimeo).

Jiménez, L. (1995) *Distribución del ingreso, shocks y políticas macroeconómicas*, Santiago: Comisión Económica Para América Latina y El Caribe (mimeo).

Jiménez, E. and W. Jiménez (2001) 'Movilidad ocupacional y desempleo en el área urbana de Bolivia', *Revista de Economía Política* II(1), La Paz: Sociedad de Economía Política.

Jiménez, W. and E. Yáñez (1997) 'Pobreza en las ciudades de Bolivia', Working Paper, La Paz: Unidad de Análisis de Políticas Sociales.

Landa, F. (2002) *La pobreza en Bolivia entre 1999 y 2001*, La Paz: Unidad de Análisis de Políticas Sociales y Económicas (mimeo).

Löfgren, H., R. Lee and S. Robinson (2001) 'A standard computable general equilibrium (CGE) model in GAMS', TMD Discussion Paper no. 75, Washington, DC: International Food Policy Research Institute (IFPRI), Trade and Macroeconomics Division.

Lora, O and W. Orellana (2001) 'El tipo de cambio real de equilibrio: Un análisis del caso boliviano de los últimos años', *Revista de Análisis* 3(1), La Paz: Banco Central de Bolivia.

Loza, G. (2000) 'El tipo de cambio, exportaciones e importaciones. El caso de la economía boliviana', *Revista de Análisis* 3(1), La Paz: Banco Central de Bolivia.

Paredes, R. (1994) *Propuesta para la reforma de la legislación laboral*, La Paz: Unidad de Análisis de Políticas Económicas (mimeo).

Pereira, R. and W. Jiménez (2001) 'Liberalización de la balanza de pagos: efectos sobre el empleo, desigualdad y pobreza', in: Enrique Ganuza, R. Paes de Barros, L. Taylor and R. Vos (eds) *Liberalización, desigualdad y pobreza: América Latina y el Caribe en los 90*, Buenos Aires: Editorial Universitaria de Buenos Aires (EUDEBA), Programa de las Naciones Unidas para el Desarrollo (PNUD) y Comisión Económica para América Latina (CEPAL).

Reinert, K. A. and D. W. Roland-Holst (1997) 'Social accounting matrices', in: J. F. Francois and K. A. Reinert (eds) *Applied Methods for Trade Policy Analysis,* Cambridge: Cambridge University Press.

UDAPE (1997) *Dossier de Estadísticas Económicas y Sociales de Bolivia No. 7*, La Paz: Unidad de Análisis de Políticas Económicas.

Vos, R, H. Lee and J. A. Mejía (1997) 'Structural adjustment and poverty in Bolivia', INDES Working Paper I-3, Washington, DC: Inter-American Development Bank.

World Bank (2000) *Poverty Diagnostic 2000*, Washington, DC: The World Bank.

Zambrana, H. (2002) *La apertura externa en Bolivia*, La Paz: Unidad de Análisis de Políticas Sociales y Económicas (mimeo).

6 Brazil – the impact of trade openness on employment, poverty and inequality

Francisco Galrão Carneiro and
Jorge Saba Arbache

Abstract

Brazil's trade reforms were very ambitious and introduced in a short period of time. Import tariffs and non-tariff barriers were reduced significantly in less than 3 years after a long period of controlled imports and avoidance of foreign competition. The expectation was that after increasing exposure to international trade the economy would embark on a fast-growth track due to improvements in productivity with positive spillover effects on inequality and poverty. There is, however, some controversy among analysts in Brazil about the effectiveness of trade liberalization in reducing inequality and poverty in practice. This chapter takes a more comprehensive approach than most existing studies to investigate the impact of greater trade openness on employment, poverty and inequality in Brazil. The empirical strategy is based on a decomposition analysis to assess the main determinants of current account deficits following trade liberalization as well as output decomposition into private sector demand, public sector expenditures and import substitution. Going beyond this aggregate analysis, we use a computable general equilibrium model to simulate different policy scenarios and use the results of this modelling approach to create counterfactual microsimulations and assess the impacts of greater trade openness on household income distribution and poverty ratios. The main finding is that trade liberalization alone is not sufficient to reduce poverty and inequality in Brazil in any significant way.

6.1 Introduction

Most Latin American and Caribbean countries adopted the reforms of the so-called Washington Consensus during the 1990s in an attempt to control inflation and resume economic growth. Brazil was not an exception in promoting trade liberalization, privatization, administrative reforms and seeking better fiscal discipline. This set of reforms was supposed to promote macroeconomic stabilization and attract long-term foreign capital that would contribute for a sustainable process of economic growth in the whole of the region.

In the majority of the countries, trade reforms were very ambitious and took place at a very rapid pace. That was also the case of Brazil, where import tariffs and non-tariff barriers were reduced significantly in less than 3 years after a long period of controlled imports and avoidance of foreign competition. The expectation was that after increasing exposure to international trade the economy would embark on a fast-growth track due to improvements in productivity with positive spillover effects on inequality and poverty.

There is, however, some controversy about the effectiveness of trade liberalization in improving inequality and poverty indicators (Carneiro and Arbache 2003). In this chapter, we review major macroeconomic developments since the 1980s and describe the main economic reforms adopted during the 1990s. Using output decomposition analyses, computable general equilibrium (CGE) simulations and counterfactual scenarios we assess the effects of trade liberalization and changes in the minimum wage on employment, poverty and inequality indicators in Brazil. The counterfactual scenarios proposed in this chapter include (1) a set of simulations that consider incentives to exports by means of a devalued exchange rate and an exogenous policy to increase export subsidies and (2) another set of experiments that propose more explicit trade liberalizing measures, such as tariff reductions and the implementation of regional free trade agreements [e.g. Free Trade Agreement of the Americas (FTAA) and World Trade Organization (WTO)]. The experiments are based on data for 1996 and draw on the most recent social accounting matrix (SAM) available for Brazil. The results, thus, must be interpreted with due care.

The chapter is organized as follows. After this introduction, Section 6.2 reviews the major macroeconomic developments over the 1990s. Section 6.3 describes (1) the results of an output growth decomposition analysis based on a Keynesian multiplier and on a sectoral decomposition methodology as developed by Chenery (1979) and (2) the aggregate performance of exports and its product and sectoral composition, as well as the role of export promotion policies in Brazil. Section 6.4 makes use of a CGE model for Brazil to simulate the impacts of greater openness on the major labour market indicators, while Section 6.5 applies the elasticities obtained with the CGE model strategy to assess the impact of different policy scenarios on poverty and inequality indicators. Section 6.6 concludes pointing to the limited scope of trade liberalization to significantly affect poverty and inequality in Brazil.

6.2 Macroeconomic background and structural reforms

The adoption of structural reforms in Brazil in the 1990s was preceded by deteriorating economic conditions that included accelerating inflation, declining investment rates, low or falling growth rates, large fiscal deficits and contraction of financial intermediation. Prior to 1990, the economic strategy was based on import substitution that prevailed for decades provoking lasting inefficiencies and inducement to poor macroeconomic management. In an attempt to revert the trajectory of accelerating inflation and slow growth, reforms of the so-called Washington Consensus were introduced during the 1990s and the country engaged in fiscal adjustment, privatization, deregulation and, above all, trade liberalization. Trade liberalization took place over a relatively short period of time, and the reductions in trade protection were substantial. Between 1990 and 1993, trade liberalization was a key policy instrument aimed at stabilizing prices.

The structural reforms, however, did not drive the economy to a satisfactory macroeconomic performance. In the first half of the 1990s, inflation was still high and growing, moving from 432 per cent in 1991 to 2,075 per cent in 1994, while the government faced a weak fiscal stance with modest fiscal surpluses (as measured by the operational fiscal balance and public sector borrowing requirements), a strongly devalued exchange rate and a rising surplus in the current account of the balance of payments and large foreign reserves. In the second half of the 1990s, this macroeconomic scenario was reverted and there was a quick deterioration in some of these variables, despite the fact that the government managed to considerably reduce inflation rates. The annual inflation rate moved from the 2,000 per cent observed in 1994 to 66 per cent in 1995 and reached the one-digit level in 1997 at 6.9 per cent.

A number of factors contributed to that economic deterioration. First, the increase in public deficits was a response to increases in the number of retired public workers, a significant real increase in the value of the minimum wage with consequent increases in pensions and social security benefits, and the deterioration of the fiscal stance of state governments. Second, the Central Bank adopted a tight and deflationary monetary policy to avoid a consumption boom after the quick fall in inflation observed in 1995. Third, with an overvalued exchange rate and low tariffs, there was a rapid deterioration in the trade balance, which registered deficits for the whole of the second half of the 1990s.

The exchange rate appreciation and the consequent trade balance deterioration that characterized most of the 1990s contributed to worsening the current account deficit. Exchange rate policy did not change until 1999, when a floating exchange rate regime was introduced. The current account deficit, which averaged 0.3 per cent of the GDP in 1994, reached 4.5 per cent in 1998. Additional factors that contributed to this deterioration were the exchange rate crisis of 1998 and the bad performance of the factor payments and services account, which was mainly due to the observed increases in interest rate payments and profit remittances abroad. These factors were a direct consequence of the high foreign real interest rates paid by Brazil to its creditors, the increase in the external debt and in foreign direct investment, which in 2000 represented some 9.7 per cent of the GDP up from an insignificant share of 0.2 per cent in 1990. By the end of the decade, the economic performance in terms of growth rates was not encouraging as the country was forced to slow down economic activity to regain control over inflation. GDP growth rates that averaged 2.9 per cent annually in the 1980s declined to a yearly average of 1.7 per cent in the 1990s.

In order to assess the external shocks that have hit the Brazilian economy over the last decade, we use the Balassa current account deficit decomposition methodology as detailed in Chapter 2 of this volume. The analysis is carried out for the period 1980–2001 during which most Latin American countries went through a series of external shocks, such as the changes in terms of trade during the 1980s, increases in international interest rates in the early 1980s, foreign direct investment boom in the early 1990s and, more recently, the Mexican crisis of the mid-1990s, oil price shocks in the second half of the 1990s, the Russian crisis of 1997 and the Brazilian crisis of 1999.

Table 6.1 shows the effect of the external shocks and domestic adjustment on the current account deficit, as measured by changes from the previous period as

Table 6.1 Brazil: decomposition of changes in current account deficit (percentage of GNP; period averages)

Period average Weights	1985–9 1980–4	1990–5 1985–9	1995–9 1990–5	1999–2001 1995–9
Observed deficit increase	−1.66	2.63	1.98	0.48
External shocks				
Total	5.15	−0.92	−4.13	−0.03
Terms of trade deterioration	3.21	2.84	−1.73	1.65
Import price effect	−2.30	1.27	−2.73	3.17
Export price effect	5.51	1.58	1.00	−1.52
Interest rate shock	1.93	−0.71	−0.39	−0.18
World trade retardation	0.02	−3.05	−2.00	−1.50
Other external variables				
Total	−2.80	1.24	1.77	1.56
Debt accumulation burden	−2.90	2.90	1.31	1.02
Change in direct investment income	0.08	−1.22	0.26	0.54
Change in remittances	−0.02	−0.34	0.17	0.02
Change in official transfers	0.04	−0.11	0.02	−0.02
Domestic adjustment				
Total	−4.05	2.88	5.59	−0.46
Domestic spending	−0.31	0.41	0.77	0.27
Consumption contraction	−0.43	0.41	0.71	0.24
Private consumption	−0.62	0.39	0.90	0.27
Public consumption	0.19	0.02	−0.19	−0.03
Investment reduction	0.12	0.00	0.06	0.03
Private investment	0.15	0.02	0.16	−1.07
Public investment	−0.03	−0.03	−0.10	1.10
Trade ratios	−3.74	2.47	4.83	−0.73
Import replacement	−1.14	2.11	3.90	−0.38
Export penetration	−2.60	0.37	0.93	−0.35
Interaction effects				
Total	0.04	−0.56	−1.26	−0.58
Import shock	0.44	0.87	−1.11	−0.05
Demand/unit imports	0.12	0.33	0.00	0.07
Displacement/price	0.32	0.55	−1.12	−0.12
Export shock	1.17	0.64	0.32	−0.42
Demand/unit exports	−0.01	0.71	0.43	−0.35
Penetration/price	1.18	−0.07	−0.11	−0.06
Debt shock	−1.57	−2.07	−0.46	−0.12
Stock/interest	−1.57	−2.07	−0.46	−0.12

Source: Chapter 2

a percentage of GNP. In the first period analysed, 1985–9, domestic absorption explained on average 4 percentage points of GNP of the shortening current account deficit of 1.7 per cent of GNP, while terms of trade moved negatively mainly due to falling export prices.

In the first half of the 1990s, however, this overall situation was reversed, and the current account deficit increased by 2.6 percentage points of GNP. In this period, shifting trade ratios and negative terms of trade shocks dominated the importance of a positive world trade shock in the widening of the current account balance. This scenario was marked by a significant fall in domestic prices after 1990 and the subsequent overvaluation of the domestic currency with the exchange rate anchor put in place in 1994.

In the third and fourth periods (1995–9 and 1999–2001, respectively), the external shocks were responsible for an average increase in the current account deficit of 2 per cent between 1995 and 1999 and of 0.5 per cent between 1999 and 2001, as a share of the GNP, respectively. In this post liberalization period, the main factors impacting the external deficit were significant increases in import substitution, decreases in the export penetration ratio, rises in the debt accumulation burden and a slight contribution of domestic policy variables.

To evaluate the role of exports in promoting economic growth in the process of macroeconomic adjustment carried out over the 1990s, we examined the results of a decomposition exercise based on a simple Keynesian multiplier (see Table 6.2). The methodology is explained in detail in Chapter 2. The results indicate that, in the 1980s, the external sector contributed positively for output growth (10.2 per cent), although by means of controlled imports and not of export growth. During this period, the public sector was the main source of output growth (16.4 per cent), while the private sector contributed negatively to output growth (−14.9 per cent).

In the first half of the 1990s, this overall situation was reversed when trade liberalization measures were implemented and the government regained control over inflation and fiscal discipline. As the government promoted economic reforms, both the private (13.7 per cent) and the public sectors (6.2 per cent) became the main sources of dynamism. The contribution of the external sector, however, was negative (−3.5 per cent). In the second half of the 1990s, exports repeated the conservative performance growing less than total imports and contributing to a negative impact of the external sector for output growth. The same pattern was observed in the post liberalization period of 1995–8, although with less intensity (−0.8 per cent). Throughout the period, the external sector contributed negatively as imports continued to grow in excess of exports. The main positive impact came from the private sector. As a result, the shares of total exports and investment in aggregate demand declined after 1990, whereas the participation of government spending and private consumption increased.

6.3 Sector and export growth

We proceed now to investigate the main determinants of aggregate demand using the methodology of sectoral decomposition developed by Chenery (1979) and

Table 6.2 Brazil: GDP growth decomposition by components of the aggregate demand, 1980–98 (per cent changes based on constant price values in R$ billion)

	Change in GDP		Private sector			Public sector			External sector		
	Observed	Calculated	Total	Investment	Savings	Total	Spending	Taxes	Total	Exports	Imports
1981/0	-4.0	-4.7	-6.3	-2.7	-3.5	-2.0	-0.6	-1.4	3.5	0.0	3.6
1982/1	0.6	1.1	-0.7	-4.9	4.2	2.4	1.9	0.5	-0.6	-4.6	4.0
1983/2	-2.1	-1.6	-7.4	-12.6	5.2	-1.7	-1.4	-0.3	7.5	9.5	-2.0
1984/3	7.5	7.7	-5.0	0.7	-5.7	1.4	-2.1	3.5	11.3	8.3	2.9
1985/4	7.2	6.1	-0.1	11.7	-11.8	5.2	5.6	-0.4	1.0	-1.0	2.0
1986/5	6.8	6.5	13.1	3.1	10.0	-1.2	4.0	-5.2	-5.5	-7.4	1.9
1987/6	3.3	2.3	-6.9	9.0	-15.9	6.5	4.3	2.2	2.6	2.3	0.4
1988/7	1.1	0.7	-5.8	1.4	-7.3	2.0	1.2	0.8	4.5	3.4	1.1
1989/8	1.2	1.3	-0.3	4.8	-5.1	5.7	4.0	1.7	-4.1	-5.5	1.4
1990/89	-5.2	-8.0	1.9	-11.7	13.6	-4.9	8.4	-13.3	-5.0	-1.0	-4.1
1991/0	0.5	2.2	1.0	-0.7	1.7	2.1	-2.8	4.9	-0.9	1.1	-2.1
1992/1	4.3	4.6	-1.2	-0.1	-1.2	1.1	-0.3	1.4	4.7	5.7	-1.0
1993/2	0.6	-0.3	2.4	4.2	-1.9	-0.6	1.5	-2.0	-2.1	-0.7	-1.4
1994/3	5.4	4.3	8.3	5.0	3.3	-2.9	2.4	-5.2	-1.1	-0.9	-0.2
1995/4	4.8	4.9	2.6	2.4	0.2	5.8	5.4	0.4	-3.5	-2.9	-0.7
1996/5	2.5	3.7	2.1	-2.3	4.4	1.8	0.2	1.6	-0.2	-0.9	0.7
1997/6	3.7	4.2	5.1	2.9	2.2	-0.3	-0.9	0.6	-0.6	1.5	-2.1
1998/7	0.9	1.2	0.4	0.5	0.0	0.7	-0.4	1.1	0.1	-0.1	0.2
1990/80	16.6	11.6	-14.9	0.4	-15.3	16.4	27.9	-11.5	10.2	1.0	9.1
1995/0	16.3	16.4	13.7	11.6	2.1	6.2	7.1	-0.8	-3.5	1.6	-5.1
1998/5	7.3	9.2	7.8	1.2	6.6	2.2	-1.1	3.3	-0.8	0.5	-1.3

Source: Own calculations based on national accounts data, several years

Table 6.3   Brazil: GDP growth decomposition – selected periods

	1975–80	1981–3	1984–7	1988–90	1991–4	1995–8
Absolute numbers						
GDP	1.30	−0.14	0.97	−0.11	0.42	0.40
Domestic demand	1.14	−0.24	0.97	0.10	0.55	0.43
Import substitution	0.01	0.03	0.09	−0.07	−0.24	−0.04
Export	0.15	0.07	−0.09	−0.15	0.11	0.01
% Contribution to GDP growth						
GDP	100.0	100.0	100.0	100.0	100.0	100.0
Domestic demand	87.6	171.1	100.1	−111.4	132.3	106.9
Import substitution	0.6	−22.3	9.2	66.4	−58.3	−9.4
Export	11.8	−48.8	−9.3	145.0	26.0	2.5

Source: Own calculations based on national accounts data, several years

explained in Chapter 2. The idea is to go beyond the aggregate output growth decomposition presented in the previous section and obtain some adequate sector detail. Output is decomposed into domestic growth, import substitution and export growth dynamics. In all periods considered from 1975 to 1998, domestic demand was always the main determinant of output growth (see Table 6.3). Import substitution contributed positively only during the period of heterodox economic plans (1984–7) as imports were restricted to avoid trade deficits and generate hard currency to face the external debt service. As inflation accelerated to hyperinflationary levels, total output decreased as a result of falling exports and growing imports.

In the first half of the 1990s, the main source of economic growth was the domestic demand followed by some export growth and a process of rapid growing imports, as trade barriers and tariffs were dropped and the exchange rate appreciated considerably. Between 1995 and 1998, the accumulated output growth was roughly the same in magnitude as the one observed for the first half of the decade, but the main source of growth was the domestic demand as exports lost dynamism and imports increased little.

From 1981 to 1994, the trade balance was always favourable to Brazil, but before and after those years the trade account was heavily negative. The surplus observed from 1981 onwards came after a strong economic adjustment following the oil and debt crisis and the major exchange rate devaluation. In a very short period, imports rose from about US$ 20.5 billion in 1992 to US$ 50 billion in 1995. Meanwhile, total exports increased from US$ 35.7 billion in 1992 to US$ 46.5 billion in 1995. The deficits from 1995 onwards were a result of the combination of trade liberalization, use of imports as a device to discipline domestic price formation and exchange rate overvaluation. Thus, the more liberal trade regime and the exchange rate overvaluation were part of a broader economic reform seeking primarily to stop inflation at the cost of increasing trade deficits.

Although the openness did improve the performance of both imports and exports, the growth rate of exports failed to match the growth rate of imports. The growth rate of exports reached 4.39 per cent in the 1980s, but declined to an annual average of 1.34 per cent in the 1990s. The share of manufactured goods in total exports rose from 45 per cent in 1980 to 61 per cent in 2000, while the share of primary goods fell from 43 to 23 per cent over the same period. Meanwhile, the terms of trade became unfavourable, demanding more exports for a given amount of imports.

Manufacturing import penetration ratio experienced a monotonic increase after 1990. From 1990 to 1998, the import penetration ratio more than doubled, jumping from 5.5 per cent in 1990 to 13.4 per cent in 1998. Interestingly enough, one cannot find clear patterns of import penetration for traditional and modern industries as it could be expected. A possible explanation for this is that Brazil faced more competition after trade liberalization not only from developed countries but also from other developing countries, which have also introduced trade reforms at the same time, such as China, India, Indonesia and Malaysia, among others (Arbache 2002). Furthermore, the need to increase exports to fund increasing imports after trade openness may have hurt middle income countries, such as Brazil.

Export intensity coefficients show a slow negative trend over time, and the trade openness period does not seem to have affected exports, since there is no apparent change in the 1990s. Thus, while import penetration increased during the decade, the export intensity coefficient remained relatively unchanged. Both trends are evidence that domestic firms have not been competitive internationally. Furthermore, there is no clear pattern related to export intensity among traditional and modern industries, as in the Heckscher–Ohlin theorem.

Unit labour costs show high volatility, which is mostly explained by changes in the real exchange rate and to a less extent by changes in real wages. In the 1980s, there was an upward movement, while the reverse took place in the 1990s. Two competing effects potentially affected the labour costs of the last decade. On the one hand, the Real appreciated in relation to the US dollar provoking an increase in the unit labour cost. On the other hand, labour productivity rose rapidly thus reducing the labour cost. Overall, it seems that the latter effect dominated the former, thus increasing the competitiveness of the economy.

The greater openness observed in the 1990s enabled the economy to import more capital goods and technology, changing the production function upwards. Higher competition disciplined price formation and lead firms to produce at a better quality and a lower price. One of the consequences of the higher level of technology was the increasing demand for skilled workers at the expense of the less skilled. The search for higher efficiency and quality levels may have forced firms to rationalize and modernize production, which tended to shift demand in favour of more skilled workers.

Export growth had a limited impact on employment generation, while import growth and the introduction of new technologies in the production process contributed to a net destruction of some 5.4 million jobs (Maia 2001). As the sectors which benefited from export growth during the 1990s were intensive in the use of capital and skilled labour, better educated and skilled workers gained in the process. Increases in informality and average unemployment rates mainly affected unskilled and less educated workers. The increasing exposure to foreign trade promoted neither improvements nor deteriorations in inequality indicators, which runs counter to the implications of the Stolper–Samuelson theorem (Green *et al.* 2001).

Based on the preceding analysis, we formulate two main hypotheses for the counterfactual model simulations. The first hypothesis is based on the skill composition of the labour market. The second is concerned with an export shock and its impact on the labour market. Regarding the first hypothesis, our results indicated that the unskilled and less educated workers suffered the adverse effects of trade liberalization in terms of job and wage losses, suggesting that a first set of microsimulations to be investigated would be the effects of a productivity shock in the labour market. Such productivity shock would be basically obtained by hypothetically raising the profile of the less advantaged group of workers in the labour market to the types of skill and education levels of the workers who benefited most from trade liberalization. Thus, one could observe how major labour market indicators would perform following a productivity shock, under the hypothesis of an overall improvement in the skill and education profile of labour market participants.

The second hypothesis is concerned with a more aggregate exercise and aims at investigating labour market outcomes following a major trade liberalization programme. As indicated, Brazilian exports seem to have responded more to quantity incentives rather than price movements. Then, a possible route for this exercise would be to hypothesize on how exports would respond to credit and tax incentives and then investigate the impact of export change on the labour market. At the same time, one could also use different levels of exchange rate and tariff reductions to assess the performance of major labour market indicators.

6.4 Counterfactual CGE model simulations

Model description

In this section, we present a brief description of the model we have used to assess the impact of trade liberalization on macroeconomic and labour market indicators in Brazil. The model solves endogenously for quantities and prices, and for the income of institutions and disaggregates the production factors and institutions in an attempt to capture the distributive impacts of economic changes. The labour factor is divided into eight categories reflecting the different types of labour force – given by their status of labour contract – and schooling. Families are divided into nine categories according to income, degree of urbanization and head of household. This disaggregation captures the different impacts economic reforms have on the labour market and income distribution and the different sources of income, respectively.

The model is constructed in a way that follows the pattern of income generation in the economy: from activities and commodities, to factors of production, to institutions and back to activities and commodities again.[1] There are 841 equations and endogenous variables.[2] The price equations are presented first, followed by equations that describe production and value-added generation. Next are equations that describe the mapping of value added to incomes by institutions (households, firms, government). The circular flow is then completed by equations showing the balance between supply and demand for goods by the various agents. Finally, there are a number of system constraints that the model economy must satisfy. These include both market clearing conditions and choice of macro-closure for the model.[3]

The general equilibrium block

The production function of the model employs three factors: labour, capital, and intermediate inputs. The function is specified in three stages. In the first stage, the different types of labour (F_1) are aggregated in a Cobb–Douglas labour demand function (L) for each sector (i):

$$L_i = \Pi_i F_{il} \beta^{li}$$

In the second stage, aggregate labour factors and capital (K) are linked through a CES function to obtain the value added for each sector (X_i):

$$X_i = \alpha_i^D \left[\alpha_i L_i^{\rho ip} + (1 - \alpha_i) K_i^{\rho ip} \right]^{1/\rho ip}$$

Finally, in the third stage, value added is associated to intermediate inputs through a Leontief function of the following form:

$$\text{INT}_i = \sum_j \alpha_{ij} X_j$$

The firm maximizes profits and the prices of inputs, production factors and output are fixed. Profit maximization is carried out with the technological constraints specified in the production function. Thus, as a result of the maximization, wages equal the marginal productivity of labour.

There are 42 sectors in which the production can be either exported or sold domestically. The producer takes the decision as to where to sell his output based on the comparison of the domestic and international prices, besides considering a restriction related to the capacity of redirecting this output to different markets. Consumers, on the other hand, choose among domestic or imported goods that are considered as perfect substitutes (see Armington 1970).

Labour market behaviour

The adjustment rule for the labour market proposed for this model incorporates a feature that ensures the existence of involuntary unemployment in equilibrium. As in Barros *et al.* (2001) we considered two alternatives for that purpose. The first is based on the hypothesis of wage rigidity that establishes that nominal wages are fixed exogenously. Thus, the adjustment in the labour market would be reached via changes in employment levels. In the model we use, four out of eight labour markets operate according to this rule: formal rural, low skill urban formal, low skill public workers and high skill public workers.

The second alternative represents a negative relationship between the unemployment rate and the wage level, such as in the wage curve literature.[4] The idea is consistent with efficiency wage arguments or trade union wage bargain stories. In the first case, the firm motivates workers to be efficient by means of attractive salaries. However, in a situation of high unemployment, workers tend to be efficient for fearing losing their jobs and the firm does not need to increase wages to encourage efficiency. In the second case, the firm may be forced to increase wages in periods of low unemployment, as trade union bargaining power tends to increase in these situations.

Thus, the wage curve rule establishes that firms take into account the state of the outside labour market at the moment of defining the wages of their labour force. If competition for a job is big (high unemployment rates), the firm can offer low wages. Therefore, Barros *et al.* (2001) assumed that middle and high skill workers in the formal urban sector, as well as the low and high skill workers in the informal sector, have their wages fixed according to this rule.

It is important to stress that the labour market closure is made per type of labour, rather than per sector. Thus, in the first stage the model defines the levels of employment, wage and unemployment for each aggregate type of labour in the different sectors of the economy. To define the levels of employment and wage of each type of labour in each sector, it is necessary to assume another behavioural rule for the labour market. This new rule assumes sector segmentation in the labour market by including an exogenous variable that represents differences in relative wages for each sector. The average wage for each type of work is then used to determine the wage of this type of work in each sector. With this, the employment level for each type of work in each sector is determined by means of the labour demand function for each type of labour and sector.

Income transfer block

In the second block of the model, the formation of the income flows appropriated by families, firms, government and rest of the world are considered. This process considers the definition of the income distribution generated in the productive process and the transfers among the economic agents.

The income distribution is generated by attributing the remuneration of capital to firms and the remuneration of labour to families. The distribution of earnings of the eight types of labour among the nine types of families is made according to the composition of these families. The government acts in this process by promoting the redistribution of the income generated in the production process through tax collections from firms and families, tariffs levied on imported goods and social security contributions. The government then redistributes this revenue among the families by means of retirement pensions and other government transfers.

Transfers to firms are made by means of interest payments on public bonds and consumption of goods.

The government finances its expenditures with tax collections and external savings. The government's income flow is defined as the amount of money requested to close the balance of payments with the balance observed for the base year in the model. Any positive excess balance is considered as government savings, which together with household savings forms the amount of resources spent in the form of investments.

Empirical implementation strategy

In this section, we use the multisectoral CGE model and apply it to the analysis of eight different simulations regarding the effects of trade liberalization measures on labour market outcomes. The SAM uses data from the Brazilian Institute of Geography and Statistics for 1996. The empirical implementation of the model follows two different stages. In the first stage, the model is solved for the base year without the imposition of any changes in the parameters or exogenous variables. Thus, the optimal solution of the model must replicate the original values of the variables for the base year. At the end of this stage, the base year values are saved for comparison with the results of the simulations, which are implemented in the second stage.

In the second and final stage, a set of exogenous variables and/or parameters is modified to mimic a given policy, in our case a trade-liberalization-oriented policy. The model is then solved to find the solution compatible with the modifications in the base model. The rationale of our simulations is explained below.

Simulation 1

In the first simulation, we impose a productivity shock of 10 per cent in the variables of the model. The idea is to investigate interindustry and employment linkages following a productivity shock, examining which sectors are likely to be the leaders in terms of output and employment generation, how exports and imports react and whether the implied effects will favour labour or capital-intensive sectors and skilled or unskilled labour.

Simulation 2

The second simulation imposes a 10 per cent increase in the prices of world imports to investigate how this would affect Brazil's macroeconomic variables as well as poverty and inequality indices.

Simulations 3 and 4

The third and fourth simulations assess the effects of a 50 per cent across-the-board change in import tariffs. At this point, the idea is to investigate how an overall and significant tariff reduction/increase strategy would affect output, salaries and employment.

Simulation 5

In the fifth simulation, export subsidy rates are raised by 10 per cent with the objective to assess the overall effects of an explicit export-oriented policy.

Simulation 6

The sixth simulation is an attempt to assess the impacts of a Free Trade Agreement of the Americas (FTAA) in which import tariffs are reduced and international prices of exports and imports change simultaneously onto the Brazilian economy. The tariff reductions and the international price changes under the FTAA have been estimated by the International Food Policy Research Institute (IFPRI) team using predictions derived from their world model.

Simulation 7

As in the case of the previous exercise, the seventh simulation is an attempt to assess the effects of a broader WTO agreement in which import tariff rates are lowered to zero and international prices of exports and imports change according to the predictions of the IFPRI's world model.

Simulation 8

In the last simulation, we impose a 10 per cent exchange rate devaluation in the model in order to see how the external sector, macroeconomic variables, wage and employment indicators react to a relative price change.

Analysing the simulation results

The aggregate results of the CGE model simulations have already been analysed in detail in Carneiro and Arbache (2003) and will only be briefly commented on here. A summary of the results for some selected variables appears in Table 6.4.

In most cases, trade liberalization experiments provoked a significant drop in tariff revenues (Simulations 3, 6 and 7). Another significant pattern was the very limited impact of trade liberalization on real GDP as only in the case of a 10 per cent shock in productivity does real GDP increase by a similar magnitude (Simulation 1).

In most of the counterfactual scenarios, unemployment rates tend to go down and average real household incomes tend to increase. The exception was the case of a 10 per cent exchange rate devaluation where the largest impacts in terms of unemployment were observed for the unskilled informal workers, while the decline in household income was larger for poor families either in the urban or the rural sector.

Table 6.4 Brazil: CGE simulations (per cent change from base year in macroeconomic variables per simulation)

Variables	Simulation 1	Simulation 2	Simulation 3	Simulation 4	Simulation 5	Simulation 6	Simulation 7	Simulation 8
Real GDP (RGDP)	10.038	−1.050	−0.008	0.009	−0.050	−0.009	−0.027	−0.084
Household savings (HHSAV)	−1.940	−1.700	0.288	−0.180	0.700	0.184	0.392	−1.889
Government savings (GOVSAV)	−94.070	−1.900	6.340	−5.980	15.173	5.406	12.616	−0.936
Depreciation (DEPREC)	−4.297	0.590	−0.267	0.290	−0.980	−0.278	−0.644	−0.454
Total savings (SAVING)	19.156	0.530	−0.706	1.010	−3.710	−0.911	−2.132	−3.080
Fixed investment (FXDINV)	21.334	0.400	−0.735	1.070	−3.980	−0.967	−2.270	−3.437
Tariff revenue (TARIFF)	8.763	10.140	−48.413	47.050	−3.610	−42.315	−98.336	5.487
Indirect taxes (INDTAX)	3.083	0.240	−0.008	−0.020	0.010	0.029	0.045	0.274
Total revenue (GR)	4.353	−0.310	−1.103	1.090	−2.660	0.961	−2.269	−0.023
Average real household income − poor families	9.053	−1.630	0.144	−0.142	0.240	0.153	0.322	−1.030
Average real household income − poor families headed by the retired	3.556	−0.730	0.079	−0.078	0.220	0.081	0.174	−0.454
Average real household income − middle income urban families	7.366	−1.690	0.151	−0.150	0.460	0.160	0.337	−0.916
Average real household income − high income urban families	5.563	−1.690	0.171	−0.170	0.580	0.177	0.377	−0.840

(Continued)

Table 6.4 (Continued)

Variables	Simulation 1	Simulation 2	Simulation 3	Simulation 4	Simulation 5	Simulation 6	Simulation 7	Simulation 8
Average real household income – poor rural families	9.936	−1.670	0.129	−0.130	0.240	0.140	0.291	−1.337
Average real household income – middle income rural families	7.856	−1.590	0.151	−0.150	0.460	0.158	0.334	−1.064
Average real household income – middle–high income families	5.750	−1.700	0.189	−0.190	0.730	0.193	0.413	−0.946
Average real household income – high income families	7.404	−1.740	0.198	−0.190	0.930	0.199	0.423	−1.091
Unemployment – low skill informal workers	−9.529	1.828	−0.427	0.415	−1.351	−0.909	−0.403	7.056
Unemployment – skilled informal workers	−4.128	2.415	−0.211	0.209	−0.796	−0.468	−0.214	1.214
Unemployment – low skill formal workers	−6.832	1.647	−0.286	0.278	−0.901	−0.614	−0.275	1.520
Unemployment – middle skill formal workers	−9.773	3.509	−0.428	0.420	−1.532	−0.930	−0.434	0.915
Unemployment – high formal skill workers	−7.425	1.760	0.025	−0.021	0.032	0.026	−0.003	0.102

In the next set of simulations in which we reduced the level of import tariff rates, raised export subsidy rates, introduced an FTAA scenario and a WTO agreement, the results coincide in showing lower unemployment rates and higher household incomes for all types of labour and families. The absolute magnitude of these changes, however, is very small. A slightly different picture was observed for the cases of a rise in world import prices, and a rise in import tariffs, where changes were in the opposite direction, but again in small magnitudes. This could indicate that greater openness may have a limited impact on labour market, poverty and inequality indicators in Brazil.

To investigate how the economy would react to a productivity shock, we run a simulation imposing a 10 per cent rise in the shift parameter of the production function of the model. In this experiment, we notice an overall drop in the unemployment rate for all types of workers with more emphasis for the highly skilled formal sector workers. Real average household incomes increase for all families.

In the next section, we set out to investigate the effects of changes in unemployment rates and real household incomes provoked by the trade liberalization experiments on the degree of inequality and poverty ratios using the methodology of counterfactual microsimulations.[5]

6.5 Microsimulations of the impact of trade on poverty and inequality

In this section, we use the parameters obtained from the CGE model in a new round of microsimulations to investigate the likely impacts of export demand shocks, exchange rate devaluation, export promotion, productivity shocks and trade liberalization on the degree of income inequality at the household level and on poverty and extreme poverty ratios.

The methodology for this analysis is discussed in detail in Vos (2002) and Chapter 3. In very broad terms, the methodology consists of creating a counterfactual in the form of labour market parameters, representing the employment and remuneration structure, which would prevail if liberalization had not taken place. The counterfactual simulations are carried out to obtain a new distribution of income in which one or several parameters of the labour market structure are changed. The relevant labour market parameters in our case are (1) the unemployment rate for each type of worker and (2) the average level of remuneration for each type of family.

The results of the counterfactual microsimulations are reported in Table 6.5. The table lists the baseline scenario and then presents the main results of each simulation. We have first estimated impact of the change in the unemployment rate (keeping average household income constant) resulting from the policy simulation obtained with the CGE model on poverty and inequality indices, and second the impact of changes in average household income (keeping unemployment rates constant) on poverty and inequality. Finally, estimates of the new poverty ratios and Gini coefficients are presented considering a simultaneous shift in both

Table 6.5 Brazil: counterfactual microsimulations of the effects of greater openness on poverty and inequality

	Increase in productivity (+10%)		Increase in import prices (+10%)		Across-the-board tariff reduction (−50%)		Across the board tariff increase (+50%)	
	P_0	Gini YPC	P_0	Gini YPC	P_0	Gini YPC	P_0	Gini YPC
Initial values	33.41	0.600	33.41	0.600	33.41	0.600	33.41	0.600
(1) U	30.58	0.590	34.11	0.605	33.57	0.603	33.43	0.600
(1 − 2) W	30.61	0.592	33.61	0.598	32.42	0.595	34.54	0.605
(1 + 2) U + W	30.55	0.591	33.61	0.601	32.99	0.598	33.98	0.602

	Rise in export subsidies (+10%)		Scenario FTAA		Scenario WTO		Exchange rate devaluation (+10%)	
	P_0	Gini YPC	P_0	Gini YPC	P_0	Gini YPC	P_0	Gini YPC
Initial values	33.41	0.600	33.41	0.600	33.41	0.600	33.41	0.600
(1) U	33.10	0.597	33.46	0.604	33.46	0.604	34.09	0.604
(1 − 2) W	32.90	0.596	33.00	0.597	32.20	0.596	34.12	0.607
(1 + 2) U + W	33.00	0.594	33.23	0.598	32.95	0.598	34.11	0.606

Note: U, unemployment rate; W, average earnings

unemployment rates and average household income. Due to space limitations, in what follows we will only refer to this last set of results.

In the base year, considering household level data for 1996, Brazil had a poverty ratio of 33.4 per cent, an extreme poverty ratio of 14.8 per cent and a Gini coefficient of 0.600. In most of the policy scenarios, poverty and inequality levels declined following a reduction in unemployment and increases in real average household income resulting from a simulation of greater economic openness. The largest impact was observed with the simulation of an overall 10 per cent increase in productivity. In this case, overall poverty declined to 30.6 per cent, absolute poverty to 13.6 per cent and the Gini coefficient to 0.591 following a simultaneous decline in unemployment rates and an increase in average real household income.

Considering the simulations of policy measures aimed at increasing the exposure of Brazil to foreign trade, the microsimulation results show that the potential to reduce poverty and inequality is somewhat limited, as overall poverty ratios declined at most by 0.5 percentage points, while inequality and absolute poverty varied very little as well. In the cases of an across-the-board 50 per cent cut in import tariffs, export subsidy reduction, the FTAA and WTO scenarios, overall poverty ratios dropped to roughly 33 per cent, while absolute poverty remained around 15 per cent and Gini coefficients stayed at around 0.599. The exception was the case of a 10 per cent exchange rate devaluation, in which unemployment increased and average real household income declined. Under this scenario, the overall poverty ratio and the Gini coefficient both increased to 34 per cent and 0.606, respectively.

Also, marginal were the effects on poverty and inequality generated by the simulations that raised import tariff rates and world import prices. In the first case, the poverty ratio increased by 0.2 percentage points and the Gini coefficient moved to 0.602, while in the second case, poverty increased by 0.5 percentage points and the Gini coefficient to 0.602.

Overall, our results are in line with previous assessments on the impacts of trade on poverty and income inequality in Brazil. Barros *et al.* (2001) and Corseuil and Kume (2003), for example, found a modest impact of trade on poverty and income inequality. Hertel *et al.* (2003), on the other hand, also found a very small change in Gini coefficients for Brazil after analysing the impacts of trade liberalization on inequality using consumption and not income as the control variable.

6.6 Conclusions

After a decade marked by debt crisis, fiscal imbalances and rapidly accelerating inflation, the 1990s inaugurated a new policy agenda aimed at strengthening the trade relationships among all capitalist economies. The links of a given economy with the rest of the world were supposedly to be strengthened by means of the adoption of the measures prescribed by the so-called Washington Consensus. These involved in broad terms solving the fiscal crisis, stopping inflation and opening up the economy to foreign competition. In Brazil, the government introduced some drastic policy changes towards trade liberalization, deregulation of markets, privatization of state enterprises and financial and capital market liberalization.

As a result of the liberalization measures adopted in the early 1990s, both imports and exports increased very rapidly, although the economy is still relatively closed to the rest of the world. Despite the growing exposure to foreign trade, output growth during most of the 1990s was mainly driven by domestic absorption. The output growth decomposition analysis using different methodologies confirmed that while export growth contributed only marginally to economic growth, domestic absorption was the main factor leading stop–go pattern of recessions and periods of growth.

It could be said, however, that on the one hand, higher trade enabled the economy to import more capital goods and technology, changing the production function upwards. And that, on the other hand, higher competition disciplined price formation and led firms to produce better quality and at lower prices. One of the consequences of the higher level of technology was the increasing demand for skilled workers at the expense of the less skilled. The search for higher efficiency and quality may have forced firms to rationalize and modernize production, shifting demand in favour of more skilled workers. In this way, we have also observed increases in informality and average unemployment levels, with most of the unemployed and informal workers represented by the less skilled and less educated.

Furthermore, increasing exposure to foreign trade has promoted neither larger improvements nor deterioration in inequality indicators. The same kind of conclusions can be drawn as regards the impacts of trade on poverty ratios in Brazil. Despite the fact that greater openness appeared in our counterfactual simulations as a scenario associated with lower poverty and inequality, the absolute magnitude of the improvement in these indicators was very modest. In our simulations, a situation in which import tariff rates were lowered to zero, as in the case of a broader WTO agreement, would be associated with a drop in the poverty ratio from 33.23 to 32.95 per cent while inequality would remain virtually unchanged. Trade liberalization thus has not given rise to increases in poverty, but has not led to major poverty reduction either.

Notes

1 The income flow in a CGE model is represented by a SAM. The different accounts in the SAM delineate the boundaries of an economy wide model. Thus, the specification of a complete model requires that the market, behavioural and system relationships embodied in each account in the SAM be described in the model (Robinson *et al.* 1999).

2 The model we use has been adapted to the Brazilian case by Barros *et al.* (2001).

3 The model is not presented in full to save space. A complete description can be found in Robinson *et al.* (1999).

4 See Blanchflower and Oswald (1998) for the theoretical foundations of the wage curve. The actual parameters used in the model have been estimated by Barros and Mendonça (1997).

5 Recent accounts of the evolution of poverty and inequality indices for Brazil can be found in Morley (2003) and Barros *et al.* (2001). Both of them notice the remarkable

reduction in poverty in Brazil observed during the 1990s, but they also point to the need to promote both (1) a sustainable economic growth strategy and (2) policies that advance in the distributive front so that the poor population can be effectively and significantly reduced.

References

Arbache, J. S. (2002) 'Trade liberalization and labor markets in developing countries: theory and evidence', in: A. Levy and J. R. Faria (eds) *Economic Growth, Inequality and Migration: National and International Perspectives*, Cheltenham: Edward Elgar Publishers.

Armington, P. (1970) 'Adjustment of trade balance: some experiments with a model of trade among many countries', *IMF Staff Papers*, 17: 488: 523.

Barros, R. P., C. H. Corseuil and S. Cury (2001a) 'Salário Mínimo e Pobreza no Brasil: Estimativas que Consideram Efeitos de Equilíbrio Geral', Texto para Discussão No. 779, Rio de Janeiro: Ipea.

Barros, R. P., C. H. Corseuil, S. Cury and P. G. Leite (2001b) 'Abertura econômica e distribuição de renda no Brasil', Proceedings of the Workshop on Trade Liberalization and the Labour Market in Brazil, Brasilia: UnB/IPEA.

Barros, R. P., R. Henriques and R. Mendonça (2001c) 'A estabilidade inaceitável: Desigualdade e Pobreza no Brasil', Texto para Discussão No. 800, Rio de Janeiro: Ipea.

Barros, R. P. and R. Mendonça (1997) 'Flexibilidade do Mercado de Trabalho Brasileiro: Uma Avaliação Empírica', Discussion Paper No. 452, Rio de Janeiro: IPEA.

Blanchflower, D. G. and A. J. Oswald (1998) *The Wage Curve*, Cambridge, MA: MIT Press.

Carneiro, F. G. and J. S. Arbache (2003) 'The impact of trade on Brazilian labor market: a CGE model approach', *World Development*, 31: 1581–95.

Chenery, H. B. (1979) *Structural Change and Development Policy*, Oxford, NY: Oxford University Press.

Corseuil, C. H. and H. Kume (2003) *Abertura Comercial Brasileira nos Anos 1990: Impactos sobre Emprego e Salarios*, Brasilia: MTE-IPEA.

Green, F., A. Dickerson and J. S. Arbache (2001) 'A picture of wage inequality and the allocation of labor through a period of trade liberalization: the case of Brazil', *World Development*, 29: 1923–39.

Hertel, T., M. Ivanic, P. Preckel and J. Cranfield (2003) 'Trade liberalization and the structure of poverty in developing countries', Paper presented at the UNU/WIDER Conference on Sharing Global Prosperity, Helsinki.

Maia, K. (2001) 'Progresso tecnológico, qualificação da mão-de-obra e desemprego', Unpublished PhD Thesis, Brasilia: Departamento de Economia, Universidade de Brasília.

Morley, S. (2003) 'Reducing poverty in Brazil: lessons learned and challenges for the future', Pro-Poor Economic Growth Research Studies, Boston Institute for Developing Economies (mimeo).

Robinson, S., A. Yúnez-Naude, R. Hinojosa-Ojeda, J. D. Lewis and S. Devarajan (1999) 'From stylized to applied models: building multisector CGE models for policy analysis', *North American Journal of Economics and Finance*, 10: 5–38.

Vos, R. (2002) 'Export-led growth strategies: effects on poverty, inequality and growth in Latin America and the Caribbean – microsimulations methodology' (mimeo).

7 Costa Rica – export orientation and its effect on growth, inequality and poverty

Marco V. Sánchez and Pablo Sauma

Abstract

Costa Rica also adopted the Washington Consensus type of reforms, but in a much more gradual and less 'orthodox' way than the other countries in the region. It has combined import liberalization with active export promotion. By the 1980s, Costa Rica already had relatively few restrictions on capital inflows. Nonetheless, further liberalization of the capital account and legislative changes easing the entry of *maquila* industries and establishment of firms in export-processing free zones led to a boom in foreign direct investment in the 1990s. Despite the inflow of foreign capital, the government managed to stop the exchange rate from appreciating, keeping it competitive during most of the 1990s with a managed floating exchange regime. Economic growth has been volatile but on average the economy expanded at an annual growth rate of 4.3 per cent during 1985–2001. Exports have been the engine of Costa Rica's growth performance, especially non-traditional exports supported by export promotion policies (tax credit certificates, export-processing free zones and *maquilas*) and, since the late 1990s, exports by the Intel plant in the country. Growth in employment lagged behind gross domestic product growth, but was still substantially higher than growth of the labour force. Most new jobs were created in the formal sector. Real labour income increased, but due to growing demand for skilled workers, labour income inequality increased significantly. Income inequality also increased at the household level. The incidence of absolute poverty has remained stable, however, since the mid-1990s, thanks to an increase in employment and average income. Simulations with the computable general equilibrium model for Costa Rica indicate that trade liberalization tends to lead to increasing inequality of income, given the combined effect of significantly higher labour income in the most dynamic economic sectors, especially those intensive in the use of skilled workers, and a reduction in labour incomes in agriculture. Simulations also show, however, that because of the generally positive outcomes for employment, trade liberalization seems to have generated positive, though small, effects towards poverty reduction. Poverty also falls under the scenario of further trade integration through the Free Trade Area of the Americas and a world-wide World Trade Organization agreement. Not all workers will benefit from trade integration, however. Those in agriculture, in particular, would face falling employment and real incomes.

7.1 Introduction

Like many other countries in the region, Costa Rica's exports have been falling in the last few years after a period of skyrocketing growth. The hypothesis of this study is that the deceleration in the pace of economic growth experienced regionally and by the various countries in the later half of the 1990s is linked precisely to the export promotion strategies that most countries adopted earlier, with a negative impact on poverty and inequality. The study aims to explain the deceleration in economic growth, measure its effects on the distribution of income and poverty and explore alternative growth strategies that would help improve the situation.

Though the analysis emphasizes the 1990s, the Costa Rica case study includes information from the mid-1980s when the current model of economic growth was implemented. The analysis is based on a new social accounting matrix (SAM) for Costa Rica for 1997[1] and on a computable general equilibrium (CGE) model. Using the matrix, and the model calibrated to it, various macrosimulations are carried out in order to identify the impact of exogenous shocks and various policies on product growth, employment, labour income and other economic variables. The impacts are then linked to a complementary exercise of simulations with micro-data (family-level data) that allows an understanding of the way in which changes in the labour market affect the distribution of income and poverty. The results of these exercises and the application of other methodologies lead to important conclusions and recommendations.

7.2 Reforms and macroeconomic performance

Economic reforms: a general overview

After a serious crisis and a short stabilization period earlier in the decade, Costa Rica began implementing a new development model in the mid-1980s. The primary elements of the model were the liberalization of trade policies with a strong emphasis on export promotion and reforms in the financial sector and state apparatus. While most of these elements were part of the 'policy package' of the 'Washington Consensus', they were never implemented in their most orthodox form in Costa Rica, nor were they implemented at the proposed speed. The process was very gradual and various adjustments (heterodox policy formulations) were made.

In terms of trade liberalization and the balance of payments in general, tariffs were lowered significantly, important bilateral and multilateral trade agreements were negotiated, exports increased sharply as a result of the policy to promote them, capital account liberalization was expanded and, in general terms, the exchange rate policy was managed in a way that supported trade liberalization and competitiveness. In the reform of the financial system, private participation was expanded in order to achieve greater efficiency, and the regulatory function of the state was strengthened, although some changes are still pending with regard to regulation and supervision of the system and other specific aspects. Not much has happened in terms of institutional reforms of the state, not even in the field of public expenditure management and tax administration.

The country has followed a very active policy of export promotion since the 1970s, but it reached new heights in the mid-1980s with the enactment of a series of incentives for non-traditional exports, coordinated by an instrument called 'export contracts'. The most significant incentive was a tax-credit certificate, commonly known as the CAT (*Certificado de Abono Tributario*), which was issued until 1999.[2] Legislation for *maquilas* and export-processing free zones was also modified as part of the export promotion strategy.

In 1990, the Legislative Assembly approved Costa Rica's entry into the General Agreement on Tariffs and Trade (GATT), and since 1995 the country has been part of the World Trade Organization (WTO). In addition to the agreements with Central America already in place since the import substitution period, the country has moved forward with the negotiation of free trade agreements in a way that is consistent with the export promotion strategy and with trade liberalization in general. To date, four agreements of this kind have been signed: with Mexico, the Dominican Republic, Chile and Canada. All are being implemented fully. Costa Rica is currently negotiating similar agreements with Panama[3] and Trinidad and Tobago that can be extended to all of the Caribbean Community (CARICOM). It also joined with the other Central American countries to negotiate a free trade agreement with the United States of America (CAFTA), which is to be subjected to legislative approval. Costa Rica is also participating actively in the effort to form the Free Trade Area of the Americas (FTAA).

Costa Rica has benefited from the Caribbean Basin Initiative (CBI) and from the General System of Preferences (GSP) of the United States. It is also a beneficiary of the general system of preferences of the European Union and, like the rest of the Central American countries, has enjoyed a special regime within that system. Since the late 1980s, the country has made significant progress towards lowering tariffs, and as the year 2000 approached, the great majority of tariffs were under 15 per cent (and almost half were at 0 per cent).

Though the Costa Rican capital account has been open for many years and foreign investors enjoy the same privileges and protections as national investors, the capital account has undergone further liberalization in recent years through the 1992 elimination of restrictions on capital movements (including the elimination of the capital registration requirements and the 1995 reforms to the Organic Law of the Central Bank, which strengthened liberalization in several ways – especially by eliminating restrictions on the purchase and sale of foreign exchange).

This greater liberalization, together with equally important attracting factors (specific legislation, closeness to US markets, availability of fair amounts of skilled labour, etc.) has resulted in a strong increase in foreign direct investment (FDI). In net terms, FDI went from 1.4 per cent of gross domestic product (GDP) in 1985 to 4.3 per cent in 1998, peaking in absolute terms in 1999 (US$ 619.5 million). Investment decreased in 2000–1 but continued to be higher than the level of 1995 and previous years. The most significant investment happened in 1997 when Intel, the world leader in microprocessor manufacturing, came to Costa

Rica. Intel began to produce in mid-1998 and had a large impact on national production and exports. The destination of investment is also changing significantly, with more investment going towards tourism and high-tech industries (in addition to Intel) and less to textile *maquilas* and agriculture.

The Central Bank plays an important role in determining the exchange rate in Costa Rica. During the economic crisis of the early 1980s, the currency market was one of the primary sources of economic instability. This led to the 1982 decision to give the Central Bank a monopoly on dollar transactions. The Central Bank kept that monopoly from the mid-1980s until 1992, and commercial banks were its only authorized agents in the foreign exchange market. To keep the exchange rate on target, a policy of small and periodic nominal devaluations (mini-devaluations) was enacted in order to maintain the parity of the colony's purchasing power and accumulate foreign exchange. Although the exchange rate was liberalized in 1992, the Central Bank soon began to intervene in the foreign exchange market[4] once again with mini-devaluations. A managed or 'dirty' float is the practice until today. The Central Bank uses the multilateral real effective exchange rate index as a reference for determining the mini-devaluations.

Macroeconomic performance

In general terms, during the period of study the macroeconomic performance on the whole has been satisfactory, but is also showing some volatility with alternating brief periods of expansion and recession. During 1985–2001, the economy achieved average GDP growth rate of 4.6 per cent (4.3 per cent if we exclude Intel). However, this includes periods of relatively high growth rate (above 6 per cent) as well as periods of low growth (below 1 per cent). GDP growth also tended to slow down between 1999 and 2001.

The average inflation rate for the period was 15.8 per cent, with spells of single-digit rates in a few years (1989 and 1993) and jumping to over 20 per cent in four years (1988, 1990, 1991 and 1995). Interest rates have been high in real terms throughout the period. Open unemployment has been low, while minimum wages increased in real terms. Furthermore, the share of aggregate investment in GDP remained constant despite the increase in foreign direct investment.

The most dynamic productive sector throughout the entire period has been *transportation, storage* and *communications*. This dynamism is explained primarily by expansion in telecommunications services, but transportation and storage also played a role because of the increased volume of international trade. The second fastest growing sector is industry. The overall results of the sector, however, are affected by high production in the *maquila* and export-processing regimes, and in the latter case by Intel's production of microprocessors. When production from these regimes is excluded, the result is a modest growth in the sector – 3.1 per cent annual average growth for 1992–2000, which is less than the previous period (1985–91). This lower growth, both compared to the special export development regimes and to the 1985–91 period, is explained in part by the low level of linkage between the activities falling under those regimes (contributing on average 8.6 per cent of total GDP during 1992–2000) and other industry. The fact that industry grew more slowly than services means that industrial activity without the support of the special regimes declined as a share of GDP from 20.9 per cent in 1991–2 to 16.9 per cent in 2000.

Other activities like tourism, which are directly related to the liberalization of trade and financial services, have shown significant dynamism, especially *commerce, restaurants* and *hotels*,[5] and to a lesser degree *financial services, insurance, real estate* and *business services.* The agricultural sector, on the other hand, has grown very little, losing importance within total output throughout the period of study. This is a result of the poor performance of traditional exports (coffee and bananas primarily) mainly due to falling export prices. Both non-traditional agricultural exports and agricultural production for the domestic market have shown greater dynamism.

Fiscal deficits of the central government have been a chronic problem. Deficits widened during the electoral cycle at the beginning of the 1990s.[6] However, the structural causes of large fiscal deficits lie beyond these cyclical factors. For one thing, since the middle of the last century, the government has progressively assumed a series of obligations not covered by an adequate tax base. The average tax burden for 1985–2001 was nearly 12 per cent of GDP not including social security contributions (which add to just over 5 per cent of GDP on average for 1990–2001). In addition, the trade liberalization process brought both export incentives and significant reductions in tariffs. This imposed a fiscal burden that was not met by new sources of government revenue and even more so because the most dynamic sectors were precisely the ones receiving fiscal incentives. The fiscal problem became more acute with the explosive growth of pension payments from the public budget as a result of generous adjustments implemented in previous years. Finally, domestic debt grew sharply in the 1990s under onerous conditions since the government had to offer very attractive interest rates in order to place the large number of debt instruments that it needed. The rise in interest rates led to substantial increase in debt service burden while reducing investment and output. The domestic public debt is nowadays not only one of the primary determinants of the fiscal deficit but also one posing strong limitations to public investment. In the year 2001, for example, interest payments on the domestic debt accounted for 20.5 per cent of all central government expenditures.

Costa Rican exports grew dramatically throughout the period of study, rising from US\$ 1,082 million in 1985 to a peak of US\$ 6,662 million in 1999 before falling to US\$ 5,006 million in 2001 (Figure 7.1). Exports without the products falling under the special regimes (export-processing free zones and *maquilas*) grew from US\$ 941 million in 1985 to US\$ 3,145 million in 1998 (peak value), falling to US\$ 2,314 million in 2001.

Since it began production in 1998, Intel exports have been very high and with a strong impact on total exports. Excluding the exports from this enterprise, but including the enterprises in the special regimes, the country's total exports increased from US\$ 1,082 million in 1985 to a peak level of US\$ 4,976 million in 1998, before falling to US\$ 4,053 million in 2001. The drop in the latter period

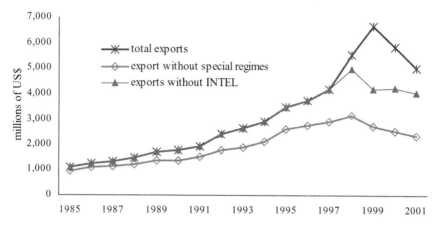

Figure 7.1   Costa Rica: exports of goods and services, 1985–2001 (millions of US$). (From Central Bank of Costa Rica and Intel.)

is related to the deceleration of the US economy, which is the principal destination of Costa Rica's exports. In the case of Intel, the decline is related to the situation in the world market for microprocessors.

Despite some annual fluctuations, traditional exports (coffee, bananas, meat and sugar) expanded between 1985 and 1995 before falling in 2001 to levels similar to those of 1990 (Figure 7.2). This decline, as said, is primarily due to falling prices. For instance, the average export price of a 46 kilogram sack of coffee declined from US$149 in 1995 to US$58 in 2001. Revenue from exports, therefore, declined significantly although the volume of exports remained essentially

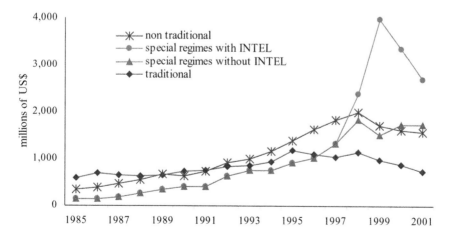

Figure 7.2   Costa Rica: traditional and non-traditional exports, 1985–2001 (millions of US$). (From Central Bank of Costa Rica and Intel.)

the same. Similarly, the average price of bananas declined from US$336 per ton in 1995 to US$277 in 2001. However, in the case of bananas, volume of export also decreased due to the European Union's imposition of a limit on purchases from Latin America in July 1993. Meat and sugar were also affected by the decline in export prices, although they account for a very small percentage of total traditional exports.

Non-traditional exports (industrial, agricultural and fishing products),[7] which have outperformed traditional exports since 1992, behave similarly to other exports (traditional and special regimes); they went through a phase of expansion peaking in 1998 before declining again. In this case, the decline is related mostly to the suspension of the CAT benefit, since exports that were only profitable because of the incentives ceased their activities, along with other 'fictitious' exports whose only objective was to acquire tax-credit certificates, as several fraud cases currently in process show. The deceleration in the US economy is also important, and has affected the placement of various products in that market.

External shocks and the domestic response

Following the methodology proposed in Morley and Vos (see Chapter 2),[8] the change in the current account deficit as a ratio to the GDP is disaggregated into four types of effects: (1) external exogenous shocks; (2) impacts of internal and external autonomous conditions; (3) responses of domestic policy and (4) a group of interaction ('residual') effects. Analysis is undertaken for 1985–2000, disaggregating for four sub-periods: 1985–91, 1992–7, 1998–9 and 2000.

Results of the analysis (Table 7.1) show that external shocks on the whole were favourable to Costa Rica in the 1990s despite declining export prices. This is mainly because of the expansion in world demand for Costa Rican products. During the same period, the increase in exports led to a significant reduction in the current account deficit, despite the increase in imports that pushed the deficit in the other direction. In the year 2000, world demand for Costa Rican products remained high, but import prices deteriorated and exports fell, causing an increase in the deficit with respect to 1998–9.

Exports and product growth: a Keynesian analysis

In order to approximate the contribution of exports to GDP growth, a Keynesian decomposition analysis was carried out that explains the growth of output as a result of the changes in exogenous or autonomous expenditures (private investment, public expenditures and exports) and of the parameters relative to imports, private savings and taxes. While it is true that those considered here are not the only determinants of that growth, the methodology proposed in Morley and Vos (see Chapter 2) contributes important elements to the investigation of the importance of the various macroeconomic aggregates during the period.

Exports clearly have led to output growth. Equally, export decline has been the main cause of the deceleration of the economy in 2000–1 (Figure 7.3).

Table 7.1 Costa Rica: decomposition of variations in the current account deficit (percentage points of GDP)

	1992–7/ 1985–91	*1998–9/ 1992–7*	*2000/ 1998–9*
Observed change in current account deficit (% GDP)	−1.8	−0.3	0.7
External shocks	−4.7	−1.6	3.1
Terms of trade effect	−1.2	−1.5	4.7
Import price effect	−3.3	−2.7	2.3
Export price effect	2.1	1.2	2.4
Impact of interest rates on public external debt	0.4	0.1	0.1
World trade effect	−3.9	−0.2	−1.7
Other external variables	−2.2	6.5	0.0
Accumulation of public external debt	−1.2	−0.5	0.1
Change in foreign direct investment income[1]	−1.4	6.3	−0.3
Change in remittances	...	0.1	...
Change in public transfers	0.4	0.6	0.1
Domestic adjustment	5.2	−3.8	−3.3
Domestic absorption	−0.1	−1.5	−2.6
Trade ratios	5.3	−2.3	−0.7
Import substitution	11.3	10.8	−1.7
Penetration of exports in world market	−5.9	−13.1	0.9
Interaction (residual) effects	−0.1	−1.4	1.0

Source: Own estimation with data from the Central Bank of Costa Rica

Note: 1 The strong impact of change in foreign direct investment income is explained primarily by Intel

Exports are single-handedly the main contributing factor to growth in each sub-period. Nevertheless, the trade liberalization process has also triggered a strong increase in imports, so that the external sector taken as a whole does not show the same dynamism as exports individually (Table 7.2). The private sector, on the other hand, through investment (including public enterprises) and savings, is the sector that, on average through the period of study, has had the greatest influence on that growth (with the only exception of 1998–9). The government sector, through the direct impact of expenditures and taxes, lost all influence on economic growth since the middle of the 1990s.

7.3 Trends in employment, inequality and poverty

Labour market

Between 1988 and 2000, employment grew at an annual average rate of 2.8 per cent, meaning 30,600 new jobs were created per year. Employment growth was

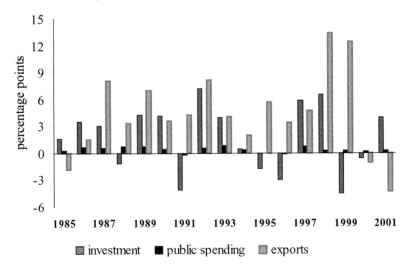

Figure 7.3   Costa Rica: contribution of changes in aggregate demand components to GDP growth, 1985–2001. (From our own estimates based on data from Central Bank of Costa Rica.)

higher than population growth (2.2 per cent), which meant that in spite of increased labour participation, the rate of open unemployment stayed relatively low (5 per cent as an average for the period). Employment growth accelerated during the 1990s to 3.1 per cent per year during 1992–2000, up from 1.9 per cent in 1989–91.

About one-fourth of employed are self-employed or employers (25.4 per cent on average between 1998 and 2000), 70.9 per cent were wage earners (of which 15.4 per cent public, 51.2 per cent private and 4.4 per cent domestic servants) and 3.7 per cent worked as unpaid family members.

One characteristic that stands out in the economic process in question is that throughout the period of the study formal sector (non-agricultural) employment grew to almost half the labour force (from 46.5 to 49.5 per cent between 1988 and 2000).[9]

Informal sector employment went from 25.5 to 30.1 per cent in the same period, while the agricultural sector reduced its participation from 28 to 20.4 per cent. It should also be noted that although the average growth rate for formal employment was less than that of informal employment (given the greater participation of the formal sector early on in the period) six of every ten new jobs created between 1988 and 2000 were in the formal sector and only four were in the informal sector. This situation contrasts significantly with what has occurred in many other countries of the region where most new jobs have been in the informal sector.

Throughout the period of study, the most dynamic sectors in terms of growth in employment were *financial services, insurance, real estate* and *other business services*; and *transportation, storage* and *communications*, with annual growth

Table 7.2 Costa Rica: contribution to GDP growth by aggregate demand component; period averages 1985–91, 1992–7, 1998–9 and 2000–1 (percentage points)

	GDP growth[1]	Private sector			Government sector			External sector			
		Total	Inv.	Sav.	Total	Exp.	Tax	Total	Exp.	Imp.	Residual
1985–91	3.7	1.2	1.6	-0.4	1.2	0.5	0.7	0.9	3.7	-2.8	0.4
1992–7	5.3	3.1	2.2	0.9	0.5	0.4	0.2	1.8	4.7	-2.9	-0.2
1998–9	8.3	-4.4	1.0	-5.4	1.3	0.3	1.0	10.8	12.9	-2.1	0.6
2000–1	1.6	2.0	1.7	0.3	0.4	0.2	0.2	-0.7	-2.7	1.9	-0.1

Source: Own estimation with data from the Central Bank of Costa Rica

Note: 1 Refers to changes observed in GDP

rates of 7.5 and 6.7 per cent on average for 1989–2000. *Commerce, restaurants* and *hotels* (5 per cent) continues to be an important sector as well. The same sectors are among those showing the highest rates of growth in output. They are also sectors that benefited from trade liberalization, export promotion and growth of tourism. The specific case of financial services is also tied to the process of financial reform.

According to household survey data, the average labour income per employed person (wages as well as profits for employers and self-employed workers) grew in real terms at 1.6 per cent per year between 1989 and 2000. Labour income inequality fell due to greater job creation for formal sector and more skilled workers. Labour productivity, measured as average output per employed person, grew at a pace of 1.4 per cent per year between 1989 and 2000.

Inequality and poverty at the household Level

Poverty rates (extreme and total) clearly declined in the early 1990s. Poverty reduction came to a standstill, however, in 1994. At that point the nation-wide poverty incidence stood at 23 per cent and extreme poverty at about 7 per cent. On the other hand, inequality in distribution of household income initially remained stable, but increased strongly from the mid-1990s onwards (Figure 7.4). Clearly, the structural adjustment that took place since the mid-1990s led to a widening of income differentials, but without increasing poverty.

7.4 Exports, employment, inequality and poverty: a counterfactual analysis

With the use of a CGE model for Costa Rica, a series of macrosimulations were performed to identify the impact of exogenous shocks and various policies on

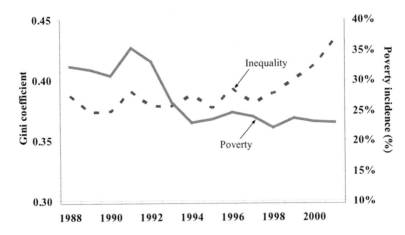

Figure 7.4   Costa Rica: household income poverty and inequality, 1988–2001. (From our own estimates based on household survey data of the National Institute of Statistics and Censuses.)

output growth, employment, labour income and other economic variables. These impacts were subsequently coupled with a complementary exercise of simulations with micro (household survey) data, which made it possible to see how changes in the labour market affect income distribution and poverty.

Basic characteristics of the Costa Rican CGE model

The Costa Rican CGE model follows the structure of the standard model that has been used as methodology for other studies in this project (see Löfgren *et al.* 2001, and Chapter 3).[10] The model distinguishes 17 production activities and the same number of groups of goods and services (see Table A7.1). At the top level of the production technology, constant-elasticity-of-substitution (CES) production functions are used. To maximize profits, producers demand factors of production that are assumed to be imperfect substitutes. Factors are grouped by capital (machines and land) and labour. Labour was disaggregated into 12 categories, combining breakdowns by sector (agriculture, formal and informal), educational level (skilled and unskilled)[11] and occupational category (wage earners and self-employed workers).[12] Household expenditures (rural and urban) are determined through a linear expenditure system in which expenditures on goods and services is a linear function of the total expenditures on consumption.[13]

The Costa Rican CGE defines the following equilibrium conditions for the various markets (closure rules). In the factor market, the sum of the quantities demanded of each factor in each of the activities is equal to the aggregated supply of each factor in all the activities. It is assumed that there can be unemployment in the various labour market segments, which implies that there are specific and fixed real wages for each activity of the economy, according to the type of work. Workers can move with relative flexibility towards other segments of the labour market if they have become unemployed. The average wage and labour supply, both per type of worker, are the variables that clear the labour market. Full employment is assumed in the factor market for capital, but capital is sector specific; that is, it is not allowed to move from one activity to another. The price of capital is flexible and ensures equilibrium between supply and demand for capital in all sectors. Based on these assumptions of the factor market, the model defines equations for value added and factor demands.[14]

The model imposes equality between the quantities supplied and demanded of each (composite) good or service. The variables that balance the market are the quantities of import supply on the import side and domestic prices on the domestic production side. The current account balance is determined by the equality between the country's expenditures and income in foreign currency. Given the prevailing condition of Costa Rica's current account deficit and the need for external financing, foreign savings equilibrate the foreign exchange market (or external accounts).[15] This implies maintaining a fixed exchange rate, which is also consistent with Costa Rica's current exchange rate regime. The system of preannounced mini-devaluations resembles more a fixed than a flexible regime. This closure implies that foreign savings are flexible in the model.[16]

The government savings are assumed to be endogenous in the model, i.e. the result of endogenous current revenue of the government (mainly taxation) and exogenous current expenditure (without including government investment). Total savings of institutions[17] must equal total investment. Total investment is the sum of the values of fixed investment (gross fixed capital formation) and change in inventories. Savings rates of domestic institutions adjust to balance the savings–investment account. The 'balancing' operates through the savings side, such that this closure is a typical case of savings-driven investment.

Because the model is homogenous of degree zero in prices, an equation is included to normalize prices. 'Normalization' can be done using virtually any nominal magnitude of the model, since it will not affect any of the real variables (Dervis *et al.* 1984: 150). In the Costa Rican CGE model, the normalization of prices is based on the consumer price index (CPI); that is to say, the CPI is the 'numéraire'. Thus, if the value of the 'numéraire' is doubled, all prices would be doubled, but the real quantities would not vary.

Calibration, parameters and elasticities

The Costa Rican CGE model is calibrated with data from a SAM, just as the literature recommends (see, for example, Taylor 1990: 7).[18] In addition to the values of their exogenous variables, the parameters used in the CGE model equations are calculated from the SAM. For this, a SAM for Costa Rica was estimated in millions of 1997 *colones*,[19] using the Cross Entropy Method.[20]

The employment data that were used to calibrate the model were obtained from a 1997 household survey. All of the elasticities used were located within the range in which the model provided a consistent solution that replicates the SAM data. To complement this and to get an idea of the values that the elasticities should take on, we examined the existing literature on models for Costa Rica that specify elasticities of substitution and transformation in international trade.[21] Table A7.1 shows the values for the CET and CES functions for output transformation and aggregation of imported and domestically produced goods and services. The elasticities of substitution among factors and between factors and aggregated intermediate goods are assumed to take a value of 0.4 and 0.5, respectively. These values are also used in the model of Dessus and Bussolo (1998). Finally, the elasticity of household expenditure on marketed goods and services is equal to one, while that of expenditure on goods and services produced in the household is equal to zero (since there is no household self-consumption).

Counterfactual simulation exercises

Impact of external shocks

Ten simulations were carried out, in five sets, for changes in the prices of export products and export value, variations in import prices, changes in the terms of trade and changes in foreign savings. The first set includes four simulations relating to a *10 per cent reduction in prices for the four major export products*: non-traditional agricultural exports (PAGNEDIS); food products, beverages and tobacco (PALIMDIS); the products falling under the special export regimes, that is, *perfeccionamiento activo* and export-processing zones (PPAZFDIS); and traditional agricultural exports (PAGTEDIS).

As the results in Table 7.3 show, if export prices fall, the model predicts reductions in total exports and GDP, as well as in employment and labour income. Furthermore, there will be increases in the fiscal deficit and current account deficit of the balance of payments. The fall in employment and labour income causes an increase in poverty.

There will also be an increase in inequality in the distribution of household income. The largest increases in both poverty and inequality are associated, primarily, with the decline in agricultural income and employment (Table A7.2). The biggest impacts on production, employment, labour income and poverty come from the fall in non-traditional export prices and in the prices for special regimes, while the smallest impact comes from the reduction in traditional export prices. This reflects the significant diversification of the Costa Rican economy. Three decades ago, this kind of shock would have had a much greater impact. The result is consistent with the situation of the country at the turn of the century when prices for these export products had declined significantly, especially that of coffee. This has had a negative effect on the economic situation in general, but much less than historically.

The second set of external shock simulations includes three simulations relating to a US$100 million increase in the value of exports as a result of an assumed increased demand for those products. The following sectors were considered: traditional agricultural exports (EAGTEINC), non-traditional agricultural exports (EAGNEINC) and special export regimes (EPAZFINC). As expected, for these simulations the model generates results that mirror those of the previous set, with increases in exports, GDP, employment and average labour incomes, and reductions in the incidence of poverty. The fiscal and current account deficits decrease as well. Inequality of income distribution does not change in just one direction but increases or decreases depending on the impact on employment and labour income of the various categories of workers (Table A7.2). Most notably, an increase in exports falling under special export regimes strongly increase inequality, while traditional agricultural exports produce a small decrease.

But in addition to understanding the impact on selected variables, these three simulations were carried out with an additional purpose: to assess the degree of integration of *export sectors with the rest of the national economy*. By looking at the impact of exogenous export growth on GDP and demand for intermediate consumption,[22] the simulations allow us to conclude that the production linkages of the export activities in export-processing zones and *maquilas* with the rest of the economy are quite low. The linkages of these industries with the economy as

Table 7.3 Costa Rica: main simulation results (percentage deviation with respect to base-year value)

Simulations	Exports (value)[1]	Current account deficit[1]	Fiscal deficit[1]	GDP[1]	Employment	Labour income	Gini[2]	Poverty incidence Extreme	Poverty incidence Total
External shocks									
Reduction in export prices									
PAGTEDIS	−0.40	0.16	2.81	−0.29	−0.11	−0.01	0.47	2.36	0.94
PAGNEDIS	−0.48	1.71	5.76	−0.92	−0.27	−0.19	0.63	4.38	1.77
PALIMDIS	−1.56	0.63	5.38	−0.25	−0.04	0.01	0.18	0.34	0.36
PPAZFDIS	−0.48	0.16	3.40	−0.46	−0.20	−0.30	−0.03	1.85	1.67
Increase in exports (value)									
EAGTEINC	2.21	−9.25	−5.58	0.61	0.08	0.14	−0.05	−0.51	−0.21
EAGNEINC	1.87	−6.66	−4.18	0.67	0.14	0.10	0.00	0.00	−0.21
EPAZFINC	1.98	−7.38	−5.16	0.70	0.19	0.28	0.23	0.00	−0.63
Increase in import prices									
PIMPINC	1.20	−46.67	25.71	−1.09	−1.19	−1.22	0.68	11.62	5.11
Deterioration in terms of trade									
DISHOCK	0.20	−4.82	5.26	−0.11	−0.28	−0.17	0.55	4.21	1.67
Increase in foreign savings									
AEXTINC	−0.40	4.62	0.71	0.11	0.04	0.04	0.08	0.17	0.16

(*Continued*)

Table 7.3 (Continued)

Simulations	Exports (value)[1]	Current account deficit[1]	Fiscal deficit[1]	GDP[1]	Employment	Labour income	Gini[2]	Poverty incidence Extreme	Poverty incidence Total
Policy									
Trade liberalization									
LIBCOM1	−0.40	17.38	34.18	0.29	0.38	0.39	0.13	−0.34	−0.26
LIBCOM2	−0.38	17.45	31.88	0.27	0.35	0.36	0.08	−0.34	−0.21
LIBCOM3	3.15	−6.18	−12.08	7.51	1.29	1.37	0.18	−0.67	−2.19
LIBCOM4	0.40	−16.47	−31.84	−0.33	−0.39	−0.40	0.23	3.37	2.24
Trade agreements									
FTASIM	−0.50	23.21	44.60	0.36	0.49	0.50	0.26	−0.34	−0.35
WTOSIM	−1.20	18.86	40.13	0.09	−0.02	0.26	0.60	3.20	0.89
Other policy simulations									
DEVAL	6.50	−69.64	−10.38	−1.02	−0.54	−0.66	−0.21	3.87	1.62
SUBEXINC	0.40	−1.42	5.37	0.01	0.08	0.06	0.13	0.00	−0.10
SALINC	−0.28	−1.02	13.83	−0.19	−0.68	5.54	−0.13	5.89*	−1.04*
Productivity									
PRODINC1	10.29	27.94	−87.76	10.76	1.07	1.15	0.18	−0.34	−1.09
PRODINC2	7.76	−26.95	−21.33	2.06	0.02	0.06	0.08	0.00	−0.16

Notes
1 Variations in real terms
2 Gini coefficient for the distribution of per capita household income
*SALINC is the only simulation in which the sign of the simulated change in extreme poverty differs from that of total poverty.

a whole are in fact no stronger than those of the primary export activities (traditional and non-traditional agricultural).

The third kind of simulation of external shocks consisted of a *10 per cent increase in the prices of imports* (PIMPINC). As expected, the model predicts a dramatic fall in imports (−9.3 per cent of their real value) and a 9.7 per cent depreciation of the real exchange rate, which results in a small increase in exports (1.2 per cent of their real value). There is, consequently, a significant reduction in the current account deficit, but also an increase in the fiscal deficit due to the reduction in import tax revenue. GDP, employment and labour income fall, while poverty and inequality rise. These results reflect the enormous importance of imports for the Costa Rican economy.

The fourth kind of simulation combines two of the previous ones to simulate a deterioration in the *terms of trade* (DISHOCK) originating from a 10 per cent decline in the international prices of traditional export products and a 10 per cent increase in the international price of chemical imports, including petroleum. In this case, the results generated by the model are identical in form to those of the simulation for increased import prices, only they are of a smaller magnitude. This simulation reflects very well Costa Rica's situation in recent years – with significant increases in the price of petroleum and decreases in the price of traditional exports, especially coffee. The small impact on GDP, employment and labour income – but not on poverty – reflects the significant transformation of the Costa Rican economy in recent years, referred to earlier, since a decline in the terms of trade of this type and magnitude in the 1970s would have presumably caused a severe economic crisis.

One last simulation in this group consisted of a *10 per cent increase in foreign savings* (AEXTINC), which is understood in the model as an inflow of foreign currency. According to the model, such a capital inflow provokes a decline in the real exchange rate (or appreciation) of 0.8 per cent, which impacts on imports (with a 0.7 per cent increase in their real value) and exports (−0.4 per cent) with an increase in the current account deficit. The model indicates very small increases in GDP, employment and labour income, and also a very small reduction (not significant) in poverty. This simulation shows the important destabilizing effect that a massive inflow of capital can have on small and open economies, affecting the competitiveness of exports because of the appreciation in domestic currency. Costa Rica experienced this type of capital inflow and its impact in the early 1990s.

Impact of policies

In the policy arena, nine simulations grouped in three sets were carried out. The first set included four simulations of trade liberalization. The first is a 50 per cent reduction in import tariffs (LIBCOM1). The second uses the same reduction in tariffs but adds a 5 per cent increase in indirect taxes to compensate for the fall in government revenue (LIBCOM2). In the third, the same reduction in tariffs is applied along with a 5 per cent increase in factor productivity in those activities whose product grew in the first of the three simulations considered here (LIBCOM3). The fourth considered the effects of a 50 per cent increase in import tariffs (LIBCOM4), in other words, a more protectionist policy.

For the first two simulations (reduction in tariffs without an increase in productivity), the model forecasts an increase in real imports (3.5 per cent in LIBCOM1) and expands both the fiscal and current account deficits. Small increases in production, employment and labour income are also foreseen along with a small reduction in poverty. In the event that productivity were to increase (LIBCOM3), the impact on the current account and fiscal deficits reverts (that is, both deficits would now shrink), GDP, employment and labour income would all grow, and poverty reduction would be relatively more pronounced. In all three previous cases, however, inequality grows. The simulation of increased protectionism (LIBCOM4) yields results that are inverse to the previous, with the exception of inequality, which also increases. Two important conclusions can be drawn from these simulation results. First, an increase in productivity appears to be one of the necessary conditions for trade liberalization to have a positive overall impact. Second, the finding that trade liberalization helps to reduce poverty, but increases inequality confirms that of previous studies (Sauma and Vargas 2001).

In a second set, we simulate the impact of *multilateral trade agreements*, specifically Costa Rica's incorporation into the FTAA and a worldwide implementation of the agreements of the WTO (FTASIM and WTOSIM, respectively). The simulations were carried out keeping in mind the variations in the international prices forecast by the International Food Policy Research Institute (IFPRI) for these scenarios, by reducing the tariffs of all import sectors of the Americas in the case of the FTAA, and by eliminating all tariffs and export subsidies (CAT) in the case of the WTO.[23]

In both cases, the model indicates a decline in Costa Rican exports and increases in the current account and fiscal deficits. GDP increases as well as employment and labour incomes, although the increase of the first two is very small in the WTO simulation. In both situations, but especially in that of the WTO, employment and labour income for the agricultural sector are the most affected since they fall while for the other sectors these variables record an increase (see Table A7.2). Unskilled workers are also affected, or benefit less, in terms of employment and labour income. The increase in inequality that appears in both cases (stronger in the WTO simulation because of the greater decline in agricultural income) should, therefore, not come as a surprise. Results are different in terms of poverty. While the FTAA simulation generates a reduction in poverty, the WTO simulation forecasts an increase, especially in extreme poverty. This is explained primarily by the dramatic decline in agricultural income[24] since most of the country's poor are in the agricultural and informal sectors (Sauma and Vargas 2001).

However, a clarification is necessary for the WTO simulation. The main difference between the results of this simulation and those of the FTAA has to do with the elimination of export subsidies and not so much with the changes foreseen in international prices and tariffs. Since the last CATs were issued in 1999, at present one would have to expect WTO results that would be similar to those encountered here in a FTAA scenario.[25] In fact, when the elimination of export subsidies is simulated separately, the model forecasts a small decline in overall exports and production, which affects agriculture in a relatively significant way. One can also see that while employment and labour income do not vary much in either the formal or informal sector, in agriculture both would fall (by 0.53 and 0.57 per cent, respectively). The results the model generates for individual simulations are not additive, but it is possible to say that the elimination of export subsidies explains most of the differences observed in the results of the FTAA and WTO scenarios, primarily in view of the outcome in production, employment and labour income for agriculture in the WTO scenario.

The third set includes simulations of *other policies*: the promotion of exports through a 10 per cent nominal devaluation (DEVAL); export promotion through a 50 per cent increase in export subsidies for selected sectors (SUBEXINC); and a 10 per cent increase in the nominal wage for the formal sector (SALINC).

In the case of the devaluation, it is important to highlight that in the base year the model supposes the real exchange rate to be that of parity, so that a nominal devaluation reflects a depreciation in the real exchange rate. This depreciation increases exports and reduces imports, and although according to the model there is a reduction in the current account and fiscal deficits, it has a negative impact on GDP, employment, labour income and poverty. The results suggest that using devaluation (real depreciation) as an instrument to boost exports may not be a good idea as this form of export promotion could have a negative impact on the economy as a whole.

The model generates another interesting result when export subsidies are incremented. This policy would lead to a positive impact on exports, GDP, employment and labour income, albeit very small. This result could be influenced by the fact that in 1997, the base year for the model, the export subsidies were very high, so that additional increases would not cause greater increases in exports and production at the margin. As mentioned earlier, the model also predicts that the elimination of export incentives would cause a small decline in overall exports and production, which seems consistent with what actually happened after the elimination of the CAT in 1999.

Finally, according to the model, raising wages in the formal sector triggers the same kind of increase in labour income and reduces total poverty. Yet, this policy has more of a negative impact on exports, GDP and employment.[26]

Increased productivity

A final simulation assumes an exogenous increase in productivity (beyond that of LIBCOM3), specifically a 10 per cent increase in total factor productivity in all production activities (PRODINC1) and a 10 per cent increase in total factor productivity but only in export sectors (PRODINC2).[27] As expected, increases of this kind are extremely beneficial for the country, since they not only increase production, employment and labour income along with exports, but also have a significant impact on the reduction of poverty and of the fiscal deficit. The impact is quite a bit higher when the increase happens across the board rather than only in the export sectors. As mentioned earlier, the productivity of labour in reality grew by 1.3 per cent as an annual average for 1992–2000. This growth is low and needs to be significantly increased in order to expand the benefits that productivity generates. In the same way, the productivity of the capital factor should increase, which theoretically could be achieved by technological innovation facilitated through trade liberalization and by attracting foreign direct investment.

7.5 Conclusions

The study shows that economic growth during the 1990s is explained in large part by the increase in exports, although domestic demand, particularly private sector spending, also played an important role. The economic deceleration of recent years is related to the fall in exports. The study also shows that the current economic process, which includes the promotion of exports, has had a positive impact on the reduction of poverty, but has also increased inequality in income distribution.

The general equilibrium model elaborated as part of the study satisfactorily explains the behaviour of the Costa Rican economy, allowing the exploration of what would have happened in various counterfactual scenarios. Some conclusions and policy recommendations derived from the study are presented as follows – using no particular order:

1. An increase in factor productivity is a necessary condition for broadening the benefits of the current economic process, but also to protect the national economy against external shocks and alleviate the fiscal problem.
2. A persistent increase in the fiscal deficit in practically all scenarios suggests that the solution to the fiscal problem requires structural reforms in the area of expenditures and taxes in accordance with the economic reality of the country and the world. But an increase in productivity is also a complementary option to these reforms.
3. Trade liberalization in particular and the current economic process in general reduced poverty in the first phase and have kept it stable since 1994. One of the principal reasons for this is the generation of formal sector jobs. The simulations carried out show an inverse relationship between formal employment and the incidence of poverty. That is to say that increases in formal employment are accompanied, in many cases, by reductions in poverty (obviously, the final poverty outcome will depend on what happens in all the segments of the labour market). Therefore, in order to maintain – and better yet – to reduce the incidence of poverty, economic policy should promote the creation of formal sector jobs.

4. In order to increase the aggregate benefits of the current economic process for the country, it becomes absolutely necessary to increase productive linkages between export sectors (especially enterprises operating in special export regimes) and the rest of the economy.

5. The simulations on the FTAA and WTO scenarios carried out by adjusting international prices and tariffs (according to projections provided by IFPRI) generate similar results. In general, a fall in exports and a rise in imports were observed, with increases in the current account and fiscal deficits, as well as in production, employment and labour income. There is an additional small impact on poverty – presumably a reduction – and an increase in the inequality of income distribution. The impacts are not of great magnitude, in general terms, which suggests that in order to expand the benefits of these agreements for the country, some other changes are necessary. The priority areas of change would be enhanced productivity and increased value added of export products. The agricultural question is especially important, since both simulations reflect the possibility of negative impacts on employment and labour income for this sector. It is necessary, therefore, to carry out a detailed product-by-product analysis and, based on the results, to define particular strategies for negotiation or for broadening the benefits for producers.

6. Given a situation of parity in the real exchange rate, a real depreciation of the exchange rate has positive repercussions for the value of exports, but at the level of the economy as a whole the result is not satisfactory. Exchange rate policy must therefore be managed in a very prudent way, to attempt to maintain – as has been done up to now – a neutral exchange rate for international trade.

7. Wage increases are not an effective means to reduce poverty. In the case studied, though the total poverty rate was reduced a little, extreme poverty increased and did so at a greater rate. Furthermore, because of its adverse impact on the main economic variables, in the long term it could provoke a much larger increase in poverty. Therefore, the minimum wage policy should be managed prudently – as has been done so far – maintaining the purchasing power of the minimum wages in order to avoid an increase in poverty. Greater upward adjustments of minimum wages should be conditioned on increases in productivity.

8. Most of the scenarios conducted cause an increase in inequality, consistent with the reduction in agricultural employment and income on the one hand, and with the increase of income in the formal sector on the other. This leads inevitably to considering the need to apply some redistributive policies.

9. Finally, the model shows the destabilizing effect that massive capital inflows can have on a small and open economy like that of Costa Rica, affecting the competitiveness of exports through the appreciation of the domestic currency. This highlights the importance of an exchange rate policy that allows the Central Bank to at least partially counteract the effects of these inflows.

Table A7.1 Costa Rica: elasticity values for functions of output transformation (CET) and aggregation of imported and domestically produced goods and services (CES)

Sector	CET	CES
Agriculture for domestic consumption (basic grains, forest products, livestock – except for cattle – and other products for internal consumption)	2.2	2.2
Traditional export agriculture (including coffee, bananas, sugar cane and cattle)	4.5	1.5
Non-traditional export agriculture (all other agricultural export sectors including fishing and maritime products)	3.0	3.0
Food products, beverages and tobacco	2.5	2.5
Textiles, clothing and leather industries	0.8	0.8
Wood and wood products	0.8	0.8
Chemical substances and products; petroleum derivatives; carbon derivatives, rubber and plastics	0.4	0.4
Paper and paper products; presses and publishing; non-metallic mineral products (except for petroleum and carbon derivatives); basic metals	0.9	0.9
Metal products (except for machinery and equipment) and other manufacturing industries	0.4	0.4
Perfeccionamiento Activo and export-processing zones (export regimes)	0.8	nt
Construction	nt	nt
Retail and wholesale trade	nt	nt
Hotels and restaurants	1.5	nt
Transport, storage, mail and telecommunications	0.4	0.4
Electricity and water supply	nt	nt
Financial and securities intermediation	1.5	1.5
Other services	1.5	1.5

Note: 'nt' stands for non-tradable sector

Acknowledgements

The authors would like to thank all the people who made this research possible, especially the Project Coordinators, Enrique Ganuza, Samuel Morley, Rob Vos, and Barbara Stallings, as well as Sherman Robinson, Eugenio Díaz-Bonilla, and Valeria Piñeiro of IFPRI, for their support in the modelling. Our thanks go also to all of the participants in the follow up workshops for the project, held in Montelimar (Nicaragua), Santo Domingo (Dominican Republic), and Buenos Aires (Argentina). Special thanks to William Calvo and Mariam Cover, officials of the Central Bank in Costa Rica, for their support in obtaining the relevant information for analysing macroeconomic performance and estimating the 1997 SAM for Costa Rica. It is important, however, to mention that all of the opinions, errors, or omissions this document may contain are the exclusive responsibility of the authors, and do not correspond to either the individuals or the institutions named.

Table A7.2 Costa Rica: impact of simulations on employment and labour income (percentage deviation with respect to base-year value)

	Total	Sector			Skill level		Employment category	
		Formal	Informal	Agriculture	Skilled	Unskilled	Wage	Non-wage
Employment								
PAGTEDIS	−0.11	0.14	0.12	−1.45	0.09	−0.28	−0.09	−0.18
PAGNEDIS	−0.27	0.00	−0.01	−1.71	−0.08	−0.42	−0.25	−0.34
PALIMDIS	−0.04	−0.05	−0.08	0.05	−0.08	−0.02	−0.04	−0.05
PPAZFDIS	−0.20	−0.41	0.04	0.04	−0.28	−0.12	−0.29	0.04
EAGTEINC	0.08	−0.31	−0.28	2.14	−0.25	0.35	0.05	0.19
EAGNEINC	0.14	−0.01	0.01	0.90	0.04	0.22	0.12	0.18
EPAZFINC	0.19	0.40	−0.04	−0.05	0.27	0.11	0.27	−0.04
PIMPINC	−1.19	−1.39	−1.48	0.07	−1.40	−1.03	−1.23	−1.09
TDISHOCK	−0.28	−0.04	−0.07	−1.57	−0.09	−0.44	−0.26	−0.36
AEXTINC	0.04	0.07	0.08	−0.17	0.07	0.00	0.04	0.03
LIBCOM1	0.38	0.45	0.48	−0.06	0.45	0.32	0.39	0.35
LIBCOM2	0.35	0.41	0.45	−0.08	0.43	0.29	0.36	0.32
LIBCOM3	1.29	1.60	0.46	2.02	1.26	1.30	1.48	0.81
LIBCOM4	−0.39	−0.46	−0.48	0.05	−0.47	−0.32	−0.40	−0.35
FTASIM	0.49	0.57	0.62	−0.02	0.59	0.42	0.51	0.45
WTOSIM	−0.02	0.45	0.37	−2.27	0.44	−0.35	−0.01	−0.02
DEVAL	−0.54	−1.01	−1.26	2.59	−1.11	−0.07	−0.58	−0.37
SUBEXINC	0.08	0.04	0.07	0.25	0.03	0.12	0.07	0.12
SALINC	−0.68	−0.89	−0.68	0.02	−0.81	−0.58	−0.73	−0.54
PRODINC1	1.07	1.29	0.56	1.44	1.31	0.88	1.17	0.81
PRODINC2	0.02	−0.01	0.03	0.09	0.05	0.00	0.02	0.03

(Continued)

Table A7.2 (Continued)

	Total	Sector			Skill level		Employment category	
		Formal	Informal	Agriculture	Skilled	Unskilled	Wage	Non-wage
Labour income								
PAGTEDIS	-0.01	0.15	0.14	-1.30	0.15	-0.17	0.13	-0.10
PAGNEDIS	-0.19	0.01	0.02	-1.82	0.01	-0.39	0.01	-0.31
PALIMDIS	0.01	0.06	-0.06	-0.08	0.03	0.00	0.01	0.02
PPAZFDIS	-0.30	-0.48	0.02	0.04	-0.36	-0.23	-0.87	0.05
EAGTEINC	0.14	-0.25	-0.23	3.32	-0.24	0.52	-0.21	0.36
EAGNEINC	0.10	0.00	-0.01	0.97	0.00	0.20	-0.01	0.17
EPAZFINC	0.28	0.47	-0.02	-0.05	0.35	0.22	0.84	-0.05
PIMPINC	-1.22	-1.33	-1.48	0.10	-1.37	-1.07	-1.24	-1.20
TDISHOCK	-0.17	-0.03	0.00	-1.42	-0.01	-0.33	-0.02	-0.27
AEXTINC	0.04	0.06	0.08	-0.17	0.07	0.01	0.04	0.04
LIBCOM1	0.39	0.43	0.48	-0.07	0.45	0.33	0.39	0.39
LIBCOM2	0.36	0.40	0.46	-0.08	0.42	0.31	0.36	0.36
LIBCOM3	1.37	1.18	1.53	2.11	1.43	1.32	1.41	1.35
LIBCOM4	-0.40	-0.44	-0.49	0.05	-0.46	-0.34	-0.41	-0.40
FTASIM	0.50	0.55	0.62	-0.04	0.58	0.42	0.49	0.51
WTOSIM	0.26	0.50	0.52	-1.74	0.53	0.00	0.48	0.13
DEVAL	-0.66	-0.95	-1.30	2.60	-1.08	-0.23	-0.64	-0.65
SUBEXINC	0.06	0.03	0.04	0.27	0.02	0.09	0.02	0.08
SALINC	5.54	9.00	-0.61	0.02	6.00	5.07	6.02	5.24
PRODINC1	1.15	1.20	0.91	1.45	1.12	1.18	1.25	1.09
PRODINC2	0.06	0.09	-0.02	0.12	0.06	0.07	0.24	-0.04

Notes

1 The estimation procedure to derive the SAM is documented in Sanchez (2004, chapter 7).
2 This incentive had a significant fiscal cost (equal to or greater than 0.9 per cent of GDP in 1988 and most of the following years until 1998), which forced modifications to be made in its application in the early 1990s. The scheme was completely abandoned after 1999.
3 A Free Trade and Preferential Exchange Agreement has been in place with Panama since 1973, but is limited in scope as it only regulates the exchange of goods under a limited coverage of the tariff universe. For this reason, a broader agreement is being negotiated.
4 As Delgado indicates (2002: 446–7), 'There is no clear documented evidence from the moment in which the Central Bank returned to the system of mini-devaluations. Exchange rate behaviour between August 1992 and January 1993 – and especially from July 1993 onwards – suggests that the Central Bank is playing a decisive role'.
5 Tourism was bolstered in 1985 with the approval of a law to promote the development of the activity.
6 Except for 1998 when there was a break in the cycle, election years (1986, 1990 and 1994) show higher fiscal deficits than those prevailing in years immediately before and after these years. The deficits in elections years become larger each time (2.6 per cent of GDP in 1986, 3.5 per cent in 1990 and 5.5 per cent in 1994). This fiscal management forces each of the governments that take office in the following years to undertake significant stabilization measures during their first years of administration. Once stabilization is achieved, they use public expenditures to increase the aggregate demand, passing on a similar problem to the next administration.
7 Sometimes special regime exports are classified with non-traditional exports, but for purposes of this study, they will be kept separate.
8 This methodology was developed originally by UNCTAD (1987), and Morley and Vos (see Chapter 2) use the methodology as adapted by Jansen and Vos (1997).
9 The 'informal sector' is considered to be the group of productive non-agricultural activities whose characteristic trait is the low endowment of capital and, therefore, a lower capital/labour relationship. Following traditional definitions, with some additional adjustments, this study considered informal sector workers to be: non-agricultural self-employed workers (excluding those who had any university education); unpaid family members; micro-enterprise workers (employers and private sector wage earners without university education in establishments of five or fewer employees); and domestic service workers. All other non-agricultural workers were considered to be part of the 'formal sector'.
10 The optimal solution of the model was obtained after running a program written in *GAMS* (Brooke *et al.*, 1998).
11 A skilled worker is assumed to have nine or more years of formal education.
12 The category of wage earners includes domestic servants, while that of self-employed workers includes independent workers, employers and family workers.
13 The Costa Rican CGE model does not include self-consumption of households.
14 According to the standard model that is used here, each activity pays a wage rate expressed as the product of an economy-wide wage for each factor (or average wage in the base solution) and an activity-specific wage distortion factor. In the Costa Rican CGE model, the activity-specific wage distortion factor is assumed to be equal to one in the case of capital (given that the capital market is assumed to be without distortions), but different from one in the case of the 12 types of labour in order to reflect the segmentation of the labour market.
15 Foreign savings are assumed to be equal to the deficit in the current account.
16 This closure rule was changed when a shock in foreign savings was simulated. In line with the functioning of the CGE model used, this scenario implied allowing the exchange rate to adjust in order to clear the foreign exchange market, whereas foreign savings were considered as an exogenous variable.

17 The CGE model institutions are: households (urban and rural), enterprises, government and the rest of the world. The savings for the rest of the world is converted into domestic currency.

18 The SAM reorders national accounts to highlight the income of productive factors as well as the use that economic institutions make of the income they receive (Pyatt and Roe 1977: 339). Its structure gives a consistent framework since, by convention, each one of its rows has a corresponding column with equal totals. This consistency, then, assures that of the CGE model; the calibration assures that in the end the (base) solution of the CGE model replicates the SAM data, which is an indication that there is a base equilibrium solution (Reinert and Roland-Holst 1997). Having proved the existence of the base solution, any changes in the parameters (or exogenous variables) of the model should lead to a new equilibrium solution and, therefore, a new SAM is generated.

19 This means that the base year for model solution is 1997.

20 This method has been previously used by some authors to estimate the SAM of some developing countries. See, for example, Thissen (2000) and Robinson *et al.* (2001). The details of the construction of the 1997 SAM of Costa Rica are presented in Sánchez (2004).

21 See, for example, Dessus and Bussolo (1998), Cattaneo *et al.* (1999) and Abler *et al.* (1999).

22 The increase in the total intermediate consumption of the economy was 1.20 per cent in EAGTEINC, 0.24 per cent in EAGNEINC and 0.25 per cent in EPZAFINC.

23 The adjustments in international prices and tariffs are the result of FTAA and WTO scenarios carried out by IFPRI, using a world computable general equilibrium model calibrated to world trade data from the Global Trade Analysis Project (GTAP).

24 While it is true that a reduction in some international prices could translate into a reduction in the cost of the basic food basket, and therefore in the poverty lines, it is unlikely that that reduction would manage to reverse the impact on poverty in the WTO case.

25 Since the model is static and calibrated with 1997 data, it was not possible to carry out a WTO simulation for the year 2000, for example, when there were no longer any export subsidies. Nevertheless, conducting the WTO simulation maintaining export subsidies would have probably generated results that would be much more difficult to interpret.

26 This simulation generates a mixed result on poverty since it reduces total poverty but increases extreme poverty. This explains why giving a wage increase only to the formal sector is not directly benefiting the poorest (extreme poverty), since they do not have wages nor are they in the formal sector. However, the increase in formal income indirectly benefits the informal sector (Sauma and Garnier 1998), which is also shown by the model. According to the model, in this particular case, the indirect effect is felt in urban areas but not in rural areas, since the total income of urban households increases, but that of rural households falls, with the consequent impact on extreme poverty.

27 Specifically, traditional and non-traditional export agriculture; food products, beverages and tobacco; and special export regimes (that is, *perfeccionamiento activo* and export-processing zones).

References

Abler, D. G., A. G. Rodríguez and J. S. Shortle (1999) 'Parameter uncertainty in CGE modeling of the environmental impacts of economic policies', *Environmental and Resource Economics,* 14: 75–94.

Brooke, A., D. Kendrick, A. Meeraus and R. Raman (1998) *GAMS: A User's Guide*, San Francisco: The Scientific Press.

Cattaneo, A., R. Hinojosa-Ojeda and S. Robinson (1999) 'Costa Rica. Trade liberalization, fiscal imbalances, and macroeconomic policy: a computable general equilibrium model', *North-American Journal of Economics and Finance,* 10(1): 39–67.

Chenery, H. B. (1979) *Structural Change and Development Policy,* Oxford: Oxford University Press.

Dessus, S. and M. Bussolo (1998) 'Is there a trade-off between trade liberalization and pollution abatement?', *Journal of Policy Modeling,* 20(1): 11–31.

Dervis, K., J. de Melo and S. Robinson (1982) *General Equilibrium Models for Development Policy,* Cambridge: Cambridge University Press.

Jansen, K. and R. Vos (1997) *External Finance and Development: Failure and Success in the Third World,* Basingstoke and New York: Macmillan and St. Martin's Press.

Löfgren, H., R. Lee Harris and S. Robinson (2001) 'A standard computable general equilibrium (CGE) model in GAMS', TMD Discussion Paper No. 75, Trade and Macroeconomics Division, International Food Policy Research Institute (IFPRI), Washington, DC: IFPRI.

Morley, S. and R. Vos (2000) *Export-led Economic Strategies: Effects on Poverty Inequality and Growth in Latin America and the Caribbean.* New York: UNDP, ECLAC, IFPRI. Research methodology for the first part of the project by the same name (mimeo).

Pyatt, G. and A. Roe (1977) *Social Accounting for Development Planning with Special Reference to Sri Lanka,* Cambridge: University Printing House.

Reinert, K. A. and D. W. Roland-Holst (1997) 'Social accounting matrices', in: J. F. Francois and K. A. Reinert (eds) *Applied Methods for Trade Policy Analysis,* Cambridge: Cambridge University Press.

Robinson, S., A. Cattaneo and M. El-Said (2001) 'Updating and estimating a social accounting matrix using cross entropy methods', *Economic Systems Research,* 13(1): 47–64.

Sánchez C., M.V. (2004) *Rising Inequality and Declining Poverty during Trade Policy Reform: Understanding the Trade-off in Costa Rica's Agriculture,* Maastricht: Shaker Publishing BV.

Sauma, P. and J. R. Vargas (2001) 'Liberalización de la balanza de pagos en Costa Rica: efectos en el mercado de trabajo, la desigualdad y la pobreza', in: Enrique Ganuza, R. Paes de Barros, L. Taylor and R. Vos (eds) *Liberalización, desigualdad y pobreza: América Latina y el Caribe en los 90.* Buenos Aires: Editorial Universitaria de Buenos Aires (EUDEBA), United Nations Development Program (UNDP) and Economic Commission for Latin America and the Caribbean (ECLAC).

Sauma, P. and L. Garnier (1998) 'Efecto de las políticas macroeconómicas y sociales sobre la pobreza en Costa Rica', in: Enrique Ganuza, L. Taylor and S. Morley (eds) *Políticas macroeconómicas y pobreza en América Latina y el Caribe.* Madrid: Mundi-Prensa Libros S.A. United Nations Development Program, ECLAC and Inter-American Development Bank.

Taylor, L. (1990) 'Structuralist CGE models', in: L. Taylor (ed.) *Socially Relevant Policy Analysis: Structuralist Computable General Equilibrium Models for the Developing World,* Cambridge, MA: The MIT Press.

Thissen, M. (2000) *Building Financial CGE Models: Data, Parameters, and the Role of Expectations. A Financial CGE Model for Egypt,* Theses on Systems, Organization and Management, University of Groningen, Groningen.

UNCTAD (1987) *International Monetary and Financial Issues for Developing Countries,* Geneva: UNCTAD.

8 Cuba – export promotion, poverty, inequality and growth in the 1990s

Angela Ferriol, Xuan Hoang, Alfredo González and Alina Hernández

Abstract

Cuba introduced important reforms during the 1990s, including special facilities to promote foreign investment inflows, the reduction of tariffs and other trade restrictions, the opening up of the foreign exchange market and the flexibility of rules regarding non-state activities. These reforms changed the way the economy functioned, but remained far from turning Cuba into a market economy. Rather, dual structures were introduced in commodity and labour markets with national currency and dollar segments. There is also segmentation in the domestic money supply for the public and for business activities. Import tariffs were reduced and export promotion policies were geared towards attracting foreign investors to the tourist industry and towards export diversification. These measures were a response to the collapse of the socialist regimes in Europe, which had provided Cuba with foreign assistance and export market access. Various domestic policy measures allowed the economy to recover gradually after 1993. Export performance responded positively to the process of opening of the economy. The share of exports of services increased, exports diversified geographically and the competitiveness of Cuba's exports to industrialized countries improved. The composition of exports has changed fundamentally since 1989, as Cuba has moved from an agriculture-led to a service-led economy. Manufacturing exports, especially those requiring more advanced technology, have not performed well. Labour productivity and average real wages increased during the 1990s, along with rising inequalities between groups of workers. This also caused rising inequality and poverty at the household level.

A computable general equilibrium model was developed which captures the particular characteristics of the Cuban economy and its segmented market structure. Counterfactual model simulations suggest that, if the tariff reform had not been applied, gross domestic product growth would have remained about the same, though consumption would have been lower. Export promotion – through a more competitive exchange rate – would be mildly positive for growth, employment and poverty reduction. Model simulations were also performed assuming different trade agreements in the World Trade Organization framework and for the hypothetical case that Cuba could enter the Free Trade Area of the Americas.

Static model simulations suggest that such scenarios would not be immediately beneficial to either growth or employment. Cubans would only benefit from such trade integration if that scenario would bring substantial productivity gains or if subsidies on agricultural products could be sustained. Other simulations related to several domestic policies showed better results, such as the promotion of investment in export sectors and others to improve factor productivity.

8.1 Introduction

The Cuban economic reforms of the 1990s are different from other experiences in the region in that they are not part of a process of liberalization or opening within the context of a market economy. It is, rather, the transformation of a socialist economy towards an adaptation aimed at becoming more competitive and flexible to respond to conditions of international markets. Therefore, while significant parallels exist with other economies in the region, differences – such as the government's much more active economic role and the greater weight given to social criteria in macroeconomic management – must be taken into account. The upshot of both of these elements, among other things, is that economic activity is more constrained by supply than demand. Furthermore, the transition mechanisms implemented to modify the previous material planning system introduce particular kinds of behaviour by economic actors – behaviour arising from an economy with a dual monetary policy and segmented consumption markets.

This chapter briefly describes the particular characteristics of Cuba's economic reform process. Macroeconomic performance is then analysed along with export performance, sectoral dynamism and its relationship to exports and other results related to productivity, employment, inequality and poverty. This is followed by the most salient results of a counterfactual analysis in which policy alternatives and their macro- and mesoeconomic effects are explored with 1999 as the base year. To do this, a computable general equilibrium (CGE) model was designed and applied for Cuba. It should be said that this is the first model that incorporates the unique aspects of Cuba's economy and the first time that a diverse set of policy options have been simulated. The study also uses a microsimulation methodology to show the microeconomic implications of the tested policy alternatives in terms of the variations in inequality and poverty that are produced. This type of exercise is also new for Cuba. Finally, the study yields some conclusions about economic policy.

8.2 Economic reforms: peculiarities of the Cuban case

During 1989–93, Cuba took its first steps to increase sources of foreign exchange income and to reduce the social impact of the external adjustment that became necessary after the fall of the socialist bloc. The constitution was amended in 1992 to include new kinds of property, the government monopoly on foreign trade was eliminated and the role of planning became more flexible. Steps were also taken to achieve permanent changes in the way the economy functioned and especially to get to a more efficient use of resources. In addition, measures were taken to achieve a greater decentralization of business management and administration. In general, the more structural measures began in 1993 and have continued with a particular sequence and pace.[1]

The opening of the economy in Cuba has been different from trade and balance of payments liberalization processes elsewhere. It has included: the creation of facilities for the entry of direct foreign investment; the reduction of tariffs and duties; the dismantling of the state monopoly of foreign trade; the creation of a domestic foreign exchange market where national producers are allowed to freely compete in buying and selling of foreign exchange; and the creation of export processing free zones. With respect to capital inflows through credits, it is important to point out that Cuba has not had access to financing from the International Monetary Fund, International Development Bank or World Bank since 1964. In addition, the economic embargo limits direct and indirect commercial access to important markets, interferes in various ways in foreign economic relations and makes obtainable credits significantly more expensive. Consequently, mobilizing available commercial credit to cover the external financing gap has been a central element of the reform. Another policy decision was to impede the entry of speculative capital.

Three main changes took place in terms of trade liberalization. The first was the emergence of a complex entrepreneurial network engaged in foreign trade activities. The second was the creation of domestic markets with transactions in foreign exchange (*exportaciones en frontera*) and the third was tariff reductions. The average tariff for Most Favoured Nation declined from 17.7 per cent in 1990 to 10.7 per cent in 1996.

One distinctive aspect of the way in which the Cuban economy began to reinsert itself into the international economy was the introduction of a dual monetary policy.[2] This was done by way of substituting material planning with a more flexible financial economic mechanism and a formula to finance basic needs and other supplies of goods and services to the population. In practice, activities linked to the external sector are generally carried out with foreign currency, and all other activities operate with the national currency. This segmentation of the economy into two sectors explains, in part, how the official exchange rate has remained at its original one-to-one rate of the *peso* against the dollar. In practice, however, because there was no way to convert dollars to *pesos*, the only important function of the official exchange rate until 2001 was to determine internal prices in domestic currency. The dual monetary policy permitted the export sector to recover quickly, but it has affected economic performance adversely in some ways by limiting the recovery of activities that function using the national currency. With the inflow of workers remittances and private transfers from abroad, some degree of dollarization of cash balances among the population emerged and this influences the liberalization process.

The year 1997 was an important moment in the reform as the banking system was restructured. Fiscal reform included a new tax law for businesses, the application of income tax for citizens for the first time in 30 years, a greater decentralization of the budget and the modernization of the country's entire budget accounting system.

Another significant aspect to keep in mind when interpreting the causal relationships that define economic processes in Cuba is the existence of heavily segmented markets and economic spheres. In addition to the differences between groups that operate with foreign exchange and those that use national currency, there is also a difference between the monetary circulation that occurs among people in general and that which occurs in business.

In 1989, the Cuban economy was basically constrained by supply. The introduction of the previously described mechanisms has meant a progressive incorporation of market elements into the determination of economic activity. The social measures of the reform began in 1990 and included the decision to keep government workers in their jobs and to conserve their nominal income even in a time of abrupt economic contraction, the almost complete transfer of available consumer goods to rationing in the initial phase and the express will to preserve health and education programmes as completely as possible. Later, new measures undertaken showed an incipient tendency towards the search for greater efficiency in social policy. Another component of reform was expanding the space for non-government activity. In addition to opening the economy to foreign investors, a significant part of government-owned agricultural land was turned over as a free concession to agricultural cooperatives and as individual parcels. Own-account activity was also made more flexible.

In addition, various markets in both foreign and national currencies were pulled out of the informal circuit at prices determined by supply and demand, though these markets remain segmented as the government continues to keep full control of certain components of the flow of goods and services demanded by the population. Nevertheless, the various components of this market influence each other a great deal, and the unofficial exchange rate establishes the link between the purchasing power of the two currencies. From 1997 on, microeconomic reforms were enacted that brought to completion these tendencies towards allowing more private initiative and decentralized decision-making in the functioning of the economy. These were called 'business improvement' policies. Though this is an ongoing process, it is a decisive step towards the success of the reforms implemented since 1993 and represents one of the unique aspects of economic reform in Cuba since it gives government enterprises the opportunity to prove their capacity to be efficient and competitive.

Before the reform, the labour market could be characterized as highly segmented and regulated. A very narrow salary scale was established as well as a single pay rate as the basis to determine wage differentials based on the complexity of labour and the skills required to perform the work.[3] Labour reforms in Cuba have very little to do with limiting job security, reducing contract labour indefinitely or other such characteristics common in the rest of Latin America. The most important change was the application of special forms of labour remuneration as a complement to the wage system.

Many of the measures included in the reforms are aimed at promoting exports, and sectoral policies are directed at a greater diversification of the export supply.

The Center for the Promotion of Exports was created to distribute the export supply, undertake market research, advise on the development of new kinds of products, design promotion programmes, reach consensus on trade missions and act as a clearing house for trade information. Fiscal incentives were also included, and overseas investments and trade linkages were promoted through agreements of association.

8.3 Macroeconomic performance

Economic growth in Cuba during the 1990s can be divided into three stages. In the first stage – between 1989 and 1993 – the external shock that came from the disappearance of the socialist bloc caused an abrupt contraction of output. Severe financial imbalances became evident, including: a high fiscal deficit, double-digit inflation (somewhat limited by the black market for consumer goods and services) and the depreciation of national currency, all within the context of a depressed economy.

A recovery period with 3.2 per cent average annual growth began in 1993 and lasted until 1999. There were two sub-periods during this time: 1994–6 and 1997–9. In 1999, gross domestic product (GDP) reached a level equivalent to 86 per cent of the 1989 GDP. Other performance results from these years are: strict control of the budget deficit from 1995 on, falling prices for consumer goods until 1997 (without any significant inflationary symptoms later) and a strong appreciation of the nominal exchange rate in the foreign exchange market segment open to the public in general. All of these had beneficial social effects. However, growth continued to be volatile (see Table 8.1).

Table 8.1 Cuba: decomposition of GDP growth, 1989–99

	Annual GDP growth	Impact on growth (%)					
		Government	Investment	Exports	Import propensity	Tax rate	Savings rate
1993–1996	2.9	5.4	35.1	124.5	−20.2	−108.3	63.6
1994	1.6	−63.4	8.7	242.1	−47.0	−428.7	388.2
1995	2.0	−15.1	79.9	61.9	−27.5	−19.4	20.1
1996	6.0	23.8	25.2	132.2	−19.5	−75.8	14.0
1996–1999	3.6	19.6	37.0	64.3	−6.9	−29.1	15.1
1997	0.6	20.8	134.1	99.1	−134.9	−65.8	46.9
1998	1.7	81.4	191.9	−228.5	85.8	−114.6	84.0
1999	8.5	11.7	6.5	98.1	−7.4	−11.3	2.4
1993–1999	3.2	11.5	33.0	85.9	−11.1	−59.6	40.1

Source: Authors' calculations based on Cuba's Statistical Yearbooks (several years)

Note: A positive sign denotes positive impact on GDP growth

Liberalization had a positive effect on Cuba's exports. After a 10 per cent average annual decline during the crisis, the export volume began to turn around in 1993, showing an 8.6 per cent annual average increase through 1999. Performance was less encouraging in 1997 and 1998, however, as compared to 1994–6. Nevertheless, in 1999, for the first time since the crisis began, the export volume of goods and services exceeded that of 1989.

Important structural changes are behind export performance. Services took an increasing share of Cuba's exports, accounting for 62 per cent of the total in 2000. In addition, the exports diversified by geographic destination, and Cuba improved competitiveness of its exports to industrialized countries. While exports were dynamic during the whole period after 1993, import rates were even more dynamic every year except for 1996 and 1999. Thus, some of the gains from liberalization were lost.

Investment also showed strong recovery from a very low level that resulted from the nearly 40 per cent decline during 1990–3. Available information shows that investment grew at annual average rate of about 16 per cent, although domestic investment in 1999 was a meagre 32 per cent of the 1989 level.

Government consumption – in which social expenditures predominate – was the aggregate demand category least affected during the crisis, while in the period of recovery it grew at a discreet 1 per cent annual average. The tax rate,[4] which had dropped during 1990–4, grew quickly after 1995 with the economic recovery and the application of a new tax law. Consequently, net taxes grew rapidly through 1999 when they reached the equivalent of 78 per cent of what the government was able to collect in 1989. Private consumption grew at a 3.9 per cent annual average between 1994 and 1999. Both periods of product growth showed similar growth in this area, though in the initial period up to 1996 the annual increases were consistently greater.

This economic performance occurred under difficult conditions in terms of external financing. In no single year after the economic reform capital flows reached more than 15 per cent of the level obtained in 1989 (see Table 8.2).

Debt service obligations remained a persistant constraint for the entire recovery period due to restricted access to new borrowing. Overall it was the main adverse component in current account adjustment, offsetting some of the increase in earnings due to the growth in world trade and favourable performance of other external variables. We elaborate this later in the analysis of external adjustment.

Table 8.2   Cuba: net capital inflows (in millions of dollars)

	1989	1993	1996	1997	1998	1999
Capital account	3,122.0	371.6	166.8	436.7	392.4	484.9
Long term		118.4	307.9	786.9	632.7	209.9
Others (net)		237.7	−133.5	−330	−223.3	275.0
Net resource flow	2,784.0	107.8	−325.8	−46.2	−56.3	−29.2

Source: Authors' calculations based on Cuba's Statistical Yearbooks (several years)

Table 8.3 Cuba: decomposition of the current account

	1989–93	1993–6	1996–9	1993–9
Change in current account deficit (% GDP, current prices)	−11.80	−0.85	0.93	0.07
Terms of trade effect	1.16	−1.91	0.24	−1.67
Interest payment shock	−0.48	0.81	−0.11	0.70
World trade effect	18.34	1.23	0.87	1.79
Current transfers effect	1.21	1.76	−0.09	1.68
Domestic absorption effect	−6.70	0.11	0.13	0.19
Displacement of imports effect	−18.00	4.42	1.18	5.46
Export penetration	−11.96	0.87	−0.27	0.70
Interaction effects	19.80	−0.42	0.01	−0.43

Source: Authors' calculations based on Cuba's Statistical Yearbooks (several years)

Table 8.1 shows that export performance appears to be the primary engine for growth, especially during the take-off period. World trade had a dynamic that, in general, exceeded that of Cuba's GDP, except in 1999. This export outcome is counteracted by rising import dependence, though exports continue to be the predominant demand factor influencing the growth rate.

The decomposition of the balance of payments current account is another element of interest (see Table 8.3).[5] In the first phase – from 1989 to 1993 – a significant reduction is observed in the ratio of the current account deficit to GDP, which cannot be interpreted as positive. In these years, the economic system did not allow economic agents to respond to changes in relative prices.

For the second period (1993–6), there is a much smaller decline in the deficit for various reasons. The beginning of the economic recovery, improvement in the terms of trade, growth in exports and better conditions in terms of the volume of world trade and flow of net current transfers were factors that allowed the current account deficit to shrink, in spite of the need to increase imports to sustain economic activity.

The current account deficit increased in the final period (1996–9). As already mentioned, this period was marked by the deceleration of the economy in 1997 and 1998. While there was a large growth in GDP in 1999, exports at current prices do not grow fast due to falling export prices. The decomposition shows that in addition to the decline in the terms of trade, national production was displaced by imports.

8.4 Exports

The composition of Cuban exports has changed considerably in a single decade. In 1989, 90 per cent of total exports were primary goods of which sugar accounted for 66 per cent. Mining, with nickel as the main product, was 8.3 per cent of the total exports. Two export items in which Cuba had clear comparative advantages – tobacco and tourism – accounted for barely 1.5 and 3 per cent, respectively, in 1989.

The disintegration of the socialist bloc changed the export structure quickly. Export values of goods fell, due to the decline in the preferential prices established in the socialist trade bloc and the loss of markets and financing. Total value of exports in 2000 was only 72.5 per cent of what it had been in 1989. This decline in exports is fully due to the deterioration of international prices as the actual volume of exports was higher.

Cuba had major problems in trying to compete in the world market at prices quite different from those prevailing under the socialist integration scheme. Sugar production continued to lose ground gradually to end contributing only 10.4 per cent of all exports in 2000. The market for raw sugar has also declined in terms of world trade in merchandise, and Cuba has lost a share of the market here as well. Other agricultural export products that were fairly important in the early 1990s, like citrus and coffee, have also seen a substantial decline. Mining products, however, have maintained their place within total exports and have increased their world market share. The nickel industry has performed especially well. Fishing products have kept up fairly well so far, but certain products like crustaceans and molluscs have performed better than the rest, gaining a share of dynamic markets.

The shares of tobacco and tourism were 3.8 and 40.4 per cent of total exports in 2000, which indicates that the strategic policy of export promotion in these cases had significant results. Exports of these items have grown considerably in recent years and have done so in expanding international markets.

Thus, in only 12 years Cuba has gone from being primarily an exporter of agricultural products to being an economy led by services. In addition to tourism, other important services are air transportation and communications. In 2000, the relative weight of Cuba in the trade of services was 2.6 times higher than it was in 1989.

Manufactured goods have not gained a significant share of Cuban exports in recent years. This has been a weak point of the reform process, since Cuba is moving from one extreme kind of specialization to another. Manufactured goods with the highest technological content, like medicines, have not performed up to their potential domestically or according to the dynamism in the world market. In the case of medicines, this is explained by the rigidities that limit competition in the markets for pharmaceutical products.

8.5 Productivity and employment

The transformations described above and the resulting growth pattern have had a clear impact on the labour market. It is important to keep in mind that the Cuban population is ageing rather rapidly. The total population increased very slowly in the 1990s at an annual average rate of 0.6 per cent, and there was similar slow growth in the working age population.

Because of the social protection mechanisms applied during the years of the economic crisis (1989–93), a paradoxical situation emerged that has been studied extensively. This period was characterized by a 5.8 per cent annual decrease in the unemployment rate, a 2.4 per cent decrease in the average participation rate and

Table 8.4 Cuba: changes in rates of economic participation, employment and unemployment (per cent)

	Employment	Unemployment	Participation
1993	−2.2	0.1	2.1
1994	−2.7	0.6	2.2
1995	−1.6	1.4	0.5
1996	0.7	−0.3	−0.4
1997	3.2	−0.6	−2.5
1998	1.6	−0.4	−1.2
1999	−0.6	−0.6	1.2

Source: Authors' calculations based on Cuba's Statistical Yearbooks (several years)

a stable employment rate. Consequently, productivity declined by 9.5 per cent per annum on average. The share of workers in the formal sector potentially threatened by underemployment is estimated at 12 per cent of the total in 1993, based on the productivity observed in 1989.

In 1993, the trend changed and unemployment began to grow, but then it declined again in 1995. The economically active population began to grow slightly from 1996 onwards and employment also grew at a faster pace from that year on. The overall analysis of these changes is shown in Table 8.4 using a decomposition proposed by Taylor (2001).

The 1996–8 period is the only one characterized by an increase in employment. This rise is mainly due to the recovery of the economy and the related reduction in labour underutilization. Productivity started to increase from 1993, but productivity growth is less associated with the displacement of workers and much more with the dynamics of the average real wage. In particular, the two years in which the highest economic growth was achieved – 1996 and 1999 – are also the years in which labour productivity grew the most, pushed by the increase in labour income.

The 3 per cent rise in employment beginning in 1996 corresponded primarily to the tradable sectors and to tourism, which increased their employment by 7.4 per cent. Activities with relatively high dynamism in terms of job creation between 1996 and 1999 include mining, tourism and commerce with annual growth rates of 71, 29 and 22 per cent, respectively, followed by agriculture with 8 per cent growth. It is important to note that demand for labour has been rising steadily in the tourism industry since 1990.

As Table 8.5 shows, the workers who benefited most from the growth in employment rates were the skilled workers, especially those in the upper-middle level (with at least 12 years of schooling). It should be noted that even during the years when the employment rate declined, the participation of skilled workers kept growing among the total number of employed.

Significant changes are also observed in employment by type of enterprise ownership. Between 1989 and 1994, cooperatives and informal labour made the greatest contribution to total employment. It is important to note that informal

Table 8.5 Cuba: contribution of skill level to employment rate (changes)

	1987–96	1997–9
Primary school or less	−0.059	0.008
Mid-level	−0.073	−0.008
Upper-middle	0.068	0.051
Higher education	0.028	0.007
Subtotal	−0.036	0.058
Unclassified	−0.031	−0.013
Total	−0.067	0.044
Skilled	0.096	0.058
Other	−0.163	−0.013

Source: Authors' calculations based on Cuba's Statistical Yearbooks (several years)

Table 8.6 Cuba: contributions to changes in employment rate by enterprise ownership

	1989–94	1994–6	1996–9
State	−0.118	−0.079	0.038
Cooperatives	0.054	0.005	−0.005
Mixed enterprises and joint ventures with foreign capital	0.000	0.007	0.012
Domestic private	−0.001	0.011	0.036
Own account	0.020	0.000	0.009
Others	−0.001	0.001	0.000
Subtotal	−0.028	−0.055	0.092
Informal	−0.074	0.045	−0.047
Total	−0.102	−0.011	0.044

Source: Authors' calculations based on Cuba's Statistical Yearbooks (several years)

employment in the case of Cuba should not be interpreted as a low-income activity since it has to do with income generated on the black market during the crisis period (1989–93). In the period 1994–6, informal activities and domestic private activities accounted for most of the increase in employment rate.[6] Formal employment gains significance after 1996, primarily in government enterprises and in the aforementioned domestic private activities. Mixed enterprises and joint ventures with foreign capital also began to make significant contributions to the employment rate (Table 8.6).

Labour productivity, for its part, increased at an annual average of 3.8 per cent after the reform. The greatest increases took place in tradable activities (7.9 per cent annual average), especially between 1993 and 1996 (Table 8.7). Productivity increased on average in most sectors after 1993, but the performance has been volatile. In 1997 and 1998 in particular generalized decreases in productivity are observed.

Table 8.7 Cuba: productivity growth (per cent change per year)

	1989–93	1993–6	1996–9	1993–9
Total	−9.5	4.9	2.7	3.8
Tradables	−10.4	11.9	4.0	7.9
Non-tradables	−9.0	0.6	1.6	1.1

Source: Authors' calculations based on Cuba's Statistical Yearbooks (several years)

A decomposition analysis of changes in productivity shows that the activity that contributed most consistently to productivity growth after 1993 was manufacturing industry. Between 1993 and 1996, the contribution of agriculture, commerce and productive services also stands out.

In general, changes in productivity were not related to sectoral reallocation of production or labour but rather to increased efficiency. Reallocation is somewhat significant only in the case of agriculture. This is the sector that in a weighted analysis contributed the most to avoiding a divergence between productivity and employment, since the change in output per capita was higher than that of productivity. Other activities that contributed in this way were construction, tourism and productive services.

Real labour income increased slightly on average during the recovery but showed significant differences in gains by type of worker. The average real remuneration for wage earners grew by 3.4 per cent between 1993 and 1999, mainly due to falling prices and the application of the special payment systems related to foreign exchange earning activities. Labour income of other workers benefited from the functioning of the informal economy during the crisis, but with a tendency to decline in the period of economic recovery, especially during 1993–6.

In this sense, the most significant thing about the decade turned out to be the increasing disparities in labour income, most starkly between workers in different production activities and between those working in different types of enterprises according to ownership. In 1989, workers with mixed income (self-employed) received average earnings 35 per cent greater than those of wage earners. That difference increased to 500 per cent during the crisis and later dropped to 200 per cent in 1999. Inequality also increased among wage earners. The average wage in export sectors like tourism, for example, was twice that of workers in non-export activities. All of this had an impact on household income.

8.6 Inequality and poverty

The crisis of the early 1990s, changes in the labour market and the dollarization of the economy greatly affected the equitable pattern in incomes and consumption that was one of the pillars of Cuban society before the 1990s. On the one hand, the diversification of labour income sources changed the significance of each specific income source and widened income disparities. On the other hand, non-labour income sources gained relevance, especially remittances and targeted government transfers. In addition, more space was given to the market in the supply of consumer goods and services.

The population at risk of poverty estimated for Cuba's urban areas grew from 6.3 per cent in 1988 to 15.0 per cent in 1996. There is no estimate for 1993 since the Household Survey was not conducted that year, but local studies show that the population at risk of poverty was probably higher than in 1996. Thus, the risk of being poor increased between 1989 and 1993 and fell again during the economic recovery. Rising poverty is related to the increase in monetary income inequality, but this was offset in part of the period by increasing mean income. A poverty profile analysis shows that the employment situation, the sector of economic activity, the sector of employment ownership and the lack of an income source in foreign exchange were all significant factors explaining different degrees of vulnerability of the population.[7]

In 1999, estimates of population at risk – not completely comparable with those of previous years[8] – show 20 per cent of the urban population at risk. Indices of the poverty gap and intensity show most of the at-risk population near the poverty line with very little inequality within this group.

Social inequality in Cuba was very low in the late 1980s. Studies carried out at the end of the decade showed a Gini coefficient of about 0.25. In 1988, for example, the urban population in the lowest income decile had 3.1 per cent of the total income, while the population in the highest income decile had 24.3 per cent. The ratio of per capita income for the lowest decile with respect to the total was 26.3 per cent, while that of the highest income decile was 285 per cent.

Estimates for 1999 show that inequality increased and the Gini coefficient was estimated at 0.37. The urban population in the lowest decile had 2 per cent of the income while the highest decile had 39 per cent, so that the ratio for the average per capita income of the first decile with respect to the total was 18 per cent and that of the highest income decile was 394 per cent.

Also according to Cuban studies, it is probable that inequality was higher in 1993 than in 1988. The fall in mean primary income for non-wage earners and the appreciation of the real exchange rate – a characteristic of the 1994–6 period – left their imprint in the form of higher inequality. Later the labour income improvements for workers employed in tradable activities and other foreign exchange generating activities, together with the stabilization of the exchange rate and prices, slowed this trend towards rising inequality.

This level of inequality, though lower than the rest of Latin America, has introduced fundamental changes in the way society functions and pushed the government to apply new concepts in its social policy.

8.7 Counterfactual analysis

This section shows the results of the counterfactual analysis undertaken. In essence, these exercises were aimed at exploring the kind of results that would have obtained for 1999, had certain international trade conditions been different or alternative domestic policies been applied, or other economic conditions for the year remained constant. The exercise also leads to conclusions about which economic policy measures might be feasible and how effective they might be.

In establishing the relationships and parameters of the model, certain assumptions were made that reflect to a lesser or greater degree the real characteristics of the economy. Later, after running the simulations and drawing economic policy conclusions from them, it is necessary to be sure that the premises of the model, pertinent to the results in question, are sufficiently realistic and that they do not contain a bias that might distort the conclusions. It is also necessary to establish an adequate balance between policies geared at short- and medium-term adjustments.

The following section will briefly explain the characteristics of the social accounting matrix elaborated for Cuba and the CGE model.

The social accounting matrix

The structure of the matrix by and large follows conventional patterns, except for the specification of commodity markets. It was constructed for the year 1999 with information from the 1999 Statistical Yearbook of Cuba, the Socio-economic Household Survey and other statistical sources. The social accounting matrix is provided in Table A8.1.

The Activity account is made up of ten economic sectors. Six of them belong to the formal sector of the economy (tourism, primary exports, other primary activities, other industries and construction, personal and business services and social services); and another four small-scale sectors related to tourism, agriculture, industry and services. The Commodities account was substituted for a similar one relative to Markets. The account is to reflect the prevailing market segmentation according to the type of demanding agent, as Enterprises and Households carry out their transactions in different markets. From this, six types of markets were defined: one export market; two markets in which Enterprises are the only ones that exercise demand; and three markets in which Households consume, that is (1) a rationed market that operates with fixed quantities and prices, (2) a market that operates in foreign exchange and (3) another market that operates with national currency. The latter two markets have flexible prices that adjust according to supply and demand.

Consequently, the sub-matrix that usually corresponds to the intersection between the Commodity–Activities accounts was substituted for another that looks at the Markets–Activities relationship. This solution better reflects the previously described particularities of the Cuban economy. It also resolves the problem posed by the fact that the last official input–output matrix was constructed in 1987 when the economic structure was considerably different from that of Cuba today.

The Factors account includes capital and labour. The latter was divided into wage earners and other workers.[9] Wage earners were subdivided into skilled and unskilled workers. The Institutions account is also conventional. Households were divided into five levels according to income and other characteristics taken from the household survey. Two new financial accounts were introduced, the

Central Cash Account (*Caja Central*) and a money balance account for households (CADECA), which identify the current monetary duality of the Cuban economy. The first institution is in charge of transactions in the business sector and the second expresses the operations of the currency exchanges that happen at the household level. This allows to differentiate between monetary flows between agents in both types of currency. The *Caja Central* account has the function of financing deficits in foreign exchange, or imports for markets that operate in *pesos*, since there is no convertibility of the Cuban *peso* in the Enterprise sector. The *Caja Central* receives contributions in foreign exchange from the surplus in pesos from the CADECA exchange house and from the government. The *Caja Central* gives contributors a quantity of money in Cuban *pesos* that is similar to the total amount of foreign exchange it receives. In other words, the transaction happens at an official exchange rate. The other account, CADECA, responds to Households' need to acquire foreign exchange or national currency at the money exchange (*Casa de Cambio*), to the degree the consumer market for goods and services market is segmented by type of currency. The balance of CADECA constitutes an additional closure to the 'standard' model. These transactions are carried out using a non-official exchange rate. The closure of the population's foreign exchange market is determined by the monetary balance of Households and is independent of the financial situation of the Enterprises, Government, and Rest of the World. The Savings–Investment and Rest of the World accounts follow conventional patterns.

General equilibrium model for cuba

The CGE model is based on the standard elaborated by the International Food Policy Research Institute (IFPRI) (see Chapter 3). It contains practically the same blocks of equations, parameters and variables. Some of the original equations had to be modified, however, and some new ones were introduced in order to make sure they corresponded to the particular characteristics of the Cuban economy. The following principles are characteristic of the model for Cuba (see Ferriol *et al.* 2003, for a formal presentation of the model's equations):

- The productive technology is of the Leontief type. CES functions are used for the rest of the demand relationships.
- Transaction costs are contained in the Trade sector.
- Government subsidies exist for production losses and for prices in the rationed market.
- There are two types of exchange rates: official and informal.
- The volumes of sales to the external market (exports) by activity are assumed to be exogenous.
- Wages are assumed to be fixed and the demand for labour is flexible, which enables us to examine the change in unemployment in the case of an exogenous shock. The endowment of capital by activity is fixed and its remuneration is flexible.

- In terms of external closure, foreign savings are assumed to be flexible and the official exchange rate is fixed. The exchange rate in the informal segment of the foreign exchange market is flexible.
- In terms of the savings–investment closure of the model, the total value of investment is exogenous and domestic and foreign savings adjusted to ensure macroeconomic equilibrium.
- The Domestic Producer Price Index (DPI) was taken as the numéraire rather than the Consumer Price Index (CPI).

In the calibration, almost all of the model's parameters can be determined from the social accounting matrix, from which the data for the simulations' base year equilibrium were drawn. In the case of Cuba, currently there are no econometric studies providing estimates for substitution elasticities and transformation elasticities. It was necessary, therefore, to consult international literature on studies of this kind in developing countries, in order to estimate these coefficients and undertake various kinds of sensitivity analyses. In the end, the decision was made to work with relatively inelastic relationships in all cases, though in different magnitudes.

In fact, if coefficients with high elasticities had been used, results obtained would have been very unrealistic. One aspect to consider, among others, is that the essential restriction faced by the Cuban economy is associated precisely with the external sector. This limits the response of domestic production to changes in international market prices. At the same time, the type of market that producers go to in the domestic economy is very well defined (in foreign currency or in *pesos*). Therefore, the following intervals were used for the elasticities used in the model:

- Substitution elasticity between labour and capital for each activity: intervals vary from 0.5 to 0.8.
- Substitution elasticity between inputs of the activities in foreign and national currencies: 0.3 for all cases.
- Demand elasticity (CET) of each market to the activities: between 0.15 and 0.25.
- Demand elasticity (Armington) between domestic and imported goods: 0.4 in all markets.

Simulations relevant to the Cuban case

This section will present the main results obtained from the simulations (see Table A8.2). First, the effects of external shocks are examined, followed by the effects that correspond to the implications of economic policy changes. Finally, some results will be discussed that take into consideration certain world trade conditions in the hypothetical event that Cuba were to be part of the World Trade Organization (WTO) or the Free Trade Area of the Americas (FTAA). In each case, the work presents the effects that each variation would produce if certain conditions from before 1999 are kept constant, since 1999 is the year in which the social accounting matrix and the CGE model were built.

The external shocks refer to the variations in the demand for exports and in the terms of trade. The level of variations simulated was framed within intervals that were considered feasible given historical tendencies of the demand for Cuban goods and services exports and given international prices.

The simulations of domestic policy changes include the following: governmental support measures to boost investment in export activities and others aimed at increasing overall productivity in the use of the factors also for export activities; a devaluation in currency; an increase in the mean wage; and tariff changes. In general, the simulated magnitude does not exceed 10 per cent of the reference indicator.

The simulations related to the WTO and the FTAA scenarios set world prices, tariff regulations and agricultural subsidies according to the results of the GTAP world model (see Chapter 3).

External shock: demand for exports

An external shock in the form of a 5 per cent increase in the demand for basic exports and assuming no change in domestic conditions would have had positive effects on economic growth. The outward shift of the demand curve for exportable goods and services would require an increase in production in export activities, which would have implied a slight structural change in favour of tourism and primary exports.

In addition, there would have been a slight growth of 0.4 per cent (155 million *pesos*) in total production and a 0.4 per cent increase in the total value added (180 million *pesos*). This would have favoured the overall employment rate by creating additional jobs for 19,000 workers, which would help unemployment drop by 7 per cent. Given the structure of the labour market, this increment would favour wage labour and skilled labour.

As a result of about a 3 per cent rise in the CPI, however, household consumption volume would fall by 1 per cent (about 160 million *pesos*). Additionally, foreign savings would have fallen by US$205 million and, therefore, there would have been less need for external credits.

In summary, in 1999 and, therefore, under conditions prevailing that year, an additional external demand of 5 per cent – a feasible amount given historical behaviour – would have been a positive factor for economic growth and employment, but this export effort could not have been accompanied by domestic supply to meet worker's growing income. Therefore, household consumption would fall with ensuing inflation.

Positive effects on growth and employment would only happen without sacrifices in domestic consumption if there was a positive export shock of at least 10 per cent. In those circumstances, value added would increase by 1.4 per cent, employment by 2.4 per cent, and consumption by 0.2 per cent.

External shock: terms of trade

Results would have also been positive if the external shock would take the form of an improvement in the terms of trade. A 16 per cent decrease in the world price of imports – corresponding to the largest decline in world petroleum prices as occurred in 1991 – would have slight favourable effects on economic growth by creating the conditions for an US$180 million increase in value added (0.4 per cent increase). The most favourable impact, however, would have been in the volume of household consumption, which would increase by more than 4 per cent (671 million *pesos*), aided by the 23 per cent reduction in unemployment, an increase in labour remunerations of 344 million *pesos*, and a more than 5 per cent reduction in consumer prices. Additionally, there would have been less dependence on foreign borrowing as foreign savings would fall by 461 million dollars.

Furthermore, an increase in export prices, together with a growth in the demand for primary exports, would stimulate economic performance. For example, an 11 per cent increase in export prices, together with an additional 6 per cent increase in the demand for primary exports, would produce a small increase in total value added. Foreign savings would fall by US$211 million. While close to 5,000 additional people would be employed as wage earners, more than 10,000 people would lose jobs in small-scale activities, and this would result in a 2 per cent increase in total unemployment. This, together with the 0.7 per cent increase in retail prices, would reduce the volume of household consumption by 131 million *pesos*. It would seem that supply constraints impede greater welfare gains from an increase in the export demand mainly oriented at primary products.[10] Consequently, adjustment went at the expense of lower household consumption.

Domestic policies: export promotion

An analysis of domestic policy simulations yielded the following results. Export promotion could be a first promising avenue for the government. Thus, a policy simulation was carried out assuming an increase in public investment to support export sectors, which would yield favourable results as long as there is an international demand for the products in question.

In this simulation, a 10 per cent increase in the fixed capital for tourism would lead to an increase in export value (US$373 million) greater than the increase in imports (US$70 million), with a consequent decrease of more than 64 per cent in foreign savings. The value added would increase by 1.3 per cent (555 million *pesos*), especially in tradable goods, and the employment level would grow by 66,000 workers, of which 83 per cent would be wage workers. Additionally, retail prices would be reduced by 6 per cent, which along with rising remunerations of 338 million *pesos* would lead to a slight increase of 0.4 per cent in the household consumption volume (66 million).

If in addition to the increase in investments in this sector and the increase in external demand there were a 2 per cent increase in investment to support primary exports and some of the non-traditional industrial exports, the effects on consumption would be less favourable than in the previous simulation, unless the global volume of exports would increase by more than 16 per cent.

Tariff cut

Trade liberalization in the form of tariff cuts was another component of the reform. By 1996, the average nominal tariff rate was already reduced substantially. Thus, we simulate what would have happened if the 17 per cent average tariff prior to 1996 would have been maintained. A simulation of a uniform tariff cut of this magnitude yields only a slight change in output. Imports would be replaced by domestic demand imports following higher prices of foreign goods, inclusive of tariffs. This, in turn, given supply constraints, would push up retail and detail prices and cause a drop in real household consumption by 0.4 per cent (58 million *pesos*). Unemployment would drop by 5 per cent and foreign savings requirements would decrease by 33 per cent. Greater protection thus would also protect jobs in the domestic industry and reduce unemployment, albeit at cost of higher inflation and lower consumption.

Devaluation

Another controversial aspect of policy change has to do with devaluation. Under 1999 conditions, a 10 per cent devaluation would have produced additional GDP increase in the order of 0.9 per cent with 1.8 per cent increases in value added for tradable goods. The resulting 15 per cent growth in unemployment along with a 0.7 per cent increase in consumer prices would have affected the volume of household consumption slightly as it would have fallen by 8.2 million *pesos* (0.05 per cent).

While a devaluation could have led to an almost 4 per cent increase in primary exports, it is likely that the social effects and the effects of rising factors payments would have counteracted the advantages. In this scenario though, value added and employment would have risen somewhat stronger than in the previous simulation, but the 3.9 per cent rise in retail prices would have also had a greater negative impact on the level of household consumption. When making the balance of pros and cons of export promotion policies in practice, one must consider in addition the fact that the government has preferred to guide reforms along paths that guarantee social protection, no matter whether this would go at cost of lesser economic growth.

Nominal wage shock

Another policy measure with lower than expected results is the application of a wage shock. Increasing the median nominal wage in the formal sector by 10 per cent would lead to a rise in the costs of production, which would have led to an 88 per cent increase in unemployment (243,000 workers), and the value added would fall by 1,035 million *pesos* (2.4 per cent). Furthermore, while retail prices would fall by 9.8 per cent, household consumption would have fallen by 8 per cent, given the steep drop in the employment level.

The model does not permit to simulate the effect of a stimulus to labour productivity. Likely, a productivity shock would have had a much more positive outcome than just a rise in nominal wages, showing likely positive repercussions on economic growth and the volume of household consumption. In the last few years of the 1990s, there was indeed a positive synergy between rising remunerations and productivity, as mentioned earlier.

In sum, under 1999 conditions and with low productivity levels, a wage shock would not bring about a significant impact on economic growth. Apparently, the magnitude of the wage increase does not sufficiently stimulate an increase in output per worker and would lead to a trade-off between productivity and employment.

Efficiency in factor use

Finally, it is worth asking if an increase in overall efficiency in the use of factors could have increased economic growth. One significant result is that a 10 per cent increase in total factor productivity in each activity would have had considerable repercussions if these increases had happened either in the Primary Export activity or in that of Other Industry and Construction. In both cases, this should be accompanied by a minimum increase of 16 per cent in exports.

Additionally, if conditions had been created to implement a generalized productivity shock, a 7 per cent increase in overall productivity would have been sufficient for the value added to increase by almost 5 per cent, but the constraint to growth would have been the international demand for exports. In that case, unemployment would have fallen by more than 50 per cent, but would require new investments to maintain that level of employment in the wage worker sector and not produce displacement of workers towards small-scale activities. Labour income would have been 5 per cent higher, household consumption would have increased by 10 per cent and foreign savings would have been 34 per cent less. Current measures to improve the business climate are aiming to create a situation like the one described above.

The examination of simulations makes it possible to distinguish which measures and shocks would have the greatest quantitative impact on growth, employment, consumption and prices without yet taking into account their implications for inequality and poverty (Table 8.8).

At first glance, one might postulate that the most effective measures of an internal nature are associated with achieving an increase in overall productivity of factors and with increasing the fixed capital of export sectors. Each of these measures could be a way of substantially transforming economic performance and its most overarching results, especially if there were to be an improvement in the terms of trade.

Table 8.8 Cuba: simulations with greatest impact

Primary impact	External shock and/or policy measure
GDP growth	Increased productivity, export promotion and improvement in terms of trade
Growth in employment	Increased productivity, export promotion and improvement in terms of trade
Growth in household consumption	Increased productivity, improvement in terms of trade and export promotion
Lower consumer prices	Improvement in terms of trade and export promotion
Lower unofficial exchange rate	Export promotion
Decrease in foreign savings	Improvement in terms of trade and export promotion

However, a more detailed analysis indicates that measures cannot be examined in an isolated fashion. To obtain positive results, an increase in total factor productivity requires an increase in the demand for Cuban exports; this is also a requirement for producing positive results through the promotion of exports. It must also be supposed that increases in fixed capital in export activities lead to an increase in the overall efficiency of factors.

In addition, an improvement in the terms of trade, especially via lower import prices, would create an environment in the external debt situation that would be very favourable for obtaining credits and in general for the functioning of the economy. As consumer prices would decline, it could also improve the social situation.

In sum, economic policy would have to integrate all of these elements, but there would also have to be conditions in the international arena that would complement policy efforts.

WTO and FTAA

Other simulations looked at the impact of the international prices that are presumed to be the result of WTO functioning and its recommendations for tariff and sub-sidy policies. If participation in this organization leads to the elimination of tariffs but does not affect government agricultural subsidies,[11] some slightly favourable results would be obtained such as increasing value added by 0.05 per cent, employment by 0.04 per cent and household consumption by 0.6 per cent.

However, if WTO agreements cut agricultural subsidies – by 50 per cent, for example – there would be adverse repercussions for growth and consumption, especially due to increased unemployment and higher retail prices. Even if these new conditions were to be verified with a 5 per cent increase in exports, the essential results would not change. The results of the simulation would be somewhat better, however, if the application of WTO agreements were to be accompanied by an increase in overall productivity levels. In this case, value added would increase by 1.8 per cent, foreign savings would go down by 22 per cent and household consumption would grow by almost 3 per cent because of a 4.2 per cent reduction in retail prices.

It is not likely that Cuba will participate in the FTAA in the medium term, but the FTAA simulation was carried out anyway. Participation would yield various unfavourable impacts, especially in employment, and with very little change in value added. Positive results would only be produced if such a simulation were accompanied by an increase in overall productivity levels for factors, in which case the value added would grow by 6 per cent and unemployment would fall by 82 per cent. The lower levels of unemployment would contribute to a 15 per cent rise in consumption in spite of a 6 per cent increase in consumer prices. Therefore, it can be supposed that in large measure any positive results would be due more to the increase in internal productivity than to joining the FTAA.

In both the WTO and the FTAA cases, results highlight the need to achieve increases in overall efficiency in the use of factors in order to obtain any benefits from international agreements on trade or integration. In this way, the simulations contribute to highlighting, once again, the importance of applying measures that elevate the internal efficiency in the use of resources in order to boost growth, employment and consumption.

8.8 Impact of simulated policies on inequality and poverty

Simulated policies assess the socioeconomic situation of households in several ways. The first is by looking at the creation of new jobs or the opposite – the displacement of employed workers and the accompanying increase in unemployment. The magnitude of the change and its decomposition depends on the sector of economic activity, skill level and type of property ownership. The second way of assessing the socioeconomic situation is by looking at the transfers the families receive from the government, other families and abroad. Once again, the magnitude and structure of these transfers according to each source is relevant. Finally, the dynamic of consumer prices and the informal exchange rate also affect the family situation and have an impact on poverty and inequality.

The methodology of microsimulations focuses attention on the impacts associated with the labour market.[12] In other words, it includes effects of changes in economic participation rates, unemployment rates, structure of employment according to sector of activity and type of property and the average level of remunerations and their structure – also by sectors – as well as the education level of the employed population.

The order in which the changes in labour market parameters are introduced supposes that the population makes an initial decision about active economic participation. Then, given a demand for labour, the individual decides if he or she wants to be a wage worker – in large-scale activities – or if he or she would rather

Table 8.9 Cuba: impact on poverty and inequality (points of deviation from 1999 base)

	Export shock	Terms of trade	Tariff increases	Devaluation	Export promotion	Increased productivity	Increase in median wage
Headcount ratio P_0	−0.023	−0.021	−0.023	−0.021	−0.020	−0.015	0.003
Poverty gap P_1	−0.008	−0.007	−0.008	−0.007	−0.007	−0.006	0.006
Gini income per capita	−0.005	−0.004	−0.004	−0.005	−0.005	−0.002	−0.014
Theil income per capita	−0.015	−0.012	−0.012	−0.013	−0.014	−0.009	−0.042
Gini labour income	−0.013	−0.010	−0.011	−0.012	−0.012	−0.005	−0.050
Theil labour income	−0.035	−0.028	−0.030	−0.031	−0.032	−0.016	−0.162

Source: Authors' calculations based on Survey of Economic Situation of Households (1999)

work in small-scale activities. These decisions and the economic performance will determine the median level of labour remunerations and the dispersion around this level, defining the median remuneration of each worker according to his or her occupation. The income and skill level of the worker also have an influence.[13] Table 8.9 shows the main results of each of the variables analysed.

If there had been an external shock of about 5 per cent in the demand for exports – as described previously – the percentage of the population in poverty in 1999 would have been 2.3 points lower, and the poverty gap for that period indicated that the average poor person would have had income closer to the poverty line. The higher employment level and primarily its new structure by sectors and labour categories would be the main contributing factors to this more favourable situation. In this case, labour income inequality would have fallen, lowering the Gini coefficient by 1.3 per cent.

Improvement in the terms of trade would have had a very similar impact on decreasing both poverty and inequality. In this case, the factors that would have had the largest impact in producing this outcome would be (most importantly) increased employment, the shift in structure of employment between wage earners and non-wage earners and changes in remuneration differentials. In these circumstances, inequality in per capita incomes as measured by the Gini coefficient would have been 1 per cent less.

Simulated domestic policies also produce generally positive effects in the form of reduced poverty and inequality. The rise in total factor productivity by at least 7 per cent, so positive for economic growth, would have caused a 6 per cent decline in the percentage of poverty (1.5 points), primarily because of employment opportunities that would have been generated. Its effects on inequality would have been rather modest, in spite of the fact that labour income inequality would decrease by 1 per cent.

Export promotion policies, for their part, would have led to a two percentage points decline in poverty with respect to 1999, also mainly induced by the aggregate employment effect. These measures would have reduced labour income inequality by 3 per cent, influencing in this way a 1.4 per cent decrease in the Gini for per capita household incomes.

An increase in the median income of workers employed in large-scale activities would have had a greater impact than the previous simulations on decreasing inequality of labour income. This inequality of labour income would have been 12 per cent less (five points), and caused the Gini coefficient to decline by 3.5 per cent. However, poverty would have increased by 1 per cent and the situation within this part of the population would have been worse, since the poverty gap index would have been almost 9 per cent greater. This is a result of a higher number of workers who are displaced from their jobs and pushed into unemployment, something that more than offsets the positive effect of higher median wages.

If tariffs were not decreased or if a devaluation were to take place, the results in terms of the population at risk of poverty and in terms of inequality would be of a similar magnitude as those simulations described earlier. In the first case, the beneficial effect would come primarily through the changes in the employment structure. In the second, increased employment and the new employment structure between wage and non-wage workers would have the bigger impact.

In general, results that lower poverty and inequality are relatively modest in all of the simulations – around two points and 0.5 points in the headcount and the Gini coefficient, respectively. Even in the case of simulations whose results were higher in terms of growth – such as the one that increased overall efficiency in the use of productive factors, the promotion of exports and improvement in the terms of trade – their impact on poverty and inequality was less dramatic. This reinforces the validity of the need to enact equitable social policies.

8.9 Conclusions

The study shows that exports have been the most important factor in Cuba's economic performance during the 1990s, though there are unstable results in terms of these changes. There are both internal and external causes for this limited dynamism.

The external shock that had the most adverse impact was the one that affected the price of Cuba's most important tradable goods, and especially an increase in the prices of basic imports. The simulations show that improvement in the terms of trade would reduce the need for external credits or other foreign capital flows and would also have an influence on lowering prices for consumers and increasing family consumption.

Limitations on the international demand for Cuban products – though overall a factor of less relevance compared to the slowing of growth during this decade – stands out in the simulations as a decisive element. Changing the practice of international trade by eliminating subsidies and other barriers to demand from the industrialized world towards developing countries would be very favourable to the Cuban economy. In addition, the application of domestic policies of diversification and an effort to increase the competitiveness of exports would be important.

The main domestic difficulties that would have to be eliminated would be, first of all, low factor productivity. Though improved overall efficiency of capital appears to have stimulated output growth in the 1990s, productivity levels remain low, and efficiency would have to be increased in order to reach greater and more stable GDP growth dynamics.

The second most important limiting factor for growth is that investment in fixed capital is insufficient to boost exports. In perspective, the development of exportable goods (especially of non-traditional primary and non-industrial products) would have to be supported by complementary government investment and actions that stimulate foreign direct investment. Both aspects would result in greater domestic production capacity to respond to internal demand, a boost to the import substitution process and a better relationship between the increase in the import rate and the growth of exports. Improved total factor productivity and the promotion of exports would also contribute to making these sectors leaders in increasing employment, favouring especially skilled wage workers.

In order to ensure that redistribution takes place that will produce a decline in inequality and poverty, everything points once again to the relevance of a pattern of growth guided by exports, but requiring greater investments in fixed capital in these activities. This will need to be accompanied by an appreciation in the unofficial exchange rate and the decrease in retail prices.

As said, for growth to resume at the required pace, total factor productivity will need to increase. The simulations showed, however, that this would tend to depreciate the national currency in the unofficial foreign exchange market. It will thus be necessary to change the pattern of supply of consumer goods and services in favour of commodities purchased in national currency. This would help reduce the incidence of the population at risk of poverty further through lower domestic prices and increased employment.

Furthermore, a package of measures would have to be designed to include other projects that protect lower income groups. The new programmes already in progress to create jobs in the eastern region of the country, programmes to educate and retrain young people and other programmes directed at the development of human capital are already moving down that path. Other targeted social assistance programmes like the extension of communitarian social work and reinforced attention to malnourished children would also contribute towards these goals. In general, a permanent objective would be for the new and existing programmes to become a new way to compensate for inequalities. These are feasible options in a country where the socioeconomic system is more rational and human.

Appendix A8

Table A8.1 Social accounting matrix – Cuba, 1999 (million pesos)

Millions of pesos	Sectors										Markets (commodities)					
	1	2	3	4	5	6	7	8	9	10	11	12	13	14	15	16
1 Tourism																
2 Primary exports												4602.0				
3 Other large-scale primary activities													1768.7			
4 Other large-scale industry and construction														8272.5		
5 Large-scale production and commercial services															7338.3	
6 Social services																356.9
7 Small-scale tourism											632.9					
8 Other small-scale prim. act													2365.2			
9 Other small-scale industry and construction																

(Continued)

Table A8.1 (Continued)

	Millions of pesos	Sectors									Markets (commodities)						
		1	2	3	4	5	6	7	8	9	10	11	12	13	14	15	16
10	Small-scale production and commercial services															2125.7	
11	Tourism	78.8					482.1										
12	Primary exports	91.7	305.5	199.1	695.4	860.1	252.8										
13	Other primary activities	73.4	756.2	492.9	1170.8	122.9	1102.9										
14	Other industrial, construction, electricity	304.8	1128.2	735.4	2673.7	1392.3	128.2										
15	Business and commercial services	286.8	133.9	87.3	266.0	1036.7	400.0										
16	Social services																
17	Skilled wage-workers remuneration	41.5	984.7	1096.2	2121.0	1722.9	3289.6										

Markets

(Continued)

Table A8.1 (Continued)

	Millions of pesos	Sectors										Markets (commodities)					
		1	2	3	4	5	6	7	8	9	10	11	12	13	14	15	16
Factors																	
18	Unskilled wage-workers remuneration	1.6	141.1	164.0	320.3	267.0	432.9										
19	Mixed income							632.9	2365.2	3244.3	2125.7						
20	Operating surplus	917.0	2543.0	0.2	1187.2	2054.7	186.2										
Institutions																	
21	Households 1																
22	Households 2																
23	Households 3																
24	Households 4																
25	Households 5																
26	Businesses																
27	Government		−1390.6	−1006.4	−161.9	−118.3							4163.7	213.2	1842.4	367.0	
28	Tariffs												5.2	124.1	258.8		
29	Subsidies												−57.4	−396.6	−85.1		
	Rest of the world												58.6	1389.1	3337.7		
30	Capital account																
	Total	1795.6	4602.0	1768.7	8272.5	7338.3	6274.7	632.9	2365.2	3244.3	2125.7	2428.5	8772.1	5463.70	16870.6	9831.0	356.9

(Continued)

Table A8.1 (Continued)

	Millions of pesos	Factors				Institutions										Total
		17	18	19	20	21	22	23	24	25	26	27	28	29	30	
1	Tourism															1795.6
2	Primary exports															4602.0
3	Other large-scale primary activities															1768.7
4	Other large-scale industry, construction, electricity											5917.8				8272.5
5	Large-scale production and commercial services															7338.3
6	Social services															6274.7
7	Small-scale tourism															632.9
8	Other small-scale prim. act.															2365.2

Sectors

(Continued)

Table A8.1 (Continued)

Millions of pesos	Factors				Institutions										Total
	17	18	19	20	21	22	23	24	25	26	27	28	29	30	
9 Other small-scale industry, construction															3244.3
10 Small-scale production and commercial services															2125.7
11 Tourism					19.2	29.8	34.2	31.2	33.5				1719.7		2428.5
12 Primary exports					391.6	1313.2	1452.4	911.0	1111.1				1188.2		8772.1
13 Other primary activities					128.2	433.1	476.1	299.5	364.6				43.1		5463.7
14 Other industry, construction, electricity					780.6	1838.3	2104.6	1511.5	1757.6				264.5	2250.9	16870.6
15 Business and commercial services					596.5	1632.2	1845.9	1243.4	1478.9				823.4		9831.0
16 Social services					47.0	72.3	80.5	76.4	80.7						356.9

Markets

(Continued)

Table A8.1 (Continued)

Millions of pesos	Factors				Institutions										Total
	17	18	19	20	21	22	23	24	25	26	27	28	29	30	
17 Wages skilled workers															9255.9
18 Wages unskld workers															1326.9
19 Mixed income															8368.1
20 Operating surplus															6888.3
21 Households 1	415.9	140.1	18.3	93.3					1355.0		820.3		8.4		2851.3
22 Households 2	1055.7	212.8	33.2	210.7					4594.3		405.7		26.4		6538.8
23 Households 3	1690.6	245.6	73.6	322.6					5509.4		474.2		46.8		8362.8
24 Households 4	2527.6	307.6	252.4	470.0					667.9		513.5		80.4		4819.4
25 Households 5	2591.8	279.7	7990.6	473.3							455.5		438.0		12228.9
26 Businesses				3365.1							149.0		56.6		3570.7
27 Government	974.3	141.1		1829.4	1.4	2.6	5.7	19.6	586.0	3179.5			198.9		13912.9
28 Tariffs												388.1			388.1
Subsidies											3216.3				0.0
29 Rest of the world				123.9							446.9				5356.2
30 Capital account					886.8	1217.3	2363.4	726.8	-5310.1	391.2	1513.7		461.8		2250.9
Total	9255.9	1326.9	8368.1	6888.3	2851.3	6538.8	8362.8	4819.4	12228.9	3570.7	13912.9	388.1	5356.2	2250.9	

Factors: 17, 18, 19, 20

Institutions: 21, 22, 23, 24, 25, 26, 27, 28, 29, 30

Table A8.2 Results of selected simulations (percentage of change relative to base year)

	External shock		Terms of trade		Devaluation		Export promotion		Tariff increase
	Simul. 1-1a	Simul. 1-1b	Simul. 1-2a	Simul. 1-2b	Simul. 2-2a	Simul. 2-2b	Simul. 2-3a	Simul. 2-3b	Simul. 2-1
	5% Increase in demand for exports[1]	10% Increase in demand for exports[2]	1% Decline in import prices	11% Increase in export prices and 6% increase in primary exports	10% Devaluation	10% Devaluation and 4% increase in primary exports[3]	9% Increase in export demand and 10% increase in tourism capital[2]	9% Increase in export demand and of capital in three activities[4]	17% Tariff[5]
Volume of production	0.40	1.73	0.97	−0.06	0.87	0.96	1.59	1.08	0.19
Volume of value added	0.42	1.40	0.36	0.07	0.75	0.88	1.30	0.86	0.00
GDP (value)	1.07	3.63	3.42	0.67	1.04	1.39	1.32	2.39	2.58
Value added tradables	0.72	2.28	−0.43	0.28	1.85	2.52	1.79	1.68	−0.01
Value added large scale	0.45	1.41	0.25	0.10	0.76	0.90	1.32	0.87	−0.03
Export volume	5.41	8.70	0.00	1.77	0.00	2.52	9.24	9.24	0.00
Export value	5.41	8.70	0.00	5.20	10.00	12.78	9.24	9.24	0.00
Import volume	0.14	1.14	7.47	−0.12	−2.91	−3.03	1.46	0.69	−3.08
Import value	0.14	1.14	−9.73	−0.12	6.80	6.66	1.46	0.69	−3.08
Foreign savings	−44.35	−63.61	−99.86	−45.76	−30.40	−52.99	−64.38	−70.80	−33.32
Employment level	0.45	2.35	1.48	−0.13	0.97	1.18	1.53	0.50	0.31

(Continued)

Table A8.2 (Continued)

	External shock		Terms of trade		Devaluation		Export promotion		Tariff increase
	Simul. 1-1a	Simul. 1-1b	Simul. 1-2a	Simul. 1-2b	Simul. 2-2a	Simul. 2-2b	Simul. 2-3a	Simul. 2-3b	Simul. 2-1
	5% Increase in demand for exports[1]	10% Increase in demand for exports[2]	1% Decline in import prices	11% Increase in export prices and 6% increase in primary exports	10% Devaluation	10% Devaluation and 4% increase in primary exports[3]	9% Increase in export demand and 10% increase in tourism capital[2]	9% Increase in export demand and of capital in three activities[4]	17% Tariff[5]
Employment in tradable activities	1.82	7.00	−0.84	0.67	3.39	5.14	3.32	1.29	0.03
Wage employment	0.89	2.93	0.38	0.16	1.19	1.61	1.91	0.45	0.00
Skilled wage employment	0.88	2.90	0.37	0.16	1.18	1.60	1.89	0.45	0.00
Skilled wage in tradables	1.78	6.83	−0.87	0.69	3.51	5.32	3.02	0.93	0.03
Unemployment	−7.06	−36.89	−23.23	2.05	−15.22	−18.42	−24.02	−7.81	−4.83
Labour income	0.48	3.02	1.82	−0.18	0.84	1.04	1.78	0.80	0.40
Household demand	−0.99	0.23	4.18	−0.81	−0.05	−0.69	0.41	−0.57	−0.36
Demand per capital H1	−0.85	0.04	3.13	−0.61	0.09	−0.45	0.70	−0.65	−0.89

(Continued)

Table A8.2 (Continued)

	External shock		Terms of trade		Devaluation		Export promotion		Tariff increase
	Simul. 1-1a	Simul. 1-1b	Simul. 1-2a	Simul. 1-2b	Simul. 2-2a	Simul. 2-2b	Simul. 2-3a	Simul. 2-3b	Simul. 2-1
	5% Increase in demand for exports[1]	10% Increase in demand for exports[2]	1% Decline in import prices	11% Increase in export prices and 6% increase in primary exports	10% Devaluation	10% Devaluation and 4% increase in primary exports[3]	9% Increase in export demand and 10% increase in tourism capital[2]	9% Increase in export demand and of capital in three activities[4]	17% Tariff
Demand per capita H2	−1.08	0.30	4.17	−0.91	0.05	−0.59	0.57	−1.46	−1.57
Demand per capita H3	−1.19	0.16	4.35	−0.90	0.06	−0.69	0.66	−1.41	−1.54
Demand per capita H4	−0.36	3.58	3.49	−0.40	0.09	−0.62	−0.21	−2.08	−0.75
Demand per capita H5	−1.28	−2.56	5.02	−1.06	−0.47	−0.98	0.35	2.70	2.89
Household consumption (value)	0.48	3.51	2.46	−0.08	1.04	0.97	0.40	1.66	2.78
Inflation (CPI)	3.27	−0.63	−5.37	0.72	0.70	3.86	−3.61	4.00	7.26
Informal exchange rate	−2.54	−10.61	3.33	−0.83	1.06	0.25	−5.62	−1.97	5.17

(Continued)

Table A8.2 (Continued)

	Productivity shock			WTO			FTAA	
	Simul. 2-4	Simul. 2-4	Simul. 2-5	Simul. WTO	Simul. WTO	Simul. WTO	Simul. FTAA	Simul. FTAA
	10% Increase in productivity of primary exports and 16% increase in demand for primary exports	7% Increase in generalized productivity and 9% in export demand	10% Increase in median wage for large-scale activities	Without eliminating agricultural subsidies	With 50% reduction in subsidies and a 5% increase in export demand	With 50% reduction of subsidies	With 5% increase in exportable demand and 9% increase in overall productivity and export demand	With 9% increase in exportable demand and 8% increase in overall productivity
Volume of production	0.52	6.17	−3.67	0.05	−0.27	2.21	−0.17	7.95
Volume of value added	0.70	4.56	−2.43	0.05	0.07	1.78	0.05	5.82
GDP (value)	−0.13	8.00	−6.18	−0.48	−0.06	0.33	0.61	10.49
Value added tradables	1.38	3.01	−0.62	0.08	1.59	1.47	0.27	3.72
Value added large scale	0.73	4.23	−2.11	0.05	0.18	1.74	0.11	5.36
Export volume	4.71	9.24	0.00	0.00	5.41	9.24	5.41	9.24
Export value	4.71	9.24	0.00	1.47	6.97	10.80	5.44	9.27
Import volume	0.84	4.20	−1.78	2.30	0.93	4.24	0.94	6.61
Import value	0.84	4.20	−1.78	4.72	3.34	6.67	0.90	6.57
Foreign savings	−30.86	−34.37	−17.65	36.78	−23.70	−22.19	−37.06	−10.32

(Continued)

Table A8.2 (Continued)

	Productivity			WTO			FTAA	
	Simul. 2-4	Simul. 2-4	Simul. 2-5	Simul. WTO	Simul. WTO	Simul. WTO	Simul. FTAA	Simul. FTAA
	10% Increase in productivity of primary exports and 16% increase in demand for primary exports	*7% Increase in generalized productivity and 9% in export demand*	*10% Increase in median wage for large-scale activities*	*Without eliminating agricultural subsidies*	*With 50% reduction in subsidies and a 5% increase in export demand*	*With 50% reduction of subsidies*	*With 5% increase in exportable demand and 9% increase in overall productivity and export demand*	*With 9% increase in exportable demand and 8% increase in overall productivity*
Employment level	−0.88	3.34	−5.65	0.04	−0.72	−3.00	−0.40	5.22
Employment in tradable activities	−4.37	−6.51	−1.28	0.14	3.40	−10.43	0.83	−6.84
Wage employment	−1.24	−2.00	−2.72	0.08	0.55	−6.03	0.25	−1.62
Skilled wage employment	−1.23	−1.99	−2.69	0.08	0.55	−5.97	0.25	−1.61
Skilled wage in tradables	−4.53	−7.15	−1.33	0.14	3.41	−11.20	0.76	−7.49
Unemployment	13.77	−52.40	88.48	−0.63	11.33	47.01	6.21	−81.70
Labour income	−1.00	5.04	−0.98	0.06	−0.86	−1.89	−0.44	7.34
Household demand	−0.20	10.41	−8.25	0.58	−3.36	2.83	−1.88	14.56

(Continued)

Table A8.2 (Continued)

	Productivity shock			WTO			FTAA	
	Simul. 2-4	Simul. 2-4	Simul. 2-5	Simul. WTO	Simul. WTO	Simul. WTO	Simul. FTAA	Simul. FTAA
	10% Increase in productivity of primary exports and 16% increase in demand for primary exports	*7% Increase in generalized productivity and 9% in export demand*	*10% Increase in median wage for large-scale activities*	*Without eliminating agricultural subsidies*	*With 50% reduction in subsidies and a 5% increase in export demand*	*With 50% reduction of subsidies*	*With 5% increase in exportable demand and 9% increase in overall productivity and export demand*	*With 9% increase in exportable demand and 8% increase in overall productivity*
Demand per capita H1	−0.15	6.51	−3.96	0.61	−2.60	1.70	−1.47	9.35
Demand per capita H2	−0.17	9.24	−5.04	0.48	−3.93	2.35	−2.28	12.97
Demand per capita H3	−0.18	9.02	−5.18	0.69	−3.90	2.39	−2.25	12.87
Demand per capita H4	−0.63	5.37	−3.83	0.66	−2.37	−0.56	−1.18	8.51
Demand per capita H5	0.07	19.39	−21.03	0.47	−3.28	7.27	−1.80	25.77

(Continued)

Table A8.2 (Continued)

	Productivity shock			WTO			FTAA	
	Simul. 2-4	Simul. 2-4	Simul. 2-5	Simul. WTO	Simul. WTO	Simul. WTO	Simul. FTAA	Simul. FTAA
	10% Increase in productivity of primary exports and 16% increase in demand for primary exports	7% Increase in generalized productivity and 9% in export demand	10% Increase in median wage for large-scale activities	Without eliminating agricultural subsidies	With 50% reduction in subsidies and a 5% increase in export demand	With 50% reduction of subsidies	With 5% increase in exportable demand and 9% increase in overall productivity and export demand	With 9% increase in exportable demand and 8% increase in overall productivity
Household consumption (value)	−0.85	9.90	−10.60	0.11	−0.63	−0.09	0.01	13.72
Inflation (CPI)	−0.85	7.63	−9.80	−4.37	3.32	−4.18	1.70	5.90
Informal exchange rate	−1.08	11.19	−23.00	0.00	−3.65	−1.78	−3.03	17.72

Notes
1 Includes the following variations in exports: 3 per cent in tourism, 6 per cent in primary exports, 5 per cent in rest of industrial activities, 10 per cent in productive commercial services and 3 per cent in own account tourism
2 Includes the following variations in exports: 12 per cent in tourism, 6 per cent in primary exports, 5 per cent in rest of industrial activities, 10 per cent in productive commercial services and 12 per cent in own-account tourism
3 Includes the following variations in exports: 4 per cent in primary exports, 5 per cent in rest of industrial activities and 5 per cent in productive commercial services
4 Includes increases of 10 per cent in tourism capital, 2 per cent in primary exports and 2 per cent in rest of industrial activities
5 In this simulation the average tariff of 17 per cent that prevailed before trade liberalization of 1996 is applied. Hence, the simulation in fact shows the impact on the economy if tariffs had not been lowered.

Acknowledgements

Special thanks to Yenniel Mendoza of the Instituto Nacional de Investigaciones Económicas (INIE) for her collaboration in providing the social accounting matrices, sector analysis and decomposition analysis of the current account used in this study. Thanks also to Nancy Quiñones of the INIE for her reflections on the economic theory of international trade and its link to the current context, and to Niek de Jong of the Institute of Social Studies of The Hague for his invaluable support in the utilization of the microsimulations software.

Notes

1 Opening to foreign capital and dismantling the state monopoly of foreign trade already began before 1993, but their impact on the economy became significant from that year onwards.
2 An analysis of monetary duality in Cuba is found in González (2000).
3 The salary scale sets a minimum wage of 100 *pesos* and a system where the highest wage can be 4.5 times higher than the lowest wage.
4 This refers to the net direct taxes of government transfers.
5 This decomposition is based on UNCTAD methodology for estimating external shocks and domestic responses (see Chapter 2). The residuals are secondary effects that primarily reflect the response of economic agents to changing terms of trade. In the case of Cuba, they are not shown in detail as they are not significant.
6 Domestic private activities include workers in credit and service cooperatives, independent farmers, individual concessions, branches of foreign companies and associations and foundations.
7 To further examine conceptual questions associated with Cuba's social system, see Ferriol *et al.* (1998).
8 In the period between 1996 and 1999, family income sources included in the estimates varied. The exchange rate used in the calculations was also different in each study.
9 Other workers include individual farmers and land tenants (*parceleros*), workers in agricultural cooperatives, own-account workers and informal sector workers.
10 Prices of primary exports were increased in the export price shock simulation.
11 This refers primarily to subsidies derived from dual monetary circulation. See CEPAL (2000).
12 The methodology was proposed by Paes de Barros and Vos. See Ganuza *et al.* (2001) and Chapter 3.
13 In this part of the chapter, people with nine or more years of study are considered skilled workers. While in Cuba's case, a worker must have a higher level of education to be considered skilled, this criterion was adopted in order to facilitate comparisons with other countries within the framework of this research project.

References

Alvarez, E. (1995) 'Impacto de la inversión extranjera en la sociedad cubana', *Revista Cuba: Investigación Económica* No. 4 (INIE).

CEPAL (2000) *La Economía Cubana. Reformas estructurales y desempeño en los noventa*, Santiago: CEPAL.

Chenery, H. B. (1979) *Structural Change and Development Policy*, Oxford: Oxford University Press.

Decaluwé, B., A. Martens and L. Savard (2001) 'La politique economique du development et les modeles d'equilibre general calculable', Agence Universitaire de la Francophonie, Les Presses de L'Université de Montreal, Canada (mimeo).

Ferriol, A., G. Carriazo, O. Echavarría and D. Quintana (1998) 'Efecto de políticas macro-económicas y sociales sobre los niveles de pobreza. El caso de Cuba en los años noventa', in: Enrique Ganuza, Lance Taylor and Samuel Morley (eds) *Política Macroeconómica y Pobreza en América Latina y el Caribe*, Madrid: Mundi-Prensa (for UNDP-ECLAC-IDB).

Ferriol, A., X. Hoang, A. González and A. Hernández (2003) 'Promoción de las exportaciones, pobreza, desigualdad y crecimiento. El caso de Cuba en los noventa', UNDP Project, Havana and New York: UNDP (mimeo).

Ganuza, E., R. Paes de Barros and R. Vos (2001) 'Ajuste del mercado laboral, pobreza y desigualdad durante liberalización', in: E. Ganuza, L. Taylor, R. Barros and R. Vos (eds) *Liberalización, desigualdad y pobreza. América Latina y el Caribe en los 90*, Buenos Aires: Ediciones Universidad de Buenos Aires.

González, A. (1997) 'Economía y Sociedad. Los retos al modelo económico', *Revista Temas* No. 11.

González, A. (2000) 'Particularidades de la dolarización en Cuba', Presentation to International Conference in Honour of Julian Alienens, Granada (Mimeo).

Löfgren, H., R. Lee and S. Robinson (2001) 'A standard computable general equilibrium model (CGE) in GAMS', TMD Discussion Paper 75, International Food Policy Research Institute, Washington, DC: IFPRI.

Mañalich, I. (1996) 'Cuba y las zonas económicas especiales en el mundo.' *Revista Cuba: Investigación Económica* No. 2 (INIE).

Mercenier, J. and T. N. Srinivasan (eds) (1994) *Applied General Equilibrium and Economic Development*, Ann Arbor: The University of Michigan Press.

Morley, S. and R. Vos (2000) 'Research methodology of the project export-led economic strategies: effects on poverty, inequality and growth in Latin America and the Caribbean', New York: UNDP (mimeo).

ONE (several years) *Anuarios Estadísticos de Cuba*, 1996–2000, Havana: National Office of Statistics.

Quiñones, N., I. Mañalich and N. Pico (2001) 'Por qué exportar', *Revista Cuba: Investigación Económica* No. 1 (INIE).

Rodríguez, J. L. (2000) 'Resultados económicos del 2000. Plan y Presupuesto para el 2001', Report of the National Assembly, December 2000, Havana.

Taylor, L. (1992) *Estabilización y crecimiento en los países en desarrollo: un enfoque estructuralista*, México: Fondo de Cultura Económica.

Taylor, L. (ed.) (2001) *External Liberalization, Economic Performance, and Social Policy*, Oxford: Oxford University Press.

Vos, R. (2002) 'Microsimulations methodology for the project export-led economic strategies: effects on poverty, inequality and growth in Latin America and the Caribbean', New York: UNDP (mimeo).

9 Ecuador – dollarization, trade liberalization and poverty

Rob Vos and Mauricio León

Abstract

Ecuador engaged in drastic economic reforms in the early 1990s. In the decade that followed there is a tale of great economic and political turmoil. In the process, the country's dependence on primary exports (oil, shrimps and bananas) has not been reduced, while the economy is likely to have become even more sensitive to terms-of-trade shocks following its decision to adopt the dollar as official means of payments thereby fully giving up independence of monetary policy. The early 1990s began with fairly successful economic stabilization helped by debt reduction under the Brady deal, use of the exchange rate as nominal anchor and a rise in trade and capital inflows following import liberalization and capital account opening. In the first half of the 1990s, modest growth was achieved and real wages were up fostering a substantial decline in (urban) poverty. Things start to breakdown after 1995 following political turmoil and several external shocks. A full-blown currency and financial crises emerged in 1999 as the domestic currency could no longer be defended. A shift towards a flexible exchange-rate regime and rise in interest rates did not evade, but rather accelerated the banking crisis as it revealed the currency mismatch and large share of bad debts in the system. Per capita income fell by 9 per cent in 1 year and poverty increased substantially during 1998–9. The crisis eventually led to the decision to dollarize the economy. Inflation hit at an unprecedented height in the first months following dollarization, but the inflation rate has gradually decelerated since and the economy has slowly recovered. Inflation has been higher though than that of the major trading partners leading to an appreciation of the hypothetical real exchange rate. Real wages have been able to recover alongside the real appreciation alike in the early 1990s. Workers remittances have become a major new source of household income following massive emigration after the economic crisis of 1999. These factors have helped reduce (urban) poverty in 2001–2. Factors associated with the structural reforms, however, seem to have pushed up income inequality. This trend has been visible throughout the 1990s, particularly due to a rise in skill-intensity of production in most traded and non-traded goods sectors pushing up the wage gap between skilled and unskilled workers. Employment growth has been as volatile as aggregate output growth, but on balance more workers have been pushed in the informal sector and a widening gap between formal and informal sector workers has further contributed to rising inequality. These trends may be associated to a large extent with the process of trade liberalization in Ecuador as shown by the CGE simulations. The simulation results indicate that the trade opening in Ecuador induced mild aggregate welfare gains, but rising income inequality due to rising wage differentials between skilled and unskilled workers implies that at the end of the day trade liberalization had no poverty-reducing impact. Scenarios of deepened trade integration, such as under the Free Trade Agreement for the Americas and a WTO scenario of free trade and no export subsidies only exacerbate these trends. Under the WTO scenario rising inequality and unfavourable relative prices for agricultural exports would even lead to a rise in poverty. To reap the benefits of trade, Ecuador's stabilization and growth strategy should thus give priority to investment in human and physical infrastructure to foster productivity growth and reduce the shortage of skilled workers.

9.1 Introduction

Ecuador's recent economic history has been characterized by drastic reforms and a good deal of economic and political turmoil. It introduced radical trade reforms in the early 1990s, along with a liberalization of the financial sector and the economy's capital account. During a decade, it switched exchange-rate regimes radically, from using the exchange rate as nominal anchor for a good part of the 1990s, to a free-floating exchange rate in 1999 and a switch to full dollarization in 2000. The macroeconomic policy shifts reflect persistent economic volatility and severe political instability. Since 1996, two elected presidents were ousted from office early into their terms and several more constitutional and unconstitutional caretaker presidents temporarily took their place. The economy collapsed in 1999 following a series of adverse external shocks, which painfully manifested the extreme fragility of the financial sector and fiscal insolvency. The move towards dollarization was an emergency response to the country's woes. It has helped bring the economy to more stable waters between 2000 and 2003 and has imposed a straightjacket on macroeconomic policy. As in the early 1990s, the real exchange rate has appreciated and this has enabled real wage increases and allowed for poverty reduction. However, this may also hamper export growth and diversification away from the country's secular dependence on primary exports.

The costs and benefits of both dollarization and trade liberalization are subject of continuous debate in Ecuador. While the main focus of this paper is to analyse the links between trade opening, export growth and poverty in Ecuador, the macroeconomic policy framework will be a related central concern. In order to isolate the effects of trade reforms, we combine a computable general equilibrium (CGE) model analysis and a microsimulation approach. The former instrument allows us to assess economy-wide effects of isolated trade policies, including the effects on employment and real incomes by groups of workers and households. We need the microsimulations to account for within-group income differentials and thereby the impact on inequality and poverty at the household level.

The CGE-cum-microsimulation analysis shows that trade liberalization in Ecuador, when isolated from other factors, appears to have led to modest improvements in growth, but at the same time has induced greater income inequality, particularly between skilled and unskilled workers, offsetting the poverty-reducing impact of aggregate income gains. This empirical finding seems at odds with predictions of standard trade theory by the Stolper–Samuelson theorem, which would expect gains from trade to accrue to the more abundant factor, being unskilled labour in a country like Ecuador. However, the limiting assumptions of the Stolper–Samuelson theorem do not apply in a typical developing country setting and in a broad sense the findings for Ecuador confirm patterns found elsewhere in Latin America and other parts of the world (see, e.g. Wood 1997; Vos *et al.* 2002). The precise interactions between macro- and microeconomic adjustment are context specific though and this is precisely what we wish to unravel in this chapter.

The remainder of this chapter is organized as follows. Section 9.2 describes Ecuador's macroeconomic performance and vulnerability to external shocks over the past few decades. Section 9.3 spells out trade reforms and export performance during the 1990s, while Section 9.4 describes the observed labour market adjustment and related trends in poverty and inequality. Section 9.5 spells out the CGE model and the social accounting matrix (SAM) which provides the accounting consistency and many of the model parameters. Section 9.6 details the microsimulations approach, compares it to other similar methods and lists its main advantages as well as its limitations. Section 9.7 reports the results of applying the macro–micro linkage analysis using the CGE model and microsimulations to assess the economy-wide and poverty and inequality effects of alternative trade liberalization scenarios and a range of external shocks. Section 9.8 summarizes the main conclusions and assesses pertaining policy trade-offs in Ecuador's economic development.

9.2 Macroeconomic performance and external shocks

Macroeconomic volatility

Ecuador is a small, primary-exporting economy with, since the early 1970s, oil as its major export commodity. Macroeconomic volatility is high, even by Latin American standards,[1] and strongly influenced by export performance and terms-of-trade fluctuations as Table 9.1 shows. The standard deviation of real GDP growth during the 1980s and 1990s was below that of the 1970s. However, due to the much slower growth pace, the relative importance of volatility (as measured through the coefficient of variation) increased in recent decades. Since 1980, the overall trend of Ecuador's terms of trade has been on the decline, albeit with continuing large fluctuations. Oil price fluctuations have an important impact on this source of volatility, but trends in other main export commodity prices (bananas, coffee and shrimps) have not been much more favourable, as visible from the non-oil terms-of-trade data in Table 9.1.

Table 9.1 Ecuador: macroeconomic volatility indicators, 1965–2001

	1965–80	1980–90	1990–2001	1965–2001
Real GDP				
Mean (%)	7.4	2.1	1.9	5.9
SD	5.7	4.3	3.2	5.4
CV	0.77	2.06	1.65	0.91
Export volume				
Mean (%)	9.3	5.2	4.1	9.2
SD	31.3	12.2	4.5	21.2
CV	3.38	2.33	1.08	2.31
Terms-of-trade				
Mean (%)	0.9	−5.2	−2.8	−2.7
SD	20.1	12.4	10.5	15.5
CV	21.40	−2.37	−3.74	−5.74
Non-oil terms-of-trade				
Mean (%)	−0.7	−4.1	−2.8	−3.2
SD	11.6	10.7	10.1	10.9
CV	−15.60	−2.62	−3.57	−3.38

Source: Central Bank, National Accounts data

Note: GDP, export volume and terms-of-trade show annual average growth rates (mean and standard deviation, SD). The coefficient of variation (CV) is the standard deviation divided by the mean

Coping with shocks and volatility before and after dollarization

These intrinsic conditions of the Ecuadorian economy will not disappear as a result of the adoption of official dollarization as its new monetary regime. More likely, the impact of these real external shocks is expected to hit harder on output and unemployment. Under a fixed exchange-rate regime – and dollarization for that matter – real wage adjustment may be slow to achieve restoration of the internal and external equilibrium in the advent of an adverse shock, hence resulting in possible high costs in terms of output contraction and employment losses. Under a more flexible exchange-rate regime with commensurately greater scope for monetary policy, real wage adjustment may take place more quickly and monetary expansion may push for some aggregate demand expansion, such as to cushion the real output effect of the shock. By limiting job and income losses this way, flexible exchange rates could perform a 'social insurance function' in a context where wages are rigid downwards.[2]

From this perspective, the move towards dollarization may not have been a very good idea and indeed these arguments are still voiced today in Ecuador by opponents of the new monetary regime. In addition, the same conditions – opponents would point out – make dollarization an unsustainable policy option as much as Argentina's currency board proved to be. Output contraction following an adverse terms-of-trade shock could push the economy into a deflationary spiral, lessening investor confidence, depletion of dollar reserves and increasing job losses and poverty, making the monetary regime socially untenable.

While this may not be an implausible scenario for Ecuador, it is not obvious that reverting to a more flexible exchange-rate regime would actually provide a greater social insurance option for the population if past experience were to be our guide. We apply two types of decompositions in order to obtain greater insight into the nature of external shocks and the consequent domestic adjustment during the 1980s and 1990s: a decomposition of the external (current account) deficit by type of shock and a decomposition of the macroeconomic growth rate by type of aggregate spending effect. The methodology for these decompositions is spelled out in Morley and Vos (2003) (see Chapter 2).

External shocks

As already suggested above, the decomposition of the current account deficit clearly shows that terms-of-trade shocks predominate Ecuador's external vulnerability (see Table 9.2). Rising oil prices helped reduce Ecuador's external deficit in the second half of the 1970s and early 1980s, but subsequently, relative export prices have shifted against Ecuador throughout the 1980s and 1990s. Not just oil prices, but also prices of other major primary commodities (bananas, coffee, shrimps and cocoa) moved – on average – unfavourably in relation to import costs. During the 1990s, Ecuador managed to reduce its external deficit substantially, despite negative period average terms-of-trade shocks of nearly 5 per cent of GDP. The rising debt accumulation burden had been another major source of rising current account deficits particularly during the 1980s, but this effect was contained during the 1990s following debt relief under the Brady plan. Unlike the rest of Latin America, Ecuador benefited from favourable world trade growth and this has been a major factor in explaining the reduction in external deficits during the 1990s, as Table 9.2 shows.[3] Worker remittances are the major component of 'other external variables' and a steeply rising source of foreign-exchange earnings from the second part of the 1990s onwards. The economic crisis of 1999 stimulated further out-migration of Ecuadorians and remittances have now become the second source of external earnings after oil exports, reaching US$1.5 billion or about 7 per cent of GDP in 2002.

Despite this recent phenomenon, Ecuador essentially remains highly vulnerable to 'real', trade-related external shocks, which theoretically speaking is not an ideal condition for a dollarized economy (Calvo 1999; Vos 2000), as it severely limits domestic policy adjustment options.

Domestic adjustment

The adverse terms-of-trade shocks have been accommodated by reductions in domestic spending levels (as shares of GDP) as the typical pattern during the 1980s and 1990s. As also shown by Table 9.2, these expenditure cuts have been more or less evenly split between public and private sector spending and between

Table 9.2 Ecuador: decomposition of external shocks and domestic adjustment, 1965–99 (per cent point changes of GDP)

	1971–5/ 1965–71	1975–82/ 1971–5	1982–5/ 1975–82	1985–90/ 1982–5	1990–5/ 1985–90	1995–9/ 1990–5
Observed change in current account deficit	*−1.2*	*0.9*	*−3.0*	*2.4*	*−2.1*	*−11.4*
External shocks (total)	7.7	−1.5	−1.8	4.7	−1.2	−1.9
Terms-of-trade effect	7.3	−5.9	−0.9	10.7	4.4	4.6
Interest rate shock	−0.1	1.1	−0.5	−3.4	−0.4	1.2
World trade retardation	0.5	3.3	−0.4	−2.6	−5.2	−7.7
Other external variables (total)	2.7	−1.6	4.8	4.6	-0.8	−3.1
Debt accumulation burden	0.0	0.5	4.4	4.8	−0.9	1.9
Other external variables	2.7	−2.1	0.4	−0.2	0.1	−5.0
Domestic adjustment (total)	−12.1	2.8	−5.0	−3.5	−1.2	−5.4
Domestic absorption	−1.7	1.8	−0.5	−1.4	−2.1	−3.1
Government consumption	0.2	1.1	−0.1	−0.5	−0.7	−0.5
Private consumption	−1.8	0.2	1.0	−0.3	−1.0	−0.4
Public investment	−0.1	0.2	−0.4	−0.1	−0.4	0.0
Private investment	0.0	0.4	−0.9	−0.3	0.2	−1.2
Change in inventories	0.1	−0.1	−0.1	−0.3	−0.1	−1.0
Trade ratio adjustment	−10.4	1.0	−4.5	−2.1	0.9	−2.3
Import replacement	2.8	0.1	−4.7	−0.4	2.4	−7.0
Export penetration	−13.2	0.9	0.2	−1.7	−1.5	4.7
Total of previous effects	−1.7	−0.4	−2.1	5.9	−3.2	−10.4
+interaction effects	0.5	1.3	−0.9	−3.5	1.1	−1.0
Measured change in current account deficit	*−1.2*	*0.9*	*−3.0*	*2.4*	*−2.1*	*−11.4*
Memo:						
Decomposition of interaction effects						
Interaction effects (total)	0.5	1.3	−0.9	−3.5	1.1	−0.9
Domestic demand and unit imports	−0.9	−0.3	0.1	−0.7	0.0	0.0
Import replacement and import price	1.0	0.0	−0.3	-0.2	−0.2	−2.4
World demand and unit exports	0.4	0.1	0.0	−0.2	0.9	0.1
Export penetration and export price	0.0	0.0	0.0	0.0	0.3	0.8
Debt stock and world interest rate	0.0	1.5	−0.7	−2.4	0.1	0.6

Source: Central Bank of Ecuador, National Accounts (SNA Revision 2 series) and balance-of-payments data

Note: All changes refer to period averages. Values with a positive sign refer to contributions (in per-centage points of GDP) to an *increase* in the current account *deficit*. Negative values refer to contributions to a *decrease* in the current account deficit

consumption and investment. The larger shifts (and volatility) are visible though in Ecuador's trade ratios. Import cuts ('replacement') dominated adjustment to external shocks in the immediate aftermath of the 1980s debt crisis (1982–5) and again during the economic crisis of the late 1990s. The trade opening of the early 1990s (see below) helped boost Ecuador's penetration into world markets and into the markets of the Andean Pact countries. Export penetration was a factor, albeit not very big, in reducing the current account deficit in the first half of the 1990s. During 1995–9, however, Ecuador lost competitiveness and the export penetration ratio deteriorated strongly nearly offsetting the gains from growing world trade.

The latter effect indicates that Ecuador's export volume growth lagged behind global trade growth. It does not mean exports failed to grow during that period. What is more, exports have been, are and likely will remain for the foreseeable future the major source of output growth. This is shown by the macroeconomic growth decomposition in Table 9.3. Export growth has been the major source of GDP growth throughout the 1980s and 1990s. As the table shows, the contribution of export growth in each of the episodes has been almost at par with GDP growth, meaning that export growth explains about 100 per cent of overall economic growth and all other components tend to offset each other. The crisis period 1995–9 is a bit of an exception. Export growth slowed down but remained positive and the import coefficient was cut to stave off a collapse of growth, but to no avail with a steep fall in private investment essentially causing the output decline. In turn, in 2000–1 private investment led the recovery after dollarization as the financial sector gradually came back to its feet and, from 2001 onwards a start was made with the construction of a second oil pipeline. The import leakage increased strongly though, which seems associated with the appreciation in the real exchange rate (see Figure 9.1) and with a boom in consumer durable purchases (cars in particular) by deposit holders who got (part of) their savings deposits in failed or ailing banks returned by the deposit insurance agency. Clearly, dollarization as such has not fully returned confidence in the banking system, as many households prefer durables and real estate to financial assets.

9.3 Trade liberalization, macroeconomic policies and export promotion

Like most other countries in Latin America, Ecuador introduced the major economic reforms along the lines of the Washington Consensus during the early 1990s (Vos 2002). Trade liberalization was the major reform measure that was implemented between 1990 and 1992. The impetus came largely from outside. The Initiative for the Americas pushed for greater integration and economic liberalization of the western hemisphere. Nowadays, this initiative is better known as the Free Trade Area of the Americas (FTAA). A decade ago, the emergence of NAFTA and Mercosur induced the Andean Pact countries to revive their regional trade agreement. In this context, Ecuador reduced its average nominal tariff from 39 per cent in 1988 to 25 per cent in 1990 and further down to around 12 per cent

Table 9.3 Ecuador: decomposition of GDP growth, 1980–2001 (contribution to compound annual GDP growth)

	Private sector			Public sector			External sector			Interaction effects (%)	GDP growth (%)
	Total (%)	Investment (%)	Savings leakage (%)	Total (%)	Government (%)	Tax leakage (%)	Total (%)	Exports (%)	Import leakage (%)		
1980–4	−1.3	−1.7	0.4	0.1	0.6	−0.5	3.2	2.0	1.2	0.1	2.1
1985–9	−0.5	0.0	−0.4	−0.3	−1.3	1.0	2.8	2.1	0.7	0.1	2.0
1990–4	1.3	1.5	−0.2	−0.7	−0.6	−0.1	2.8	3.5	−0.7	0.0	3.4
1995–9	−2.6	−2.3	−0.2	−0.4	−0.5	0.1	2.2	0.2	2.1	0.3	−0.5
2000–1	5.9	6.4	−0.5	−0.1	−0.7	0.5	−2.8	0.8	−3.6	0.1	3.0

Source: Central Bank of Ecuador, National Accounts (SNA revision 2 series)

Note: See Morley and Vos (2003) for the decomposition methodology

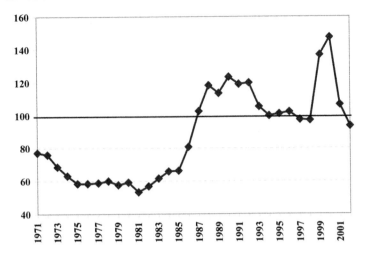

Figure 9.1   Ecuador: real exchange rate (trade-weighted), 1971–2002 (index, 1994 = 100). (From Central Bank of Ecuador.)

in the period after 1992 (see Table 9.4). The dispersion in tariffs was also substantially reduced from 34.5 to 6.0, as measured by the standard deviation of tariffs.

The capital account of the balance of payments was also fully liberalized by the end of 1992 and simultaneous measures were taken to lift restrictions on the domestic financial sector. Price subsidies and controls on domestic fuel prices were lifted, albeit subsidies on basic utilities (electricity, cooking gas) were sustained for a longer period, mainly for political reasons. Privatization of state enterprises also began to be implemented. The first half of the 1990s also marked a shift in macroeconomic policies with a stronger stabilization effort than during the 1980s (see Vos 2002). The nominal exchange rate was used as a nominal anchor, which together with the capital account opening led to a real exchange-rate appreciation and higher domestic interest rates. Figure 9.1 showed the historical pattern of the real exchange rate with a tendency towards appreciation during the oil boom and consequent 'Dutch disease' in the 1970s (Vos 1989), a prolonged depreciation during the 1980s and renewed appreciation with the stabilization plans and economic reforms of the 1990s. This turned out to be unsustainable. With the decline in oil prices and the severe damages caused by the 'El Niño' phenomenon in 1997–8 (Vos *et al.* 2000), the government ran out of foreign exchange reserves and the exchange rate could no longer be defended. The subsequent float and devaluation of the national currency (sucre) in early 1999 pushed the financial system over the edge as two-thirds of bank lending was dollar-denominated. The ensuing financial crisis and economic and political turmoil led to full dollarization in January 2000. As the conversion rate at dollarization

Table 9.4   Ecuador: tariff reform and structure, 1986–2001

	Nominal tariff rates									
	1986	*1990*	*1991*	*1992*	*1994*	*1995*	*1996*	*1997*[1]	*2000*[1]	*2001*[2]
Average	39.1	24.6	15.5	9.3	11.9	11.3	11.3	13.9	16.9	11.3
Minimum	0	0	0	0	0	0	0	2	0	0
Maximum	290	80	50	37	40	40	35	38	40	35
Number of items with *ad valorem* rate	8,991	7,187	6,525	6,251	6,251	6,699	6,637	6,637	6,688	6,688
Standard deviation	34.5	19.3	10.9	6.0	6.3	6.5	6.4	7.2	8.6	6.3

Source: Ministry of Economy

Notes
1 Includes tariff surcharges
2 The surcharges clause was eliminated in 2001

was set very high,[4] there was a de facto maxi-depreciation of the exchange rate. The domestic inflation rate shot up in consequence in the first months following dollarization. Convergence of the domestic price level to international inflation has been slow since and by the end of 2002 the annual rate of inflation stood around 10 per cent more than double that of Ecuador's major trading partner, the USA. The real exchange rate has been appreciating steadily again since 2000.[5]

How did these policy reforms impact on export performance? We should add that the Ecuadorian government also took a large number of legal reforms to facilitate and promote exports. Vos and León (2003) describe these in some detail, but note that none of these had a very large impact on the relative profitability of export production via price effects (e.g. subsidies) or on general conditions that could stimulate exports in a more structural way (such as export credits, marketing, or special infrastructure). This would leave import liberalization, real exchange-rate adjustment and foreign direct investment as major factors influencing export performance. Import liberalization also led to strong declines in effective protection rates also after correcting for the real exchange-rate appreciation of the early 1990s (see Vos and León 2003). Also, dispersion in effective protection rates across manufacturing industries fell, but sectors producing non-basic consumption goods, intermediates and capital goods still benefit from greater protection. These sectors also show on average greater export dynamics during the 1990s. However, a cross-sectional analysis of changes in effective protection and export growth for manufacturing industries at the two-digit level of industry classification showed no significant correlation. Looking at the export performance during the 1990s, there was a relatively strong export volume growth of both agricultural and manufacturing products, but most was achieved in the first half of the decade.

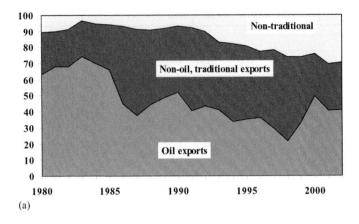

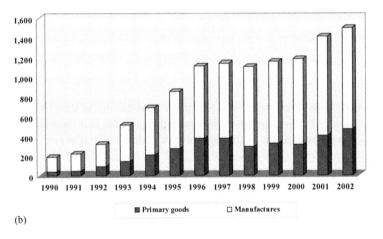

Figure 9.2   Ecuador: (a) export structure, 1980–2002 and (b) non-traditional exports, 1991–2002 (millions of US$). (From Central Bank of Ecuador.)

During 1990–5 agricultural exports increased at an annual rate of 6.3 per cent and manufactured exports at 9.5 per cent. Nearly all export diversification towards non-traditional commodities took place during the first part of the 1990s. The share of non-traditional exports increased from around 10 per cent in the 1980s to 25 per cent by 2001 (Figure 9.2a), but both volume and value of such exports stagnated in the second half of the 1990s (Figure 9.2b). This is consistent with the aggregate finding of the previous section, which showed that export dynamics more or less collapsed in the second half of the 1990s despite the real exchange-rate depreciation towards the end of the decade.

Our interpretation of these events is that the growth and diversification of exports during the 1990s is most closely associated with trade liberalization in the context of the Andean Pact and the enlarged market created along with it. As

Table 9.5 Ecuador: skill intensity of labour demand,[1] 1990–9

	Ratio of skilled/unskilled workers		
	1990	*1995*	*1999*
Agriculture	0.07	0.18	0.20
Oil and mining	0.55	0.89	1.18
Manufacturing	0.63	0.68	1.00
Construction	0.24	0.68	0.81
Commerce	0.76	1.53	1.14
Transport and communications	0.79	2.71	4.40
Financial services	5.62	7.70	8.74
Other services	1.56	0.44	0.46
Total	0.52	0.53	0.59
Traded goods	0.19	0.24	0.27
Non-oil, traded goods	0.19	0.20	0.22
Non-traded goods	1.01	0.85	0.99

Source: INEC, *Censo de Población* 1990; *Encuesta de Condiciones de Vida* 1995 and 1999. Data are national, i.e. covering the whole labour force, urban and rural

Note: 1 Unskilled workers are those with less than nine completed grades of formal education (primary plus 2 years of secondary education); skilled workers have 9 or more years (grades) of formal education

market size in the neighbouring countries is rather limited for Ecuador's manufactures and economic growth has also stagnated there, non-traditional export growth lost momentum. Foreign direct investment has been important in the emergence of new export activities during the 1990s. The most noticeable one is cut flowers (roses in particular), but the relative importance of this new industry (as that of others) still is rather limited generating less than 4 per cent of export earnings at the beginning of the new millennium. It remains clear though, that despite the drastic trade reforms, Ecuador remains heavily dependent on primary exports with the associated vulnerability to external shocks discussed earlier. The investment in a second oil pipeline will step up oil exports in the coming years. This will provide additional export earnings, but further deepen vulnerability to terms-of-trade shocks and speed up the depletion of the country's natural resource endowment.

9.4 Labour market adjustment and poverty during the 1990s

The effects of trade reforms and export promotion on the labour market and poverty will be analysed in the next section using a general equilibrium approach. Before studying the counterfactual simulations, it is useful to look at observed labour market trends first. As analysed in a previous study (Vos 2002), labour demand shifted in the 1990s towards skilled workers in formal employment inducing a rising wage differential between skilled and unskilled workers and between formal and informal sector workers. Table 9.5 shows the rise in the skill intensity of labour demand since 1990.

Figure 9.3 Ecuador: skilled and unskilled wage gap, 1988–2001 (ratio of mean income skilled to unskilled workers). (From INEC, Urban Household Surveys, 1988–2001.)

Figure 9.4 Ecuador: urban unemployment rate (right-hand scale) and wage gap (left scale) between formal and informal sector workers, 1988–2001. (From INEC, Urban Household Surveys, 1988–2001.)

Figures 9.3 and 9.4 show that rising labour income inequality was a sustained trend throughout the 1990s, at least in urban areas for which consistent series of household surveys are available. Average real wages increased until 1996 and (urban) poverty fell significantly alongside, as shown by Figure 9.3. During the

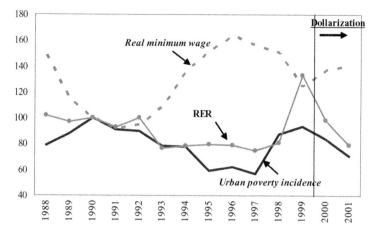

Figure 9.5 Ecuador: real wage, real exchange rate and urban poverty trends (index, 1990 = 100). (From INEC, Urban Household Surveys, 1988–2001.)

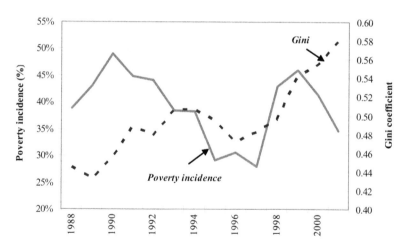

Figure 9.6 Ecuador: urban poverty and inequality, 1988–2001. (From INEC, Urban Household Surveys, 1988–2001.)

initial period after liberalization, poverty thus declined despite a strong rise in inequality (also at the household level, as shown by Figure 9.4).

The trade opening and growing world demand for Ecuadorian products thus could not prevent the economy from slipping into a crisis. Real wages fell dramatically and all gains in poverty reduction were lost in 1998 and 1999 as a consequence of the crisis (see Figures 9.5 and 9.6). Inequality continued to rise during the crisis. Dollarization provoked a renewed tendency towards real exchange-rate appreciation and a recovery of real (urban) wages during 2000–2. Following the pattern of the early 1990s, this more radical exchange-rate based stabilization process allowed for a recovery of consumption, and a demand and relative price shift in favour of non-traded goods and assets to accompany overall recovery in economic activity. Unemployment declined with some improvement in income conditions and a drop in income poverty. This could point at a beneficial social impact of dollarization. The short-run impact is as described and we should add various rounds of nominal wage increases decreed by the government. One may doubt of course whether the process is sustainable, as export competitiveness has declined and fiscal solvency is increasingly put at risk.

The question we wish to focus on now is to what extent the trade opening contributed to or counteracted the observed trends in poverty and inequality. As many things happened at the same time, we need a rigorous method to isolate the trade reform effects. For that purpose, we apply a CGE model for Ecuador to analyse the effects on sector output, employment and factor incomes. This model is spelled out in the next section. We hypothesize that the rise in income inequality is caused to a significant degree by labour market adjustment related to trade reform and exchange-rate adjustment. Labour demand seems to have shifted in favour of skilled labour in both traded and non-traded goods sectors, following trade liberalization and public sector reforms. This went to the detriment of unskilled labour demand. Unskilled workers, by and large, were pushed into either unemployment or low productivity, non-wage employment in informal trade and services. These observed shifts in employment structure and related widening of earnings differentials also seem to have produced greater inequality at the household level, but overall real income and employment growth during the first half of the 1990s outweighed this effect to allow for poverty reduction. Our question here is: what has trade liberalization precisely got to do with these outcomes?

9.5 A SAM and CGE model for Ecuador

In order to isolate the effect of trade liberalization on poverty and income distribution we use a CGE model for Ecuador. The CGE allows us to obtain counterfactual simulation results of trade policy on sectoral output, employment and remunerations by different labour categories. The microsimulation methodology described further below then translates those labour market adjustment results into the impact on income distribution and poverty at the level of individuals and households.

The core specification of the CGE is based on a static trade model developed at the International Food Policy Research Institute (IFPRI) (see Löfgren *et al.* 2001; Chapter 3), following a neoclassical–structuralist model tradition originating in Dervis *et al.* (1982). The CGE distinguishes production activities, commodities and institutions (household groups, government, enterprises and the rest of the world). For producers, profits are maximized subject to a production function, which may be a constant elasticity of substitution (CES), Leontief or a nested CES function. Each production activity uses labour, capital and land up to the point where the marginal revenue product of each factor is equal to its price. Factor prices and rents may differ across activities when factors are sector-specific (not mobile) across activities and/or when there is a fixed remuneration for particular factors and these are affected by unemployment. In the Ecuador model, we assume that the total stock of land, capital, and unskilled labour is fixed and sector specific, and the supply of skilled labour is endogenous and responsive to variations in the real wage for skilled labour. Factor substitution as defined through the production functions is assumed to be imperfect and substitution elasticities are generally low, but vary across the 17 activities distinguished by the model. Factors include capital (land and fixed capital) and four labour categories split by occupational category (wage earners and self-employed) and education (skilled and unskilled). In commodity markets (for 17 products) sellers maximize sales revenue deciding on allocation of total supply between exports and the domestic market according to a constant elasticity of transformation (CET) function. Import demand imperfectly substitutes for demand for domestic commodities through Armington specification. Export supply of certain commodities specific to the Ecuadorian economy (like crude oil) is assumed to be more or less fixed and little responsive to relative prices. Household consumption includes marketed commodities, which are valued at market prices including commodity taxes and transaction costs, and self-consumption valued at activity-specific producer prices. A linear expenditure system (LES) is used to define the allocation of household consumption across different commodities.

Three macroeconomic balance equations complete the model: the (current) government balance, the external balance (the current account of the balance of payments) and the savings–investment balance. We have run the simulations using alternative 'closure rules' for these macroeconomic balances. For the simulations reported here we apply the following closures considered most relevant for Ecuador's case in the period immediately after the liberalization process. Fiscal adjustment is characterized by rigidities, hence we 'close' the government balance endogenously, keeping discretionary spending items and tax rates fixed. Ecuador's macroeconomic adjustment typically has been demand-driven and without a binding savings constraint on investment (e.g. Izurieta 2000). Hence, we assume a closure whereby savings follow investment. This is also consistent with an external closure, which allows for (some) endogeneity in foreign savings adjustment and a fixed exchange-rate regime. During much of the 1990s (until about 1999 and again in 2000 following dollarization), Ecuador mostly used the exchange rate as a nominal anchor to its macroeconomic policies, justifying a closure of the external balance with endogenous foreign savings. Capital account liberalization also eased access to foreign capital, at least during the first part of the 1990s, followed by increased recurrence to borrowing from multilateral agencies during the latter part of the decade. However, we will also test the sensitivity of some of the simulations to this closure rule and run this for the case of a flexible exchange rate.

The CGE is calibrated to the 1993 SAM for Ecuador. The SAM for Ecuador is part of a broader, 'extended system of social accounts' with satellite tables for employment and demographic data, labour and household income distribution indicators, and stock data for opening and closing financial assets. The SAM was constructed in full compliance with the new SNA (see Round 2003) by a team of experts from the Institute of Social Studies, the national statistical office of Ecuador (INEC) and the Secretariat of the Social Cabinet of Ecuador (Frente Social) (see Vos *et al.* 2002). The SAM was slightly aggregated to fit the specifications of the CGE. The financial sector and capital accounts were aggregated for the present purpose. Hence, the main focus is on the real side of the economy. The SAM also provides the key, base year parameter values of the model and ensures the overall accounting consistency. The elasticities for production functions, commodity demand and the LES were derived from partial equilibrium econometric estimates and other existing CGE models for Ecuador. Vos and León (2003) report the details for these estimates. Table A9.1 of the Appendix presents the values for the main elasticities as used in the model. Since the model is homogeneous of degree zero in prices, a price normalization equation is added to the model. This equation defines the 'numéraire' of the model, which is the composite consumer price index in the Ecuador model.

9.6 Microsimulation methodology

The CGE model only provides simulation results for between-group differentials in terms of employment and factor remuneration. The impact on household incomes and consumption is also limited to differentials between highly aggregate groups and moreover assumes a fixed, SAM-based distribution structure of factor incomes to household groups. The CGE model thus misses the full distribution effect and hence also lacks detail for a meaningful assessment of the poverty impact of the policy simulations. The main transmission channel of the modelled impact of trade reforms on poverty and distribution runs through the labour market, as discussed in the next section. In the microsimulations, we take the result of the CGE simulations as to which groups are affected by the trade reforms and subsequently ask ourselves how this may have affected the full income distribution, and hence poverty. The microsimulation methodology applied here is that developed in Ganuza *et al.* (2002) and discussed in Chapter 3.

In its application to Ecuador, the methodology used here follows Vos and De Jong (2001) and consists of creating a counterfactual in the form of labour market parameters, representing the employment and remuneration structure, which would prevail – allegedly – if liberalization had not taken place. This counterfactual may be obtained by either (CGE) model simulations to generate a case of 'with-and-without' or by taking the structure prevailing at the beginning of the liberalization or crisis period to get a sophisticated 'before-and-after' comparison. We adopt the former approach here, but see Vos and De Jong (2001) for an application of the latter.

The counterfactual labour market parameters according to each of the CGE 'macrosimulations' are applied to national data from the 1995 Living Standard Measurement Study (LSMS) household survey.[6] The 1995 LSMS also provided the main data source for the construction of the household and factor income distribution accounts of the SAM that underlies the CGE model for Ecuador (see Vos *et al.* 2002). The counterfactual 'microsimulations' should then show what poverty and income distribution would have been in the absence of trade liberalization (or what they are expected to be in case of further liberalization).

We could label the combination of the CGE model and the microsimulations approach as a 'top–down' modelling of macro–micro linkages because the CGE model communicates with the microsimulation model without a further feedback effect.

9.7 CGE macro–microsimulations: effects of trade liberalization and external shocks on employment and factor incomes

Trade liberalization and export promotion

To isolate the impact of trade liberalization, we perform five counterfactual policy scenarios. First, a nominal tariff increase to simulate the trade regime prior to the liberalization of the 1990s. The average nominal tariff in Ecuador was 40 per cent in 1986 and 25 per cent in 1990 and after 1993 the rate was about 12 per cent. We simulate the counterfactual trade liberalization by raising tariffs to 1990 levels (on average about a 100% increase). Second, we simulate the impact of a further uniform tariff reduction of 50 per cent. Next, we adopt two alternative trade integration scenarios. The third scenario would adopt the tariff structure as proposed under the Free Trade Area for the Americas (FTAA) agreement. Tariffs would become zero for trade among countries of the integration block. Average tariffs are reduced according to the weight of the countries of the Americas in total imports by commodity. The fourth scenario involves the elimination of all export subsidies and taxes according to WTO regulations. In both the FTAA and the WTO scenarios we incorporate the expected effect of each scenario on world export and import prices, as these would affect Ecuador. These outcomes for world market prices were derived from running a global scenario of FTAA and WTO simulations using the global trade model (GTAP).[7] The fifth scenario would go against WTO regulations and promote exports directly and unilaterally by raising export subsidies.

The main simulation results for macroeconomic aggregates, employment and factor incomes are reported in Table 9.6. The results clearly suggest that, under a fixed exchange-rate regime, trade liberalization has had mild positive effects on the economy. A return to trade protection (scenario 1) would lead to a small but visible output loss. From both scenarios 1 and 2 it is clear that the effect on export growth is almost negligible, whereas the import demand increases steeply as a consequence of the import liberalization. This causes a widening of the trade deficit and higher demand for foreign savings. We assume (see above) that Ecuador would have access to foreign borrowing under such a scenario resulting in a real exchange-rate appreciation. This endogenous result will have

Table 9.6 Ecuador CGE: trade policy scenarios (simulation results represent deviations in percentage from the baseline)

	Base (level)	Tariff increase to prereform level	Uniform tariff decrease (−50%)	FTAA scenario	WTO scenario	Export subsidy increase (+100%)
		1	2	3	4	5
Macroeconomic aggregates						
Real values						
GDP at factor cost	25,574.1	−0.7	0.3	0.4	1.0	0.2
Absorption	28,463.6	−2.2	1.1	1.4	1.7	0.3
Household consumption	19,869.4	−3.1	1.6	2.0	2.4	0.0
Investment	5,412.1	0.0	0.0	0.0	0.0	0.0
Government consumption	3,182.0	0.0	0.0	0.0	0.0	0.7
Exports	7,128.3	−0.3	0.1	0.3	2.6	0.7
Imports	8,126.9	−5.1	2.8	3.4	4.7	−0.8
Real exchange rate (index)	100.0	0.9	−0.5	−0.7	0.8	−0.7
Export price index	100.0	0.0	0.0	0.0	2.4	0.0
Import price index	100.0	0.0	0.0	−0.2	0.8	0.0
World price index of tradables	100.0	0.0	0.0	−0.1	1.6	0.0
Domestic price index of non-tradables	100.0	−0.9	0.5	0.6	0.7	0.1
Terms of trade (index)	100.0	0.0	0.0	0.2	1.5	0.0
Percentage of nominal GDP						
Investment	19.0	0.6	−0.3	−0.4	−0.7	−0.1
Private savings (households and firms)	8.6	0.2	−0.1	−0.1	0.9	0.2
Foreign savings	6.5	−1.3	0.7	0.8	0.1	−0.1
Trade deficit	3.5	0.4	−0.2	−0.3	−1.8	−0.3
Government savings	5.4	1.6	−0.9	−1.1	−1.7	−0.2
Tax income from import duties and tariffs	1.8	1.7	−0.9	−1.1	−1.8	0.0
Direct tax revenue	9.9	−0.2	0.1	0.1	0.3	0.0
Employment (thousands)						
Skilled wage earners	885.8	0.0	0.0	0.0	0.0	0.0
Unskilled wage earners	1,297.1	−2.1	1.1	1.3	2.9	0.6

(Continued)

Table 9.6 (Continued)

	Base (level)	Tariff increase to prereform level	Uniform tariff decrease (−50%)	FTAA scenario	WTO scenario	Export subsidy increase (+100%)
		1	2	3	4	5
Skilled self-employed	400.8	0.0	0.0	0.0	0.0	0.0
Unskilled self-employed	1,093.3	−1.9	1.0	1.2	2.7	0.5
Total employment	3,677.1	−1.3	0.7	0.8	1.8	0.4
Real factor income (per worker/unit of capital)						
Skilled wage earners	4.9	−3.9	2.0	2.7	3.6	0.5
Unskilled wage earners	1.5	0.4	−0.2	−0.2	−0.4	−0.1
Skilled self-employed	5.6	−3.0	1.6	2.2	3.4	0.5
Unskilled self-employed	1.5	−0.2	0.1	0.2	0.5	0.1
Capital (index)	1.1	−2.9	1.5	1.8	4.5	0.5

counteracted the trade policy-induced incentive towards tradable goods production, but the larger external resource flow allows for an increase in domestic absorption and household consumption. This positive aggregate demand effect also allows for overall employment growth, but with widening wage gaps between skilled and unskilled workers as average remunerations grow faster for skilled workers (either wage earners or self-employed). Real incomes would deteriorate for unskilled workers. These outcomes are quite consistent with the observed patterns of labour market adjustment during the early 1990s during which trade liberalization went together with larger capital inflows and real exchange-rate appreciation.

The trade integration scenarios under FTAA and WTO show a very similar pattern as unilateral tariff reductions albeit with stronger effects on growth, employment and wage differentials. The WTO arrangement appears to yield more gains for Ecuador, as it would produce a favourable terms-of-trade effect for Ecuador.[8]

We also ran the above policy scenarios under an alternative external balance closure, i.e. a flexible exchange rate and fixed foreign savings. The outcomes are very similar suggesting that the exchange-rate regime is not critical to the impact of these trade reform scenarios. This does not hold for the fifth scenario, in which we increase export subsidies. The initial effect of the subsidy increase would be a (mild) stimulus to export growth and a reduction of the trade deficit. Under a fixed exchange-rate closure this would lead to less foreign savings, offsetting most of the growth and employment effects in export sectors induced by the subsidy. Under a flexible exchange-rate regime some of the economy-wide positive effects of the export-subsidy policy are retained in terms of output and employment growth. However, as in the other trade policy scenarios, also a uniform export subsidy scheme would enhance labour income inequality between skilled and unskilled workers.

These results of trade liberalization and free trade for the Americas appear more favourable than what would be in the beliefs of many economic analysts in Ecuador, let alone antiglobalists. Yet, free trade supporters have not much reason to be triumphal either. As said, the positive welfare effects are not very big and in part rely on the model assumption that a widening trade gap can always be financed. While Ecuador did have increased access to foreign capital in the beginning of the 1990s, this was much less so towards the end of the decade. Moreover, the relatively small aggregate growth effects, widening factor income inequality and falling real incomes for unskilled workers put in doubt whether trade liberalization actually helps to reduce poverty. This is confirmed by the microsimulation results. As a matter of fact, none of the trade reform scenarios are poverty reducing. In effect, the rise in wage differentials fully offsets the poverty-reducing effects of rising employment and average labour earnings. This is clearly indicated by the reversal of the sign for both the change in poverty and inequality in step 4 of the sequential simulations which add the wage differential effect (W_1) to the employment shifts (see Table 9.7).

However, a return to preform trade protection levels is not a solution either. The tariff increase under scenario 1 would on average be twice that of the simulated trade liberalization scenario and there would be stronger (negative in this case) employment and average wage effects. These now outweigh the reduced labour inequality in the preform context. As shown in the last row of Table 9.7, the poverty incidence would have been 2.6 per cent higher in 1995, had tariffs been kept at their preform levels of 1990 (scenario 1), suggesting a negative impact of trade protection.

The trade liberalization scenarios 2, 3 and 4 all induce increases in primary income inequality. Employment shifts across households determine whether rising labour income inequality is also affecting per capita income inequality and poverty. Household income inequality increases in the WTO scenario 4 and explains the slight rise in poverty following the worldwide elimination of export subsidies. In this case the rise in inequality, particularly due to widening wage differentials (steps 1–4 in the microsimulations), implies that the aggregate income gains do not benefit those at the bottom end of the scale. In the case of scenarios 2 (uniform tariff reduction) and 3 (FTAA) the reduction in the unemployment rate helps reduce income inequality, but this effect is neutralized by the rising wage gaps between skilled and unskilled workers and across sectors (W_1). The latter effect also eliminates all poverty-reducing effects despite the rise in the average real wage (W_2). In short, further trade liberalization in Ecuador by itself will not help reduce poverty. Interestingly, the counterfactual of a reversal towards more trade protection suggests that the poor will not be better off either in that case. The macrochanges then appear detrimental for the poor. Under the given CGE model assumptions, there are aggregate employment losses as the trade gap narrows, less foreign savings flow in and the real exchange rate depreciates. The

Table 9.7 Ecuador: microsimulation results of CGE simulations – impact of trade liberalization on poverty and inequality (per cent changes from observed values in 1995)

	Tariff increase to prereform (+50%) 1			Uniform tariff decrease (−50%) 2			FTAA scenario 3			WTO scenario 4			Export subsidy increase 5		
	P_0	Gini YPC	Gini YPI	P_0	Gini YPC	Gini YPI	P_0	Gini YPC	Gini YPI	P_0	Gini YPC	Gini YPI	P_0	Gini YPC	Gini YPI
Observed 1995	31.9	0.529	0.555	31.9	0.529	0.555	31.9	0.529	0.555	31.9	0.529	0.555	31.9	0.529	0.555
(1) U	2.5	0.8	0.1	−1.4	−0.4	0.0	−1.8	−0.5	0.0	−4.0	−1.2	0.0	−0.6	−0.2	0.0
(1–2) U + S1	2.4	0.8	0.1	−1.4	−0.4	0.0	−1.8	−0.5	0.0	−4.2	−1.3	0.0	−0.8	−0.2	0.0
(1–3) U + S1 + O	2.3	0.8	0.1	−1.5	−0.4	0.1	−1.9	−0.5	0.1	−4.3	−1.3	0.0	−0.8	−0.2	0.0
(1–4) U + S1 + O + W1	1.2	0.3	−0.4	1.0	0.3	0.3	1.3	0.4	0.5	1.6	0.5	0.6	0.0	0.1	0.1
(1–5) U + S1 + O + W1 + W2	2.4	0.2	−0.4	0.2	0.3	0.3	0.2	0.4	0.5	0.1	0.5	0.6	−0.1	0.1	0.1
(1–6) U + S1 + O + W1 + W2 + M	2.6	0.1	−0.4	0.3	0.1	0.3	0.4	0.3	0.4	0.3	0.3	0.6	0.0	−0.1	0.1

Note: The table reports sequential (cumulative) simulations. The different steps are defined as follows: U = unemployment effect, S1 = sectoral employment shift (export vs. domestic sectors), O = occupational shift (wage earners, self-employed), W1 = shift in relative remuneration, W2 = shift in mean labour remuneration, M = shift in educational level of labour categories. See text for definition of the steps. P_0 refers to poverty incidence; Gini YPC and Gini YPI refer to Gini coefficients for per capita household income and primary (labour) incomes, respectively

reduction in wage inequality after reversing trade liberalization in this case does not outweigh this contraction of incomes and employment for the poor.

The model simulations should be taken with some caution though, as the CGE only considers the static gains and distributive effects of trade. Trade opening could induce productivity gains forced by world market competition. In Ecuador productivity, gains in traded goods sectors have been rather modest at around 2 per cent per annum during the 1990s and prior to the 1999 crisis (Vos 2002; Vos and León 2003). However, running the tariff reduction simulation together with an exogenously imposed 'productivity shock' in export sectors of that size does not alter the previous conclusions in a major way. Export growth is stronger, the employment effect weaker and the impact on wage differentials is bigger. However, see also further below under shocks.

Other policy experiments and external shocks

We also simulate a few other experiments with the CGE model for Ecuador. First, we simulate a set of terms-of-trade shocks (scenarios 6–8). Next, we simulate two types of foreign-exchange booms: exogenous increases in foreign savings (external borrowing) and a rise in workers remittances (scenarios 8–10). Finally, we experiment with the impact of a currency devaluation (assuming Ecuador still had a currency of its own) and a productivity shock to export sectors (scenarios 11 and 12). Scenarios 6–10 are meant to identify how the Ecuadorian economy seems to respond to external shocks of that nature. Scenarios 11 and 12 complement the trade liberalization and export promotion analysis.

Scenarios 6 and 8 simulate an adverse terms-of-trade shock in the form of a 25 per cent decline in oil prices (the average size of annual oil price fluctuations in recent periods). The static effects of such a shock on the real economy are not as devastating as one might think. Under the assumption of a fixed exchange-rate closure (scenario 6), much of the adverse effect of the shock will be accommodated by a rise in endogenous foreign savings. This assumes adjustment can take place by accumulating more external debt, which would have to grow by 2 per cent of GDP (Table 9.8). The model does not consider the sustainability of such adjustment over time. The exchange rate would even slightly appreciate as a result and exports would suffer, but non-traded goods production and absorption benefit. Total employment expands, but real wages shift in favour of skilled workers, while more unskilled workers are pushed into self-employment reducing the average labour income for that group of workers. The upshot is that poverty increases slightly mainly due to the labour inequality effect (see Table 9.9). Interestingly, under a closure of a flexible exchange rate and fixed foreign savings (simulation 8), the detrimental inequality effects can be avoided and poverty does not decline. The real exchange rate depreciates depressing import demand and expanding export growth and unskilled wage earners are the main beneficiaries in the process. This confirms the earlier hypothesis that in an economy vulnerable to real (commodity price) shocks a fixed exchange rate may provide less social protection to wage earners than under a more flexible regime (see also Lustig 1999; Rodrik 1999), but see below under scenario 11.

Table 9.8 Ecuador CGE: external shocks and other policy scenarios (simulation results represent deviations in percentage from the baseline)

| | Base (level) | Fixed exchange rate | | Flexible exchange rate | | | Fixed exchange rate | |
| | | Oil price shock (−25%) | Import price shock (+10%) | Oil price shock (−25%) | Rise in foreign savings (+10%) | Rise in workers' remittances (+10%) | Devaluation (+10%) | Productivity shock in export sectors (+10%) |
		6	7	8	9	10	11	12
Macroeconomic aggregates								
Real values								
GDP at factor cost	25,574.1	0.3	−1.1	0.2	0.1	0.1	0.0	3.5
Absorption	28,463.6	0.3	−3.4	−1.9	2.8	2.8	−4.0	3.4
Household consumption	19,869.4	0.4	−4.8	−2.8	4.0	4.1	−5.7	4.9
Investment	5,412.1	0.0	0.0	0.0	0.0	0.0	0.0	0.0
Government consumption	3,182.0	0.0	0.0	0.0	0.0	0.0	0.0	0.0
Exports	7,128.3	−0.3	−0.5	2.9	−3.8	−3.8	5.7	4.2
Imports	8,126.9	0.0	−7.8	−4.3	5.9	5.9	−7.5	4.3
Real exchange rate (index)	100.0	−3.0	6.7	3.0	−7.3	−7.3	11.2	−1.8
Export price index	100.0	−7.7	0.0	−7.7	0.0	0.0	0.0	0.0
Import price index	100.0	0.0	10.0	0.0	0.0	0.0	0.0	0.0
World price index of tradables	100.0	−3.7	5.2	−3.7	0.0	0.0	0.0	0.0
Domestic price index of non-tradables	100.0	−0.8	−1.4	−1.4	0.8	0.7	−1.0	1.9
Terms of trade (index)	100.0	−7.7	−9.1	−7.7	0.0	0.0	0.0	0.0
Percentage of nominal GDP								
Investment	19.0	0.2	1.4	0.6	−0.6	0.1	0.8	−0.8
Private savings (households and firms)	8.6	−0.6	0.6	1.3	−2.1	0.7	3.4	−0.8

(Continued)

Table 9.8 (Continued)

	Base (level)	Fixed exchange rate		Flexible exchange rate			Fixed exchange rate	
		Oil price shock (−25%)	Import price shock (+10%)	Oil price shock (−25%)	Rise in foreign savings (+10%)	Rise in workers' remittances (+10%)	Devaluation (+10%)	Productivity shock in export sectors (+10%)
		6	7	8	9	10	11	12
Foreign savings	6.5	2.1	0.8	0.5	1.9	0.0	−3.1	−0.1
Trade deficit	3.5	2.0	0.7	0.1	2.2	0.0	−3.6	0.0
Government savings	5.4	−1.3	0.2	−1.1	−0.4	−0.5	0.6	0.1
Tax income from import duties and tariffs	1.8	0.0	0.1	0.1	0.0	0.0	0.0	0.0
Direct tax revenue	9.9	−0.2	−0.1	−0.3	0.1	0.0	−0.1	0.0
Employment								
Skilled wage earners	885.8	0.0	0.0	0.0	0.0	0.0	0.0	0.0
Unskilled wage earners	1297.1	1.1	−3.3	0.5	0.9	0.8	−1.0	0.7
Skilled self-employed	400.8	0.0	0.0	0.0	0.0	0.0	0.0	0.0
Unskilled self-employed	1093.3	1.2	−2.9	1.0	0.4	0.5	−0.3	2.8
Total employment	3677.1	0.7	−2.0	0.5	0.4	0.4	−0.4	1.1
Real factor income (per worker/unit of capital)								
Skilled wage earners	4.9	0.6	−6.1	−2.3	3.6	3.5	−5.1	5.8
Unskilled wage earners	1.5	0.2	0.6	0.4	−0.2	−0.1	0.3	−0.9
Skilled self-employed	5.6	1.4	−4.8	0.6	1.2	1.3	−1.4	4.4
Unskilled self-employed	1.5	−0.6	−0.3	−0.4	−0.2	−0.2	0.4	1.1
Capital (index)	1.1	−6.0	−4.5	−5.8	−0.3	−0.4	1.0	3.0

Table 9.9 Ecuador: microsimulation results of CGE simulations – impact of trade liberalization on poverty and inequality (per cent changes from observed values in 1995)

	Oil price shock (−25%) 6			Import price shock (+10%) 7			Oil price shock (−25%) 8			Rise in foreign savings (+10%) 9			Rise in workers' remittances (+10%) 10			Devaluation (+10%) 11			Productivity shock in export sectors (+10%) 12		
	P_0	Gini YPC	Gini YPI	P_0	Gini YPC	Gini YPI	P_0	Gini YPC	Gini YPI	P_0	Gini YPC	Gini YPI	P_0	Gini YPC	Gini YPI	P_0	Gini YPC	Gini YPI	P_0	Gini YPC	Gini YPI
Observed 1995	31.9	0.529	0.555	31.9	0.529	0.555	31.9	0.529	0.555	31.9	0.529	0.555	31.9	0.529	0.555	31.9	0.529	0.555	31.9	0.529	0.555
(1) U	−1.6	−0.5	0.0	3.8	1.2	0.0	−1.0	−0.3	0.0	−0.9	−0.3	0.0	−0.9	−0.3	0.0	0.9	0.3	0.0	−2.4	−0.8	0.0
(1-2) U + S1	−1.7	−0.5	0.0	3.7	1.2	0.0	−1.2	−0.4	−0.1	−0.9	−0.3	0.0	−1.0	−0.3	0.0	0.6	0.2	0.0	−2.4	−0.7	0.1
(1-3) U + S1 + O	−1.8	−0.5	0.0	3.6	1.2	0.1	−1.2	−0.4	0.0	−1.1	−0.2	0.1	−1.1	−0.3	0.1	0.6	0.3	0.1	−2.4	−0.6	0.2
(1-4) U + S1 + O + W1	0.2	0.2	0.2	1.8	0.3	−0.8	−0.5	−0.3	−0.2	1.2	0.5	0.5	1.3	0.5	0.5	−0.8	−0.4	−0.5	2.7	1.1	1.2
(1-5) U + S1 + O + W1 + W2	0.1	0.2	0.2	3.6	0.3	−0.8	−0.2	−0.3	−0.2	0.6	0.5	0.5	0.6	0.5	0.5	0.3	−0.4	−0.5	0.2	1.2	1.2
(1-6) U + S1 + O + W1 + W2 + M	0.2	0.0	0.2	3.7	0.1	−0.8	−0.2	−0.5	−0.2	0.6	0.3	0.5	0.8	0.3	0.5	0.4	−0.7	−0.6	0.8	1.0	1.1

Note: The table reports sequential (cumulative) simulations. The different steps are defined as follows: U = unemployment effect. S1 = sectoral employment shift (export vs. domestic sectors), O = occupational shift (wage-earners, self-employed), W1 = shift in relative remuneration, W2 = shift in mean labour remuneration, M = shift in educational level of labour categories. See text for definition of the steps. P_0 refers to poverty incidence; Gini YPC and Gini YPI refer to Gini coefficients for per capita household income and primary (labour) incomes, respectively

A uniform import price shock (simulation 7) would be more detrimental though as it would directly affect the cost structure and relative prices in the entire economy and not just start with a loss concentrated in oil revenues. Under a fixed exchange-rate regime import demand collapses, but also closes the trade gap not inducing any new external borrowing as under the adverse oil-price shock. Employment falls in most parts of the economy, as much as real earnings and poverty rises (Tables 9.8 and 9.9).

We report exogenous foreign exchange earnings shocks only for the case of a flexible exchange-rate regime, as under the endogenous foreign savings closure such additional earnings would dissipate immediately through the external account and exercise hardly any effect on the economy. The two types of shocks produce similar results. The real exchange rate appreciates and exports fall. Absorption and average household consumption increase, but earnings shift against unskilled workers, which is the main cause of the rising inequality and poverty despite the positive foreign-exchange injection into the economy.

A nominal exchange-rate devaluation (scenario 11) has a contractionary effect under the conditions of Ecuador's economic structure of the 1990s. Ecuador's export structure is relatively labour-extensive and household consumption is composed of a high share of tradables. In consequence, devaluation does not provide the major impulse to employment in export sectors, while it depresses the real consumption wage. Unskilled workers would suffer most job losses and self-employed in agriculture (farmers) win only slight employment gains, but real wages and household incomes fall for all groups with skilled workers and urban middle income groups suffering the larger loss in purchasing power. Income inequality would fall, but this cannot compensate for losses in employment and real incomes to stave off an increase in poverty (see Table 9.9, scenario 11). This finding appears consistent with the poverty and real wage trends in Figure 9.5, where poverty reduction is associated with episodes of real exchange-rate appreciation. Earlier model-based policy analysis for Ecuador by De Janvry and Sadoulet (2001) based on a dynamic real-financial CGE obtains a similar outcome for the preliberalization period. Hence, given its present economic structure, a return to a less rigid monetary regime than that of dollarization would add degrees of freedom for economic policy-makers, such as the option of a devaluation, but by itself does not constitute an effective instrument to protect the poor against the effects of bad economic weather. On the other hand, sustained real exchange-rate appreciation cannot be a feasible solution for the medium-run either as it would undermine export competitiveness, impede badly needed export diversification and require unsustainable external debt accumulation.

Under dollarization, increased productivity will be a key factor in overcoming such trade-offs. Our static CGE model does not endogenize dynamic effects of trade on productivity growth. Scenario 12 therefore presents an exogenous productivity shock to export sectors. This induces positive effects on aggregate growth and exports (Table 9.8). Aggregate employment also rises, but with rigid nominal wages for unskilled wage earners (as assumed in the model) real earnings for this group fall, income inequality rises and poverty increases despite the productivity rise (Table 9.9).

9.8 Concluding remarks

Ecuador has experimented with drastic economic reforms during the 1990s. It liberalized trade along with many other parts of the economy and three times switched exchange-rate regime to end up with a fully dollarized economy. The economy has gone through turmoil as a result of a mixture of adverse external shocks, structural economic weaknesses, policy mistakes and political upheavals. Assessing the impact of specific shocks and policy reforms in this context is therefore difficult. Using decomposition methods to evaluate the importance of shocks and output growth determinants, we find that Ecuador remains mostly vulnerable to terms-of-trade shocks and export growth is key to understanding overall output growth. Ecuador's reforms have not helped the country to cut loose of its primary-export commodity dependence and new major investment in a second oil pipeline will only increase such dependence for the coming decades at the expense of future generations by accelerating the depletion of the natural resource base.

To isolate the effects of trade reforms on export growth, employment and poverty, we use a static CGE model for Ecuador. We find that import liberalization has yielded positive welfare gains. The 'macrosimulations' of the CGE model suggest that further trade opening and trade integration within the FTAA would generate mild positive growth and employment effects. However, this will come at the cost of rising labour income differentials. The main winners in terms of labour earnings are skilled workers in formal, traded goods sectors and the losers are the unskilled workers. The WTO scenario for Ecuador would exacerbate this effect on inequality. To assess the impact on poverty and inequality at the household level, information is needed as to how individual workers are expected to move. The microsimulations procedure resolves this. The results show that trade liberalization in Ecuador helps to reduce poverty on account of a positive aggregate employment effect, but that at the end of the day it is poverty-enhancing after considering the rising labour income inequality. Efficiency gains in export sectors (as simulated through an exogenous productivity shock) only seem to exacerbate the trade-off between aggregate growth effects and poverty reduction, as income inequality increases even further.

During periods of macroeconomic stabilization and real exchange-rate appreciation (1992–5 and since dollarization) real wages could increase and poverty decline. However, such short-run policies compromise export competitiveness and diversification and exacerbates the country's external debt overhang. Enhanced export earnings from increased oil production after completion of the second oil pipeline will be managed in a stabilization fund under the new Fiscal Responsibility Law. Our analysis of the growth and poverty effects of trade opening would suggest much of this should go into investment to support productivity growth and, above all, education to meet demands for skilled labour. The need for sustained access to foreign capital forces the government to prioritize repayment of existing external debt obligations, likely leaving too little for overdue investment in physical and social infrastructure. This will then continue to jeopardize the need for all Ecuadorians to be able to reap the benefits from trade.

Appendix A9

Table A9.1   Ecuador CGE: main elasticity values

Production and trade elasticities	Factor substitution CES ρ_i	Import demand Armington σ_{qi}	Export supply CET σ_{ti}
Bananas, cocoa, coffee	0.60		0.4
Cut flowers	0.80	0.8	0.8
Shrimp production and fishing	0.80	1.2	1.5
Other agriculture and livestock	0.80	0.9	0.6
Oil and mining	0.20	0.8	
Electricity, gas and water	0.90	0.2	0.2
Manufactures: food processing	0.90	0.9	0.9
Manufactures: non-food processing	0.60	0.8	0.6
Construction	0.80		
Commerce	0.80		1.0
Hotels and restaurants	0.90		
Transport and communications	0.90	0.8	1.0
Financial and enterprise services	0.95	1.5	1.5
Government services	0.20		
Social services (education and health)	0.20		
Other social and personal services	0.95	1.5	1.0
Domestic services	0.20		

Consumption demand elasticities (LES)	Urban households[1]			Rural households[2]	
	High education	Medium education level	Low education	Agriculture	Non-agriculture
Bananas, cocoa, coffee	0.81	0.83	0.88	0.87	0.84
Cut flowers	1.20	1.20	1.20	1.50	1.50
Shrimp production and fishing	0.81	0.83	0.88	0.87	0.84
Other agriculture and livestock	0.71	0.73	0.77	0.87	0.84
Oil and mining	0.72	0.74	0.78	1.02	0.98
Electricity, gas and water	0.72	0.74	0.78	1.02	0.98
Manufactures: food processing	0.66	0.74	0.78	0.85	0.81
Manufactures: non-food processing	1.12	1.15	1.22	1.27	1.22
Construction					
Commerce	0.72	0.74	0.78	1.02	0.98
Hotels and restaurants	0.72	0.74	0.78	1.02	0.98

(Continued)

Table A9.1 *(Continued)*

Consumption demand elasticities (LES)	Urban households[1]			Rural households[2]	
	High education	Medium education level	Low education	Agriculture	Non-agriculture
Transport and communications	0.72	0.74	0.78	1.02	0.98
Financial and enterprise services	1.13	1.17	1.23	1.11	1.07
Government services	1.01	1.00	0.99	1.00	1.00
Social services (education and health)	1.13	1.17	1.23	1.11	1.07
Other social and personal services	1.13	1.17	1.23	1.11	1.07
Domestic services	1.13	1.17	1.23	1.11	1.07
Frisch parameter	−2	−3	−4	−4	−2

Source: Vos and León (2003)

Notes
1 Urban households are classified by educational level of the head of the household
2 Rural households are classified by the main sector of employment of the head of the household

Notes

1 See for comparative analyses, e.g. IDB (1995) and Rodrik (1999).
2 Rodrik (1999) and Lustig (1999).
3 See Morley and Vos (Chapter 2) for an analysis of such trends during the 1980s and 1990s for the rest of Latin America and the Caribbean.
4 The conversion rate was fixed at 25,000 *sucres* per dollar, i.e. at about the highest point of the nominal exchange rate during the days of high uncertainty and turmoil preceding the announcement of dollarization. There was a fear that insufficient (cash) dollars was available to convert the entire stock of national currency and coins. Likely this was a misperception and a much lower conversion rate (say, at 18,000 per dollar) would have been sufficient (Vos, 2000) and could have avoided the initial inflationary impact as well as the severe erosion of financial asset values redistributing wealth from deposit holders to the banks.
5 The trend is similar for the bilateral real exchange rates for all Ecuador's trading partners.
6 In Ecuador the survey is known as the *Encuesta de Condiciones de Vida* (ECV) and was conducted by the national statistical office (INEC).
7 These scenarios were run at IFPRI in Washington and we are grateful to Eugenio Diaz-Bonilla and Sherman Robinson for sharing the detailed results. See Hertel and Tsigas (1997) for a discussion of the GTAP model.
8 This may not hold for any economy. A recent CGE study for Mexico showed, for instance, that the WTO scenario would be much less favourable as the cut in export subsidies would adversely hit Mexico's agricultural sector as well as its *maquila* sector (Morley and Díaz-Bonilla, 2003).

References

Almeida dos Reis, J.G. and R. Paes de Barros (1991) 'Wage inequality and the distribution of education: a study of the evolution of regional differences in inequality in metropolitan Brazil', *Journal of Development Economics*, 34: 117–43.

Bourguignon, F., M. Fournier and M. Gurgand (2001) 'Development with stable income distribution: Taiwan, 1979–1994', *The Review of Income and Wealth*, 47(2): 1–25.

Calvo, G. (1999) 'On dollarization', University of Maryland (mimeo), www.bsos.umd.edu/econ/ciecalvo.htm

De Janvry, A. and E. Sadoulet (2001) 'Has aggregate income growth been effective in reducing poverty and inequality in Latin America?', in: Nora Lustig (ed.) *Shielding the Poor*, Washington, DC: Brookings Institution and Inter-American Development Bank.

Dervis, K., J. de Melo and S. Robinson (1982) *General Equilibrium Models for Development Policy*, Cambridge: Cambridge University Press.

Frenkel, R. and M. González Rozada (2000) 'Liberalización del balance de pagos. Efectos sobre el crecimiento, el empleo y los ingresos en Argentina – Segunda parte', Buenos Aires: CEDES (mimeo).

Ganuza, E., R. Paes de Barros and R. Vos (2002) 'Labour market adjustment, poverty and inequality during liberalisation', in: R. Vos, L. Taylor and R. Paes de Barros (eds) *Economic Liberalisation, Distribution and Poverty: Latin America in the 1990s*, Cheltenham: Edward Elgar.

Hertel, T. W. and M. E. Tsigas (1997) 'Structure of GTAP', in: T. W. Hertel (ed.) *Global Trade Analysis: Modeling and Applications*, Cambridge: Cambridge University Press.

IDB (1995) *Economic and Social Progress in Latin America: Overcoming Volatility*, Washington, DC: Johns Hopkins University Press (for Inter-American Development Bank).

Izurieta, A. (2000) *Crowding-out or Baling-out? Fiscal Deficits and Private Wealth in Ecuador, 1971–99*, PhD thesis, The Hague: Institute of Social Studies.

León, M. and R. Vos (2000) *Pobreza Urbana en el Ecuador, 1988–98: Mitos y Realidades*, Quito: Abya-Yala Publishers.

Löfgren, H., R. Lee and S. Robinson (2001) 'A standard computable general equilibrium (CGE) model in GAMS', TMD Discussion Paper No. 75, Trade and Macroeconomics Division, International Food Policy Research Institute, Washington, DC: IFPRI.

Lustig, Nora (1999) 'Crisis and the poor. Socially responsible economics', Poverty and Inequality Advisory Unit, Washington, DC: Inter-American Development Bank.

Morley, S. and C. Díaz-Bonilla (2003) 'Do the poor benefit from increased openness? The case of Mexico', Paper presented at UNDP workshop *Export-Led Growth, Poverty and Inequality in Latin America and the Caribbean*, Buenos Aires (January; mimeo).

Morley, S. and R. Vos (2003) 'Bad luck or wrong policies? External shocks, domestic adjustment and the growth slowdown in Latin America', The Hague and Washington, DC: Institute of Social Studies and IPRI (mimeo).

Paes de Barros, R. (1999) 'Evaluando el impacto de cambios en la estructura salarial y del empleo sobre la distribución de renta', Rio de Janeiro: IPEA (mimeo).

Paes de Barros, R. and Ph. Leite (1998) 'O Impacto da Liberalizaçao sobre Distribuiçao de Renda no Brasil', Rio de Janeiro: IPEA (mimeo).

Rodrik, Dani (1999) 'Why is there so much economic insecurity in Latin America?', Harvard University (mimeo).

Round, J. I. (2003) 'Constructing SAMs for development policy analysis: lessons learned and challenges ahead', in: Rob Vos (ed.) *Economic Systems Research: Special Issue on Accounting for Poverty and Income Distribution Analysis*, Vol. 15(2), pp. 161–84.

Vos, R. (1989) 'Ecuador: windfall gains, unbalanced growth and stabilization', in: E. V. K. FitzGerald and R. Vos (eds) *Financing Economic Development. A Structural Approach to Monetary Policy*, Aldershot: Gower.

Vos, R. (2000) *Development and the Colour of Money. Should Developing Countries Have Their Own Currency?*, The Hague: Institute of Social Studies.

Vos, R. (2002) 'Ecuador: economic liberalization, adjustment and poverty, 1988–99', in: R. Vos, L. Taylor and R. Paes de Barros (eds) *Economic Liberalisation, Distribution and Poverty: Latin America in the 1990s*, Cheltenham: Edward Elgar.

Vos, R. and N. de Jong (2001) 'Rising inequality during economic liberalisation and crisis: macro or micro causes in Ecuador's case?', ISS Working Paper No. 326, The Hague: Institute of Social Studies.

Vos, R. and M. León (2003) 'Dolarización, Dinámica de Exportaciones y Equidad. Cómo Compatiblizarlas en el Caso de Ecuador?', Estudios e Informes del SIISE No. 5, Quito: STFS.

Vos, R., M. León, M. Carvajal, J. Alarcon, N de Jong, J. van Heemst and collaborators (2002a) *Matriz de Contabilidad Social para el Ecuador, 1993*, Quito: ISS-INEC-SIISE.

Vos, R., L. Taylor and R. Paes de Barros (eds) (2002b) *Economic Liberalisation, Distribution and Poverty: Latin America in the 1990s*, Cheltenham: Edward Elgar.

Vos, Rob, Margarita Velasco and Edgar de Labastida (2000) 'Los efectos económicos y sociales de El Niño, 1997–98,' in: Enrico Gasparri, Carlo Tassara, and Margarita Velasco (eds) *El Fenómeno de El Niño en el Ecuador, 1997–99*, Quito: Ediciones Abya-Yala, pp. 27–121.

Wood, A. (1997) 'Openness and wage inequality in developing countries: the Latin American challenge to East Asian conventional wisdom', *The World Bank Economic Review* 11(1): 33–57.

10 Mexico – do the poor benefit from increased openness?

Samuel A. Morley and Carolina Díaz-Bonilla

Abstract

In the last 15 years Mexico has shifted to an outward-looking, export-oriented growth strategy. The strategy seems to have been more successful in Mexico than in almost any other country in the region. Exports have tripled since 1990 and the growth in per capita income since 1995 is among the highest in Latin America. The purpose of this chapter is to estimate the distributional, employment and poverty implications of this change in growth strategy. After reviewing the very turbulent macroeconomic environment in Mexico since 1980, we develop a CGE-microsimulation model and use it to simulate the impact of Mexico's trade liberalization and increased openness on output, employment, poverty and the distribution of income. We find that increased openness, whether measured by lower tariffs, capital inflows or an increase in the demand for exports, is expansionary. Output and employment both increase and poverty declines, but there is at the same time a slight increase in inequality and extreme poverty. This is partly because the new growth strategy has been skill-intensive, causing a widening of wage inequality between skilled and unskilled labour in the urban sector and between agriculture workers and everyone else. These favourable effects of increased openness on poverty at the national level hide very different effects for the urban and rural sector. Increasing export demand or capital inflows hurt agricultural workers because they lead to both an appreciation of the exchange rate and a movement of capital out of agriculture and a contraction of agricultural wages and output. Overall, poverty falls but both rural poverty and extreme poverty increase because most extreme poverty is found in rural families.

These poverty results are very different from the observed rise in poverty since 1984. Our results say that trade reform is not the reason for rising poverty. The counterfactual simulations enable us to separate the effects of trade reforms from all other factors that were changing at the same time. By themselves the reforms helped the poor (while slightly increasing inequality). But these positive effects were overshadowed by the spike in inflation and subsequent stabilization in the mid-1980s and by the financial crisis and recession in 1995–6.

10.1 Introduction

In the last 15 years Mexico has made a clear and important change of development strategy by implementing a wide range of economic reforms. Since 1985, it has reduced its average tariff from 34 to 14 per cent, reduced barriers to foreign investment, dismantled most price subsidies, privatized a wide range of state enterprises and joined NAFTA. The neoliberal model, which these reforms were intended to implement, envisioned an increase in economic growth led by exports. Mexico appears to be one of the shining success stories of this approach. Exports have tripled since 1990 and the export ratio has risen from less than 15 per cent in the late 1980s to 35 per cent in 1999. Growth overall was not particularly impressive until quite recently, and was interrupted by a severe crisis in 1995. But, thanks in part to NAFTA, per capita income has grown by 4 per cent per year from 1995 through 2000, among the highest growth rates in Latin America.

All of this makes Mexico an important case study for anyone interested in examining the effectiveness of the export-led growth strategy or the impact of that strategy on poverty and the distribution of income. The purpose of this chapter is to address the question of the distributional, employment and poverty implications of Mexico's shift to greater openness. Were the new leading sectors relatively skill-intensive and did they therefore make the distribution more unequal? Did they raise or lower employment and poverty? We use a small CGE model to simulate the effect of increased openness on disaggregated goods and factor markets and a microsimulation model to show the effect of the policy changes on poverty and distribution. Unfortunately, our results with respect to the distribution must be regarded as tentative because of the serious problem of underreporting of profits in the survey of Mexico's statistical office (INEGI 2000).

10.2 Macroeconomic overview: 1980–99

Between the end of the Second World War and the explosion of the first debt crisis in 1982, Mexico was one of the fastest growing countries in the world. Growth rates were high and relatively stable. GDP per capita almost tripled between 1950 and 1982, and there were only 3 years during that entire 32-year period in which there was a decline in per capita income. The performance in the last 20 years has been markedly inferior. Overall, the growth rate since 1980 has been far lower than it was earlier. In fact, per capita income did not get back to its 1981 level until 1998 (see Figures 10.1 and 10.2). Even if we exclude the 1980s, which reflect the aftermath of the 1982 debt crisis, and look just at the 1990s, the growth rate is lower. The growth comparison is still unfavourable even if we start in 1995 after NAFTA. Export-led growth has certainly improved Mexico's performance relative to the 1980s but it has yet to match the growth rates reached between 1950 and 1980.

Not only is the overall growth rate lower, it is also far less stable. There have been three severe recessions since 1980: the debt crisis of 1982–3, the oil shock of 1986 and the Tequila Crisis in 1995. The declines in per capita income in each

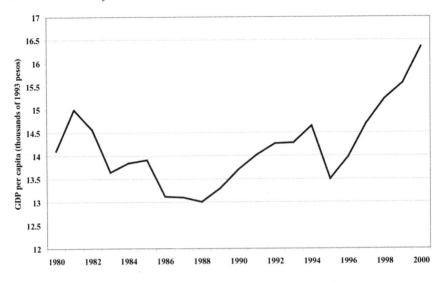

Figure 10.1   Mexico: real GDP per capita (thousands of 1993 pesos).

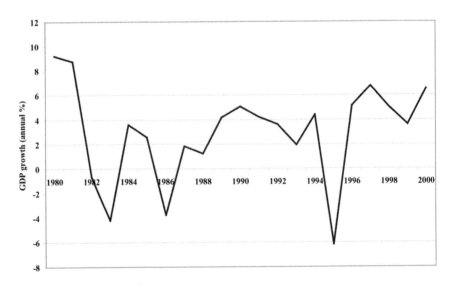

Figure 10.2   Mexico: GDP growth (annual per cent).

of the three were greater than anything experienced in the comparatively mild recessions of 1953, 1959 and 1977. (Per capita income fell 18 per cent in 1982–3, 7 per cent in 1986 and 6 per cent in 1995.)

   The recessions were more severe than they had been earlier and the recoveries from those recessions were weaker. As the reader can see in Figure 10.2, only once

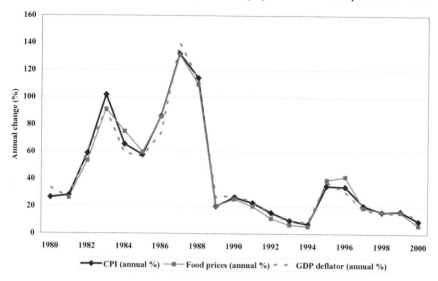

Figure 10.3 Inflation in Mexico, 1980–99.

did the growth rate of GDP exceed 5 per cent in either the 2-year recovery during 1984–5 or the longer recovery between 1987 and 1994. It is only in the last several years that Mexico has approached the rapid growth rates observed in the 1950s, 1960s and 1970s.

Stabilization and inflation

There are two other macroeconomic features of the period after 1980 that should be noted before going into our decomposition analysis. The first is the successful fight against inflation in the late 1980s and the second, linked to the inflation battle, is the appreciation of the real exchange rate. Figure 10.3 shows the inflation part of the story.

Most of the 1980s were dominated by the repercussions of three negative shocks: the debt crisis that exploded in 1982, a severe earthquake in 1985 and the drastic decline in oil prices in 1986. All of these unfavourable events put severe pressure on the balance of payments and internal price stability. Up to 1986, the government response to the heavy debt burden and deteriorating external markets for oil was a policy of aggressive devaluations and restrictive monetary policy. At the same time the government was forced by rising government deficits to reduce price controls and dismantle an expensive system of price subsidies in government enterprises. The net result of all of these measures was a serious increase in the inflation rate, which rose from 25 per cent in 1980 to over 120 per cent in 1987.

By 1987, thanks to a solution to the external debt problem (Brady bonds and debt–equity swaps) and better export markets, the economy began to recover. But the recovery was not particularly vigorous. Investment stayed below 15 per cent of GDP, and private consumption remained weak (through 1989), reflecting the severe contraction in real wages that had taken place during the preceding inflation. Government expenditure as a fraction of GDP fell sharply over the remainder of the decade as it struggled to reduce its deficit and hold on to the gains that had been made in the fight against inflation. Rising imports contributed to the overall weakness of the recovery. Responding to a combination of recovery of the economy, appreciation of the exchange rate and significant reductions in tariffs and non-tariff import restrictions, imports doubled between 1986 and 1996, more than offsetting the significant rise in export earnings.

The other feature of the inflation control programme was a very sharp appreciation of the real exchange after 1986. This was partly the result of a policy decision to stabilize key prices under the control of the government in order to bring down inflation. In an open economy inflation is highly correlated with the exchange rate. Thus, not devaluing should, in theory at least, reduce the inflation rate. At the same time, it was thought that maintaining a fixed exchange rate would bolster the confidence of foreign investors, who did in fact dramatically increase their investment in Mexico after 1989. But, of course, inflation did not stop but only fell to a much lower level. The result of all this was an appreciation of the real exchange rate and increasing current account deficits financed by the capital inflows. These imports supplied a good deal of the increase in aggregate demand in a non-inflationary way, but they also cut into the potential markets for Mexican production. In effect, using the exchange rate as an anchor helped in the battle against inflation, but the cost was the penalty it imposed on domestic production.

Labour market outcomes

Real wages were a casualty of the inflation and the struggle to control it. (See Figure 10.4.) Real wages typically fall during episodes of rapid inflation because of the time lag between adjustments for past losses of purchasing power. This is true even when there is no explicit attempt to use the control over wages to control inflation. These tendencies are invariably exacerbated by recession, as they were in Mexico in 1983 and 1986. By 1987 the minimum wage had fallen over 40 per cent and the average wage over 25 per cent, relative to their 1980 levels. Poverty has also risen sharply in two periods since 1984. Both appear to be related to the macroeconomic crisis, the first the spike in inflation and subsequent stabilization in the mid-1980s and the second the financial and balance of payments crisis in 1995.

As we have seen, inflation control was an important part of the policy package implemented by the Salinas Government after 1988. One component of the programme in addition to fiscal retrenchment is relevant to us here and that is the real wage. The government permitted the minimum wage to continue to decline in real terms, while average wages began to recover along with the economy (see Figure 10.4). This feature of the Mexican labour market will be important to bear in mind when we examine changes in the distribution of income and earnings in a later

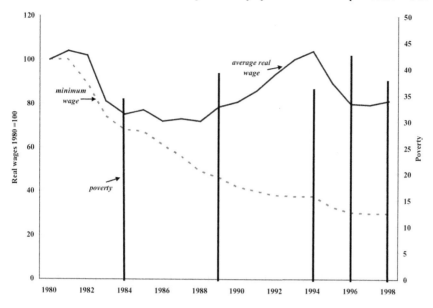

Figure 10.4 Mexico: real wages and poverty, 1980–98. [Wage data are from Ros and Bouillon (2001) and poverty data from CEPAL (1998).]

section of this chapter since it is likely to imply a regressive widening of wage differentials.

10.3 Opening the Mexican economy

It is just in the last 5 years that Mexican export growth has begun to reflect the hopes of those who implemented trade reform. As can be seen in Figures 10.5 and 10.6, up to the beginning of NAFTA in 1994, increased openness meant only a rising import share. Exports as a share of GDP were lower in 1994 than they had been 10 years earlier, and this was due mainly to the reduction in the manufacturing sector. Imports are another story. Their share rises steadily after 1986, particularly in manufacturing. This reflects both the reduction in tariff rates that began in 1986 and a steady appreciation of the real exchange rate. What Mexico had before NAFTA was the same pattern observed in many other countries – big tariff reductions, capital inflows, real exchange rate appreciation, a flood of imports and rising deficits in the trade account. Neither exports nor the economy grew very rapidly under this mix of policies.

All that changed dramatically with NAFTA. Total exports rose from US$51 billion in 1993 to $166 billion in 2000. Part, but only part, of that was *maquila*.[1] Non-*maquila* exports grew from $30 billion to $86 billion and 80 per cent of that came from manufactured exports. Imports went up too, after a decline during the recession

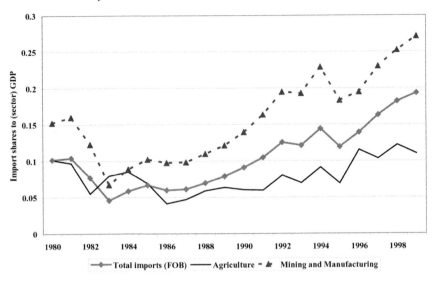

Figure 10.5   Mexico: imports/GDP ratio by sector (excluding *maquila*).

in 1995. But this time, unlike the late 1980s, the growth in imports was matched by rising exports. Thanks to NAFTA and access to the rapidly growing US market in the 1990s, increased openness meant not just the replacement of domestic industry by imports, but also a switch in the structure of production towards the internationally competitive parts of the economy.

We have shown non-*maquila* exports and imports in Figures 10.5 and 10.6 because of the large share of imported inputs that are embedded in *maquila* exports. The gross value of *maquila* exports comprised US$80 billion or almost half of the Mexican exports in 2000. But US$62 billion of that amount represented imported inputs. If one compares the value added in *maquila* plus the domestically supplied intermediate goods to total exports (which are non-*maquila* exports plus the value added in *maquila*) one gets a better picture of the contribution of this sector to export growth. We show that calculation in Figure 10.7 for 1990–2000. *Maquila* value added increased from just under US$4 billion in 1990 to US$18 billion in 2000 and the net contribution of *maquila* to adjusted exports rose from 9.5 to 13.6 per cent. This is a significant share, but it is far lower than what appears in the unadjusted data. The point is that the success of Mexico in the post-NAFTA period is far from being a *maquila* story. More than 85 per cent of the growth in the export sector was elsewhere.

10.4 A decomposition analysis of the sources of growth since 1980

We turn now to a closer look at the determinants of the changes in the level of output in Mexico since 1980. We start with a purely mechanical decomposition

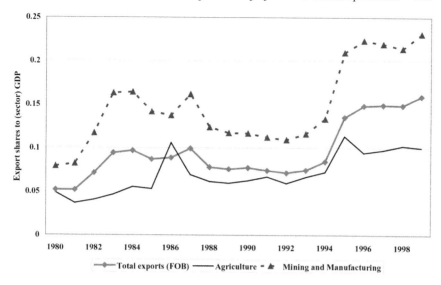

Figure 10.6 Mexico: exports/GDP ratio by sector (excluding *maquila*).

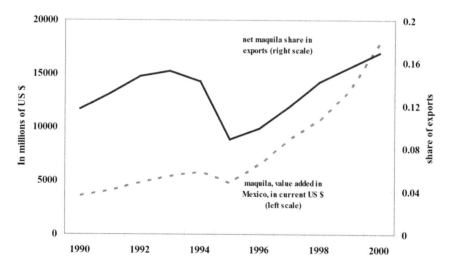

Figure 10.7 Mexico: net *maquila* exports.

of aggregate demand into its components and a simple Keynesian model of the determinants of aggregate demand. The model assumes that exports, investment and government expenditure are exogenous, while government receipts, household consumption and imports are simple linear functions of aggregate income.

Table 10.1 Contributions to growth in Mexico

	1980–3	1984–5	1986	1987–94	1995	1996–9
Investment	−6.491	1.209	−2.359	0.996	−2.490	0.952
Saving	−0.708	0.166	0.798	0.094	−1.066	−0.204
Government expenditure	0.956	0.331	0.107	0.173	−0.046	0.047
Taxes less transfers	−0.252	−0.091	−0.061	0.209	0.248	0.086
Exports	2.746	0.054	0.328	0.752	1.676	1.279
Imports	5.426	−0.650	0.223	−1.185	0.679	−1.095
Total	*1.678*	*1.019*	*−0.963*	*1.038*	*−0.998*	*1.065*
Actual growth (per annum) (%)	*1.2*	*3.2*	*−3.8*	*3.7*	*−6.2*	*5.5*

Note: In recession years a positive entry indicates an increase in aggregate demand

Several clear and important patterns emerge from the growth disaggregation. The first is the key and procyclical role of investment. It is far and away the most important determinant of the economic cycle in Mexico, particularly in the three recession periods, 1980–3, 1986 and 1995. (In the first period, the recession actually occurred in 1982 and 1983.) More than anything else, those three recessions were caused by a collapse of investment and the subsequent recoveries were led by investment (and also by exports for the recovery of the last recession). Of course, this begs the question of what caused those big fluctuations in investment. The model considers investment to be exogenous, but it is undoubtedly linked to trade policy, foreign investment and investor confidence, and other factors.

Fiscal policy was strongly countercyclical in the early 1980s, but has been weakly procyclical thereafter. Government expenditure was highly expansionary in the downturn of 1980–3 and weakly expansionary in the subsequent recovery of 1984–5. But then, the pattern changed. In the sharp recessions of 1986 and 1995, government spending was still expansionary, but it was a good deal less expansionary than it was in any of the previous or subsequent periods of recovery and growth. Government expenditures tended to rise most rapidly when the economy itself was expanding, and then rise much less or even contract when the economy was contracting. To some extent, countercyclical tax receipts offset this pattern on the expenditure side.[2] They tended to rise in recovery and decline in recession.

Consider now the role of exports and imports shown in the table. First, both are strongly countercyclical. Big reductions in imports helped cushion the impact of falling investment in all three recessions. And rising imports reduced upward pressure on demand during each expansion. Exports were also a big source of demand in each recession.

What seems surprising at first glance here is the relatively small role played by external trade in the three expansions, particularly the most recent one. Mexico has embarked on a new, export-oriented development model, based on a reduction of trade barriers and its NAFTA agreement with the United States and Canada. One would expect that this change would show up in a rising role for exports as a source of aggregate demand. And they do rise, moving from 5.4 per cent of total growth in 1984–5 to 128 per cent in 1996–9. But this was more than offset by rising imports during the 1980s and almost offset in the most recent period. The new development model has clearly made Mexico a more open economy, but external markets have not been a particularly important source of demand because the rising tide of imports has almost completely offset the significant increases in exports that were achieved.

Critics have charged that the new export-oriented development model and the dismantling of trade barriers was simply a pretext to increase the markets in developing countries for products from developed countries. The Mexican experience seems to validate this critical view. Exports increased by US$39 billion between 1996 and 1999, but imports increased by an even greater US$54 billion. But unless one takes a mercantilist view of the role of trade, this is roughly what one should expect. Indeed, if a country maintained current account balance during growth, imports ought to offset exports. The point of trade is not to increase aggregate demand, even though it opens up external markets. Rather, it is to permit countries to provide the commodities desired by their citizens more efficiently by specializing in the production of that subset of goods in which they have a comparative advantage and importing the rest.

This benign view of trade should be adjusted for economies operating below capacity output. In that situation imports do replace domestic production and reduce employment even if they are offset by exports. This distinction is relevant for Mexico. As we have seen, the growth of output in Mexico was quite slow for almost the entire period between 1980 and 1996. Throughout most of that period the economy was almost certainly operating below capacity output. To have imports more than offsetting the positive impetus to production from exports in the period between 1987 and 1994 must be one of the reasons why the overall growth rate during that expansion was so slow. During that period the combination of an appreciating exchange rate, falling tariffs, fewer import restrictions and rising capital inflows led to a rise in production-replacing imports. This was not simply a pattern of switching production over from inefficient import substitutes to more efficient exports.

Exchange rate appreciation must have been an important part of the explanation for this pattern. There was a significant appreciation between 1988 and 1995 when Mexico used an exchange rate anchor to help bring down the inflation rate. But Mexico would undoubtedly have grown more rapidly had it used the exchange rate not as an anchor to reduce inflation but rather to help keep the economy closer to its production frontier. That is exactly what President Zedillo did after the 1995 Tequila Crisis, and the result was higher growth in both exports and output. Imports grew too, but they did not completely offset exports as they had between 1987 and 1994. Nor did they prevent the economy from attaining the highest growth rates since 1981 and the lowest levels of unemployment.

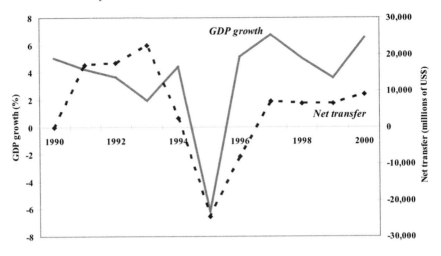

Figure 10.8 Net resource transfers and economic growth in Mexico.

Growth, investment and foreign capital

The preceding decomposition is not an entirely satisfactory way of understanding what is driving the growth process. For one thing, as mentioned above, it assumes that investment is exogenous. For another it ignores the impact of foreign capital. But in Mexico, even a casual examination of the historical record suggests that variations in capital flows are a big part of the story. Figure 10.8 charts growth and net resource transfers (NRTs) where the latter are defined as net capital inflows from the capital account less the net payment of interest and profts from the current account.

The collapse of foreign investment in the two debt crises in 1982–3 and 1995 is clearly an important contributing factor in those two recessions. Also, the surge in foreign investment after the resolution of the debt problem in 1990 and the liberalization of financial markets and the capital account transactions under Salinas must have contributed to recovery in the 1989–94 period.

There are a number of different ways by which capital inflows may affect the growth rate. The most direct is through its relationship to fixed investment. A good deal of foreign capital was linked directly to investment since it came as foreign direct investment expressly to build productive capacity in Mexico. Also, capital inflows permitted Mexico to run significant trade deficits and appreciate the exchange rate. This reduced the relative price of imported capital goods, which also would be a stimulus to domestic investment. Those same capital inflows helped finance rising government deficits and a boom in household consumption in the 1986–94 period, all of which were expansionary. But capital inflows are a two-edged sword. While the exchange rate appreciation they permitted may have had a positive effect on investment, they could have had a quite strong negative impact on tradable goods production in Mexico. As we showed in the previous section, this is exactly what happened in the slow expansion between 1990 and 1994. Capital flowed back into Mexico but a good deal of the expansionary effect was swamped or offset by a big increase in imports.

We ran some simple regressions to measure more formally the relationship between NRTs, investment and growth. As discussed above, our hypothesis is that growth is positively related to investment, which in turn is positively related to NRT. We found that both NRT and investment are positively related to growth. However because of the multicollinearity between the two, NRT is not significant in a simple regression of growth on the two variables. To control for the multi-collinearity, we reran the growth regression, substituting for *I/Y*, the residual of the regression of *I/Y* on NRT. Now, both *I/Y* and NRT have a highly significant positive impact on the growth rate. What this correction does is to assign to NRT both the direct influence it has on the growth rate and the indirect influence it has through its relationship to *I/Y*. The regression predicts that, other things being equal, a US$1 billion increase in NRTs will increase the growth rate by about 0.1 percentage point. A 1-percentage point increase in the investment rate would increase the growth rate by a much bigger 0.62 percentage point. Thus, the growth rate is sensitive to capital inflows, but variations in the investment rate have a far bigger quantitative impact.

10.5 A CGE model for Mexico

We have seen a very large increase in openness and export dependence in Mexico. What are the implications of this fundamental shift in production structure and growth strategy for poverty and distribution? This turns out to be a very difficult question to answer because we never can observe the Mexico we would have observed with some different growth strategy. Nor is time series econometrics of much help. Too many things happen at the same time to allow one to separate out the effect of export growth with any degree of confidence. An alternative approach is to build a model with two separate components: (1) a fairly simple general equilibrium model incorporating key behavioural relationships for producers, households, exporters, importers, investors and the government to determine the effect on factor prices and quantities of changes in internal or external conditions and (2) a household-based microsimulation model to trace how these changes in the factor markets affect the distribution of household income and levels of poverty. We now briefly describe these two components of the overall model.[3]

The CGE

The CGE model that we have developed for Mexico follows closely the so-called standard model developed at the International Food Policy Research Institute (IFPRI) (see Löfgren *et al.* 2001) and previously adapted for Mexico by Harris (2001).

We made three important modifications of the general CGE model for the Mexico case. We added an informal sector as an activity, a separate *maquila* activity and commodity (including a downward sloping export demand equation), and modified the labour market by including an upward sloping labour supply curve. The informal sector uses urban unskilled labour and domestic commodity inputs. Since we are unable to estimate with any confidence the amount of capital in the sector, we treat production as if it were a linear function of labour and domestically produced intermediate inputs. This implies that the sector is not integrated into the internal market for capital. On the commodity side, all informal output is sold domestically and there are no imported intermediate inputs.

Maquila is treated as an activity and a commodity. We have not separated it within the different subsectors of manufacturing. Its production function has the same form as those of the other sectors of manufacturing using both imported and nationally produced intermediates, as well as labour and capital. Where the treatment is different is in the commodity account. No *maquila* output is sold domestically; it is all exported. In addition, we assume that the sector faces a downward-sloping international or US demand curve for its output. Thus, we take US income as exogenous, and determine the output of *maquila* and its price simultaneously.

In the simulations reported here we have replaced the small-country assumption used in the export sectors in the general CGE with the assumption that Mexico faces downward sloping demand curves for its manufactured exports, most of which go to the United States. This is a more realistic portrayal of Mexico's export sectors, where the boom was mainly in manufacturing, and essentially non-*maquila*. This change will permit us to examine the effect of an increase in US demand for Mexican manufacturing outside the *maquila* sector. For comparability, we keep the same assumption in the other simulations shown in the results tables.

We assume that the supply of capital, land and skilled labour is fixed, and that in the medium-run simulations reported here these factors move across sectors to equate the factor wage.[4] The total supply of agricultural unskilled labour is fixed but the supply of unskilled labour to non-agricultural activities and the real wage for that labour are jointly determined by factor demand and an upward sloping supply curve for unskilled labour.

The social accounting matrix

The social accounting matrix (SAM) used in this chapter is based on the 1996 SAM for Mexico developed by Harris (1999). We have modified her SAM, aggregating across regions and agricultural activities and disaggregating *maquila* and informal sectors. The final SAM is disaggregated into four agriculture sectors, ten manufacturing sectors, *maquila* construction, informal and three service sectors. The labour force is divided into agricultural labour and urban labour, both disaggregated by gender. Within the urban labour force there are four kinds of labour, unskilled and skilled, male and female. Unskilled labour is defined as those with no more than high school education. We ran earnings regressions with dummy variables for different subsectors and were unable to reject the hypothesis that after controlling for personal characteristics there are no significant sectoral differences in average wages, except in the informal sector. Therefore, we assumed that average wages for urban unskilled labour are equal and fixed in real terms for all sectors other than the informal. The model solution determines the skill differential in the urban formal sector and the urban–rural wage differential for unskilled labour. The SAM has one type of capital, which is assumed to be fixed across sectors in the short-run and to be transferable between sectors in the medium-run simulations reported here. The informal sector, however, is treated as if it used no capital or, equivalently, used capital which is fixed and not transferable. The SAM also includes factor payments to land used exclusively in the four agricultural activities.

10.6 Policy experiments and simulation results

Policy experiments

Mexico has undergone a profound switch in its growth strategy, opening its domestic markets to imports and relying on export expansion to lead it to a higher and sustainable growth path. Exports plus imports as a share of GDP in Mexico have risen from 29 per cent in 1990 to 53 per cent in 1999. Increased openness was not limited to the current account. Mexico also became far more integrated into international capital markets by liberalizing capital account restrictions and enjoyed unprecedented access to foreign capital. The purpose of the simulations that we will report here is to address two basic questions. First, openness implies increased exposure to foreign capital shocks, changes in the exchange rate, terms of trade shocks and trade agreements such as the World Trade Organization (WTO) and Free Trade Area of the Americas (FTAA). What is the impact of increased openness on the wage structure, output and employment? Has it favoured skilled labour? Second, what has been the impact on poverty and income distribution? Has it impacted the rural and urban poor differently? In this section, we will report the results of simulations of several of these changes on sectoral output levels, factor supplies and relative factor prices. In the next sections of the chapter we will describe how we modelled the link between the factor markets and the distribution of household income, and how the changes from the CGE simulations affect poverty and distribution.

Maquila: One of the really dramatic stories of the 1990s is the expansion of Mexican *maquila* exports to the United States after the NAFTA agreement came into effect late in 1994. *Maquila* exports doubled between 1996 and 2000, and even though there was a big increase in *maquila*-related imports at the same time, value added still rose by over 75 per cent. Here, we simulate the impact of the observed increase of 110 per cent in *maquila* production between 1996 and 2000. This simulation is shown in the tables as MAQINCR.

Increased demand for Mexican exports: This experiment is intended to reflect the general dependence of manufacturing in Mexico on export demand from the United States. Remember that all manufacturing sectors are assumed to face a downward sloping demand curve for exports. In this experiment we assume that the external demand curves for all manufacturing exports rise by 50 per cent. We assume that this increase is primarily due to growth in the United States. This experiment is labelled MAQINCR2 in the results tables.

Tariffs: Tariffs were increased and decreased by 50 per cent for each sector from the level observed in 1996 (TARINCR and TARDECR).

Export subsidies: In this simulation we reduced export taxes (or increased the subsidy to exports) by 10 per cent across all exporting sectors (EXPSUBS).

Capital inflow shocks: One of the implications of increased integration into world capital and goods markets is increased sensitivity to foreign capital shocks. We did two simulations, first an increase in foreign capital inflows equal to 10 per cent of the value of exports (FSAVINCR) and second, a 10 per cent devaluation (DEVAL). Note that the devaluation is equivalent to a reduction in foreign saving and should be thought of as forced by a reduction in foreign capital.

Trade agreements: These simulations examine the effect on Mexico of the forecast change in world prices and import tariff levels that result from the WTO and FTAA agreements. The WTO scenario considers abolishing all import tariffs (OMC). Under the FTAA scenario, average import tariffs are reduced but not abolished (ALCA).

Terms of trade shocks: Here, we examine the effect of a 10 per cent rise in all Mexican import prices (PWMINCR) and a 10 per cent increase in the price of Mexico's agricultural exports (PWEINCR).

Results of the simulations

The results of the simulations are summarized in Tables 10.2–10.4. All the tables tell roughly the same story. Increased openness, whether expressed by an increase in the demand for Mexican exports of *maquila* or of all manufactured goods, capital inflows or a reduction in tariffs, all cause an increase in total output and employment, an appreciation of the exchange rate and a shift in the structure of production away from agriculture and towards non-traded goods. There is also a rise in two key wage differentials – that between urban and rural unskilled workers and the urban skill differential, measured here as the ratio of workers with university degrees to those with high school education or less. Lowering tariffs is also expansionary, but its sectoral impact is different because with foreign saving assumed to be constant, lower tariffs cause a devaluation and a slight rise in exports.

Sectorally, increasing the demand for *maquila* or for all exports of manufactures reduces the output and the exports of both agriculture and manufactures other than *maquila*. This may seem surprising. The reason is that we are forcing the economy to increase the output of *maquila*. To do that the other non-agricultural sectors have to release skilled labour and capital, and agriculture has to release capital. To make that happen there is a significant appreciation of the exchange rate (7.9 per cent for the across the board increase in the demand for exports and 2.8 per cent if the increase is limited to the *maquila* sector). In effect, the economy responds to an

Table 10.2 Mexico: CGE model simulations – results for total and sectoral GDP

		Base	MAQINCR	MAQINCR2	FSAVINCR	TARINCR	ALCA	OMC	PWMINCR	TARDECR	DEVAL	EXPSUBS	PWEINCR
Real GDP from value added		2287.1	2294.5	2307.6	2299.8	2285.1	2288.0	2281.4	2253.8	2289.1	2260.4	2307.2	2287.9
	(% Change)		0.3	0.9	0.6	−0.1	0.0	−0.2	−1.5	0.1	−1.2	0.9	0.0
Agriculture	Real GDP	150.2	149.2	146.1	147.1	150.1	150.7	146.2	151.4	150.3	157.0	152.4	156.7
	(% Change)		−0.7	−2.7	−2.0	0.0	0.4	−2.7	0.8	0.0	4.6	1.5	4.4
Manufacturing	Real GDP	543.8	527.9	533.2	530.9	542.6	543.6	545.9	549.3	545.0	575.0	557.6	538.3
	(% Change)		−2.9	−2.0	−2.4	−0.2	0.0	0.4	1.0	0.2	5.7	2.5	−1.0
Services	Real GDP	1288.4	1282.4	1297.2	1312.8	1287.5	1288.4	1286.7	1264.5	1289.3	1235.2	1298.6	1287.6
	(% Change)		−0.5	0.7	1.9	−0.1	0.0	−0.1	−1.9	0.1	−4.1	0.8	−0.1
Maquila sector	Real GDP	28.5	57.4	52.5	26.5	28.5	29.1	26.9	15.9	28.5	32.1	24.6	28.2
	(% Change)		101.3	84.3	−7.0	0.0	2.0	−5.5	−44.1	0.0	12.8	−13.6	−1.1
Informal sector	Real GDP	276.2	277.7	278.6	282.5	276.4	276.2	275.7	272.7	276.0	261.0	274.0	277.0
	(% Change)		0.5	0.9	2.3	0.1	0.0	−0.2	−1.3	−0.1	−5.5	−0.8	0.3

Table 10.3 Mexico: CGE model simulations – changes in foreign sector

	Base	MAQINCR	MAQINCR2	FSAVINCR	TARINCR	ALCA	OMC	PWMINCR	TARDECR	DEVAL	EXPSUBS	PWEINCR
Real exchange Rate	1.000	0.972	0.921	0.950	0.999	1.002	0.982	1.033	1.002	1.100	0.915	0.989
(% Change)		-2.82	-7.90	-5.05	-0.15	0.22	-1.78	3.27	0.15	10.00	-8.50	-1.06
Total Exports	998.83	1228.75	1179.18	896.59	994.69	998.20	1004.90	979.94	917.42	1119.54	1003.04	1219.33
(% Change)		23.02	18.06	-10.24	-0.42	-0.06	0.61	-1.89	-8.15	12.08	0.42	22.07
Total Imports	967.96	1206.67	1195.20	977.42	964.16	967.66	974.11	949.15	812.31	1076.23	971.81	955.94
(% Change)		24.66	23.48	0.98	-0.39	-0.03	0.64	-1.94	-16.08	11.18	0.40	-1.24

Table 10.4 Mexico: CGE model simulations – changes in wage differentials

	Base	MAQINCR	MAQINCR2	FSAVINCR	TARINCR	ALCA	OMC	PWMINCR	TARDECR	DEVAL	EXPSUBS	PWEINCR
Average wages of urban to rural												
Males	5.40	5.68	6.28	5.87	5.40	5.34	5.27	4.98	5.40	4.56	5.36	4.61
(% Change)		5.29	16.42	8.66	-0.03	-1.16	-2.44	-7.80	0.02	-15.55	-0.75	-14.58
Females	17.24	18.19	20.42	19.22	17.25	16.99	17.44	15.88	17.22	13.75	16.68	14.22
(% Change)		5.51	18.48	11.47	0.09	-1.42	1.18	-7.88	-0.10	-20.23	-3.26	-17.54
Average wages of skilled to unskilled												
Males	3.61	3.65	3.67	3.62	3.60	3.61	3.60	3.54	3.61	3.61	3.65	3.60
(% Change)		1.11	1.68	0.21	-0.13	0.04	-0.12	-1.87	0.13	-0.08	1.12	-0.16
Females	3.22	3.22	3.26	3.27	3.21	3.22	3.21	3.14	3.22	3.12	3.26	3.21
(% Change)		0.13	1.34	1.49	-0.13	0.03	-0.23	-2.39	0.13	-2.96	1.34	-0.07

increase in export demand by keeping exports more or less constant and transferring factors to the non-traded goods sector. Thus, increasing export demand does not necessarily translate into export-led growth, if one holds foreign savings constant. It translates into exchange rate appreciation instead. All of this is regressive in the sense that wage differentials move against unskilled and agricultural labour. One should not conclude from this that export-led growth or the export sectors in general are skill-intensive. Other than *maquila*, both the output and the exports of all the other traded goods sectors fall due to the rise in imports. This tells us that traded goods production overall is intensive in the use of unskilled labour. It is non-traded goods and *maquila* that are skill-intensive.

Another important point that is illustrated in these simulations is that the increase in openness is expansionary. In every case aggregate output increases in response to rising export demand, falling tariffs, rising export share and inflows of foreign capital. Conversely, devaluation is contractionary. That is because each of these changes increases the demand for unskilled labour, part of which is satisfied by an increase in the participation rate and an increase in the supply of unskilled labour. Most of the increase in output comes from this increase in the supply of unskilled labour, not the reallocation of factors between sectors. But all of this occurs at the same time that the skill differential and the urban–rural differential for unskilled labour both increase. These increases in the two differentials certainly increase earnings inequality and they probably increase the inequality of the distribution of household income as well. But at the same time, the increase in the total number of jobs for the unskilled will undoubtedly increase the amount of income going to those at the bottom of the income pyramid, which will probably reduce the poverty rate. In other words, the increase in openness may well increase inequality and reduce poverty at the same time.

Terms of trade shocks, represented here by a 10 per cent increase in the prices of agricultural exports in PWEINCR or of the price of all imports in PWMINCR, have the expected effects. The rise of world import prices causes a 1.5 per cent reduction in GDP, a 3 per cent devaluation and a very sharp reduction in the quantity of imports, particularly in *maquila*. But skill differentials move in favour of rural workers and the unskilled. The export price shock increases GDP by 0.03 per cent, causes a 1.1 per cent appreciation of the real exchange rate and small changes in total exports and imports. Rural workers and the unskilled are favoured once again.

The WTO and FTAA simulation give opposing results for Mexico. Eliminating tariffs and export subsidies worldwide under WTO is expected to have a very large impact on commodity prices, particularly in agriculture where prices in some sectors such as rice, wheat and dairy are expected to rise by more than 20 per cent. Curiously, the reallocation of factors of production towards favoured sectors with the biggest price increases actually leads to a reduction in output in the agriculture sector as a whole. The net result is that moving to the WTO reduces output in Mexico. The opposite is the case for the FTAA simulation, partly because the changes in external prices are much smaller and move homogeneously across sectors.

10.7 The impact of export-led growth on poverty and distribution: the microsimulations

The microsimulation approach

This section of the chapter will focus on the poverty and income distribution effects at the household level of each of the simulation scenarios presented above. The important methodological problem is how to select the individuals who will change sectors when there is a change in labour demand in a simulation. The first part of this section will explain how we dealt with this problem, and the second will present the results of the simulations.

As discussed in Chapter 3, it is not a simple task to decide how to model the movements in the labour market at the individual and household levels (which would correspond to new poverty rates and income distributions). Several microsimulation methodologies have been proposed for this in the literature. One specifies a household income generation model through which a system of equations calculates price, income, demographic and labour effects on household income and for which the labour market outcomes are based on estimated labour supply and earnings functions (see, for example, Bourguignon *et al.* 1998, 2001; Alatas and Bourguignon 2000).

Bourguignon *et al.* (2002) estimate a similar microsimulation model and join it to their macro CGE component to create a 'top-down' model that takes into account the heterogeneity of households (and resolves the sectoral movements of individuals) in calculating poverty and inequality. A third methodology developed by Almeida dos Reis and Paes de Barros (1991) uses a random selection procedure for movements of labour between sectors.

The methodology that we use in our chapter combines parts of the above methods while also adding a new procedure to the microsimulation.[5] Although we do not model a fuller household behavioural model as in Robilliard *et al.* (2001), we will use a similar top-down methodology to join the CGE and a simplified version of the microsimulations model. However, we will not randomly select the individuals in the simulations as done by Almeida dos Reis and Paes de Barros. Rather, we will use econometric analysis to: (1) determine the probability of movement of each individual based on his characteristics, (2) estimate the monetary return to being in the formal rather than the informal sector and (3) estimate the potential wages of non-workers who enter the labour force.

The microsimulation approach allows one to go from labour market outcomes to the household distribution using information from household surveys. These surveys consist of demographic and income information for each member of each household. These data were first used to calculate the totals within each of the six labour categories used in the CGE model: agricultural (AG), unskilled (less than high school education, HS) and skilled (university or more, UN) men and women. Beyond these six main groups, the unskilled category is further subdivided into a formal and informal labour force. An informal sector worker is defined to be a non-agricultural worker or employee in a firm with less than five employees, an employer or owner of a firm of one to five workers or a self-employed worker. These workers can have no more than a high school education and must reside in the urban sector.

In our simulations, the total amount of skilled and agricultural labour remains fixed. However, as mentioned earlier we allow the total supply of unskilled labour to vary. Therefore, for each simulation the CGE model calculates the change in the total number of unskilled men and women in the labour force and the change in the number of (unskilled) men and women in the informal sector. These totals are passed down to the microsimulation model, which must determine which specific people move. This we did econometrically rather than randomly.

We focused first on the simulation of moving people from the informal to the formal sector (or vice versa) and then of moving people from being inactive to working in the informal sector (or vice versa). This ladder-type movement which we have imposed is a simplification that does not allow a large jump from one state to another. For example, a shock to the economy that causes an increase in the demand for formal sector workers will pull these workers from the pool of informal workers available and not directly from inactive workers.

The probability of moving is calculated through the use of probit regressions on each person's personal characteristics. For each informal worker we calculate the probability of moving to the formal sector and for certain inactive individuals the probability of entering the labour force as an informal worker. (We exclude children, retired or incapacitated individuals.) For the former, we regress (separately for males and females) a dummy variable 'formal' on a number of personal characteristics. The estimated coefficients are then the basis for calculating the probability of being in the formal sector for every individual in that probit regression. For the latter, we regress a work dummy (which takes on a value of 1 if the individual is working or frictionally unemployed) once again on a number of personal characteristics and use these estimated coefficients to calculate for each potential worker the probability of entering the labour force. The individual observations in the household survey are now ranked in order of their probability of moving, and those with the highest probabilities move first until the total demand for workers in the formal and informal sectors, as calculated in the CGE model, is attained.

After choosing the people who are moving from the informal to the formal sector or from outside the labour force into the informal sector (or vice versa), incomes are adjusted to account for this change. For those workers moving between the formal and informal sectors, the adjustment comes through the coefficient on the formal dummy in an income regression calculated over all workers. This coefficient represents the average return of working in the formal rather than the informal sector, and is thus used to shift up the income of the new formal sector workers accordingly. (In the case of a decrease in the demand for formal sector workers, those who move down to the informal sector would decrease their income by this factor.)

The movement from outside the labour force into the labour market is somewhat more complicated since these individuals have no previous income. The new workers thus receive the potential income that corresponds to their personal characteristics as estimated from a regression of income on all informal sector workers. However, this implies that all workers with the same known character-istics will receive the same mean income. To avoid artificially reducing income variation we attach an error term to each individual who moves between sectors. The error terms from which we choose are those calculated from the income regression of informal sector workers. We make no assumption about the distrib-ution of the pool of error terms, but rather draw randomly from this pool and attach the error term to the new worker.

Once all the new workers have been given their corrected income, we take the new economy-wide average wage as calculated from the CGE simulation results for each labour type (AGM, AGF, HSM, HSF, UNM, UNF) and adjust the income of *all* workers (whether they moved or not). This results in the final version of wage income per worker for a given simulation. Summing up all income sources for all workers in a household, and dividing by the number of total members, results in the new total household per capita income, which is then used to calcu-late poverty and inequality changes.

Results of the microsimulations

We present three FGT (1984) poverty indices in Table 10.5: the headcount ratio (P_0), the average normalized poverty gap (P_1) and the average squared normalized poverty gap (P_2). These estimates, which relate to total per capita household income, are calculated for both the poverty line and the extreme poverty line, and for both the urban and the rural sectors as well as for the nation as a whole.[6] Gini and Theil measures of inequality are presented in Table 10.6.

Impact on poverty and inequality

In the CGE simulations we found that increased openness whether measured by lower tariffs, capital inflows or an increase in the demand for exports was expansionary. Both output and employment increased, but in most simulations there was also a widening of wage inequality. The microsimulations reported in Table 10.6 show that these changes all reduce poverty but increase inequality at the same time. Note that the changes in poverty and inequality are small for tariff reductions because the level of tariffs is so small to begin with.

The finding that export-led growth and trade liberalization reduce poverty is an important result that runs counter to much of the literature and the empirical evidence on the impact of the reforms on poverty (see Alarcón and McKinley 1997; Berry 1998; Ganuza *et al.* 2001; Ros and Bouillon 2001). Undoubtedly, this is because this result is strikingly different from what actually happened to poverty in the postliberalization period. Trade liberalization began in earnest between 1986 and 1989. Yet, between 1984 and 1989, according to CEPAL, poverty rose from 34 to 39 per cent. Later, between 1989 and 1996, when most of the remaining reform agenda was adopted, poverty rose again from 39 to 43 per cent

Table 10.5 Mexico: macro–microsimulation results – effects on poverty

		Base	MAQINCR	MAQINCR2	FSAVINCR	TARINCR	ALCA	OMC	PWMINCR	TARDECR	DEVAL	EXPSUBS	PWEINCR
P₀: headcount ratio (proportion poor; % change from base level)													
Poverty	Urban	52.71%	-1.11	-3.84	-2.39	0.19	-0.06	0.19	4.97	-0.27	4.13	-3.28	-0.04
	Rural	84.92%	-0.005	0.34	0.01	0.00	-0.22	-0.14	0.60	-0.14	-0.25	-0.54	-1.26
	Total	61.52%	-0.691	-2.26	-1.48	0.12	-0.12	0.06	3.32	-0.22	2.48	-2.24	-0.50
Extreme	Urban	23.11%	-2.31	-6.45	-4.55	0.48	-0.07	0.45	9.30	-0.41	7.83	-6.05	-0.64
poverty	Rural	66.10%	0.64	1.96	0.83	0.19	-0.06	-0.06	0.31	-0.09	-1.03	-0.74	-2.64
	Total	34.87%	-0.78	-2.09	-1.76	0.33	-0.06	0.19	4.64	-0.25	3.24	-3.30	-1.68
P₁: average normalized poverty gap (% change from base level)													
Poverty	Urban	23.70%	-1.77	-5.28	-3.44	0.36	-0.15	0.41	8.54	-0.42	7.37	-4.80	-0.47
	Rural	53.03%	0.74	2.20	1.08	0.09	-0.31	-0.39	-0.05	-0.09	-2.30	-1.16	-3.75
	Total	31.72%	-0.62	-1.86	-1.38	0.24	-0.22	0.04	4.61	-0.27	2.95	-3.13	-1.97
Extreme	Urban	8.52%	-2.10	-5.89	-4.53	0.73	-0.31	0.66	17.47	-0.47	14.57	-6.77	-1.90
poverty	Rural	34.86%	1.46	4.42	2.21	0.13	-0.54	-0.74	-0.67	-0.14	-4.62	-1.78	-6.67
	Total	15.73%	0.06	0.36	-0.44	0.37	-0.45	-0.19	6.47	-0.27	2.93	-3.74	-4.79
P₂: average squared normalized poverty gap (% change from base level)													
Poverty	Urban	13.85%	-1.96	-5.62	-3.92	0.51	-0.21	0.51	11.91	-0.46	10.14	-5.66	-0.99
	Rural	38.06%	1.20	3.64	1.81	0.12	-0.45	-0.61	-0.45	-0.12	-3.73	-1.55	-5.52
	Total	20.47%	-0.35	-0.91	-1.01	0.31	-0.33	-0.06	5.62	-0.29	3.09	-3.57	-3.29
Extreme	Urban	4.46%	-1.76	-4.69	-4.13	0.99	-0.43	0.85	24.14	-0.36	20.13	-7.44	-3.13
poverty	Rural	22.51%	2.12	6.47	3.26	0.16	-0.73	-1.04	-1.30	-0.16	-6.45	-2.21	-8.76
	Total	9.40%	0.78	2.62	0.71	0.45	-0.62	-0.39	7.47	-0.23	2.71	-4.01	-6.82

Note: Poverty (and extreme poverty) estimate relates to total per capita household income

Table 10.6 Mexico: macro–microsimulation results – effects on inequality

	Base	MAQINCR	MAQINCR2	FSAVINCR	TARINCR	ALCA	OMC	PWMINCR	TARDECR	DEVAL	EXPSUBS	PWEINCR
Gini coefficient (% change from base level)												
Labour income[1]	0.5918	0.23	0.86	0.29	−0.07	−0.04	−0.17	−0.90	0.00	−1.17	0.08	−0.68
HPCI	0.5732	0.35	0.88	0.38	−0.04	−0.02	−0.11	0.19	0.04	−0.06	0.15	−0.63
Theil index (GE1) (% change from base level)												
Labour income	0.7222	0.23	1.07	0.04	−0.15	−0.03	−0.24	−1.58	−0.02	−1.53	0.13	−0.62
HPCI	0.6739	0.37	0.93	0.17	−0.08	0.00	−0.14	0.12	0.06	0.07	0.24	−0.65

Note: 1 Gini for HPCI (household per capita income) includes households with zero income (see Figure 10.4). These rising poverty trends are what led many observers to conclude that trade liberalization and financial liberalization hurt the poor. Our results say that trade reform is not the culprit. Our counterfactual simulation is able to separate out the effects of the trade reforms from all of the other factors that were changing at the same time. By themselves, the reforms helped the poor (while slightly increasing inequality). These positive effects were overshadowed by the spike in inflation and subsequent stabilization in the mid-1980s and by the financial crisis and recession in 1995.

These favourable effects of increased openness on poverty at the national level hide very different effects for the urban and rural sectors. Increasing export demand or capital inflows hurt agricultural workers because they both lead to an appreciation of the exchange rate and a movement of capital out of agriculture and a contraction of agricultural wages and output. Overall, poverty falls but both rural poverty and extreme poverty increase because most extreme poverty is found in rural families. A far more favourable effect is seen if the increase in export demand comes from a rise in the world prices of agricultural commodities as shown in the simulation labelled PWEINCR.

The experiment labelled OMC (WTO) simulated the effect of the sharp increase in world agricultural prices that would result from eliminating all trade barriers and export subsidies. In the previous section we found that it reduced total GDP slightly, while the ALCA (FTAA) scenario had almost no effect. The favourable effect of OMC on agriculture leads to a reduction in rural poverty, rural extreme poverty and inequality, but to an increase in urban poverty. For the ALCA experiment, poverty and inequality decrease under all definitions, but the magnitude of change is close to zero in some cases.

The last experiment (DEVAL) shows that overall devaluation is contractionary. Here, we see that it increases both urban and national poverty levels. However, because agriculture produces traded goods, a devaluation helps agriculture. Rural poverty and extreme poverty both fall and there is a reduction in inequality, especially of earnings.

10.8 Conclusion

Mexico's increased openness has increased output and employment and reduced poverty. But it has slightly increased inequality and extreme poverty at the same time. This is partly because this new growth strategy was skill-intensive and caused a widening of wage inequality between skilled and unskilled labour in the urban sector and between agriculture workers and everyone else. In the simulations, agriculture is hurt by anything that causes an appreciation of the exchange rate. Lower tariffs, increased demand for exports or bigger inflows of foreign capital, all measures of openness, cause an appreciation of the exchange rate and a movement of capital out of agriculture. This contributes to a fall in the relative wages of agriculture workers and a rise in rural poverty, particularly among the poorest families. As a result, while increased openness reduces the conventional measures of poverty (the headcount ratio and the poverty gap), those at the very bottom of the income distribution in the rural sector are made worse off. Conversely, the reduction of export subsidies under the WTO scenario reduces extreme poverty because of the rise in world prices of agricultural commodities.

Acknowledgements

The authors gratefully acknowledge the assistance of David Coady, Rebecca Lee Harris and Karen Thierfelder in the preparation of this chapter.

Notes

1 *Maquila* is defined in the Mexican national accounts as the assembly of goods for export primarily from imported inputs. All of *maquila* output is exported and most of its inputs are imported.
2 Note that one will be misled if one judges fiscal policy by the behaviour of G/Y. It appears to be countercyclical, with spikes in both 1986 and 1995. In the latter case, that happens despite the fact that G declines, because the fall in G in percentage terms is far less than the fall in GDP.
3 For a more complete description of the methodology, data sources and simulations, see our IFPRI working paper, Díaz-Bonilla and Morley (2003).
4 We also ran a short-run closure in which capital was fixed within each sector to get an idea of the short-run cost of adjustments to changes in exogenous conditions. See Díaz-Bonilla and Morley (2003).
5 See Díaz-Bonilla and Morley (2003) for a fuller description of the methodology.
6 Poverty lines come from Panorama Social 2000–1 from CEPAL. Our estimates of the level of poverty are much higher than those of CEPAL displayed in Figure 10.4 because we did not make any corrections for underreporting of income in such parameters as home production and profit.

References

Alarcón, Diana and Terry McKinley (1997) 'The paradox of narrowing wage differentials and widening wage inequality in Mexico', *Development and Change*, 28(3): 505–30.

Alatas, V. and F. Bourguignon (2000) 'The evolution of the distribution of income during Indonesian fast growth: 1980–1996', Princeton University (mimeo).

Almeida dos Reis, J. G. and R. Paes de Barros (1991) 'Wage inequality and the distribution of education: a study of the evolution of regional differences in inequality in metropolitan Brazil', *Journal of Development Economics*, 34: 117–43.

Berry, Albert (ed.) (1998) *Poverty, Economic Reform and Income Distribution in Latin America*, Boulder: Lynne Rienner.

Bourguignon, F., F. Ferreira and N. Lustig (1998) 'The microeconomics of income distribution dynamics, a research proposal', Washington, DC: The Inter-American Development Bank and the World Bank.

Bourguignon, F., M. Fournier and M. Gurgand (2001) 'Development with stable income distribution: Taiwan, 1979–1994,' *The Review of Income and Wealth*, 47(2): 1–25.

Bourguignon, François, Anne-Sophie Robilliard and Sherman Robinson (2002) 'Representative versus real households in the macro-economic modeling of inequality', Washington, DC: World Bank and IFPRI (mimeo).

CEPAL (2000–2001) *Panorama Social de America Latina*, Santiago: United Nations.

Cogneau, D. and A. S. Robilliard (2000) 'Growth, distribution, and poverty in Madagascar: learning from a microsimulation model in a general equilibrium framework', IFPRI TMD DP no. 61 and DIAL DT/2001/14, Washington, DC: IFPRI.

Díaz-Bonilla, Carolina and Samuel Morley (2003) 'The effects of export-led growth on employment, poverty, and inequality: the case of Mexico', IFPRI, TMD Working Paper, Washington, DC: IFPRI.

Ferreira, F. and R. Paes de Barros (2000) 'The slippery slope: explaining the increase in extreme poverty in urban Brazil, 1976–1996', Washington, DC: World Bank (mimeo).

Foster, J., J. Greer and E. Thorbecke (1984) 'A class of decomposable poverty measures', *Econometrica*, 52: 761–5.

Ganuza, E., R. Paes de Barros and R. Vos (2001) 'Efectos de la liberalización sobre la pobreza y la desigualdad', in: E. Ganuza, L. Taylor, R. Barros and R. Vos (eds) *Liberalización, Desigualdad y Pobreza. América Latina y el Caribe in los 90*, Buenos Aires: Ediciones Universidad de Buenos Aires (for UNDP), pp. 77–116.

Harris, Rebecca L. (1999) 'The distributional impact of macroeconomic shocks in Mexico: threshold effects in a multi-region CGE model', IFPRI-TMD Working Paper #44, Washington, DC: IFPRI.

Harris, Rebecca L. (2001) 'A computable general equilibrium analysis of Mexico's agricultural policy reforms', IFPRI, TMD Working Paper #65, Washington, DC: IFPRI.

Löfgren, Hans, Rebecca Lee Harris and Sherman Robinson (2001) 'A standard computable general equilibrium (CGE) model', IFPRI, TMD Working Paper #75, Washington, DC: IFPRI.

Lustig, Nora and Miguel Székely (1998) 'México: Evolución Económica, Pobreza y Desigualdad', in: E. Ganuza, Lance Taylor and S. Morley (eds) *Política Macroeconómica y Pobreza en América Latina y el Caribe*, Madrid: Mundi-Prensa (for UNDP).

INEGI (2000) *Cuenta Satélite del Subsector Informal de los Hogares 1993–1998*, Mexico City: INEGI.

Morley, Samuel A. (2001a) *The Income Distribution Problem in Latin America*, Santiago: CEPAL.

Morley, Samuel A. (2001b) 'Growth and distribution in an era of structural reform: the case of México 1980–1999', Washington, DC: IFPRI (mimeo).

Ros, Jaime and César Bouillon (2001) 'La liberalización de la balanza de pagos en México: Efectos en el crecimiento, la desigualdad y la pobreza', in: E. Ganuza, R. Paes de Barros, L. Taylor and R. Vos (eds) *Liberalización, desigualdad y pobreza: América Latina y el Caribe en los 90*, Buenos Aires: Ediciones Universidad de Buenos Aires (for UNDP), pp. 713–64.

Székely, Miguel (1998) *The Economics of Poverty, Inequality and Wealth Accumulation in Mexico*, London: Macmillan.

Székely, Miguel (2001) 'The 1990s in Latin America: another decade of persistent inequality, but with somewhat lower poverty', Inter-American Development Bank, OCE Working Paper #454, Washington, DC: IDB.

Székely, Miguel and Mariannne Hilgert (1999) 'The 1990s in Latin America: another decade of persistent inequality', Inter-American Development Bank, OCE Working Paper #410, Washington, DC: IDB.

Torre, Rodolfo de la (2000) 'La Distribución Factorial del Ingreso en el Nuevo Modelo Económico en México', CEPAL, Serie Reformas Económicas #58, Mexico: CEPAL.

11 Peru – impact analysis of trade liberalization on poverty and inequality

Alonso Segura Vasi and Juan García Carpio

Abstract

Trade liberalization was one of the central elements of Peru's economic reform programme in the 1990s, accompanied by efforts to increase the competitiveness of its export sector. This chapter analyses the policy measures adopted by Peru and their impact on the economy, employment, income levels, poverty and inequality.

Exports formed the driving force of economic recovery and balance-of-payments adjustment. Productivity also increased in the tradable sectors. In this sense, the Peruvian experience shows that a stable macroeconomic environment, a programme to modernize the institutional framework protecting private investment and the improvement of basic infrastructure services are important for attaining growth in the export sector. This strategy was based on liberalizing trade and finance and acquiring a significant flow of external financial resources through privatizations, concessions and better access to capital markets. The pattern of growth in the export sector, however, shows that growth was sustained primarily by the recovery of traditional sectors responding to new conditions of competitiveness and lower barriers for entry into other markets, and less by the diversification of non-traditional products with greater value added. In part, this was due to a delay in certain key reforms related to competitiveness (such as ports and infrastructural support services for foreign trade).

The impact of this strategy on employment and income levels was not what had been hoped for, even though it was accompanied by an increase in social expenditures for poverty reduction. Though more jobs were created, there was no significant improvement in real income in tradable sectors while income inequality increased.

A counterfactual computable general equilibrium model analysis shows that Peru has probably benefited from trade liberalization and export promotion. Macroeconomic indicators improve as visible in (simulated) increases in economic activity, consumption and employment and improvement in the trade and fiscal balances. These changes do not occur at the magnitude that one would hope, however. The country is vulnerable to external shocks that accompany liberalization, in part because exports per capita are very low, exports concentrate mainly on primary products and the economy is heavily dependent on complementary imports for consumer goods and productive inputs, causing a chronic tendency towards widening trade deficits. Furthermore, devaluation of the exchange rate has contractionary effects that can counteract the positive impact of other liberalization measures.

Employment growth is very little, but mainly favouring unskilled workers. Outcomes in terms of labour income are mixed, differing by type of worker, but rural workers witness income declines. On balance, trade reform does not translate into a substantial poverty reduction, while it tends to increase income inequality. Integration through trade agreements like the Free Trade Area of the Americas and the World Trade Organization would allow a generalized improvement in employment levels and would lead to a more visible reduction in poverty, as the country would benefit more from a rise in world export prices.

11.1 Introduction

Peru, like many other Latin American countries, made trade liberalization and the promotion of high levels of competitiveness in exports one of the central elements of its growth policy and its economic reform programme. Exports were the engine of the economic recovery during the 1990s and productivity grew in tradable sectors. The effect of this strategy on employment and income levels, however, has not been as great as expected.

In the first part of this chapter, we assess the Peruvian economic situation and the policy regime adopted during the 1990s, highlighting the impact of external shocks on the balance of payments and the effect of export growth on the main macroeconomic accounts. The second section describes the evolution of the exports and analyses the importance of export promotion policies in stimulating growth. The impact of export growth on employment and labour productivity is analysed in the third section.[1] The next section includes the implementation of the computable general equilibrium (CGE) model, built on the basis of a social accounting matrix (SAM), and analyses the impact of different kinds of external shocks and economic liberalization measures on macroeconomic indicators like activity level, consumption, investment, balance of trade, employment and income. Finally, through a microsimulation technique, the impact on poverty and inequality is assessed.

11.2 Evolution of the economy in the 1990s

The macroeconomic panorama before the reforms

After poor performance in the previous decade, the Peruvian economy experienced significant growth during the 1990s (Table 11.1). This recovery was accompanied by a gradual reduction in inflation, a decline in the fiscal deficit, currency stability and greater access to foreign capital.

Previously, in the 1970s and 1980s, the Peruvian external sector went through periods characterized predominantly by protectionist policies based on import

Table 11.1 Peru: main economic indicators, 1980–2000

	1980–5	*1986–90*	*1991–5*	*1996–2000*
GDP (growth rate, %)	−0.18	−1.54	5.58	2.56
Average inflation (%)	104.94	2342.20	113.30	6.92
Non-financial public sector (% of GDP)				
Current account savings	0.77	−2.64	1.79	3.14
Overall balance	−1.53	−6.60	−3.14	−1.59
Total liquidity (% of GDP)	17.00	9.04	13.08	22.88
Total credit to private sector (% of GDP)	36.92	27.11	9.70	23.80
Money supply (growth rate, %)	156.86	1523.13	108.38	10.84
Current account balance (% of GDP)	−2.99	−5.37	−6.04	−4.87

Source: Central Reserve Bank of Peru

substitution with high tariffs, wide tariff dispersion, quotas and prohibitions on imports, multiple exchange rates and various other anti-export biases. These periods were occasionally interrupted by brief and frustrated attempts at liberalization.

The tariff structure in July 1990 (high tariffs and a wide range) favoured inputs and capital goods, while a significant percentage of industrial production benefited from tariff and non-tariff prohibitions and restrictions. This system generated distortions in the form of negative effective rates protection for export products compared to non-export production that enjoyed high levels of effective protection.

The structural reform programme in the 1990s

In the early 1990s, an economic programme was implemented that sought to reduce inflation, eliminate price controls and government intervention in economic activity, unify the currency system and re-establish fiscal and monetary discipline. Regarding trade policy, the level and range of tariffs were reduced and the primary tariff barriers and controls on current and capital accounts were eliminated. In addition, the foreign exchange market was liberalized establishing a floating exchange rate regime and efforts were made to attract foreign investment. From 1990 on, tariffs have been reduced and made more uniform (Table 11.2).[2] Furthermore, the customs system was reformed through modernization, improvement of quality and efficiency standards and the delegation of responsibilities to the private sector.

These policies led to significant export growth during the 1990s (see Figure 11.1) at average per capita rates of 5.8 per cent during the first five years, and even greater rates in the second half of the decade, exceeding the Latin American average.

Structural reforms also included other aspects that helped improve competitiveness such as labour market reforms (in particular, flexibility of hiring and firing practices in the labour market), social security reform (creation of a private system based on individual capital accounts), tax reform (a smaller number of taxes, generalized use of the value-added tax and the simplification of income

Table 11.2 Peru's tariff reform process, 1990–2000

	Number of rates	*Simple tariff average*	*Standard deviation*
July 1990	39	46.5	25.7
August 1990	24	38.1	12.4
September 1990	3	26.3	13.3
January 1991	4	26.3	13.3
March 1991	3	16.8	3.9
March 1992	2	17.6	4.4
July 1992	2	17.6	4.4
June 1993	2	16.3	3.4
April 1997	4	13.5	3.5
January 1998	4	13.5	3.5
July 2000	5	11.8	4.4

Source: Abusada *et al.* (2001); BCRP, Monthly Economic Report; Macroconsult, May 2001

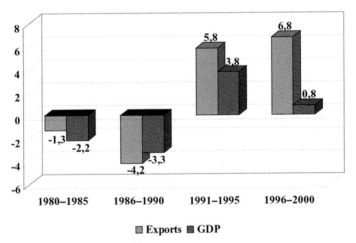

■ **Exports** ■ **GDP**

Source: Central Reserve Bank of Peru.

Figure 11.1 Peru: GDP and export growth, 1980–2000 (average per capita growth rates).

tax), financial liberalization (the elimination of interest rate controls, liquidation of state-owned development banks and new regulatory and supervisory frameworks) and the promotion of private investment (a new legal framework for investments, privatizations and concessions and autonomous regulating bodies).

Nevertheless, after 1997 there were a series of exogenous shocks, such as international financial crises and the *El Niño* phenomenon, which negatively affected the external context and reduced the availability of resources for financing private activity. In addition, the pace of implementation of the reform programme slowed, particularly in the areas of privatizations and concessions and trade reform. In particular, the paralysis of the transportation concessions programme (airports, ports and highways) slowed the process of modernizing the support infrastructure for the export sector.

External shocks and balance of payments adjustment

The current account balance showed a growing deficit in the first part of the study period. Deficits started to decline in 1998. The deterioration registered between 1991 and 1995 is explained by the growth of imports and factor income payments by the public and private sectors. The adjustment registered in 1999 and 2000 happened within the context of an economic crisis, where the balance of trade improved because of a decline in the demand for imports. According to the methodology of current account decomposition (Table 11.3), the deterioration of the current account deficit during 1991–5 as compared to the 1985–90 period was in the order of 4.5 per cent. This is explained primarily by factors related to adjustment in domestic spending (7.5 per cent), highlighting a greater preference for imported products (5.2 per cent) as a result of the liberalization policies and the relative reduction in the percentage of exportable production (1.9 per cent). At the same time, factors related to external shocks improved the current account balance by 5.0 per cent, due fundamentally to the growth in world trade (5.4 per cent). The decrease in world interest rates also had a positive effect on the current account balance, while greater profit remittances to foreign countries had a negative effect (1.9 per cent).

Comparing 1996–2000 with the early 1990s, it is apparent that external shocks are generating greater effects than internal factors, translating into a slight improvement in the ratio of current account over gross domestic product (GDP) (–0.5 per cent). Growth in imports (2.8 per cent) and greater dynamism of exports (–1.1 per cent) stand out as significant internal factors. In terms of external shocks, further growth in world trade (–1.0 per cent), falling import prices (–1.2 per cent) and a decline in export prices (0.7 per cent) have all had an influence. The payment of profit remittances has also grown in Peru (1.7 per cent), though less than in other countries.

In both periods, private remittances and public transfers reduced the current account deficit. A contraction in consumption also contributed towards reducing the deficit. Growth in private investment had a negative influence, however, since it was primarily financed by foreign investment.

Macroeconomic adjustment and growth of exports

The macroeconomic decomposition methodology shows that sources of GDP growth during the 1990s were primarily growth in investments and exports (Table 11.4). In the 1990–5 period, investment and exports explained 80 and 17 per cent of output growth, respectively. During 1996–2000, growth is explained primarily by exports, since the decline in investment was compensated by greater expenditures on public consumption.

Growth in investment happened primarily from 1993 to 1997. Investment showed record contributions to growth in 1994 and 1995 (12.8 and 8.6 percentage

Table 11.3 Peru: decomposition of the change in current account due to external shocks

Period	1991–5	1996–2000
Weights	1985–90	1991–5
Increase in deficit	4.54	−0.50
External shocks		
Total	−4.96	−1.40
Deterioration in terms of trade	1.57	−0.50
Price effect of imports	−0.68	−1.23
Price effect of exports	2.25	0.73
Interest rate shock	−1.17	0.06
Slowing of world trade	−5.37	−0.96
Other external variables		
Total	0.79	−0.11
Accumulated debt burden	−0.32	−1.29
Change in income from direct investments	1.85	1.65
Change in remittances	−0.35	−0.24
Change in public transfers	−0.39	−0.23
Domestic adjustment		
Total	7.53	1.19
Internal demand	0.36	0.00
Contraction of consumption	−0.21	−0.31
Private consumption	−0.19	−0.36
Public consumption	−0.02	0.05
Reduction in investment	0.57	0.31
Private investment	0.46	0.34
Public investment	0.11	−0.03
Trade ratios	7.17	1.19
Import substitution	5.24	2.81
Penetration of exports	1.93	−1.61
Interaction of effects		
Total	1.18	−0.19
Imports shock	−0.17	−0.21
Demand/imports	0.13	0.00
Displacement/price	−0.30	−0.21
Export shock	1.28	0.03
Demand/exports	1.63	−0.06
Displacement/price	−0.34	0.09
Debt shock	0.06	−0.02
Stock/interests	0.06	−0.02

Source: Central Reserve Bank of Peru

points of GDP growth, respectively). The 'boom' is mainly explained by higher investment following privatizations of state enterprises (10.2 and 7.8 points, respectively). During the 1998–2000 period, the investment contribution to growth was negative. Exports grew consistently from 1994 on. At the same time, public consumption, which had fallen between 1990 and 1994, began to recover in 1995.

Table 11.4 Peru: decomposition of GDP changes, 1991–2000 (in new 1994 *soles*)

	1991	1992	1993	1994	1995	1996	1997	1998	1999	2000
Effects of exogenous components										
Exogenous components	83,760	83,401	87,375	98,577	107,039	109,709	117,110	116,485	117,590	121,267
Public consumption	19,766	19,727	19,915	19,791	20,528	21,823	22,193	22,387	24,294	25,791
Investment	38,264	37,610	41,143	50,052	57,526	55,747	60,547	58,396	52,998	51,551
Exports	25,730	26,064	26,316	28,734	28,985	32,139	34,369	35,703	40,298	43,924
Share in GDP growth (%)										
Public consumption	23.6	23.7	22.8	20.1	19.2	19.9	19.0	19.2	20.7	21.3
Investment	45.7	45.1	47.1	50.8	53.7	50.8	51.7	50.1	45.1	42.5
Exports	30.7	31.3	30.1	29.1	27.1	29.3	29.3	30.6	34.3	36.2
Contributions to growth (% points)										
Public consumption	−0.03	−0.05	0.23	−0.14	0.75	1.21	0.34	0.17	1.64	1.27
Investment	1.11	−0.78	4.24	10.20	7.58	−1.66	4.38	−1.84	−4.63	−1.23
Exports	1.09	0.40	0.30	2.77	0.25	2.95	2.03	1.14	3.94	3.08
Total GDP growth (%)	2.17	−0.43	4.76	12.82	8.58	2.49	6.75	−0.53	0.95	3.13

Source: Central Reserve Bank of Peru

Growth and structure of exports

Peruvian exports are characterized by their concentration in primary and semi-processed products – mostly from mining and fishing – that are normally subject to significant variations in international volumes and prices. Non-traditional products, especially manufactured goods, are a smaller percentage of foreign sales but have shown a growing dynamism in recent years.

In the 1990s, the average value of exports grew at an average rate of 8.4 per cent with similar rates for traditional (8.4 per cent) and non-traditional (8.4 per cent) products. Among the traditional products, the highest levels of growth occurred in fishing (8.6 per cent), mining (8.6 per cent) and petroleum and petroleum products (10.1 per cent). Agricultural products (11.3 per cent), chemicals (10.4 per cent), non-metallic minerals (11.0 per cent) and metals (9.6 per cent) grew the most among the non-traditional products. Textiles (6.7 per cent), non-traditional fishing products (7.5 per cent) and iron and steel products (6.2 per cent) achieved below-average growth rates.

The highest growth in the export sector occurred between 1993 and 1997, when total exports grew at an annual average of 13.9 per cent (13.5 per cent for traditional products and 16.2 per cent for non-traditional products) and traditional agricultural and fishing products grew at rates of 17 per cent. Non-traditional agricultural, textile and fishing products grew at annual average rates of 18.7, 15.4 and 14.8 per cent, respectively.

Labour market adjustment

In general terms, there were no great changes observed in employment or income trends as a result of structural reforms. The direction of changes in the labour market was favourable, since the number of jobs increased faster than the working-age population. The unemployment rate increased slightly due to a rise in labour participation. Real incomes have increased and there has been no clear growth in informal activity. Thus, while both employment and income showed improvement in comparison to the crisis situation of the early 1990s, long-term trends were continued. The labour market faces the same problems of ten years ago: a high level of informal activity and a very low median income level, reflected in an urban poverty rate of 40 per cent.

Employment expanded in all economic activities during the 1990s (Table 11.5).[3] Between 1989 and 1992, employment had stagnated, with labour market adjustments mainly taking place in real labour income and pensions and fewer people entering the labour market. Beginning in 1993, employment growth accelerated, absorbing those who were entering the labour market for the first time and those who had previously left the labour market. Employment increased mainly in the private sector, compensating the job losses in the public sector caused by the reform programme.

Thus, the trends in employment and incomes from 1994 on suggest that the adjustment after the reform programme mainly took the form of employment growth and little change in real remunerations. By type of worker, job creation was pretty much across the board, not favouring any particular labour category.

Table 11.5   Peru: change in employment by type of activity, 1985–2000

	1985	1994	1997	2000
Total	7,409,461	9,074,477	10,394,767	11,227,834
Agriculture and fishing	3,194,710	3,156,341	3,402,141	3,660,881
Mining	66,650	67,297	64,234	64,004
Manufacturing industry	887,548	1,132,014	1,153,036	1,090,245
Construction, electricity	254,131	360,570	558,757	430,112
Commerce, restaurants, hotels	1,494,341	2,256,378	2,604,929	2,892,939
Business services	156,185	269,634	383,518	362,431
Other services	1,355,896	1,832,244	2,228,152	2,727,223
Tradables	*4,148,908*	*4,355,651*	*4,619,411*	*4,815,130*
Non-tradables	*3,260,553*	*4,718,826*	*5,775,356*	*6,412,705*

Source: Instituto Cuánto, National Living Standards Survey (ENNIV) 1985, 1994, 1997 and 2000

Looking by sector, employment growth happened primarily in non-tradable sectors (23 per cent between 1994 and 1997) dominated by private sector firms. In this sense, trade liberalization led to a restructuring of employment, though, unlike other reform experiences, there was no contraction in levels of employment in manufacturing, in spite of the reduced role of this sector compared to commerce, transportation and services. According to the national living standards survey, ENNIV, the annual average growth of overall employment at the national level was 5 per cent between 1994 and 1997.

One important effect of the reform programme was the reduction in the costs of layoffs. This influenced the recovery of the formal sector. Nonetheless, informal employment conditions continue to affect half of the urban labour force.

Trends in labour productivity

Output growth in tradable sectors like manufacturing, agriculture and fishing did not produce a commensurate recovery in employment and consequently labour productivity increased in the sector (Table 11.6). In the case of mining, increased productivity was associated with a reduction in employment levels. The services and commerce sectors showed lower productivity. The sector probably functioned as residual employer with growth in employment surpassing GDP growth, absorbing many workers (as self-employed) from other sectors.

11.3 CGE analysis of the impact of trade liberalization and shocks

Social accounting matrix

The primary sources of information used in the elaboration of the SAM were the Input–Output Table, designed by the National Institute of Statistics and Information (INEI) for 1994 (base year for national accounts), and the *Instituto*

Table 11.6   Peru: change in labour productivity index 1985–2000 (index 1985 = 100)

	1985	*1994*	*1997*	*2000*
Agriculture and fishing	100.0	131.7	140.0	157.1
Mining	100.0	75.5	86.7	103.8
Manufacturing industry	100.0	92.2	103.3	114.7
Construction, electricity	100.0	128.1	108.5	129.9
Commerce, restaurants, and hotels	100.0	73.3	77.4	70.6
Business services	100.0	62.3	51.0	44.2
Other services	100.0	71.6	70.2	61.6
Total	100.0	90.7	93.3	90.7
Tradables	*100.0*	*104.5*	*111.8*	*120.7*
Non-Tradables	*100.0*	*77.6*	*77.2*	*68.7*

Source: Central Reserve Bank of Peru and National Employment Surveys

Cuanto's Living Standards Survey (ENNIV) for 1994, which has information about expenditures on each kind of goods and services and about the total income of each type of household by category.

The SAM contains accounts for government institutions, enterprises and three types of households: rural, urban with skilled household head and urban with unskilled household head.[4] There are 22 accounts for the different branches of economic activity (and goods and services) including: extractive sectors (agricultural, fishing and mining), various kinds of manufacturing (consumer or capital goods and inputs), electricity and water, construction, commerce, transportation and communications and service activities (including government). Production factors include capital and 12 types of labour classified according to gender (male, female), area (urban, rural), skill level (skilled, unskilled) and labour category (independent, wage labour). Employment in rural areas was not subdivided between wage earners and independent workers because of sample size limitations of the survey (wage labour is uncommon in rural areas, especially for women). Taxes are disaggregated in accounts for direct taxes on institutions, sales taxes and import duties. Finally, the SAM looks at accounts for the external sector, transaction costs (only the costs of marketing) and the savings–investment account.

Total annual household expenditures do not include payment of direct taxes (income tax, etc.), transfers or expenditures for the purchase of houses (since, if it is a recent purchase, it is considered residential investment in national accounts), and it includes the own production and consumption of products (valued at retail prices).[5] To determine the labour income of each member of the household, monthly income from primary and secondary activities have been considered along with bonuses, payment in kind and other income from work, without including own consumption (this is included in the residual operating surplus account in the input–output matrix).[6]

Total expenditures and income were disaggregated by type of household according to the proportions observed in the ENNIV. Remunerations by types of economic activity were also distributed according to the type of worker according to the survey information.

General equilibrium model

The model includes variables for quantities (and associated prices) of imports, exports, domestic production, production sold internally and level of activity for each product. Sources of income, institutions' expenditure decisions, factors, the external sector and trade margins are also modelled. In addition, a series of balance equations serve to define the model's closures and to guarantee equilibrium (i.e. the number of equations equal to the number of unknowns). Finally, in this case an equation is also included for real wages paid to the labour factor at buyer's prices. This allows the closure of the factors market to be modified and allows quantities as well as nominal remunerations to vary.

The model estimated for Peru does not include taxes levied on production or value added taxes. However, the general sales tax (IGV) can affect the Peruvian economy similar to a value added tax.

The model's key parameters were derived from various sources. Consumption elasticities by type of household were estimated using survey data from the National Institute of Statistics (INEI)[7] consumption by type of good and income level (high income, middle income and low income). Data on the goods most representative for each activity in the SAM were selected and weighted for their share in total consumption. For those goods not covered by the survey data (like furniture or machinery and equipment), elasticities were taken from the standard model of the project. The elasticity of substitution between factors in the production function, and the elasticities for the Armington function (which aggregates national and imported goods) and for the CET function (which aggregates domestic production and production for export) of each type of good, took the basic values utilized in the standard model. Finally, the elasticity of substitution between value added and intermediate demand for the supply of each good was set at 0.6, and the elasticity in the aggregation function of the same good produced by different branches of activity was 4, which are within the feasible range for these elasticities and are similar to those used in other studies.

Closures used in the model

For the system of macroeconomic constraints, the closure used in the majority of simulations is that of a flexible government deficit (fixed direct tax rates), fixed foreign savings (flexible exchange rate) and flexible investment (the marginal propensities to save of non-governmental institutions remain fixed).

The labour market closure allows the possibility of unemployment. The quantity of capital, on the other hand, is assumed to remain constant but can move between sectors, varying the level of nominal remuneration but maintaining equal rates of return in each sector (the wage distortion factor is one in all cases).

Simulations of the impact of trade liberalization and external shocks on the economy

Policy measures and external shocks simulated with the CGE model

In order to analyse the impact of liberalization on the Peruvian economy, simulations were carried out to measure the effects of the following on household income: a series of economic policy measures for trade liberalization or export promotion, a series of external shocks and the adoption of trade integration agreements. The experiments conducted are as follows:

1.   A 50 per cent change in tariffs (increases or decreases).
2.   A 10 per cent devaluation in the exchange rate.
3.   Estimated shocks of 10 per cent increases in prices of imports and exports.
4.   A 10 per cent increase in foreign savings in order to observe the impact of liberalization policies that give incentives for capital inflows, especially that of foreign direct investment.[8]
5.   A 10 per cent increase in productivity, in order to observe the impact of greater productive efficiency through a modification of the efficiency parameter in the CES production function of each branch of economic activity.
6.   A 50 per cent increase in export demand for main products (agricultural products; fishing, fishmeal and fish oils; mineral products and non-iron metallic products; and clothing).
7.   Impact of change in tariffs, export subsidies and international prices due to establishment of the Free Trade Area of the Americas (FTAA) and the agreements of the World Trade Organization (WTO).[9]

Simulations results

EFFECTS ON MACROECONOMIC INDICATORS AND HOUSEHOLD CONSUMPTION[10]

The results of the macroeconomic simulations show that a 50 per cent reduction in tariffs increases exports by 3.4 per cent and imports by about 2.8 per cent, thus reducing the trade deficit by a bit less than 1 per cent of GDP. The economy grows about 0.4 per cent (see Table 11.7). Though government income from import duties declines by almost 1 per cent, there is a positive effect on the total amount of indirect taxes, and direct taxes increase (varying according to the closure). An increase in tariffs has the converse effect in all cases, but the magnitudes vary slightly. (It is interesting to note that the government deficit decreases by a smaller amount than its increase with the opposite measure.)

The most significant type of shock is that of devaluation, which has a negative impact on the economy. A nominal devaluation of 10 per cent causes a 9.6 per cent decrease in the level of domestic absorption, due primarily to the negative impact on investment (41.2 per cent), which is the variable that adjusts strongly for the greater restriction in foreign capital. Though its effect on exports and

Table 11.7 Peru: CGE simulations – effects on macroeconomic indicators

	Base year (level)	50% Tariff cut (flexible gov. deficit)	50% Tariff cut (fixed gov. deficit)	50% Tariff increase	10% Devaluation	10% Increase import prices	10% Increase export prices	10% Increase foreign savings	10% Increase productivity	20% Increase in export demand	10% Increase wages	FTAA	WTO
Real values	(billions of new soles)					(percentage change from baseline)							
GDP	98.29	0.39	0.51	-0.39	-1.52	-0.96	0.45	0.08	13.89	1.03	-1.99	0.56	0.51
Absorption	94.00	0.35	0.55	-0.35	-9.59	-2.45	1.19	0.68	13.66	3.03	-2.00	0.54	0.34
Household Consumption	64.73	1.05	0.14	-0.98	-0.81	-2.11	1.06	0.07	12.14	2.78	-1.55	1.44	1.77
Investment	20.63	-1.69	2.06	1.45	-41.19	-4.54	2.06	2.89	24.15	5.07	-4.23	-2.04	-3.99
Government Consumption	8.64												
Exports	12.55	3.41	4.15	-3.10	40.50	1.33	0.71	-2.72	18.59	0.08	-2.85	4.78	6.54
Imports	21.55	2.86	3.48	-2.59	-16.33	-8.33	5.28	1.49	14.84	12.87	-2.31	4.28	4.84
Real exchange rate	87.23	1.23	1.41	-1.18	11.33	6.61	-4.39	-1.20	1.38	-9.73	-0.13	1.60	2.55
Nominal exchange rate	100.00	1.52	1.68	-1.44	10.00	0.14	-6.01	-1.08	0.89	-13.61	0.17	2.50	2.07
Export price index	100.00						5.22			13.15		-0.51	0.62
Import price index	100.00					10.00						-0.48	1.26
World price, tradables	100.00					5.59	2.30			5.80		-0.49	0.97
Domestic price, non-tradables	114.64	0.28	0.27	-0.26	-1.19	-0.82	0.58	0.12	-0.48	1.25	0.30	0.39	0.50
Consumer price index	100.00												
Terms of trade	100.00					-9.09	5.22			13.15		-0.03	-0.63

(*Continued*)

Table 11.7 (Continued)

	Base year (level)	50% Tariff cut (flexible gov. deficit)	50% Tariff cut (fixed gov. deficit)	50% Tariff increase	10% Devaluation	10% Increase import prices	10% Increase export prices	10% Increase foreign savings	10% Increase productivity	20% Increase in export demand	10% Increase wages	FTAA	WTO
Percentage of GDP	(%)												
						(change in percentage points from baseline)							
Investment	20.99	−0.56	0.21	0.52	−8.54	−0.19	0.03	0.57	1.91	0.04	−0.48	−0.67	−1.20
Private savings (households and enterprises)	19.33	0.22	0.12	−0.2	0.37	−0.09	0.15	−0.01	0.29	0.3	−0.09	0.25	0.50
Foreign savings	5.78	0.07	0.07	−0.07	−7.92	0.14	−0.42	0.50	−0.65	−0.95	0.11	0.11	0.11
Trade deficit	9.16	−0.65	−0.61	0.60	−9.03	−0.19	−0.07	0.60	−0.25	−0.13		−0.70	−1.42
Government savings	−3.08	−0.85	0.01	0.78	−0.97	−0.23	0.27	0.08	2.13	0.63	−0.47	−1.03	−1.80
Import duties	1.77	−0.84	−0.84	0.78	−0.15	0.05	−0.04	0.01	0.04	−0.09	−0.01	−1.01	−1.77
Indirect taxes	3.48	0.03	0.86	−0.03	0.01		−0.01		−0.04	−0.01	0.01	0.04	0.06
Indirect taxes and import duties	9.77	0.90	1.16	−1.06	−11.16	−3.54	0.99	0.50	14.33	1.27	−2.21	1.19	0.85
Household welfare	(billions of new soles)					(percentage change from baseline)							
Real consumption of households													
Rural households	11.33	1.02	−0.02	−0.96	−0.64	−2.11	1.29	0.07	12.28	3.18	−1.34	1.30	2.02
Urban households with unskilled head	23.88	1.18	0.30	−1.10	−0.71	−2.35	1.43	0.08	13.02	3.44	−1.77	1.63	2.01
Urban households with skilled head	36.13	1.09	0.20	−1.02	−0.77	−2.08	0.97	0.04	11.51	2.58	−1.39	1.52	1.76
Indirect compensation of households													
Rural households	11.33	0.94	−0.10	−0.89	−0.95	−2.07	1.19	0.10	12.57	3.04	−1.50	1.19	1.92
Urban households with unskilled head	23.88	1.07	0.19	−1.00	−0.71	−2.18	1.28	0.08	13.06	3.13	−1.80	1.50	1.79
Urban households with skilled head	36.13	1.00	0.12	−0.94	−0.88	−1.98	0.83	0.05	11.41	2.31	−1.33	1.40	1.60

Note: The column with base year values measures real indicators aggregated to the base year prices

imports is significant (exports increase by 40.5 per cent and imports decline by 16.3 per cent), the activity level decreases by 1.5 per cent.[11] The effect on the balance of trade is a 9 percentage point fall as a ratio to GDP that is compensated for by an 8.5 per cent decline in investment. Thus, it is investment and not household consumption that is the most affected (the participation of GDP continues to be the same). In the case of the government, the change in levels of activity and imports causes an increase in the deficit that is greater than 1 per cent of GDP.[12]

A 10 per cent shock in the prices of imported goods has a significant negative effect on economic activity, which decreases by 1 per cent. This effect occurs both at the level of absorption, which falls 2.5 per cent, especially on the investment side (−4.5 per cent), and at the level of imports, which falls at a similar percentage as the increase in prices (8.3 per cent), suggesting that imported goods are not luxury or non-basic goods for households and businesses, but rather take the form of basic needs like food and clothing and necessary raw materials (which cannot be substituted by national products). The real exchange rate increases (6.6 per cent) while the nominal rate does not vary. Increasing the price of primary export goods yields converse effects, showing the vulnerability of the economy to external shocks (especially because of the effect of the prices of fishmeal and fish oil and of textile products), and makes GDP grow by 0.5 per cent because of the increase in domestic absorption and in exports, which grow slightly. Since imports grow 5.3 per cent at the same time, there is a decrease in the nominal exchange rate (6 per cent).

A 10 per cent increase in foreign savings increases the absorption level by only 0.7 per cent and GDP stays practically the same. The first part is due to the fact that the investment level is growing by 2.9 per cent, which represents 0.5 per cent more of GDP, but this is reflected in a 2.7 per cent decline in exports and a 1.5 per cent increase in imports, which is why the balance of trade deficit grows 0.6 GDP points. The exchange rate adjusts, appreciating (falling) by about 1 per cent. In addition, the increase in the tax collection level brings a very small decrease in the government deficit (less than 0.1 per cent GDP).

An increase in productivity has a multiplier effect, benefiting the economy as a whole and increasing GDP by 13.9 per cent. The level of exports grows by 18.6 per cent, imports are less (14.8 per cent) and investments show the best growth (24.15 per cent). In addition, the government deficit falls by 2.1 GDP points due to the strong increase in tax collection.

A 20 per cent increase in primary export goods leads to almost no growth in total exports since other sectors are exporting less after adjusting to the exchange rate (the real exchange rate appreciates by almost 10 per cent and the nominal rate by 13.6 per cent), which also makes imports grow by 12.9 per cent. Nevertheless, the effect on the activity level is positive (1 per cent) as a result of a more than 5 per cent growth in investment.

Under the FTAA and WTO scenarios, exports increase and have a positive effect on levels of domestic absorption. They also have significant effects on the growth of imports (4.3 and 4.8 per cent respectively), but this is less than the effect on exports (4.8 and 6.5 per cent), and so they have a favourable impact on the balance of trade – 0.7 per cent GDP points in the case of the FTAA and 1.4 points for the WTO. In both cases, the production level grows by 5 per cent. Finally, the direct negative impact on tax collection is not counteracted by the increase in GDP (though direct taxes grow very little). Thus, the fiscal deficit increases by 1 and 1.8 per cent of GDP, respectively.

With respect to household consumption and welfare (measured through the 'indirect compensation' of each household),[13] urban households with unskilled household head and rural households tend to benefit from liberalization and are more vulnerable to external shocks. In general, when consumption rises (or falls) the indirect compensation of the household does so as well (since the household income would have to rise – or fall – to obtain the new level of wellbeing at basic prices). For example, lower tariffs would favour the urban household with an unskilled household head more, but with devaluation, consumption falls, especially in the unskilled urban household (by 0.8 per cent). The increase in foreign savings makes consumption fall slightly, and an increase in import prices causes about a 1.5 per cent reduction according to the type of household, while an increase in export prices has the opposite effect. Higher exports are reflected in a 2.8 per cent increase in consumption, which is clearly higher for the unskilled urban household and the rural household. Finally, the FTAA and WTO agreements lead to a general increase in the level of household consumption (though less for rural homes in the case of the FTAA and more for these same homes within the WTO).

EFFECTS ON PRODUCTION BY ACTIVITY

Lowering tariffs has a positive effect for most activities.[14] This effect happens especially in the cases of fishing, fishmeal and fish oil; mining; and textiles. A devaluation leads not only to a decline in the level of production of most activities but also to a significant increase in production for activities directed fundamentally towards export. The activities that benefit the most are fishing and fishmeal, which grows more than 116 per cent (its export grows 150 per cent); textile products, which grow by 18.5 per cent; and extraction of minerals, oil and gas, which grows by 11.1 per cent. Chemical and pharmaceutical products also grow by 5.3 per cent. As expected, the activities with greater domestic orientation are the most negatively affected, such as construction, which falls 39 per cent; machinery and transportation equipment, which falls 17.1 per cent; and furniture, rubber and plastic, which falls by 7.2 per cent.

An increase in the price of imported goods benefits fishing, fishmeal and fish oil; basic chemical products; and machinery and equipment (these latter compete with imports), and hurts the construction sector, industries like beverages and tobacco, milling and bakeries; and chemical and pharmaceutical products. An increase in export prices, on the other hand, favours the fishing sector, which grows 15.9 per cent; minerals, which grow by 1.7 per cent; and also some agro-industrial sectors along with service activities, transportation and construction.

Increased foreign savings, which implies growth in the balance of trade deficit, has a different effect according to the export orientation of the branches of activity. It works against fishing and fishmeal, mining and textiles since they are mainly export sectors, and it favours domestic activities like construction, machinery and equipment, and furniture, rubber and plastics.

In addition, the general increase in productivity produces more benefits for export activities like fishing and mining as well as branches of activities that provide inputs like furniture, rubber and plastics; machinery and equipment; and construction. Agricultural and agro-industrial production grows a little less (around 12 per cent), however. An increase in export volume benefits especially the fishing sector (which grows 15.4 per cent) and to a lesser degree minerals (7 per cent) and textiles (6.2 per cent), but the agricultural sector does not benefit. Of the non-tradables, construction grows 4.9 per cent and commerce and transportation also grow. This suggests that fishing, mining and textiles sectors could benefit increasingly from policies of export promotion and that they could lead growth in production in other labour-intensive sectors. This, in fact, is in line with what has been observed.

Finally, in terms of the free trade agreements, the FTAA would favour growth in activities related to fishing and fishmeal, mining and agro-industrial activities. Its effect on the agricultural sector would be slightly negative (1.7 per cent) due to the fact that the adjustment after integration with the other countries of the Americas that produce similar agricultural products would cause international prices to fall slightly. At the same time, WTO agreements, which would allow the prices of various products to rise (agricultural products and their derivatives and especially those related to fishing), would lead to significant growth in these activities. (Fishing would rise 15.5 per cent while agro-industrial products would also rise considerably.) Finally, in both scenarios, commerce and services in general would benefit.

EFFECTS ON EMPLOYMENT BY TYPE OF JOB AND REMUNERATION

As Table 11.8 shows, lowering tariffs has a generally positive effect on employment, but this effect is small. In no case is it greater than 2 per cent when tariffs fall 50 per cent, and it is even less with a flexible government deficit. If there is a fixed deficit, lowering tariffs makes urban employment grow faster than rural employment and makes the urban employment of men improve the most. In addition, if production levels are affected by different activities in different ways, the effect of lowering tariffs would be a slight increase in remuneration for skilled urban workers (especially independent workers) and a decrease in the remuneration of rural workers (especially unskilled workers who are the most common in rural areas).

Devaluation impacts negatively on employment except in the case of the employment of unskilled women, presumably because of its impact on the textile sector oriented to the external market. The most negatively affected are the independent urban workers (employment of unskilled workers falls 3.3 per cent and

Table 11.8 Peru: CGE simulations – effects on employment and remunerations

Employment categories	Base year (level)	50% Tariff cut (flexible gov. deficit)	50% Tariff cut (fixed gov. deficit)	50% Tariff increase	10% Devaluation	10% Increase import prices	10% Increase export prices	10% Increase foreign savings	10% Increase productivity	20% Increase in export demand	10% Increase wages	FTAA
	(millions of persons)				(percentage change from baseline)							
Male-urban-unskilled-wage earner	0.56	1.24	1.96	−1.16	−0.87	−2.60	2.22	0.15	15.27	5.07	−12.02	1.78
Male-urban-unskilled-self-employed	0.69	1.35	1.93	−1.26	−3.13	−3.26	1.88	0.31	17.21	4.08	−2.14	1.94
Male-urban-skilled-wage earner	1.18	1.12	1.39	−1.05	−0.59	−2.01	1.16	0.01	12.22	3.28	−11.35	1.61
Male-urban-skilled-self-employed	0.74	1.04	1.53	−0.99	−5.79	−2.96	1.29	0.40	14.81	3.40	−1.33	1.48
Male-rural-unskilled	1.73	0.73	0.98	−0.72	−1.98	−1.94	1.23	0.14	14.01	3.37	−1.84	0.67
Male-rural-skilled	0.42	1.19	1.32	−1.11	−0.97	−2.45	1.32	0.12	11.99	3.05	−0.04	1.71
Female-urban-unskilled-wage earner	0.13	1.33	1.21	−1.23	2.34	−1.98	1.15	−0.17	13.50	2.84	−11.22	1.83
Female-urban-unskilled-self-employed	0.77	1.77	1.46	−1.63	−0.21	−3.34	2.10	0.05	16.25	4.95	−2.39	2.35
Female-urban-skilled-wage earner	0.71	1.14	1.05	−1.07	−0.60	−2.20	1.14	0.05	10.55	2.86	−10.92	1.60
Female-urban-skilled-self-employed	0.49	1.51	1.22	−1.40	−0.47	−2.88	1.61	0.05	13.52	3.89	−1.41	1.88
Female-rural-unskilled	1.28	1.42	1.15	−1.32	2.70	−2.28	1.87	−0.16	14.64	4.28	−2.16	1.74
Female-rural-skilled	0.17	1.13	1.14	−1.06	−2.90	−2.60	1.46	0.23	10.20	3.48	0.55	1.60
Total	8.85	0.00	0.00	0.00	0.00	0.00	0.00	0.00	0.00	0.00	0.00	0.00

(Continued)

Table 11.8 (Continued)

	Base year (level)	50% Tariff cut (flexible gov. deficit)	50% Tariff cut (fixed gov. deficit)	50% Tariff increase	10% Devaluation	10% Increase import prices	10% Increase export prices	10% Increase foreign savings	10% Increase productivity	20% Increase in export demand	10% Increase wages	FTAA
Average nominal factor income	(thousands of new soles)				(percentage change from baseline)							
Male-urban-unskilled-wage earner	3.68	−0.12	−0.21	0.11	−2.25	−0.30	−0.21	0.16	0.58	−0.57	10	−0.28
Male-urban-unskilled-self-employed	2.57	0.06	−0.23	−0.05	1.81	0.19	0.10	−0.13	−0.36	0.36	−0.37	−0.10
Male-urban-skilled-wage earner	7.68	0.03	−0.02	−0.02	−1.17	−0.38	0.06	0.11	0.88	−0.15	10	0.00
Male-urban-skilled-self-employed	4.95	0.24	0.04	−0.22	1.96	−0.19	0.31	−0.10	1.06	0.60	−0.82	0.24
Male-rural-unskilled	1.00	−0.35	−1.05	0.31	2.83	1.17	−0.91	−0.30	−2.56	−1.27	0.07	−0.92
Male-rural-skilled	2.16	−0.55	−1.03	0.49	2.85	1.37	−0.55	−0.27	−0.49	−0.47	−1.48	−1.42
Female-urban-unskilled-wage earner	2.84	0.08	0.00	−0.08	−0.12	−0.33	0.42	0.05	0.22	0.72	10	−0.02
Female-urban-unskilled-self-employed	1.10	−0.05	0.06	0.04	−0.27	0.00	0.08	0.03	0.33	0.22	−0.37	−0.12
Female-urban-skilled-wage earner	4.79	0.10	0.03	−0.09	0.21	−0.22	0.27	0.01	0.79	0.48	10	0.07
Female-urban-skilled-self-employed	1.67	0.12	0.21	−0.12	−0.36	−0.36	0.29	0.05	1.69	0.68	−0.95	0.16
Female-rural-unskilled	0.33	−0.86	−1.13	0.77	−0.96	1.42	−1.25	−0.06	−3.08	−1.65	0.31	−1.71
Female-rural-skilled	1.95	−0.19	−0.52	0.17	2.53	0.70	−0.34	−0.23	1.65	−0.19	−1.88	−0.70
Labour	0.00	0.00	0.00	0.00	0.00	0.00	0.00	0.00	0.00	0.00	0.00	0.00
Capital	0.99	1.24	1.32	−1.15	−0.14	−2.43	1.59	0.06	13.59	3.82	−1.81	1.64

of skilled workers 5.8 per cent), who work primarily in construction, machinery and transport equipment, and furniture, as well as in commerce and various services. In addition, devaluation leads to a decline in wages for urban wage workers and to an increase for urban and rural independent workers (greater than 2 per cent).

An increase in the price of imported goods has a clear negative effect on all types of employment, but much less so for employment in rural areas. At the same time, it negatively affects remunerations of urban workers and positively affects those of rural workers. This could be due to the fact that rural areas produce agricultural and mineral goods that can compete with imports and because their productive activities do not use imported inputs. The opposite occurs with the shock in export prices, since their increase has a positive effect on employment (though it favours employment more in the urban areas), while remunerations tend to fall in rural areas.

An increase in foreign savings has a significant positive effect but it is differentiated, favouring the employment of workers in urban areas, especially men, and among them, especially skilled labour. With the exception of urban wage workers and urban women, this shock has a slight negative effect on wages, especially for the rural worker.

Increased productivity has a much more significant positive effect on employment in activities that use unskilled labour (especially independent urban workers with 16 per cent), and it favours the employment of men. This effect is accompanied, however, by a slight decline in remuneration, which in the case of rural women is greater than 3 per cent. This decline does not happen among skilled urban workers (whose remunerations grow by 1 per cent, especially among independent workers).

An increase in the demand for exports strongly increases the demand for employment, especially for unskilled urban workers (between 4 and 5 per cent) who usually are employed in the branches of activity that grow the most. In terms of remunerations, rural workers and urban male wage workers are negatively affected (independent workers increase their income), though wages for urban women grow due to sectors like textile, which use a great deal of female labour.

The FTAA would have a generally positive effect on employment, especially among urban independent workers (which is consistent with the case of an increase in exports), but it would have less benefit for rural employment because of the impact on agricultural activities. This could be due to competition with imported agricultural products that encounter lower tariffs and to the fact that the labour most in demand would be for the most competitive activities. In this case, wages of rural workers fall around 1 per cent and those of unskilled urban workers fall slightly. In contrast, the WTO scenario would lead to a greater increase in employment, especially for men, if it allowed a significant increase of national production. However, it would be much more favourable for urban areas (primarily for unskilled urban labour). In addition, it would increase remuneration for almost all types of workers (by about 0.5 per cent). Thus, under the integration agreements that are currently the real options for liberalization, since both total employment and remuneration increase, results indicate that any possible trade-offs between employment and remuneration are outweighed by the positive effects on economic activity levels. It would seem, then, that these agreements, especially the WTO, lead to a general improvement in the labour market.

11.4 Impact of external shocks and trade reform on poverty and inequality

In order to determine changes in poverty and inequality levels, microsimulations were carried out for each of the external shocks simulated with the CGE model. Another microsimulation was carried out using the labour market structures for the year 2000.[15] This last exercise is to simulate, in reduced form, the effects of the changes observed between 1994 and 2000, since the level of liberalization in this year was the highest.

Labour market structure for the microsimulations

The microsimulation methodology used for this project was developed by Paes de Barros (1999) and detailed by Vos (2002) (see also Chapter 3). This focus considers the labour market structure to be determined by labour force participation rates and unemployment rates for individuals of various kinds, employment structure by production activity, employment category and the skill level for each type of individual worker and the average remuneration of category.[16] The objective is to learn how labour income and per capita household income levels – and thus, poverty and inequality – would change if the economic structure were determined by values different from these indicators. This information is obtained by imposing this structure through random assignments from the survey data. Changes in poverty are measured using poverty rates calculated by comparing the national poverty line with total per capita household income,[17] and extreme poverty is estimated using the cost of the minimum food basket as the poverty line. The Gini coefficient for per capita household income was used to measure inequality.

For the microsimulations, sectors were divided into tradables and non-tradables. Extractive and industrial activities were defined as tradable, while construction, commerce and service activities are the non-tradables. Employment categories distinguish between independent workers and wage earners, and education levels distinguish between skilled and unskilled labour.

Phases of the microsimulations

The microsimulations methodology was implemented in the following phases:[18]

1. Modification of employment structure.
2. Since the CGE model does not include decisions about participation in the labour force, no distinction is made between the effect of changes in participation rates and that of a change in unemployment. This phase therefore only

considers changes in the aggregate employment rate (EAP employed/working age population).[19]

3. Modification of the employment structure by sector of economic activity and by occupational category.
4. Modification of employment structure by remuneration levels of occupational category.
5. Modification of remuneration differentials by activity and occupational category.
6. Modification of average remuneration.
7. Modification of employment structure by skill level and occupational category.

The effects of the various phases were estimated consecutively (phases 1 and 2, phases 1 through 3, and so forth until reaching phases 1 through 6).[20] Each phase of simulations was carried out 32 times to obtain adequate reliability in the average result.

Effects of trade liberalization and external shocks on poverty and inequality

Changes at the macroeconomic level lead to changes in employment, mean labour incomes and labour income inequality, and thereby to changes in household income and in poverty and inequality. Outcomes have been calculated at the national level, distinguishing between rural and urban areas. They are presented in Table 11.9.[21]

In general, poverty and inequality of per capita income move in opposite directions as a reaction to liberalization measures or shocks. Labour income inequality tends to move in a differentiated manner, remaining constant or falling slightly in most cases.[22] The observed effects have the expected signs, though it is difficult to trace all the transmission channels through which these results were generated.[23]

The tariff cut slightly decreases poverty by 0.5 per cent – primarily because of the effect on the urban household incomes – and increasing tariffs has the inverse effect. Devaluation affects poverty in a differentiated way since rural poverty remains almost unaltered but urban poverty grows by almost 1 point, increasing poverty at the national level by 0.5 per cent. Extreme poverty also grows slightly (0.5 per cent). These effects are probably due to changes in the level of employment and not so much in real incomes. Devaluation raises the costs of production of some activities and favours export activities, causing an increase in lower paid jobs in extractive activities and activities intensive in the use of unskilled labour. Because of this, poverty would increase in spite of the improvement in the relative income of workers in these activities. In the case of rural areas, the impact on income levels would counteract the negative impact of employment.

Raising the price of imported goods has a slightly negative effect on rural poverty, and increases poverty by 1.2 per cent in urban areas, where industrial activities use imported goods as inputs. This occurs because – though employment

Table 11.9 Peru: microsimulations – effects of trade policy measures and external shocks on poverty and inequality (32 repetitions)

	Rural				Urban				Total			
	Poverty incidence[1]		Income inequality[2] (Gini)		Poverty incidence[1]		Income inequality[2] (Gini)		Poverty incidence[1]		Income inequality[2] (Gini)	
	Total poverty	Extreme poverty	Per capita incomes	Labour incomes	Total poverty	Extreme poverty	Per capita incomes	Labour incomes	Total poverty	Extreme poverty	Per capita incomes	Labour incomes
Base level 1994	61.04	35.73	43.29	71.87	40.97	10.30	43.99	51.99	48.20	19.47	47.97	60.59
Labour market structure of 2000												
Phase 1	58.08	33.91	48.64	72.25	36.65	8.95	43.52	52.22	44.34	17.91	48.64	60.83
Phases 1–2	57.91	33.58	48.35	72.04	36.65	8.88	43.49	52.22	44.28	17.75	48.53	60.76
Phases 1–3	57.91	33.58	48.35	72.04	36.62	8.88	43.49	52.17	44.26	17.75	48.53	60.73
Phases 1–4	63.18	38.58	48.06	72.34	38.74	10.22	44.08	52.94	47.51	20.40	49.47	61.65
Phases 1–5	61.05	36.18	48.42	72.34	36.15	9.23	44.03	52.94	45.09	18.91	49.53	61.65
Phases 1–6	61.11	36.31	49.18	72.54	36.28	9.31	44.12	53.18	45.20	19.00	49.74	61.86
50% Tariff cut (flexible gov. deficit)												
Phase 1	60.72	35.56	44.03	71.75	40.30	10.13	43.96	51.99	47.63	19.26	48.09	60.46
Phases 1–2	60.72	35.56	44.76	71.74	40.25	10.10	43.94	51.99	47.60	19.24	48.21	60.46
Phases 1–3	60.72	35.56	44.76	71.74	40.25	10.10	43.94	51.99	47.60	19.24	48.21	60.46
Phases 1–4	60.87	35.93	44.72	71.74	40.10	10.07	43.94	52.01	47.56	19.36	48.25	60.49
Phases 1–5	60.88	35.96	44.71	71.74	40.16	10.10	43.95	52.01	47.60	19.39	48.25	60.49
Phases 1–6	60.88	35.96	44.88	71.74	40.16	10.10	43.94	52.01	47.60	19.38	48.29	60.49

(Continued)

Table 11.9 (Continued)

	Rural				Urban				Total			
	Poverty incidence[1]		Income inequality[2] (Gini)		Poverty incidence[1]		Income inequality[2] (Gini)		Poverty incidence[1]		Income inequality[2] (Gini)	
	Total poverty	Extreme poverty	Per capita incomes	Labour incomes	Total poverty	Extreme poverty	Per capita incomes	Labour incomes	Total poverty	Extreme poverty	Per capita incomes	Labour incomes
50% Tariff cut (fixed gov. deficit)												
Phase 1	60.67	35.52	45.18	71.73	40.16	10.05	43.92	51.97	47.52	19.19	48.29	60.44
Phases 1–2	60.63	35.53	44.28	71.72	40.14	10.09	43.96	51.97	47.50	19.23	48.13	60.43
Phases 1–3	60.63	35.53	44.28	71.72	40.14	10.09	43.96	51.97	47.50	19.23	48.13	60.43
Phases 1–4	60.89	36.00	44.23	71.70	40.02	10.08	43.96	51.99	47.51	19.39	48.18	60.46
Phases 1–5	60.88	35.98	44.23	71.70	39.96	10.07	43.96	51.99	47.47	19.37	48.18	60.46
Phases 1–6	60.88	35.98	44.24	71.71	39.96	10.07	43.96	51.98	47.47	19.37	48.18	60.46
50% Tariff increase												
Phase 1	61.40	36.18	43.40	71.76	41.51	10.76	44.18	51.98	48.65	19.89	48.11	60.49
Phases 1–2	61.35	36.13	43.39	71.73	41.48	10.80	44.16	51.99	48.61	19.90	48.08	60.48
Phases 1–3	61.35	36.13	43.39	71.73	41.47	10.80	44.16	51.98	48.61	19.90	48.08	60.47
Phases 1–4	61.41	36.15	43.39	71.74	41.54	10.83	44.17	51.98	48.67	19.93	48.09	60.48
Phases 1–5	61.39	36.13	43.39	71.74	41.50	10.82	44.17	51.98	48.64	19.91	48.09	60.48
Phases 1–6	61.39	36.13	43.40	71.74	41.49	10.82	44.17	51.98	48.64	19.91	48.09	60.48
10% Devaluation												
Phase 1	61.42	36.42	43.53	71.93	41.80	11.10	44.33	52.07	48.85	20.19	48.20	60.66
Phases 1–2	61.32	36.28	43.50	71.90	41.76	11.04	44.22	52.02	48.78	20.10	48.11	60.62
Phases 1–3	61.32	36.28	43.50	71.90	41.75	11.03	44.21	51.98	48.78	20.10	48.10	60.60

(Continued)

Table 11.9 (Continued)

	Rural				Urban				Total			
	Poverty incidence[1]		Income inequality[2] (Gini)		Poverty incidence[1]		Income inequality[2] (Gini)		Poverty incidence[1]		Income inequality[2] (Gini)	
	Total poverty	Extreme poverty	Per capita incomes	Labour incomes	Total poverty	Extreme poverty	Per capita incomes	Labour incomes	Total poverty	Extreme poverty	Per capita incomes	Labour incomes
Phases 1–4	61.16	36.28	43.52	71.99	42.03	11.21	44.27	52.08	48.90	20.21	48.11	60.67
Phases 1–5	61.07	36.22	43.53	71.99	41.91	11.16	44.26	52.08	48.79	20.16	48.11	60.67
Phases 1–6	61.08	36.21	43.53	71.99	41.91	11.16	44.26	52.08	48.79	20.16	48.11	60.67
10% Increase in import prices												
Phase 1	61.82	36.76	43.58	71.78	42.18	11.41	44.47	52.01	49.23	20.51	48.33	60.53
Phases 1–2	61.68	36.65	43.54	71.71	42.11	11.37	44.39	51.98	49.14	20.45	48.26	60.49
Phases 1–3	61.68	36.65	43.54	71.71	42.10	11.37	44.39	51.97	49.13	20.45	48.26	60.48
Phases 1–4	61.53	36.58	43.57	71.73	42.27	11.43	44.40	51.97	49.18	20.46	48.24	60.47
Phases 1–5	61.46	36.51	43.58	71.73	42.20	11.40	44.40	51.97	49.12	20.42	48.24	60.47
Phases 1–6	61.46	36.51	43.58	71.74	42.20	11.40	44.40	51.97	49.11	20.42	48.24	60.47
10% Increase in export prices												
Phase 1	60.56	35.46	44.87	71.74	40.19	10.04	43.98	51.98	47.50	19.17	48.23	60.46
Phases 1–2	60.37	35.39	47.03	71.72	40.16	10.13	43.96	51.99	47.42	19.20	48.64	60.46
Phases 1–3	60.37	35.39	47.03	71.72	40.16	10.14	43.96	51.99	47.42	19.21	48.63	60.46
Phases 1–4	60.63	35.75	46.99	71.72	40.00	10.09	43.95	52.01	47.40	19.31	48.67	60.50
Phases 1–5	60.67	35.86	46.97	71.72	40.05	10.13	43.96	52.01	47.45	19.36	48.67	60.50
Phases 1–6	60.65	35.86	47.00	71.74	40.05	10.13	43.96	52.00	47.45	19.36	48.68	60.50

(Continued)

Table 11.9 (Continued)

	Rural				Urban				Total			
	Poverty incidence[1]		Income inequality[2] (Gini)		Poverty incidence[1]		Income inequality[2] (Gini)		Poverty incidence[1]		Income inequality[2] (Gini)	
	Total poverty	Extreme poverty	Per capita incomes	Labour incomes	Total poverty	Extreme poverty	Per capita incomes	Labour incomes	Total poverty	Extreme poverty	Per capita incomes	Labour incomes
10% increase in foreign savings												
Phase 1	61.03	35.73	43.69	71.76	40.88	10.27	43.99	52.02	48.11	19.42	48.04	60.49
Phases 1–2	61.01	35.73	43.33	71.74	40.88	10.25	43.99	52.01	48.11	19.40	47.97	60.48
Phases 1–3	61.01	35.73	43.33	71.74	40.87	10.25	43.98	52.01	48.10	19.40	47.97	60.48
Phases 1–4	61.18	35.88	43.33	71.74	40.79	10.30	43.99	52.00	48.11	19.49	47.99	60.49
Phases 1–5	61.22	35.96	43.33	71.74	40.82	10.32	44.00	52.00	48.14	19.53	47.99	60.49
Phases 1–6	61.22	35.96	43.38	71.76	40.82	10.32	44.00	52.00	48.14	19.53	48.00	60.50
10% increase productivity												
Phase 1	56.59	32.31	47.60	71.66	35.53	8.77	44.00	51.91	43.09	17.22	48.81	60.38
Phases 1–2	56.47	32.29	47.70	71.61	35.56	8.89	44.03	51.91	43.07	17.29	48.85	60.36
Phases 1–3	56.47	32.29	47.70	71.61	35.55	8.89	44.03	51.89	43.06	17.29	48.85	60.35
Phases 1–4	56.91	32.19	47.13	71.44	35.13	8.62	43.90	51.91	42.95	17.08	48.74	60.35
Phases 1–5	57.11	32.46	47.09	71.44	35.36	8.82	43.91	51.91	43.17	17.31	48.74	60.35
Phases 1–6	57.11	32.47	47.09	71.43	35.43	8.87	43.87	51.87	43.22	17.34	48.70	60.32
20% increase in export demand												
Phase 1	59.70	35.02	47.16	71.74	38.98	9.80	43.90	51.97	46.42	18.85	48.61	60.45
Phases 1–2	59.69	35.01	46.92	71.72	39.06	9.80	43.84	51.98	46.47	18.85	48.51	60.45

(Continued)

Table 11.9 (Continued)

	Rural				Urban				Total			
	Poverty incidence[1]		Income inequality[2] (Gini)		Poverty incidence[1]		Income inequality[2] (Gini)		Poverty incidence[1]		Income inequality[2] (Gini)	
	Total poverty	Extreme poverty	Per capita incomes	Labour incomes	Total poverty	Extreme poverty	Per capita incomes	Labour incomes	Total poverty	Extreme poverty	Per capita incomes	Labour incomes
Phases 1–3	59.69	35.01	46.92	71.72	39.04	9.80	43.84	51.98	46.46	18.85	48.50	60.45
Phases 1–4	59.95	35.26	46.84	71.69	38.90	9.72	43.82	51.99	46.46	18.89	48.53	60.48
Phases 1–5	60.02	35.33	46.83	71.69	38.99	9.76	43.82	51.99	46.54	18.94	48.53	60.48
Phases 1–6	60.02	35.33	46.82	71.69	38.99	9.76	43.81	51.98	46.54	18.94	48.52	60.47
FTAA												
Phase 1	60.66	35.56	44.48	71.76	40.05	10.07	43.97	51.98	47.45	19.22	48.20	60.45
Phases 1–2	60.74	35.54	44.13	71.75	40.02	10.05	43.91	51.99	47.46	19.20	48.10	60.45
Phases 1–3	60.74	35.54	44.13	71.75	40.02	10.05	43.91	51.99	47.46	19.20	48.10	60.45
Phases 1–4	61.02	36.03	44.08	71.75	39.93	10.03	43.92	52.01	47.50	19.36	48.15	60.49
Phases 1–5	61.02	35.98	44.08	71.75	39.86	10.01	43.92	52.01	47.46	19.34	48.15	60.49
Phases 1–6	61.02	35.98	44.09	71.75	39.86	10.01	43.92	52.01	47.46	19.34	48.15	60.49
WTO												
Phase 1	60.35	35.35	44.96	71.76	39.90	10.03	43.95	51.99	47.24	19.12	48.23	60.49
Phases 1–2	60.28	35.33	45.78	71.75	39.87	9.98	43.94	51.99	47.19	19.08	48.37	60.49
Phases 1–3	60.28	35.33	45.78	71.75	39.86	9.99	43.93	51.98	47.19	19.09	48.37	60.48
Phases 1–4	60.28	35.55	45.73	71.74	39.69	9.90	43.93	52.02	47.08	19.11	48.39	60.52
Phases 1–5	60.47	35.59	45.71	71.74	39.85	9.95	43.93	52.02	47.26	19.16	48.38	60.52
Phases 1–6	60.47	35.59	45.89	71.76	39.85	9.95	43.92	52.01	47.26	19.15	48.42	60.52

Notes: 1 Poverty incidence estimated based on per capita household incomes
2 Inequality measures are based on per capita household income and per worker labour incomes

and income structures are similar – employment and labour income levels decrease, causing total poverty to increase by 1 per cent. On the other hand, when export prices are increased, urban poverty falls by 1 per cent, rural poverty by 0.5 per cent and total poverty by 0.7 per cent.

Increasing foreign savings has almost no effect on total poverty levels or on inequality. However, increased productivity has a significant effect on poverty, lowering it by more than 4 per cent. Poverty rates fall more in urban areas than in rural areas (5.5 and 4 per cent, respectively). The level of urban inequality does not change much, but in rural areas it rises almost 4 points because of changes in employment level of each type.

An increase in the demand for export goods has the expected, though small, effect of decreasing rural poverty by 1 per cent and urban poverty by 2 per cent. Total poverty decreases by 1.7 per cent. Traditional agriculture's larger participation in employment is counteracted in part because of its lower relative income.

Finally, in the case of the trade agreements, the FTAA only improves the situation in urban areas where poverty falls 1 per cent causing the national poverty rate to drop by 0.8 per cent. Poverty does not fall in rural areas. With the WTO agreement, urban poverty and total poverty decrease 1 per cent, though inequality grows slightly. In this case, rural poverty goes down a little (0.5 per cent), causing extreme poverty to fall slightly, but rural income inequality increases by more than 2 per cent.

In sum, trade liberalization measures in general tend to reduce poverty in both urban and rural areas. However, the impact is rather small and certainly much smaller than the impact expected by many observers. The simulated impact also differs from observed patterns. For example, in the period of devaluations after 1994, both poverty and extreme poverty fell (rather than the simulated increase). However, the observed decline in this period was probably due in part to the expansion of targeted social and poverty reduction programmes, an aspect not taken into account in the simulations. Possibly as an upshot of the rise in social spending, an increase in productivity could be recorded in the tradables sector from 1996 onwards. This productivity increase may have favoured lower income groups most. Further, the rise in income inequality as simulated in the trade reform scenarios is consistent with observed patterns after 1994 and, to a lesser degree, through to the end of the decade.

11.5 Concluding remarks

The analysis described earlier leads to the following conclusions about the experience of Peru's export sector during the 1990s:

- Peru's experience suggests that the following conditions are important for achieving export growth: (1) a stable macroeconomic environment, (2) a programme to modernize the institutional framework protecting private investment and (3) improving basic infrastructure services. These reforms have been accompanied by aggressive trade liberalization measures and financial liberalization and supported by a large inflow of external financial resources obtained through a programme of privatizations and concessions and through improved access to foreign capital markets. The capital inflow helped finance widening deficits in the current account balance. At the same time it enhanced dependence on foreign capital.

- These policies showed little concern, however, with the recovery of employment levels and real incomes of workers or with reducing inequality in the distribution of wealth, despite the fact that the reform policies were accompanied by an increase in social expenditure for poverty reduction.
- The pattern of growth in the export sector was sustained primarily by the recovery of traditional sectors, which responded to new conditions of competitiveness and to reductions in barriers to entry into other markets and, to a lesser degree, by a diversification towards processed traditional products with greater value added. The traditional pattern of an economy based on primary exports has not been reversed. Delays in implementing reforms in other key areas for competitiveness – such as ports and infrastructure services to support foreign trade – may explain the smaller response of the non-traditional exports.
- The export sector was an important source of aggregate demand for the economy during the 1990s, allowing the overall pace of growth to be maintained, jobs to be created and improvements to be made in productivity in tradable sectors, among which extractive activities (mining, fishing and agriculture) stand out. However, this strategy did not generate a significant improvement in the real income of the tradable sectors, but we do observe greater income inequality.
- Counterfactual analysis shows that Peru would probably benefit from further trade liberalization and export promotion. Macroeconomic indicators all improve, with economic activity, consumption and employment rising while both the trade deficit and the government deficit fall. Households benefit in general and urban households headed by skilled workers see the greatest improvement in their levels of consumption. The overall impact is rather small, however.
- Findings show that the country is highly vulnerable to external shocks that frequently accompany the liberalization process. This is probably due in part to per capita exports being very low, but more importantly to the heavy dependence on primary exports and to the high import dependence on complementary consumer goods and inputs, causing a persistent trend towards a widening trade deficit. In addition, a devaluation of the exchange rate tends to have contractionary effects on the economy offsetting the positive impact of other liberalization measures.
- In general, households tend to benefit from increasing levels of consumption following trade liberalization measures. Urban households with unskilled household heads show the greatest gains in terms of consumption levels. Employment levels improve, but not significantly. Unskilled workers gain most in terms of new jobs. The outcome for household incomes is mixed, depending on the type of employment of household members and tends to be negative in rural areas. Thus, whether or not rural workers or rural households

see improvements in their situation will depend more on exogenous changes in the prices or demand for the goods produced in these areas.

- In this sense, favourable macroeconomic indicators do not translate into a substantive improvement in the indicators for poverty and income distribution. Poverty reacts very little to greater liberalization or to positive exogenous shocks and the smallest impact is in the rural areas (linked to tradable sectors). Income inequality remains high and tends to increase further (in part because of the differential effects on labour incomes in tradable and non-tradable sectors, and between rural and urban workers). The magnitude of the latter effect depends on what kind of shock occurs in the economy and its effect on rural areas where there is a tendency towards a greater increase in inequality. Thus, achieving a significant reduction in poverty will be difficult because, all other things being equal, it would require, for example, an export growth in the order of 50 per cent. Alternatively a much more redistributive pattern of export growth would be needed to make a visible impact on poverty reduction.
- In any case, results of this analysis suggest that fishing and the elaboration of fishmeal, and, to a lesser degree, mining and textiles, would be the sectors that gain most from existing export promotion policies and which could lead the growth in production in other labour-intensive sectors (like construction, commerce and transportation). In order to achieve higher economic growth, the development of these sectors should be promoted further with investment and/or foreign assistance that allow greater absorption of technology and improvements in efficiency. In this way, employment would grow and poverty levels could fall.
- Trade integration through agreements such as the FTAA and the WTO agreements would allow a generalized improvement in employment levels and would lead to a reduction in poverty, especially if the WTO agreements are adopted. In this sense, integration with the world economy through the WTO would be important and would allow Peru to take advantage of its export sectors and achieve an increase in productivity in the tradable sectors, which would lead to a significant improvement in production, employment and income in these sectors, and, therefore, in the national economy.
- Finally, economic liberalization would have a net positive impact if it generated significant increases in productivity levels. To the extent this goal can be achieved, significant reductions in poverty levels can be attained, but inequality would increase in rural areas. In this sense, in order to achieve adequate growth based on export sectors, it would be important to design and implement policies that permit productivity increases in tradable sector businesses and in the sectors that are intensive in the use of unskilled labour.

Notes

1 These first three sections are based on a document prepared as part of the first stage of this project by Armando Cáceres with the collaboration of Juan Manuel García.
2 See Abusada *et al.* (2001).

3 See Saavedra (1998).
4 People with more than 9 years of education are considered skilled.
5 Values are deflated using the Consumer Price Index of Metropolitan Lima (IPC).
6 These types of income are calculated for people over 14 years of age (since the survey does not report information for minors), and have been attributed to the branch of their principal activity.
7 Instituto Nacional de Estadísticas e Informática, INEI (1997).
8 Though the sectors in which this capital was invested have not been taken into account.
9 In order to reconcile the disaggregation of the International Food Policy Research Institute (IFPRI) estimated prices and tariffs, the proportion of each good in total trade and in imports, respectively, were used as weights.
10 The analysis was also done using the closure in which savings is adjusted to maintain investment in order to see how results changed. Though growth in the various GDP demand categories varies, the overall effect on growth is similar. Because of this, the effects on employment and income are not very different. (For this reason differences in the results of the microsimulations carried out later are not very significant either.)
11 Though one must keep in mind that, in this case, the exchange rate is considered fixed, while in reality it is a managed float.
12 This shock in exchange rate has various effects if capital cannot be moved between activities (short term) and is slightly less recessive (GDP falls 1 per cent though absorption falls by 3.5 per cent). In this case, investments fall 10 per cent and exports increase by only 9 per cent, because of restrictions on capital mobility.
13 This measures the income needed if the market prices were the base prices for generating the same level of wellbeing (indirect utility) that the household obtains with the new incomes and prices after the simulation. The 'equivalent variation' can be obtained as a difference that measures the equivalent change in income.
14 Though the activities of services oriented to the domestic market could be affected when the government decides to maintain a fixed deficit instead of a flexible one.
15 Obtained from the 2000 Living Standards Survey.
16 This is modelled using the average remuneration for all individuals and the average relative wage of each type of wage labour with respect to this value.
17 Total per capita household income has been calculated using the new levels of labour income for household members, but keeping constant the non-labour income such as capital and transfer income because of difficulties in reflecting changes in the latter on levels reported in the survey (there is a serious problem of under-recording).
18 To adequately implement the microsimulations with the CGE results, some corrections were made in the surveys since the income employment structures of the model are not exactly the same as those of the survey. The base simulation with the estimated parameters does not exactly replicate the SAM data. Furthermore, the SAM only keeps the income structure by type of worker in each branch of economic activity, but the income per activity is different from that of the survey. In order to ensure that the CGE and survey data are compatible, these differences are corrected for by modifying the weight of the individuals in the survey by type of worker and re-scaling the average income levels by branch of economic activity and type so that they become the same as the base simulation.
19 It takes the employment rate, rather than the unemployment rate, because given the fixed participation rate in the CGE model some simulations lead to employment levels higher than the economically active population.
20 People who go on to be employed and who do not have a particular job sector or category were randomly assigned to each sector according to existing percentages in their type of job.
21 A simulation was also carried out for the labour market structure in the year 2000. Results showed that the rural poverty remained constant, urban poverty fell more than 4 points and poverty at the national level fell 3 points. The direction of impact is the

same as that observed in the case of poverty measured by income. Extreme poverty rises in rural areas (less than 0.5 per cent) and at the national level it falls very slightly (0.5 per cent). This result is due, above all, to higher employment rates between 1994 and 2000 (increase in labour participation and market adjustment through quantities). However, the change in relative income by branch of activity and type of worker counteracts this tendency, especially in the rural areas.

22 In this case the tendency for inequality to decrease in the simulations is due, above all, to the closure used for the labour market, which keep relative wages constant in CGE model simulation. In reality, these would have been affected by liberalization as we saw in the first microsimulation (in this respect the latter is not comparable to the rest).

23 A more detailed analysis of these effects should be done in function of the SAM structure and the estimated parameters of the model.

References

Abusada, C. *et al.* (2001) 'La Reforma Incompleta', Lima: Research Centre of the University of the Pacific and the Peruvian Institute of Economics, IPE, August.

Adelman, I. (1984) 'Beyond export led growth', *World Development,* 12: 937–49.

Bourguignon, François, *et al.* (1989) 'Macroeconomic adjustment and income distribution: a macro–micro simulation model', Development Centre Technical Papers, Paris: OECD.

Cáceres, Armando (2001) 'Estrategias de crecimiento liderado por exportaciones: Efectos sobre el crecimiento, desigualdad y pobreza – El caso de Perú', Lima: Development Analysis Group.

Instituto Nacional de Estadística e Informática (1997) 'Elasticidad y demanda de los principales bienes y servicios,' Lima: INEI.

Instituto Nacional de Estadística e Informática (2001) 'Multiplicadores de la economía Peruana: Una aplicación de la tabla insumo producto 1994,' Lima: INEI (March).

Löfgren, Hans (2000) 'External shocks and domestic poverty alleviation: simulations with a CGE model of Malawi,' Washington: IFPRI (mimeo).

Löfgren, H., R. Lee and S. Robinson (2001) 'A standard computable general equilibrium (CGE) model in GAMS,' TMD Discussion Paper No. 75. Trade and Macroeconomics Division, Washington, DC: International Food Policy Research (IFPRI).

Morley, S. (2000) 'The effect of growth and economic reform on the distribution of income in Latin America,' *CEPAL Review* 71.

Morley, Samuel and Rob Vos (2000) 'Export-led economic strategies: effects on poverty, inequality and growth in Latin America and the Caribbean,' New York: UNDP, ECLAC, IFPRI.

Paes de Barros, R. (1999) 'Evaluando el impacto de cambios en la estructura salarial y del empleo sobre la distribución de la renta,' Río de Janeiro: IPEA (mimeo).

Saavedra, Jaime (1998) 'Crisis real o crisis de expectativas? El empleo en el Perú antes y después de las reformas estructurales,' Working Document No. 25, Lima: GRADE.

Saavedra, Jaime and Juan José Díaz (1999) 'Distribución del ingreso y del gasto antes y después de las reformas estructurales,' Economic Reform Series No. 34, ECLAC, Santiago: ECLAC.

Saavedra, Jaime, Máximo Torero and Juan José Díaz (2000) 'Liberalización de la balanza de pagos: Efectos sobre el crecimiento, el empleo y desigualdad y pobreza: El caso de Perú,' Lima: Development Analysis Group (GRADE).

Vos, Rob (2002) 'Export-led economic strategies: effects on poverty, inequality and growth in Latino America and the Caribbean – micro-simulations methodology,' New York: UNDP (mimeo).

12 Uruguay – export growth, poverty and income distribution

Silvia Laens and Marcelo Perera

Abstract

Uruguay began liberalizing its economy in the 1970s. The process continued through the 1990s when the country joined Mercosur. The reforms were mainly oriented at liberalizing trade and financial flows, much less was done in terms of privatization and public sector reform. Uruguay established itself as a regional financial and offshore banking centre. In the early 1990s, inflation was stabilized on the basis of high capital inflows and a stabilization policy that used the exchange rate as a nominal anchor. The ensuing real exchange rate appreciation harmed export growth with the rest of the world and, along with the surge in capital inflows, pushed up import demand. Real appreciation of the exchange rate against Uruguay's trading partners in Mercosur was virtually nil and exports benefited from the new set of trade preferences within the group. This made macroeconomic performance in Uruguay strongly dependent on the business cycle in Argentina and Brazil. When these two countries shifted away from a fix on the nominal exchange rate, starting with the floating of the Brazilian *real*, Uruguay's exports were severely hit pushing the economy into recession. The recession was deepened with Argentina's crisis at the turn of the century. Uruguay's economic recovery from the sharp decline in the first half of the 1980s thus lasted until 1998. Employment increased, despite job losses in agriculture and manufacturing following productivity growth associated with the opening process. Employment growth was particularly strong in services. Job shedding in manufacturing was also associated with a fall-out of many firms in import-competing sectors. Real labour incomes also increased during this period of growth. Skilled workers were the main beneficiaries as structural adjustment made production more skill intensive. Labour income inequality increased, but overall employment and real wage increases allowed for a visible reduction in poverty. These trends reversed after 1998. Simulations with the computable general equilibrium for Uruguay confirm the positive effects of trade liberalization in the context of an appreciated exchange rate on growth and poverty reduction. The simulations also suggest that further negotiated trade liberalization in the context of the Free Trade Area of the Americas or the World Trade Organization (WTO) would reinforce these effects. With further unilateral trade liberalization export growth would require maintaining the exchange rate competitive, while employment growth would be served with allowing for some appreciation of the currency. In the case of negotiated, multilateral trade liberalization the nature of the exchange rate regime does not appear to matter for Uruguay in order to reap the gains from trade. World market prices would move in favour of Uruguay's exports, particularly under a WTO scenario that would benefit its agricultural exports. Unskilled workers would be the principal beneficiaries of such a scenario and poverty and inequality would be reduced. It seems to confirm Uruguay's paradoxical relationship with trade integration. Mercosur brought both trade benefits and greater vulnerability to the volatility of the economies of its large neighbours, Argentina and Brazil, while WTO equally would bring trade gains but enhance the country's vulnerability to the volatility in primary commodity markets.

12.1 Introduction

During the last 25 years, Uruguay gradually adopted several reforms along the lines of the Washington Consensus oriented to increase the economic ties between Uruguay and the rest of the world to achieve macroeconomic stability and to put the market at the centre of the resource allocation process. This set of reforms did not include major privatization or deep restructuring of the public sector, but focused on the liberalization of trade and financial flows.

The purpose of this chapter is to analyse the effects of some of the policies adopted and some of the shocks received on income distribution and poverty. The chapter is divided in two main parts. It starts with an overview of macroeconomic trends, with particular emphasis on the incidence of external shocks and domestic policies on the external balance. Next, the role of exports in gross domestic product (GDP) growth is examined at the macro level and by sector. Subsequently, the export performance and composition are studied, paying attention to the competitiveness indicators. The descriptive part of the paper ends with an overview of labour market adjustment.

The second part of the paper deals with counterfactual simulations carried out using a computable general equilibrium (CGE) model. Several experiments were performed trying to illustrate the effects that some specific policies or exogenous shocks might have had on the Uruguayan economy. Subsequently, the results obtained from the CGE simulations are inserted in a microsimulation methodology to assess the impact on the income distribution and poverty. Data from the Continuous Household Survey (CHS) are used to simulate these effects at the household level, taking into account the changes in the labour market obtained with the CGE. The chapter ends with the main conclusions.

12.2 Macroeconomic performance and economic reforms

Uruguay's reforms

The Uruguayan case differs from much of the rest of Latin America in terms of timing and sequencing of the reforms. The process started in the mid-1970s, with great transformations in the financial sector, but only minor progress was made in liberalizing trade. By the end of the 1970s, financial flows were completely liberalized, paving the way for the establishment of a regional financial and off-shore banking centre (Noya *et al.* 1998).

Trade protection had a strong anti-export bias until the 1970s. Thereafter, reforms were carried out gradually focusing on the liberalization of imports. Starting from a maximum of 150 per cent in 1980, tariff reductions were introduced through-out the decade until reaching a maximum tariff of 20 per cent by January 1993 (CINVE 1983, 1986; Laens *et al.* 1993; Laens 1997). Export production was strongly subsidized in the 1970s, but most incentives were dismantled by the end of that decade. From then on, the incentives were limited to a duty draw-back regime, indirect taxes rebates, special credit lines, tax exemptions for investment projects on export activities and bilateral trade agreements (Macadar 1988; Favaro and Sapelli 1989).

In the 1990s, trade policies were dominated by the creation of the Mercosur (an imperfect customs union among Argentina, Brazil, Paraguay and Uruguay). It enhanced access of Uruguayan exports to a very large market (the sum of Argentina and Brazil). At the same time, the growing competition threatened import-substitution production activities in the domestic market.

The Uruguayan economy in the 1990s

The Uruguayan economy recovered in the second half of the 1980s after a sharp decline in the first years of that decade. The performance was better in the 1990s, when GDP growth averaged 3 per cent per year. In fact, the rate of growth was much higher up to the end of 1998 when the first signs of another slowdown appeared. A deep recession set in after the Brazilian devaluation in 1999. This negative per-formance was deepened after the Argentine crisis (Table 12.1).

At the beginning of the 1990s, macroeconomic policy focused on stabilization to counter high inflation and widening fiscal deficits, using the exchange rate as a nominal anchor. At the same time, taxes were raised in order to reduce the fiscal imbalance. This policy was successful in curbing inflation, but the national currency became overvalued, hindering export growth and stimulating imports. Despite a surplus on the non-factor services balance, the current account showed increasing deficits after 1993.

Currency appreciation affected exports to most trading partners, but Uruguay's exports remained competitive in Argentina and Brazil for most of the 1990s, as these countries had adopted similar stabilization policies. This situation changed dramati-cally when the Brazilian currency was allowed to float in January 1999, affecting Uruguayan exports directly and indirectly (through its impact on Argentina).

The impact of external shocks on GDP growth

The vulnerability of the Uruguayan economy to external shocks has become more evident in the 1990s. The current account deteriorated, even in the context of a

Table 12.1 Uruguay: main economic indicators

Year	GDP[1]	Annual inflation[1]	Fiscal balance[2]	Current account deficit[2,3]	Imports of goods and services[2]	Exports of goods and services[2]	Gross capital formation[2]	Unemployment Rate[4]
1980	6.0	63.5	0.1	6.6	20.6	15.0	16.7	7.3
1981	1.9	34.0	−0.1	4.5	18.6	14.7	15.7	6.6
1982	−9.4	19.0	−14.7	5.2	17.2	14.0	15.1	11.9
1983	−5.9	49.2	−12.2	3.6	23.6	25.7	13.7	14.7
1984	−1.1	55.3	−8.9	2.2	20.4	25.5	10.7	14.0
1985	1.5	72.2	−6.8	1.7	19.9	26.7	8.4	13.1
1986	8.9	76.4	−5.2	−1.5	23.7	27.3	8.7	10.1
1987	7.9	63.6	−4.1	1.6	25.4	23.2	10.3	9.1
1988	1.5	62.2	−4.5	−0.6	24.9	24.5	12.4	8.6
1989	1.1	80.4	−6.2	−1.6	25.9	26.0	11.7	8.0
1990	0.3	112.5	−3.0	−2.0	25.6	29.5	10.8	8.5
1991	3.5	102.0	−1.8	−0.7	29.2	29.3	12.6	8.9
1992	7.9	68.5	0.3	0.8	33.9	29.6	13.8	9.0
1993	2.7	54.1	−1.7	1.8	38.7	31.3	15.3	8.3
1994	7.3	44.7	−2.8	2.3	42.7	33.6	15.2	9.2
1995	−1.4	42.2	−1.5	1.3	42.0	33.5	14.7	10.3
1996	5.6	28.3	−1.4	1.2	44.3	35.0	15.3	11.9
1997	5.0	19.8	−1.4	1.1	47.7	37.6	16.1	11.4
1998	4.5	10.8	−0.9	1.8	49.1	36.1	16.5	10.1
1999	−2.8	5.7	−4.0	2.3	47.6	34.4	15.6	11.3
2000	−1.4	4.8	−4.1	2.8	48.4	37.1	13.8	13.6
2001	−3.1	3.6	−4.2	2.9	46.4	35.1	12.9	15.3

Source: Elaborated with data from Central Bank of Uruguay (BCU) and Statistical Office (INE)

Notes
1 Annual cumulative variation
2 Percentage of GDP
3 Negative sign indicates current account surplus
4 1980–5: Montevideo. 1986–2001: urban areas

Table 12.2   Uruguay: current account deficit decomposition (percentage of GNP)

Period	Average change from the base period				
	1985–9	1990–4	1995–2000	1995–8	1999–2000
Base period	1980–4	1985–9	1990–4	1990–4	1995–8
Observed deficit increase	−4.65	2.09	0.49	0.02	1.17
External shocks	−6.61	−2.59	−5.89	−4.78	−3.02
Terms of trade	−1.39	2.16	−1.66	−1.79	0.14
Import price effect	−5.02	−4.56	−4.40	−4.09	−1.10
Export price effect	3.63	6.71	2.74	2.30	1.23
Interest rate	−2.45	−2.30	0.17	0.24	−0.22
World trade	−2.77	−2.45	−4.40	−3.23	−2.94
Other external variables	*3.43*	*−1.37*	*−0.79*	*−0.90*	*0.39*
Accumulated external debt	2.82	−2.71	0.55	0.29	0.76
Net factor rent and transfers (exc. interests)	0.61	1.34	−1.34	−1.19	−0.36
Domestic policy actions	*−0.03*	*5.77*	*7.60*	*6.32*	*3.53*
Domestic spending	−1.54	0.22	0.68	0.48	0.60
Consumption reduction	−0.82	−0.24	0.34	0.05	0.83
Private consumption	−0.69	0.07	0.56	0.29	0.80
Public consumption	−0.13	−0.31	−0.23	−0.24	0.04
Investment reduction	−0.72	0.46	0.35	0.43	−0.23
Trade coefficients	1.51	5.55	6.92	5.84	2.93
Import substitution	5.20	6.89	5.23	5.05	0.41
Export penetration	−3.68	−1.34	1.69	0.78	2.52
Interaction effects	*−1.44*	*0.28*	*−0.44*	*−0.62*	*0.27*
Imports shock	−1.13	−1.63	−1.16	−1.03	−0.04
Demand/import. unit	0.07	0.01	−0.01	0.00	−0.02
Replacement/price	−1.21	−1.64	−1.15	−1.03	−0.02
Exports shock	0.67	0.95	0.68	0.39	0.37
Demand/ export. unit	0.07	0.58	0.91	0.47	0.52
Penetration/price	0.61	0.37	−0.23	−0.09	−0.15
Debt shock	−0.98	0.97	0.04	0.03	−0.06
Stock/interest	−0.98	0.97	0.04	0.03	−0.06

Source: Elaborated with BCU data

growing economy. Following the methodology proposed by Morley and Vos (see Chapter 2), the current account balance was decomposed in order to analyse the effect of external shocks. The results are shown in Table 12.2.

World trade, the interest rate and the terms of trade had positive effects and contributed significantly to the reduction of the current account deficit in 1985–9. Domestic adjustment also contributed mostly to a reduction of the external imbalance, particularly through increased export penetration in world markets. This factor contributed with almost 4 per cent of gross national product (GNP). However, a steep rise in imports ('import desubstitution') more than offset this determinant of deficit reduction.

In 1990–4, the current account deficit increased by more than 2 per cent of GNP. The terms of trade deteriorated, but the world interest-rate effect and,

Table 12.3 Uruguay: exogenous demand factors and their contribution to GDP growth (percentages calculated from 1983 constant prices)

Periods	Exports (%)	Government consumption (%)	Investment (%)	GDP
1980–1985	2.0	−0.9	−4.7	−3.7
1985–1990	2.6	0.5	0.8	3.9
1990–1995	1.7	−0.3	2.7	3.9
1995–2000	2.1	0.3	−0.3	2.1
1995–1998	3.3	0.4	1.3	5.1
1998–2000	0.2	0.2	−2.4	−2.1

Source: Elaborated with BCU data

especially, the growth of world trade offset this negative effect. Greater export penetration helped reduce the deficit further, but again import 'desubstitution' pushed strongly towards a deficit shifting the current account by almost 7 per cent of GNP. Between 1995 and 2000 the external variables again had a positive effect while the domestic variables, mainly the rise in the import share, determined the increase of the deficit. In particular, the terms of trade and world demand moved favourably. These benefits were not fully captured due to the lack of export penetration, particularly in the final years of the decade.

Macroeconomic adjustment and export growth

The performance of the Uruguayan economy in the 1990s can also be evaluated through the demand factors that explain GDP growth, in order to identify where the sources of growth did lie. A Keynesian framework is adopted for that purpose, following Morley and Vos (see Chapter 2) and the results are presented in Table 12.3.

GDP growth has been export-led from 1983 onwards. However, as the output multiplier decreased all along the period, the effects of each demand factor were attenuated. The reduction of the multiplier is basically related to the increase in the import leakage coefficient, especially between 1990 and 1995. Additionally, the savings propensity fluctuated in the 1980s, but declined sharply in the 1990s. Overall, exports were the most important source of growth until 1998, but this effect vanished later on, partly due to their weak performance during the last years of the decade and partly due to the multiplier decrease.

Summary of the basic macroeconomic and growth problems

The brief overview in the previous sections can be summed up as follows. Starting from an external situation of severe deficit in the first half of the 1980s, the Uruguayan economy recovered strongly, reaching a positive current account balance by the end of that decade. However, in the 1990s this trend reversed and by the year 2000 the current account deficit reached 2.8 per cent of GNP. The expansion of world trade and the greater export penetration was far outweighed by a strong growth of imports, particularly in the first half of the 1990s. This outcome may be attributed to domestic policies, particularly in the 1990s when stabilization policy cheapened imports and made exports less competitive.

The analysis of sources of GDP growth confirms these conclusions about external adjustment. Exports were the key factor in explaining growth, but the smaller macroeconomic multiplier diminished their impact.

In sum, during the 1990s the economy improved in terms of GDP and export growth, but became more vulnerable to fluctuations in neighbouring countries. The decade ended with a severe recession. The recession deepened after Argentina's financial crisis at the end of 2001.

12.3 Sector and export growth

Sector performance and determinants

From 1983 to 2000, the sectoral composition of GDP shifted away from agriculture and manufacturing. The share of the agricultural sector fell from 12.5 to 10.1 per cent and that of manufacturing from 24.1 to 17.8 per cent. In turn, the most dynamic sectors were commerce, restaurants and hotels and transport, storage and communications.

Following the methodology suggested by Morley and Vos (2000) (see also Chapter 2), sectoral GDP can be decomposed by main sources of growth (see Table 12.4). In the second half of the 1980s, exports were a main factor explaining output growth in most sectors, particularly in the case of textiles, clothing and leather. At the same time, all sectors were negatively affected by 'desubstitution', as imports increased their share in domestic absorption. Both results are consistent in a process of trade opening.

In the 1990s, these sectoral growth patterns changed significantly. Between 1990 and 1995, when the real exchange rate fell *vis-à-vis* most trading partners except Argentina, there was a strong import 'desubstitution' effect in all manufacturing sectors. Domestic demand expansion partly offset this effect, but exports were no longer an important source of growth in most sectors, except those selling their products to Argentina.

In the second half of the decade, the bilateral real exchange rate with Brazil depreciated, allowing exports to recover and retake their role as a key source of growth in all manufacturing sectors. In turn, import 'desubstitution' and domestic demand became less important in explaining GDP growth. The different effect of exports in both halves of the decade is due to the changing composition of exports to Argentina and Brazil. Agro-industrial commodities dominated exports to Brazil, while exports to Argentina were more diversified. Finally, between 1998 and 2000 GDP declined in all sectors, affected both by falling external demand and domestic absorption.

Table 12.4 Uruguay: decomposition of sectoral product growth (percentages of sectoral GDP)

Sector	1985–90			1990–5			1995–8			1998–2000		
	Dom. absorc.	Imp. subst.	Exp. growth	Dom. absorc.	Imp. subst.	Exp. growth	Dom. absorc.	Imp. subst.	Exp. growth	Dom. absorc.	Imp. subst.	Exp. growth
Agriculture and forestry	1.2	−1.3	0.7	5.7	−1.2	1.1	3.3	0.1	−0.7	−0.5	−0.6	−3.8
Fishing	60.4	−0.0	−70.1	−138.0	−3.0	146.5	144.0	0.6	−140.1	10.5	−23.3	−2.3
Quarrying and mining	−3.2	−0.3	0.2	−2.3	22.4	−0.0	2.6	20.6	0.2	55.6	−62.8	−0.3
Manufacturing	3.5	−5.5	5.9	8.1	−8.9	−0.6	6.3	−7.4	5.3	−6.7	2.2	−0.8
Food., bever. and tobacco	−4.8	−0.2	8.7	7.8	−4.0	−2.0	−8.3	−3.0	17.2	−0.0	−0.3	−3.2
Text., cloth. and leather	−11.8	−2.3	14.9	9.4	−7.5	−6.0	5.5	−8.0	−2.1	−5.9	−3.6	−1.8
Paper and printing	4.3	−3.5	0.4	10.0	−10.9	2.3	12.4	−3.8	5.8	−2.8	−1.3	2.0
Chemicals	8.3	−6.7	3.2	4.7	−6.5	−0.3	8.4	−6.3	1.7	−4.1	1.8	0.5
Non-metal. miner.	13.7	−0.8	3.4	4.6	−6.0	0.1	1.2	−2.4	2.1	−12.1	−4.6	−1.7
Basic metals	12.8	−11.2	0.8	4.0	−12.5	3.2	10.0	−12.6	6.5	−14.6	10.6	−0.8
Mach. and equipment	19.5	−15.1	0.8	11.7	−20.0	1.9	14.6	−10.3	2.6	−11.4	3.7	−0.5
Wood, furnit. and others	0.4	−5.0	3.6	17.0	−18.8	0.4	10.9	−6.9	0.2	−14.9	8.1	0.7

Source: Elaborated with BCU data. See Chapter 2 for methodology

Export growth and composition

After a sharp fall in the first half of the 1980s, merchandise exports showed a steady expansion until 1998 at an average annual rate of 9.5 per cent. After 1998, they suffered a large setback due to the change in real exchange rate with Brazil and later affected by the Argentine crisis. In the 1990s, most of export growth was concentrated in trade with Mercosur. By 1998, the share of merchandise exports to Mercosur countries reached 55 per cent. In the case of services exports, this share is even higher.

The composition of exports to Mercosur differs from that to the rest of the world. More than 95 per cent of exports to countries outside Mercosur consist of agricultural commodities and traditional manufactured goods. These commodities account for 71 per cent of Uruguayan exports to Mercosur, the remaining share coming from non-traditional manufacturing activities. Much of exports to Mercosur consist of intra-industry trade (Laens and Osimani 2001).

Competitiveness indicators

As indicated, the stabilization plan of 1991 generated an overvalued national currency with respect to all trading partners except Argentina, which had adopted a currency board system at that time. Brazil introduced a stabilization plan of its own in 1994, equally leading to an overvaluation of its currency. Competitiveness of Uruguay exports to Brazil improved significantly in consequence.

Figure 12.1 shows the trends in the bilateral real exchange rates with respect to the currencies of Argentina, Brazil and seven other main trading partners (United States, Germany, United Kingdom, Italy, Japan, France and the Netherlands). The observed pattern in the real exchange rates explains the strong increase in the share of Mercosur in total exports during most of the 1990s. The sudden depreciation of Brazil's currency is a major determinant of export performance after 1999.

Increased trade links with the other Mercosur countries has also increased the sensitivity of Uruguay's growth performance to the degree of macroeconomic stability in the neighbouring countries.

Labour market adjustment

Until 1993, neither supply nor demand for labour presented large fluctuations and the rate of unemployment stabilized between 8 and 9 per cent (see Figure 12.2). From 1993 to 1995, supply outpaced demand and unemployment went up. The employment situation worsened after 1995 when labour demand lagged behind GDP growth (except for a sharp, temporary rise in 1998). When recession started in 1999 the demand for labour declined continuously and unemployment reached a peak of 16 per cent in 2001.

The composition of unemployment changed after 1996, showing increasing shares for workers of 24 years and older, household heads and previously employed and lower shares for new entrants. This shift appears to be the result of a labour-saving restructuring of production sectors.

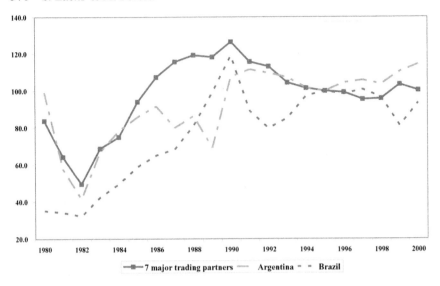

Figure 12.1 Uruguay: real exchange rate (trade weighted). Index 1998–9=100. (From Database of Instituto de Economía, Facultad de Ciencias Económicas.)

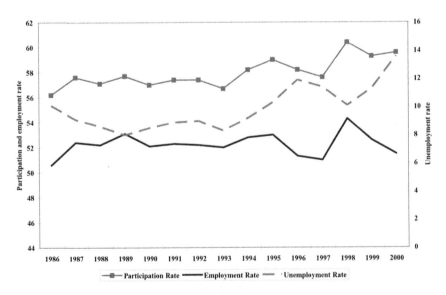

Figure 12.2 Uruguay: participation, employment and unemployment rates. (From INE.)

This restructuring process also affected employment composition by sectors. Between 1991 and 2000, the share of manufacturing employment fell strongly (from 21 to 15 per cent of total urban employment) while the share of services increased. Public sector employment decreased, affecting mainly middle-aged workers many of whom became either self-employed, retirees or unemployed (Bucheli *et al.* 2001).

All these changes in the labour market are consistent with the process of opening up. The strong import 'desubstitution' affected employment in import-competing activities. The shrinkage or restructuring of these sectors, together with the volatility of export sectors, affected both the quantity and quality of employment. Vaillant and Casacuberta (2002) find an important reduction of unskilled jobs and a rise in skilled employment, especially in jobs that require basic skills. On the other hand, the decline in public sector employment induced an increase in unskilled, informal jobs.

Changes in productivity and employment

There was an economy-wide increase in productivity in the 1990s, but the increase in traded-goods sectors (primary and manufacturing) was above average (Vaillant and Casacuberta 2002). A sectoral decomposition of employment by sectors as reported in Bucheli *et al.* (2001) was updated to 1999.

Changes in output per person of working age (*X/PET*) and changes in apparent productivity (*X/L*) can explain the slight employment increase between 1991 and 1999, but the relative weights of each determinant vary by sector. Output per person of working age increased in all sectors except manufacturing. However, as apparent productivity increased substantially, employment growth fell. In the case of manufacturing, the productivity rise reinforced rising unemployment as the restructuring process was mainly of a labour-saving nature.

Wage trends

Income distribution has been relatively stable since 1986, with a slight deterioration in the second half of the 1990s (the Gini coefficient climbed to 0.432 after oscillating for many years between 0.40 and 0.42). This trend is not the same for all income sources. Vigorito (1999) shows that wage income became more concentrated, especially for public employees. The findings of Gradin and Rossi (1999) and CEPAL (2000) are consistent with this concentration trend of wage income. Education level is the main factor explaining the increasing inequality of wage incomes (Bucheli 2000).

Summing up

In sum, export performance has been strongly influenced by the trend in the real exchange rate, favouring sales to Mercosur countries and hampering exports to the rest of the world. Exports have been a key factor in explaining GDP growth in most sectors, but the opening process also brought about a significant increase in the share of imports in domestic absorption. The combined effect of these opposite trends was a restructuring process within each sector and many firms either redirected output from the domestic market to Mercosur or went out of business and disappeared.

The restructuring process had a major impact on the labour market. Employment in manufacturing and agriculture lost ground in favour of service sector jobs. Productivity increased and income distribution remained relatively stable. However, by the end of the decade inequality increased, mainly due to greater disparity in wage incomes between skilled and unskilled workers.

12.4 Counterfactual CGE model simulations

The model

The model used for counterfactual simulations is an application of the standard model developed by Löfgren *et al.* (2001) and described in Chapter 3. It is a single-country static model for Uruguay, in which the treatment of the 'rest of the world' was changed compared to the standard model, as three trading partners were assumed: Argentina, Brazil (the two largest Mercosur countries)[1] and the rest of the world. The behaviour of these three trading partners is exogenous to the model. The greater detail in the treatment of the external sector enables the simulation of different trade policies *vis-à-vis* the Mercosur or all other countries.

The model distinguishes 21 production activities listed in Table 12.5: two primary activities, 15 manufacturing industries (keeping the greatest possible detail in food processing), one non-manufacturing industry and three services. Each activity produces one homogeneous commodity.

Output is obtained by combining intermediate inputs with primary factors following a constant elasticity of substitution (CES) at the top level of the production function. In turn, value added is a CES combination of three production factors (skilled labour, unskilled labour and capital). Factor supply is fixed and there is no international factor mobility. Both types of labour are perfectly mobile across sectors. Two contrasting alternative assumptions are made concerning capital: either it is a sector-specific factor (a more plausible assumption in the short run) or it is perfectly mobile across sectors (more likely to be true in the long run).

Output is allocated to the domestic market or export markets through a constant elasticity of transformation function. In the domestic market, goods and services are geographically differentiated, so supply is a combination of imports and domestic output following an Armington specification (Armington 1969). There are no production taxes.

On the demand side, there are four representative households, taking into account the labour characteristics of the head of the household: (a) wage or salary worker, (b) self-employed worker, (c) employer and (d) others (mainly retired). Household income is endogenous: net factor returns are assigned to each representative household in fixed proportions. Labour payments are net of social security taxes, while

Table 12.5 Sector classification of SAM for Uruguay

Name	ISIC code rev. 2	Concept
AGRO	11 and 12	Agriculture, hunting, forestry and lumber
OPRI	13 and 20	Other primary activities (fishing, mining and quarrying)
FRIG	3111	Meat products
LACT	3112	Dairy products
MOLI	3116	Wheat and rice mills
RABT	Rest of 31	Other food, beverages and tobacco
TEXT	321	Textiles
VEST	322	Clothing
CUER	323 and 324	Leather, leather products and footwear
PAIM	341 and 342	Paper, paper products and printing
QUIM	351 and 352	Chemical products
PETR	353 and 354	Petroleum products
CAPL	355 and 356	Rubber and plastic products
NMET	36	Non-metallic mineral products
MEMQ	37, 381 to 383	Basic metal and metal products, machinery and equipment
TRAN	384	Transport equipment
OMAN	331, 332, 385 and 39	Rest of manufacturing industry
ELCO	40 and 50	Electricity, gas, water supply and construction
CORE	60	Wholesale and retail trade, restaurants and hotels
TRAC	70	Transport and communications
OSER	80 and 90	Other services

there is no deduction on capital returns. Households also receive transfers from government. Social security transfers received from the government are fixed for each household in real terms. With its income, each representative household buys goods and services and saves a fixed proportion of net income. Household consumption of different goods and services is determined following a linear expenditure system (LES).

Government collects tariffs on imports, indirect taxes (on domestic and imported goods) and social security contributions. There are no direct taxes (except for social security contributions). Together, these types of taxation represent a high percentage of total government revenue, since Uruguay has no personal income tax and the amounts collected through property taxes or corporate income tax are relatively low.

The government uses its revenues to buy a composite of domestic and imported goods and services, transfer social security benefits to households, send factor payments abroad and give tax rebates to exporters. The payments to public employees are included in the services sector. Government and investment demands are fixed quantities.

The small country assumption is adopted in the case of imports, so that the country faces a perfectly elastic supply curve. In the case of exports, geographic differentiation is assumed, so the country faces a downward sloping demand curve in each of its trading partners' markets.

The macro closures of the model are the following:

1. Government: flexible savings.
2. External sector: two alternative closures were used (flexible and fixed foreign savings). The closure with flexible foreign savings (fixed exchange rate) is more appropriate to depict the prevailing situation in Uruguay during the 1990s, when a crawling peg along a fixed trend with a narrow fluctuation margin determined the exchange rate. This regime did not prove to be sustainable in the long run, so the closure with fixed foreign savings (flexible exchange rate) is more appropriate to illustrate the long-run situation.
3. Savings–investment: the model is investment driven.

Model calibration and data

The benchmark year for the calibration of the model parameters is 1995. The input–output (IO) table updated by Lorenzo *et al.* (1999) was adopted as the core of the social accounting matrix (SAM). Additional data from other sources were used to obtain more details in some cases and to complete the SAM.

The total of imported inputs used in each sector was distributed by sector of origin using microeconomic data from the 1995 Annual Manufacturing Survey carried out by the National Statistics Institute (INE). This survey was also used to disaggregate indirect taxes and tax rebates to exporters in the manufacturing sector.

Imported and exported goods were classified by country of origin or destination (Argentina, Brazil, rest of the world) using trade data from the Central Bank of Uruguay (BCU). The average exchange rate for the year 1995 was used to obtain the equivalent in pesos of imports and exports valued at CIF or FOB dollar prices. In the case of trade in services (where tourism has a very large share), the balance-of-payments estimate was allocated to Argentina, Brazil and the rest of the world according to the share of tourists coming from each country.

Total revenue from tariffs and indirect taxes on imports was obtained from National Accounts. It was distributed by commodities according to the average tariff rate of 1995 (both within Mercosur and *vis-à-vis* third countries). The 1995 Income and Expenditure Household Survey carried out by INE was used to disaggregate total private consumption by representative household and to distribute total factor returns and social security transfers by households. The column for the change in inventories in the SAM was obtained as a residual, thereby including also all the estimation errors.

The resulting SAM was checked against national accounts for consistency. However, the match with the national accounts is not perfect because the initial IO table had been adjusted to include informal output and consumption and because some of the data in national accounts has been modified recently. The RAS method was used to balance the SAM. The resulting SAM is included in Table A12.1.

To calibrate the model, elasticity parameters were obtained from secondary sources. The values for the elasticity of factor substitution were chosen taking into account the existing estimates for Uruguay (Cassoni 1998). The values for the elasticity of substitution between goods from different geographic origin were selected in the range of those estimated by Jomini *et al.* (1994). The same criterion was applied to determine the elasticity of export demand. In the case of the LES parameters, the income elasticities were estimated with data from the Income and Expenditures Household Survey. The Frisch parameter was set equal to −4. All elasticities are presented in the Appendix.

Simulations results

Several simulations were carried out to identify the effects of different policies or external shocks. All of them (except experiments 5 and 11) were performed under two different sets of 'closures': (1) capital is mobile across sectors, the exchange rate is flexible and wages too are flexible and (2) capital is a sector-specific factor, the exchange rate is fixed and real wages (skilled and unskilled) are fixed. The first type of closure is more likely to hold in the long run, while the second reflects more accurately the situation that might be found in the short run.

The following experiments were performed:

Policy simulations

1. TARCUT: 50 per cent across-the-board tariff cut.
2. TARINC: 50 per cent increase in all tariffs.
3. FTAA: Free Trade Area of the Americas (change in tariffs and prices).
4. WTO: trade liberalization under WTO (100 per cent tariff cut and change in prices).
5. DEVAL: 10 per cent devaluation of the domestic currency (closure no. 2 was modified to contemplate a fixed exchange rate).
6. SUBSID: 20 per cent increase in tax rebates for exported goods.
7. TARMER: 100 per cent tariff cut within Mercosur and no change in rest of world tariffs.

Exogenous shocks

8. PWMINC: 10 per cent increase in the world price of imports.
9. PWINC: 10 per cent increase in world prices of exports.
10. PRODUC: 10 per cent across-the-board productivity increase.
11. FORSAV: 10 per cent increase in foreign savings (only under the assumption of fixed foreign savings or flexible exchange rate).
12. PWMER: 10 per cent decrease in Mercosur prices of export-competing goods.
13. SHKMER: 10 per cent decrease in export demand from the Mercosur countries.

We add TARMER, PWMER and SHKMER as specific simulations for the case of Uruguay, as the external shocks originating in the Mercosur have a significant influence on its economic performance. Tables 12.6a and 12.6b show the changes from the baseline in macroeconomic variables, factor employment and average factor income, when the trade policy simulations were carried out, under both closures. Tables 12.7a and 12.7b present the same results for the simulations dealing with exogenous shocks.

Trade policy simulations

Tariff reduction (TARCUT, TARMER) and tariff increase (TARINC). The counterfactual simulations with the CGE model indicate that liberalization policies have a positive, but very weak, effect on GDP in the short-run closure and no effect at all when all variables are flexible. This is true both in the case of a 50 per cent tariff reduction across the board (TARCUT) and in the case of a 100 per cent tariff reduction in Mercosur with no change *vis-à-vis* the rest of the world (TARMER). It should be borne in mind that the latter was simulated as a unilateral policy, since the other partners' liberalization was not considered and no change in the other partners' prices is modelled. Therefore, the results do not include the 'market access' effect of a negotiated liberalization. Rather, they only reflect the 'domestic market opening' effect, so that the likely total effect is underestimated.[2]

When a fixed exchange rate is assumed (second closure), the domestic currency appreciates, absorption and household consumption increase, and tariff reductions mainly increase imports, without too much change in exports. However, when the nominal exchange rate adjusts under closure type 1, the real exchange rate depreciates and stimulates exports at a rate doubling that of imports. In turn, the depreciation of the domestic currency negatively affects absorption and household consumption.

These results highlight the importance of the exchange rate regime when adopting a trade liberalization policy, as the expected positive results on exports are only found when the exchange rate is allowed to adjust flexibly. Additionally, under closure type 2, with a fixed exchange rate and fixed real wages, labour income falls but employment rises in the tariff reduction scenarios. In contrast, when all variables are free to adjust, labour income will rise, particularly in the case of unskilled labour.

Unsurprisingly, a rise in trade protection simulated in the experiment TARINC generates the opposite results to the import liberalization experiments. GDP, absorption and trade decrease under closure type 2. Under closure type 1, the effects on GDP disappear, but the decline in exports is larger due to a depreciation of the real exchange rate. This result suggests that the anti-export bias of protection would appear more clearly in the long run, when all variables have adjusted. Labour income increases when the real wage remains fixed, but employment falls. When wages and the nominal exchange rate adjust (closure type 1), factor income declines, particularly in the case of unskilled labour.

Negotiated, multilateral tariff reductions (FTAA and WTO): In the simulations of a hemispheric free trade area (FTAA) or a multilateral liberalization (WTO), tariffs and world prices were changed in accordance with the data provided by the

Table 12.6a Uruguay: CGE simulations of trade policies. Real variations of macroeconomic indicators, factor employment and income (percentage change from base year)

| | Closure type 1 (long run) | | | | | | |
	TARCUT	TARINC	FTAA	WTO	DEVAL[1]	SUBSID	TARMER
Absorption	−0.1	0.1	−0.1	0.2	−6.5	0.0	−0.1
Household consumption	−0.2	0.1	−0.1	0.3	−9.2	0.0	−0.2
Investment	0.0	0.0	0.0	0.0	0.0	0.0	0.0
Government consumption	0.0	0.0	0.0	0.0	0.0	0.0	0.0
Exports	1.8	−1.7	2.2	5.0	12.5	0.3	1.3
Imports	0.9	−0.8	1.3	6.1	−14.6	0.2	0.6
GDP at market prices	0.0	0.0	0.0	0.0	−1.7	0.0	0.0
Real exchange rate	1.1	−1.1	1.2	0.6	8.2	−0.2	0.8
Nominal exchange rate	1.7	−1.6	2.0	−0.3	10.0	−0.1	1.2
Export price index	−0.8	0.8	−0.9	2.5	−5.3	−0.1	−0.6
Import price index	0.0	0.0	−0.1	1.0	0.0	0.0	0.0
Tradables world price index	−0.4	0.4	−0.5	1.7	−2.5	−0.1	−0.3
Nontradable domestic price index	0.2	−0.2	0.2	0.8	−0.9	0.0	0.1
Terms of trade	−0.8	0.8	−0.8	1.4	−5.3	−0.1	−0.6
Factor employment							
Skilled labour	—	—	—	—	—	—	—
Unskilled labour	—	—	—	—	—	—	—
Capital	—	—	—	—	—	—	—
Average factor income							
Skilled labour	0.3	−0.3	0.4	0.6	−2.9	0.0	0.2
Unskilled labour	0.5	−0.5	0.6	2.3	−0.1	0.1	0.3
Capital	0.4	−0.4	0.5	2.0	−0.1	0.1	0.3

Note
1 In this simulation, capital is mobile across sectors, the wage is flexible but the exchange rate is fixed

Table 12.6b Uruguay: CGE simulations of trade policies. Real variations of macroeconomic indicators, factor employment and income (percentage change from base year)

	Closure type 2 (short run)						
	TARCUT	TARINC	FTAA	WTO	DEVAL	SUBSID	TARMER
Absorption	1.2	−1.2	1.5	0.5	−6.5	−0.1	0.9
Household consumption	1.8	−1.7	2.1	0.8	−9.2	−0.1	1.3
Investment	0.0	0.0	0.0	0.0	0.0	0.0	0.0
Government consumption	0.0	0.0	0.0	0.0	0.0	0.0	0.0
Exports	0.2	−0.2	0.4	4.7	8.6	0.4	0.2
Imports	3.6	−3.3	4.5	5.2	−13.2	0.0	2.7
GDP at market prices	0.6	−0.6	0.8	0.4	−2.7	0.0	0.4
Real exchange rate	−0.3	0.3	−0.5	1.2	8.7	−0.1	−0.2
Nominal exchange rate	0.0	0.0	0.0	0.0	10.0	0.0	0.0
Export price index	−0.1	0.1	−0.1	2.4	−3.9	−0.2	−0.1
Import price index	0.0	0.0	−0.1	1.0	0.0	0.0	0.0
Tradables world price index	0.0	0.0	−0.1	1.7	−1.9	−0.1	0.0
Nontradable domestic price index	0.3	−0.3	0.4	0.5	−0.7	0.0	0.2
Terms of trade	−0.1	0.1	0.1	1.3	−3.9	−0.2	−0.1
Factor employment							
Skilled labour	0.8	−0.7	1.0	0.5	−2.8	0.0	0.6
Unskilled labour	0.7	−0.7	0.9	0.7	−2.0	0.0	0.5
Capital	—	—	—	—	—	—	—
Average factor income							
Skilled labour	−0.1	0.1	−0.2	0.1	1.3	0.0	−0.1
Unskilled labour	−0.1	0.1	−0.2	0.4	1.5	0.0	−0.1
Capital	—	—	—	—	—	—	—

Table 12.7a Uruguay: CGE simulations of exogenous shocks. Real variations of macroeconomic indicators, factor employment and income (percentage change from base year)

	Closure type 1 (long run)					
	PWINC	PWMINC	PRODUC	FORSAV	PWMER	SHKMER
Absorption	1.9	−2.1	8.8	12.0	−1.3	−0.7
Household consumption	2.7	−2.9	12.4	17.0	−1.8	−1.0
Investment	0.0	0.0	0.0	0.0	0.0	0.0
Government consumption	0.0	0.0	0.0	0.0	0.0	0.0
Exports	2.8	−2.2	9.2	−19.8	−1.2	−0.5
Imports	10.7	−10.1	4.2	35.7	−6.0	−3.2
GDP at market prices	0.4	−0.6	9.7	2.1	−0.4	−0.2
Real exchange rate	−3.4	4.0	1.5	−14.0	1.9	1.0
Nominal exchange rate	−6.5	−2.4	3.2	−16.6	4.3	2.3
Export price index	8.7	1.0	−4.2	11.0	−5.7	−3.0
Import price index	0.0	10.0	0.0	0.0	0.0	0.0
Tradables world price index	4.2	5.7	−2.0	5.3	−2.7	−1.4
Nontradable domestic price index	0.8	−0.8	−0.4	2.0	−0.5	−0.2
Terms of trade	8.7	−8.2	−4.2	11.0	−5.7	−3.0
Factor employment						
Skilled labour	—	—	—	—	—	—
Unskilled labour	—	—	—	—	—	—
Capital	—	—	—	—	—	—
Average factor income						
Skilled labour	2.1	−2.2	10.0	6.1	−1.6	−0.9
Unskilled labour	1.9	−1.9	8.9	1.1	−1.0	−0.5
Capital	1.6	−1.6	8.2	1.0	−0.9	−0.5

International Food Policy Research Institute (IFPRI), generated with a multicountry model for the world economy (GTAP).

The introduction of these tariff and prices changes in the Uruguayan model shows that the effects of both experiments on GDP are very low or non-existent, depending on the closure adopted. Absorption and household consumption increase in the short run but they decline in the FTAA simulation under closure type 1.

The effect on trade flows of both experiments is positive, but the magnitude is clearly more important in the case of the multilateral liberalization (WTO). Furthermore, the closure is not relevant in terms of the effects of the multilateral liberalization on trade flows, as both imports and exports increase significantly under either closure. The magnitude of trade growth is much larger in the case of WTO or FTAA than in the TARCUT or TARMER simulations. This is because

Table 12.7b Uruguay: CGE simulations of exogenous shocks. Real variations of macroeconomic indicators, factor employment and income (percentage change from base year)

	Closure type 2 (short run)					
	PWINC	PWMINC	PRODUC	FORSAV	PWMER	SHKMER
Absorption	−1.9	−4.6	16.6	—	0.9	0.5
Household consumption	−2.7	−6.5	23.5	—	1.3	0.7
Investment	0.0	0.0	0.0	—	0.0	0.0
Government consumption	0.0	0.0	0.0	—	0.0	0.0
Exports	9.8	−1.0	8.1	—	−5.7	−3.0
Imports	0.1	−13.3	14.1	—	0.0	0.0
GDP at market prices	−0.3	−2.4	15.6	—	0.0	0.0
Real exchange rate	2.4	6.3	−1.2	—	−1.7	−0.8
Nominal exchange rate	0.0	0.0	0.0	—	0.0	0.0
Export price index	5.3	0.4	−3.8	—	−3.6	−1.8
Import price index	0.0	10.0	0.0	—	0.0	0.0
Tradables world price index	2.5	5.4	−1.8	—	−1.7	−0.9
Nontradable domestic price index	0.2	−0.8	−0.7	—	−0.1	0.0
Terms of trade	5.3	−8.7	−3.8	—	−3.6	−1.8
Factor employment						
Skilled labour	0.2	−2.9	10.3	—	−0.3	−0.2
Unskilled labour	0.6	−2.5	9.1	—	−0.5	−0.3
Capital	—	—	—	—	—	—
Average factor income						
Skilled labour	0.7	0.6	0.1	—	−0.4	−0.2
Unskilled labour	0.8	0.6	−0.1	—	−0.4	−0.2
Capital	—	—	—	—	—	—

in the WTO and FTAA simulations the market access effect of a negotiated liberalization is considered.

Under closure type 1, factor income increases in the FTAA and the WTO simulations, particularly in the case of unskilled labour. However, when rigidities are assumed according to closure type 2, labour income decreases in the FTAA simulation even though employment rises.

It is important to notice that the sectoral results are quite different in the FTAA simulation as compared with the WTO simulation. This can be explained by the different composition of Uruguay's trade with Mercosur (which in turn affects trade within the FTAA) as compared with trade with the rest of the world. The big winners in the WTO liberalization would be the sectors that process meat products, dairy products, wheat and rice mills, especially in the long-run closure. This outcome reinforces the vulnerability of Uruguay's economy to the fluctuations that characterize primary commodity markets. In the case of the FTAA the gains are not so high but they would also include the leather industry, transport and communications and other services.

Increase in tax rebates to exports (SUBSID): The experiment with an increase in the tax rebate (SUBSID) on exports has no significant effect, no matter the closure rule. Only a slight increase in exports would be attained, which would mainly affect the leather industry. The almost negligible effect of this type of policy can be explained by the present level of export incentives, which is very low and covers exclusively a small percentage of indirect taxes rebate. Therefore, if exports were to be stimulated through such an instrument, the present policy needs to be redesigned to become more useful in a way that is compatible with the WTO rules on subsidies.

Devaluation: The devaluation experiment shows the results that would be obtained if the exchange rate remained fixed but at a higher level than the base value. The effect would be recessive, especially in the short run, when capital cannot reallocate and real wages are fixed. The only positive effect is observed in exports, particularly under closure type 1 when capital is mobile and wages are flexible. GDP, absorption and particularly imports would be harmed by this policy. In the short run, employment would be negatively affected while in the long run, when wages are allowed to adjust, labour income would decline. Skilled labour would be the greatest loser, either because of lower employment or lower income. Welfare for all households would be lower as they would significantly reduce consumption.

Exogenous shocks

Import prices increase (PWMINC): The increase in the world price of imports deteriorates the terms of trade, which fall more than 8 per cent. Most macroeconomic indicators are negatively affected by this negative shock: GDP, absorption and household consumption fall, especially under short-run conditions (closure type 2). Imports show a sharp decline, which is hardly attenuated under the flexibility conditions of closure type 1. Exports also decrease in all sectors. The activities with a stronger export-orientation are harmed most by this shock, while import-competing industries are not affected to the same extent. The recessive adjustment translates into less employment in the short run and lower labour income in the long run. This experiment is most illustrative of the impact of external shocks, e.g. of an oil price hike, as oil is the main imported commodity in Uruguay.

Export prices increase (PWINC): The effects of this experiment mirror those of import price increases. The results of PWINC illustrate the sensitivity to increases in world prices of beef, wool, dairy products or other goods that make up a large share of Uruguayan exports. In this experiment, exports are up, particularly in the short run as all tradable sectors increase their exports. However, non-tradable sectors (services) decline in terms of GDP, absorption and consumption. When all variables are free to adjust (closure type 1), the benefits of the world price increase of exports become more evident, as GDP, absorption and household consumption increase. Labour income rises, with skilled labour being the most favoured. The comparison of the results under the two different closures shows that the benefits of an increase in the world price of exports can only be fully obtained if the wages and the exchange rate can freely adjust and if capital can be reallocated according to the new conditions.

Productivity increase (PRODUC): This experiment assumes a uniform total factor productivity increase in all sectors. The effects on GDP, absorption and household consumption are clearly positive, whatever the closure adopted. Trade flows also rise, but in the short run the trade deficit goes up, as the growth of imports is larger than the growth of exports. This can be explained by the maintenance of a fixed nominal exchange rate and the subsequent fall in the real exchange rate. Under closure type 1 the effects are attenuated and the increases in absorption and consumption are not as high as in the case of the short-run assumption about capital mobility. Employment increases strongly if we assume labour market adjustment with a fixed real wage (closure type 2). In turn, once adjustment is achieved, productivity gains allow all factor incomes to rise. All household groups benefit from a general rise in productivity, but employers (owners of capital) are the ones that benefit the most.

Increase in foreign savings: This simulation was carried out exclusively under closure type 1, assuming that foreign savings were fixed but 10 per cent higher than the initial level. The results show a positive impact on GDP, absorption and household consumption due to the increase in available funds throughout the economy. However, as the real exchange rate appreciates by 14 per cent, exports suffer a sharp decline. In contrast, imports increase significantly pushing up its share in domestic absorption. Exports decline in all sectors and, in consequence, also output declines in most sectors except services, where all of the increase in GDP is concentrated. Skilled labour benefits most and all household groups are able to increase their consumption levels. A surge in capital flows has clearly positive effects, but obviously – as also Uruguay has experienced – sudden stops may be proportionally detrimental.

Decrease in export prices or export demand from the Mercosur (PWMER and SHKMER): As indicated, the Uruguayan economy has become highly vulnerable to the evolution of the economies of the largest Mercosur partners (Argentina and Brazil). Two simulations were carried out in order to assess the effects of negative shocks coming from these neighbouring economies. The experiment PWMER shows the impact of a decrease in the relevant prices for Uruguayan exports to Argentina and Brazil (as caused by a devaluation in those countries). Under the short-run closure, there would be no negative impact on GDP, absorption and consumption despite the significant fall in exports. However, when all the variables adjust flexibly to the new situation, the real exchange rate depreciation in Uruguay would attenuate the export decline but instead induce a decrease in GDP and, especially, in household consumption. Employment and factor incomes would fall, affecting skilled labour in particular.

The SHKMER simulation is intended to show the effects of a downward shift in external demand from the Mercosur countries. This would be the case if these neighbour countries would suffer a recession. Under closure type 2 the negative effect of this shock would affect exports most strongly and sectors strongly oriented at the Mercosur market would be hit severely. In contrast, even though these also suffer some export losses, sectors mainly exporting to the rest of the world would not face a reduction in their activity level. However, under flexible adjustment (closure type 1), all macroeconomic variables deteriorate, despite the fact that exports drop as much, as the real exchange rate would depreciate. As in the previous experiment, labour would suffer a reduction of employment and income. The damage would be higher for unskilled labour in the short run and for skilled labour in the long run.

The results of both simulations confirm the vulnerability of the Uruguayan economy to the performance of its neighbouring countries, given the high share of exports oriented to these markets.

12.5 Impact on poverty and inequality at the household level

The simulations with the CGE model can only provide a picture of the effects of particular policies at the macro or sectoral level. In order to simulate the effects of those same policies on poverty and inequality, the methodology presented in Ganuza *et al.* (2001) was adopted (see also Chapter 3). Basically, it consists of the simulation of a labour market structure different from the actual one and the measurement of the poverty and income distribution indicators corresponding to the simulated structure.

The microsimulations methodology was applied to the existing labour market structure in 1995 (same year used for parameter calibration in the CGE). The base parameters that define the labour market structure were calculated from the 1995 CHS carried out by the INE. This survey is representative for urban areas (population living in towns of 900 persons or more).

New labour market parameters were calculated from the results of the CGE model and they were used as counterfactual labour market structures. By introducing these new parameters on the CHS data, poverty indicators and Gini and Theil coefficients were estimated for each one of the simulations carried out with the CGE. The poverty indicator measures the percentage of the population under the poverty line. The results of these microsimulations illustrate the consequences that some policies or some exogenous shocks may have on poverty and inequality.

In the microsimulations derived from CGE results under closure type 1 (flexible wages, factor mobility and flexible exchange rate), the labour force (economically active population) is fixed and there is full employment. Therefore, the participation rate and the unemployment rate are maintained in their base value for 1995. On the contrary, in the simulations carried out under closure type 2, the real wage is fixed and employment is flexible, so that the unemployment rate varies.

The microsimulations were run in SPSS in a given sequence, changing one relevant parameter at a time, according to the results previously obtained in the simulations performed with the CGE under both closures. Each phase of the sequence was run independently and sequentially. The results reported here are those obtained through the cumulative (sequential) process. The parameters that were changed in each phase of the sequence are as follows:

- Phase 1: unemployment rate (only under closure type 2).
- Phase 2: share of the tradable sector employment for skilled and unskilled (male and female) workers.[3]
- Phase 3: skilled and unskilled (male and female) wages relative to the average wage.
- Phase 4: level of the average wage.
- Phase 5: share of unskilled labour (male and female) in the tradable and non-tradable sectors.

Tables 12.8a and 12.8b show the results of the microsimulations corresponding to the trade policy simulations, while Tables 12.9a and 12.9b present the results of those derived from the exogenous shocks simulations.

The first thing to notice is that most results are statistically significant in a 95% confidence interval. This is particularly true when all four or five phases are accumulated in sequence. In general, the size of the effects (positive or negative) is rather small. The grey-shadow cells indicate the cases when poverty or income inequality increases (being statistically significant), meaning an aggravation of the initial situation.

The across-the-board tariff reduction simulated in TARCUT seems to have very positive effects, as both poverty and income inequality decline, no matter which closure is adopted. Under closure type 1, the increase in average income is crucial for the reduction of poverty, while inequality is mostly improved by the larger ratio of employment in the tradable sector. Under the assumptions of closure type 2, the increase in employment is particularly relevant to explain the poverty decline. Similar comments can be made concerning the simulation of a 100 per cent tariff reduction *vis-à-vis* the Mercosur countries (TARMER), the only difference being the size of the improvement (somewhat smaller than in TARCUT).[4]

In the simulation of a tariff increase (TARINC), the results are quite different according to the closure adopted. Under the long-run conditions of closure type 1, a worsening of poverty (0.3 per cent) is observed, due to the generalized reduction of factor income, but hardly no effect is found on inequality (there is only a slight concentration of labour income). In contrast, under closure type 2 poverty increases, mainly as a result of a rising unemployment, which is not totally offset by an increase in factor income. Household income becomes more concentrated while labour income inequality falls.

In the case of a negotiated liberalization (simulations FTAA and WTO), poverty is reduced, particularly under the WTO scenario and under closure type 1. This is basically explained by the increase in factor income (or in employment under closure type 2). The FTAA simulation has a positive effect on income distribution in the short run, but under the long-run conditions its effect is neutral. The WTO simulation in contrast improves the distribution of income (both total and labour income), as unskilled labour is most favoured by this policy.

Table 12.8a Uruguay: microsimulations of trade policies. Poverty incidence, Gini coefficient for household and labour income (percentage variation from base year)

					Closure type 1		
		Initial value	Phase 1	Phases 1 + 2	Phases 1 + 2 + 3	Phases 1 + 2 + 3 + 4	Phases 1 + 2 + 3 + 4 + 5
TARCUT	Poverty	0.228	—	0.0	−0.1*	−0.4*	−0.4*
	Gini HH	0.417	—	−0.1	−0.1*	−0.1*	−0.1*
	Gini LabY	0.468	—	−0.1	−0.1*	−0.1*	−0.1*
TARMER	Poverty	0.228		0.0	0.0	−0.3*	−0.3*
	Gini HH	0.417		0.0	0.0*	0.0*	0.0*
	Gini LabY	0.468		0.0	0.0	0.0	0.0
TARINC	Poverty	0.228	—	0.0	0.0	0.3*	0.3*
	Gini HH	0.417	—	0.0*	0.0*	0.0*	0.0*
	Gini LabY	0.468	—	0.0*	0.0*	0.0*	0.1*
FTAA	Poverty	0.228	—	0.0	−0.1*	−0.6*	−0.6*
	Gini HH	0.417	—	0.0*	0.0*	0.0*	0.0*
	Gini LabY	0.468	—	0.0*	0.0*	0.0*	0.0*
WTO	Poverty	0.228	—	0.0	−0.7*	−1.9*	−2.0*
	Gini HH	0.417	—	0.0*	−0.3*	−0.3*	−0.3*
	Gini LabY	0.468	—	0.0	−0.3*	−0.3*	−0.2*
SUBSID	Poverty	0.228	—	0.0	−0.1*	−0.1*	−0.1*
	Gini HH	0.417	—	0.0	0.0*	0.0*	0.0*
	Gini LabY	0.468	—	0.0*	0.0	0.0	0.0*
DEVAL	Poverty	0.228	—	−0.1	−1.4	0.6	0.4
	Gini HH	0.417	—	0.0*	−0.4*	−0.4*	−0.4*
	Gini LabY	0.468	—	0.1*	−0.4*	−0.4*	−0.4*

Note
*Significant at the 5 per cent level

An increase in tax rebates on exports (SUBSID) has a negative effect on poverty and on income distribution in the short run, but this effect disappears when the long-run assumptions are adopted. Under closure type 1, the effect on income distribution is nil and there is a slight decrease in poverty as a result of a small rise in unskilled labour income.

The simulation of a 10 per cent increase in the nominal exchange rate (DEVAL) has mixed results under both closures. Under the short-run assumptions (closure type 2), poverty increases due to the rising unemployment, but as real wage is fixed, the rise in relative factor income compensates the effect of unemployment. Thus, when all the phases are accumulated, the devaluation has a positive effect on poverty. The opposite happens when closure type 1 is adopted, because the adjustment of wages to the new situation decreases average labour income and increases poverty. In turn, the increase of unemployment in closure type 2 worsens total income distribution, but when all variables are adjusted in closure type 1, total income distribution and labour income distribution improves.

In the simulations dealing with exogenous shocks in prices, the results are quite consistent. The increase in import prices (PWMINC) or the decline in export

Table 12.8b Uruguay: microsimulations of trade policies. Poverty incidence, Gini coefficient for household and labour income (percentage variation from base year values)

				Closure type 2			
		Initial value	*Phase 1*	*Phases 1 + 2*	*Phases 1 + 2 + 3*	*Phases 1 + 2 + 3 + 4*	*Phases 1 + 2 + 3 + 4 + 5*
	Poverty	0.228	−0.7*	−0.8*	−0.8*	−0.6*	−0.7*
TARCUT	Gini HH	0.417	−0.1*	−0.2*	−0.2*	−0.2*	−0.2*
	Gini LabY	0.468	−0.1*	−0.1*	−0.1*	−0.1*	−0.1*
	Poverty	0.228	−0.5*	−0.6*	−0.6*	−0.5*	−0.5*
TARMER	Gini HH	0.417	−0.1*	−0.1*	−0.1*	−0.1*	−0.1
	Gini LabY	0.468	−0.1*	−0.1*	−0.1*	−0.1*	−0.1
	Poverty	0.228	1.4*	1.2*	1.2*	0.6*	0.5*
TARINC	Gini HH	0.417	0.2*	0.1*	0.2*	0.2*	0.1*
	Gini LabY	0.468	−0.2*	−0.1*	−0.2*	−0.2*	−0.2*
	Poverty	0.228	−1.1*	−1.2*	−1.2*	−1.0*	−1.1*
FTAA	Gini HH	0.417	−0.2*	−0.2*	−0.2*	−0.2*	−0.2*
	Gini LabY	0.468	−0.1*	−0.1*	−0.1*	−0.1*	−0.1*
	Poverty	0.228	−0.8*	−0.8*	−0.9*	−1.2*	−1.2*
WTO	Gini HH	0.417	−0.2*	−0.2*	−0.2*	−0.2*	−0.2*
	Gini LabY	0.468	−0.1*	−0.1*	−0.1*	−0.1*	−0.1*
	Poverty	0.228	0.4*	0.4*	0.4*	0.4*	0.3*
SUBSID	Gini HH	0.417	0.1*	0.1*	0.1*	0.1*	0.1*
	Gini LabY	0.468	−0.1*	−0.1*	−0.1*	−0.1*	−0.1*
	Poverty	0.228	3.8*	3.3*	3.5*	−0.2	−0.3*
DEVAL	Gini HH	0.417	0.6*	0.5*	0.6*	0.6*	0.5*
	Gini LabY	0.468	−0.1*	0.0	−0.1*	−0.1*	−0.1*

Note
*Significant at the 5 per cent level

prices to the Mercosur (PWMER) have clearly negative effects on poverty under both closures, due to rising unemployment and lower factor income. Inequality worsens in the short-run assumptions, but when the exchange rate and the wages adjust and all factors can reallocate, there is no distribution effect (in the case of PWMINC) or this effect is slightly positive (in PWMER).

Very similar results are obtained in the simulation of a negative demand shock from the Mercosur (SHKMER). On the contrary, the effect of an increase in all export prices (PWINC) is a reduction of poverty, due to an increase in employment and factor income and an improvement in inequality in the short run. However, the latter effect cannot be observed in closure type 1.

The last two simulations have clearly positive effects on poverty reduction. The increase in foreign savings (FORSAV) and the generalized productivity rise (PRODUC) make poverty go down by a significant amount due to the decline of unemployment or to a higher factor income. However, in both cases the improvement in terms of poverty is accompanied by a worsening of inequality in both household and labour income distribution, which can be explained by the significant rise in skilled labour income, the most favoured factor in these simulations.

Table 12.9a Uruguay: microsimulations of external shocks. Poverty incidence, Gini coefficient for household and labour income (percentage variation from base year values)

					Closure type 1		
		Initial value	Phase 1	Phases 1 + 2	Phases 1 + 2 + 3	Phases 1 + 2 + 3 + 4	Phases 1 + 2 + 3 + 4 + 5
PWINC	Poverty	0.228	—	−0.1	0.0	−2.3*	−2.3*
	Gini HH	0.417	—	0.0	0.0	0.0	0.0
	Gini LabY	0.468	—	0.0	0.0	0.0	0.0
PWMINC	Poverty	0.228	—	−0.1	−0.2*	1.4*	1.4*
	Gini HH	0.417	—	0.0*	0.0*	0.0*	0.0*
	Gini LabY	0.468	—	0.0*	0.0*	0.0*	0.0*
PRODUC	Poverty	0.228	—	0.0	0.3*	−9.1*	−9.2*
	Gini HH	0.417	—	0.0	0.1*	0.2*	0.2*
	Gini LabY	0.468	—	0.0	0.2*	0.2*	0.2*
FORSAV	Poverty	0.228	—	−0.5	0.6*	−3.2*	−3.2*
	Gini HH	0.417	—	−0.2	0.5*	0.5*	0.4*
	Gini LabY	0.468	—	−0.1	0.7*	0.7*	0.7*
PWMER	Poverty	0.228	—	−0.1	−0.3*	0.7*	0.6*
	Gini HH	0.417	—	0.0	−0.1*	−0.1*	−0.1*
	Gini LabY	0.468	—	0.0	−0.1	−0.1	−0.1
SHKMER	Poverty	0.228	—	0.0	−0.3*	0.4*	0.3*
	Gini HH	0.417	—	0.0	−0.1*	−0.1*	−0.1*
	Gini LabY	0.468	—	0.0	0.0	0.0	0.0

Note
*Significant at the 5 per cent level

According to all these results, when closure type 1 is adopted, the crucial parameter to determine the poverty situation is the average wage level (modified in phase 4 of the microsimulations), while the ratio between skilled and unskilled wages (modified in phase 3) is most important to determine the changes in income distribution.

When closure type 2 is adopted, the unemployment rate (modified in phase 1) is the parameter with the highest impact on poverty, followed by the average wage level, which in some simulations compensates the former. Unemployment is also crucial to determine inequality, but the share of labour in the tradable and non-tradable sectors also has an important effect.

12.6 Conclusions

The Uruguayan economy showed good performance in the 1990s even though by the end of the decade (1999) it entered into a recession which had not been overcome by 2003. The external accounts were balanced at the beginning of the decade but deteriorated gradually, mainly as a result of domestic factors, like the exchange rate policy, which provoked an increase in the import coefficient and attenuated the positive effect of export growth.

Table 12.9b Uruguay: microsimulations of external shocks. Poverty incidence, Gini coefficient for household and labour income (percentage variation from base year values)

					Closure type 2		
		Initial value	*Phase 1*	*Phases 1 + 2*	*Phases 1 + 2 + 3*	*Phases 1 + 2 + 3 + 4*	*Phases 1 + 2 + 3 + 4 + 5*
	Poverty	0.228	−0.6*	−0.6*	−0.6*	−1.4*	−1.5*
PWINC	Gini HH	0.417	−0.1*	−0.2*	−0.2*	−0.2*	−0.2*
	Gini LabY	0.468	−0.1*	−0.1*	−0.1*	−0.1*	−0.1*
	Poverty	0.228	4.6*	3.9*	3.9*	0.9*	0.8*
PWMINC	Gini HH	0.417	0.7*	0.6*	0.7*	0.7*	0.6*
	Gini LabY	0.468	−0.1*	−0.1*	−0.2*	−0.2*	−0.2*
	Poverty	0.228	−16.0*	−16.1*	−16.3*	−16.6*	−16.9*
PRODUC	Gini HH	0.417	−3.0*	−3.1*	−3.1*	−3.1*	−3.1*
	Gini LabY	0.468	0.1*	0.1*	0.1	0.1	0.1
	Poverty	0.228	1.1*	0.9*	0.8*	0.8*	0.8*
PWMER	Gini HH	0.417	0.2*	0.2*	0.2*	0.2*	0.1*
	Gini LabY	0.468	−0.1*	−0.1*	−0.2*	−0.2*	−0.2*
	Poverty	0.228	0.9*	0.8*	0.7*	0.8*	0.7*
SHKMER	Gini HH	0.417	0.2*	0.1*	0.1*	0.1*	0.1
	Gini LabY	0.468	−0.1*	−0.1*	−0.2*	−0.2*	−0.1*

Note
*Significant at the 5 per cent level

Export growth observed in the 1990s was crucially determined by the creation of the Mercosur and by trends in the real exchange rate. The stabilization policy adopted in 1991, using the exchange rate as nominal anchor, generated an appreciation of the local currency *vis-à-vis* most trading partners, except the Mercosur countries. This led to a strong concentration of exports by destination (more than 50 per cent went to Argentina or Brazil) and to an increase in macroeconomic vulnerability to the business cycle of these economies.

In this general context, there was a shift in the driving forces of the growth pattern. In the first half of the 1990s, domestic demand was the main source of growth, while in the second part (until 1998) export expansion became the engine of growth. This process was accompanied by a generalized productivity increase and a slowdown in employment generation. By the end of the decade, unemployment affected a large share of Uruguayan workers. In addition, the composition of employment changed, with a sharp decrease in the share of manufacturing and a significant growth in the share of services. Wages showed an increasing inequality, mainly related to the widening income differentials between skilled and unskilled workers.

The diversity of growth-determining factors throughout the decade makes it difficult to identify causal linkages. The counterfactual simulations carried out in this paper intended to disentangle the forces at work and their impact. Most of the shocks and policies simulated actually were part of the events that happened along the decade, so the findings presented here give hints to help understand the process.

The CGE model simulations show that tariff reduction policies have positive effects on exports but their impact is not very important on GDP and absorption, which are only positively affected when we assume that existing rigidities do not enable full adjustment. In turn, the microsimulations show that these types of policies have small, but positive, effects on poverty alleviation and reduction of income inequality. In contrast, trade policies that raise tariffs or export subsidies are not effective to stimulate growth and may worsen poverty and income inequality, especially when the exchange rate and the real wage remain fixed.

The simulations of negotiated tariff reduction (in the framework of the FTAA or a multilateral agreement in WTO) do not show much effect on GDP, despite a strong export increase. However, the impact of these scenarios on poverty and income distribution is clearly positive. The liberalization in the framework of WTO negotiations renders the best results in poverty alleviation and improvement of income distribution. However, it should be taken into account that this negotiation reinforces a growth pattern based on exports of primary commodities, which are quite volatile.

Given the characteristics of the model, the simulation of a devaluation policy only captures trade effects. A devaluation is contractionary, despite large positive effect on exports. The impact of a devaluation on poverty and income distribution depends to a large extent on the existence of rigidities in the labour market and the foreign exchange market. It also depends crucially on the necessary period to reallocate the production factors. In the long run, a devaluation would increase poverty but it would reduce income inequality.

The exogenous shocks may have a strong impact on the macroeconomic variables, on poverty and income distribution. The results show clearly the negative effect of any increase in the world price of imports or any decrease in the price of exports. Poverty worsens even though inequality might be reduced in the long run. A similar impact would be obtained from a downward shift in export demand.

Other types of favourable shocks, like an increase in foreign savings or a rise in productivity has significant positive effects on macro variables, but generates greater inequality in the distribution of income, especially labour income. However, this type of shock would have a quite large positive effect on the alleviation of poverty.

In reality, a complex set of exogenous shocks and domestic policy adjustment occurred simultaneously during the 1990s. The factors isolated by the CGE analysis appear to have combined to a growth process (until 1998) with a parallel improvement in poverty measures and income distribution. Many other relevant aspects of the process were necessarily ignored for analytical reasons (such as the role of financial flows). However, the analysis carried out in this chapter hopefully will shed some light on factors that determined the performance of the Uruguayan economy in the 1990s.

Acknowledgement

The authors acknowledge the collaboration of Carolina Firpo who helped with data collection and processing.

Appendix A12

Table A12.1 Uruguay: basic social accounting matrix 1996 (millions of pesos)

	Activities	Commodities	Factors	Households	Taxes and tariffs	Government	Savings–investment	Change in inventories	Rest of the world	Total
Activities	0	200,477	0	0	0	0	0	0	0	200,477
Commodities	85,306	0	0	90,607	0	14,700	18,420	4,230	21,660	234,923
Factors	115,171	0	0	0	0	0	0	0	0	115,171
Households	0	0	99,373	0	0	20,778	0	0	0	120,151
Taxes and tariffs	0	10,817	15,798	0	0	0	0	0	0	26,615
Government	0	0	0	0	26,615	0	0	0	0	26,615
Savings–investment	0	0	0	29,544	0	-8,863	0	0	1,969	22,650
Change in inventories	0	0	0	0	0	0	4,230	0	0	4,230
Rest of the world	0	23,629	0	0	0	0	0	0	0	23,629
Total	200,477	234,923	115,171	120,151	26,615	26,615	22,650	4,230	23,629	774,461

Notes

1 No separate account was introduced for Paraguay as its share in Uruguayan trade is very low.
2 A multicountry model is needed in order to assess both effects.
3 The tradable sector is defined as the sum of AGRO, OPRI and all manufacturing sectors in the CGE.
4 It should be remembered that the TARMER simulation did not include any change in tariffs or prices in the other Mercosur partners, so it does not generate the total effect of the negotiated tariff reduction.

References

Armington, P. (1969) 'A theory of demand for products distinguished by place of production', *IMF Staff Papers*, Vol. 16.

Bucheli, M. (2000) 'El empleo de los trabajadores con estudios universitarios y su prima salarial', Documento N° 8/00, Montevideo: Departamento de Economía, Universidad de la República.

Bucheli, M., R. Diez de Medina and C. Mendive (2001) 'Uruguay: Equidad y pobreza ante la apertura comercial de los noventa: un enfoque a través de microsimulaciones', in: E. Ganuza, L. Taylor, R. Barros and R. Vos (eds) *Liberalización, desigualdad y pobreza. América Latina y el Caribe en los 90*, Buenos Aires: Ediciones Universidad de Buenos Aires (para PNUD y CEPAL).

Cassoni, A. (1998) 'Estimaciones econométricas de elasticidades de sustitución entre factores de producción', *Impacto de la apertura comercial del Mercosur sobre el mercado laboural uruguayo*. Documento N° 4, Montevideo: CINVE – GEOPS, Oficina de Planeamiento y Presupuesto, Programa de Fortalecimiento de las Areas Sociales (unpublished).

CEPAL (2000) *La contribución de las distintas fuentes de ingreso a la evolución de la desigualdad en el Uruguay urbano. 1986–1997*, Montevideo: CEPAL, Oficina de Montevideo.

CINVE (1983) *Industria y protección en un lcontexto de apertura externa: Uruguay 1978–1982*, Montevideo: Ministerio de Economía y Finanzas.

CINVE (1986) *Estudio sobre la reestructura de la protección arancelaria*, Montevideo: Ministerio de Economía y Finanzas (unpublished).

Favaro, E. and C. Sapelli (1989) *Promoción de exportaciones y crecimiento económico*, San Francisco: ISC Press.

Ganuza, E., R. Paes de Barros and R. Vos (2001) 'Efectos de la liberalización sobre la pobreza y la desigualdad', in: E. Ganuza, L. Taylor, R. Paes de Barros and R. Vos (eds) *Liberalización, Desigualdad y Pobreza: América Latina y el Caribe en los 90*, Buenos Aires: Editorial de la Universidad de Buenos Aires (for UNDP and CEPAL).

Gradin, C. and M. Rossi (1999) 'Polarización y desigualdad salarial en Uruguay, 1986–97', Documento N° 16/99, Montevideo: Departamento de Economía, Universidad de la República.

Jomini, P., R. McDougall, G. Watts and P. S. Dee (1994) *The SALTER Model of the World Economy: Model Structure, Database and Parameters*, Canberra: Industry Commission.

Laens, S. (1997) 'Apertura comercial e integración: reflexiones a partir de la experiencia uruguaya', Asunción: CADEP (mimeo).

Laens, S., F. Lorenzo and R. Osimani (1993) 'Macroeconomic conditions and trade liberalization: the case of Uruguay,' in: A. Canitrot and S. Junco (eds) *Macroeconomic*

Conditions and Trade Liberalization, Washington, DC: Inter-American Development Bank.

Laens, S. and R. Osimani (2001) 'The determinants of intraindustry trade: the case of Uruguay,' Paper presented to the Jornadas Anuales de Economía, Banco Central del Uruguay.

Löfgren, H., R. Lee Harris and S. Robinson (2001) 'A standard computable general equilibrium (CGE) model in GAMS,' Discussion Paper No. 75, Washington, DC: Trade and Macroeconomics Division, IFPRI.

Lorenzo, F., R. Osimani and P. Caputti (1999) 'Matriz de Insumo Producto y Contabilidad Social para la economía uruguaya. Año 1995,' *Impacto de la apertura comercial del Mercosur sobre el mercado laboural uruguayo,* Documento Nº 3, Montevideo: CINVE – GEOPS, Oficina de Planeamiento y Presupuesto, Programa de Fortalecimiento de las Areas Sociales (unpublished).

Macadar, L. (1988) 'Uruguay: Fomento de exportaciones industriales y distribución del ingreso', in: R. Urriola (ed) *Políticas de industrialización en América Latina,* Quito: ILDES.

Morley, S. and R. Vos (2000) Export-led economic strategies: effects on poverty, inequality and growth in Latin America and the Caribbean. Research methodology, New York: UNDP (mimeo).

Noya, N., C. Casacuberta and F. Lorenzao (1998) 'The Uruguayan experience', in: J. J. Fanelli and R. Medhora (eds) *Financial Reform in Developing Countries,* London: Mcmillan.

Vaillant, M. and C. Casacuberta (2002) 'Trade and wages in Uruguay in the 1990s', Montevideo: Departamento de Economía, Facultad de Ciencias Sociales (mimeo).

Vigorito, A. (1999) 'Una distribución del ingreso estable. El caso de Uruguay, 1986–1997', Serie Documentos de Trabajo DT 6/99, Montevideo: Instituto de Economía, Facultad de Ciencias Económicas y de Administración.

Index

For Product Safety Concerns and Information please contact our EU
representative GPSR@taylorandfrancis.com Taylor & Francis Verlag GmbH,
Kaufingerstraße 24, 80331 München, Germany

Printed and bound by CPI Group (UK) Ltd, Croydon, CR0 4YY
08/05/2025
01864519-0001